Constitutional Reform as a Remedy for Political Disenchantment in Australia

Bede Harris

Constitutional Reform as a Remedy for Political Disenchantment in Australia

The Discussion We Need

Springer

Bede Harris
School of Accounting and Finance
Charles Sturt University
Albury, NSW, Australia

ISBN 978-981-15-3598-7 ISBN 978-981-15-3599-4 (eBook)
https://doi.org/10.1007/978-981-15-3599-4

This Springer imprint is published by the registered company Springer Nature Singapore Pte Ltd.
The registered company address is: 152 Beach Road, #21-01/04 Gateway East, Singapore 189721, Singapore

This book is dedicated to my wife, Veronica,
and to my daughter, Elizabeth,
and to Tabby, Buttons and Adeline, who
watched as I wrote it.

Preface

This book is about both politics and constitutional change. It invites the reader to adopt a completely new approach to constitutional reform – one which is unfettered by the past and which involves a blank-slate consideration of what our constitution should look like. It is deliberately subversive in that its purpose is to identify flaws of the current constitution so as to encourage the reader to reject the status quo and consider alternatives.

The book is also the product of observing Australian politics and teaching constitutional law for the past 20 years. As a migrant to Australia who had lived in countries that either were undergoing or had undergone significant constitutional change, the absence of debate on this topic in Australia came as a surprise.

First, debate on constitutional reform is rare among politicians and the general public. The statement by renowned constitutional law academic Geoffrey Sawer that Australia is a "frozen continent" in so far as constitutional change is concerned remains as true now as it did when it was made more than 50 years ago. This is despite the fact that a constitution, like any other statute, requires regular scrutiny and updating when necessary. Indeed, given that the constitution is the foundation upon which all law rests and also determines the balance of power between the individual and the state, the case for regular review becomes all the more strong.

Second, there was – and still is – a prevailing view that Australia's constitution does not need improvement. This is despite the fact that, as I will endeavour to show in this book, our constitutional arrangements are severely – and very obviously – deficient in a number of respects. It was as if the evolution in constitutional doctrine that occurred elsewhere in the world during the twentieth century was thought to be of no application here and consequently of no relevance to the constitution.

My third observation was that, there is a significant lack of public knowledge and understanding of how the constitution works, as was revealed by the generally low level of debate on an Australian republic, on rights protection during the National Human Rights Consultation process and on Indigenous constitutional recognition. This makes it obvious that civics education in Australia is in drastic need of improvement. Of even greater concern is the fact that constitutional debate takes place without reference to the more fundamental question of what theory does (or should) underpin a constitution.

The fourth and final observation, and the one which has led me to write this book, is that there is enormous and growing dissatisfaction with how the country is governed. Yet despite this, voters do not make the obvious connection between how government is conducted and the *rules* by which government is conducted which are, of course, found in the constitution. It is only by changing the constitution in such a way as to remedy the shortcomings which enable sub-standard government to occur that the roots of political dissatisfaction will be addressed.

The notorious conservatism of voters when presented with constitutional amendments (only 8 of 42 referenda held over the past 119 have succeeded) is understandable in that people are naturally reluctant to change which they do not understand. Politicians – particularly those from the Coalition and Labor – are adept at stoking fear of change because many of the necessary constitutional reforms would be adverse to those parties' political interests. Yet this gives rise to a terrible paradox: Notwithstanding voter distrust of current political processes, fear of change means that there is little appetite to change those processes – which acts to the benefit of the very politicians with whom the public has become disillusioned. The purpose of this book is to explain how the things that are a source of popular dissatisfaction with government have their roots of constitutional flaws and to show that we have nothing to fear, and much to gain, from reforming our constitutional law. The book ends with an Appendix containing a proposed new constitution which embodies the changes argued for in the body of the book.

One thing this book does not do – at least until the final chapter – is to engage in speculation about which changes would or would not be palatable to voters. Too often, debate on constitutional reform in Australia proves abortive from the start because commentators say "Voters will never accept that" or "Constitutional change is too difficult in Australia." It is that type of thinking that has prevented us from answering the hard questions that need to be addressed if our system of government is to be improved. In this project – as in life – logic dictates that one should first decide what needs to be done before turning to practical questions relating to how to do it. The setting of goals, which are matters of principle, should not be subordinated to technical questions of how to achieve them, which are matters of pragmatics. Only once we have determined the goals we want to achieve should attention be focused on what difficulties there may be and how they can be overcome – and overcome them we can if we approach the task with optimism and ingenuity.

We must abandon the current pessimistic tone of discussion about constitutional reform which, because it is designedly focussed by those who have a vested interest in the status quo on reasons why the constitution should *not* be reformed, inevitably favours their interests. We also need to broaden our approach to debate on constitutional matters, which is currently marked by insularity and an unwillingness to learn from other countries or to adopt solutions devised by them. The questions that Australia faces are not unique: They have been addressed – and successfully answered – by many other countries. Such problems as those resistant to constitutional change put forward as reasons why we should not reform our constitution turn out, on closer inspection – and with the benefit of the experience of other countries – not to be the insurmountable obstacles to the reform they are presented to be. Adopting a new way of thinking about constitutional reform will improve our system of government and thereby help Australia achieve its enormous potential.

Albury
March 2020

Bede Harris

Acknowledgements

I would like to acknowledge the assistance provided by the library staff at Charles Sturt University, the National Library of Australia and the Australian National University. I would also like to acknowledge the help of Lucie Bartonek, Neelofar Yasmeen and Marielle Klijn at Springer Nature who oversaw the project at its various stages and Arul Vani Parttibane who corrected the proofs. Finally, I would also like to acknowledge the permission given by Oxford University Press for the use of Figure 3.1 which illustrates Commonwealth and state legislative capacities.

Contents

About the Author

Bede Harris was born in Zimbabwe. After graduating with a BA(Mod) from Trinity College, University of Dublin, he studied law in South Africa and graduated with an LLB from Rhodes University. He began his academic career at the University of Natal, Pietermaritzburg. He subsequently taught at the University of Waikato in New Zealand, where he obtained his DPhil. He was awarded a Fulbright Senior Scholarship and attended the American Studies Institute at Lafayette College in the United States. He is currently a Senior Lecturer in Law at Charles Sturt University and is the Author of six books and over 50 book chapters and articles on constitutional law, human rights, Indigenous legal issues, corporations law and consumer law.

Table of Cases

Adelaide Company of Jehovah's Witnesses v Commonwealth (1943) 67 CLR 166
Al Kateb v Godwin (2007) 233 CLR 307
Alister v The Queen (1984) 154 CLR 404
Alley v Gillespie [2018] HCA 11
Amalgamated Society of Engineers v Adelaide Steamship Company Ltd (1920) 28 CLR 129
Anderson v Commonwealth (1932) 47 CLR 50
Anderson v Dunn 19 US (6 Wheat.) 204 (1821)
Atwater v City of Lago Vista 532 U.S. 318 (2001).
Attorney General (Cth); Ex rel McKinlay v Commonwealth (1975) 135 CLR 1
Attorney-General (Victoria); ex rel Black v Commonwealth (DOGS Case) (1981) 146 CLR 559
Australian Broadcasting Corporation v Lenah Game Meats Pty Ltd 208 CLR 199 (2001)
Australian Capital Television Pty Ltd v Commonwealth (No 2) (1992) 177 CLR 106
Australian Conservation Foundation v Commonwealth (1980) 146 CLR 493
Bates v Little Rock 361 U.S. 516 (1960)
Behrooz v Secretary, Department of Immigration and Multicultural and Indigenous Affairs (2004) 219 CLR 486
Boumediene v Bush 553 U.S. 723 (2008)
Chu Kheng Lim v Minister for Immigration, Local Government and Ethnic Affairs (1992) 176 CLR 1
Coe v Commonwealth (No 2) (1993) 118 ALR 193
Coleman v Power (2004) 220 CLR 1
Combet v Commonwealth (2005) 224 CLR 494
Commonwealth v Australian Capital Territory (Marriage Equality Case) (2013) 250 CLR 441
Commonwealth v Construction, Forestry, Mining and Energy Union (2000) 171 ALR 379
Commonwealth v Yarmirr (2001) 208 CLR 1
Cormack v Cope (1974) 131 CLR 432

Democratic Alliance v The Acting National Director of Public Prosecutions 2012 (3) SA 486 (SCA)
Egan v Chadwick (1999) 46 NSWLR 563
Egan v Willis (1998) 195 CLR 424
Egan v Willis and Cahill (1996) 40 NSWLR 650
Eisenstadt v Baird 405 U.S. 438 (1972)
Entick v Carrington (1765) 19 St. Tr. 1030
Ferreira v Levin 1996 (1) BCLR 1 (CC)
Fose v Minister for Safety and Security 1997 (3) SA 786 (CC)
Freedom Under Law v Acting Chairperson: Judicial Service Commission 2001 (3) SA 549 (SCA)
Griswold v Connecticut (1965) 381 US 479
Government of the Republic of South Africa v Grootboom 2000 (11) BCLR 1169 (CC)
Hamdan v United States 696 F.3d 1328 (DC Cir, 2012).
Hicks v United States of America CMCR 13-004 18 February 2015
Ingram v Commonwealth and Peacock (1980) 54 ALJR 395
John Fairfax Publications Pty Ltd v Ryde Local Court (2005) 62 NSWLR 512
Kruger v Commonwealth (1997) 190 CLR 1
Lange v Australian Broadcasting Corporation (1997) 189 CLR 520
Lawrence v Texas 539 U.S. 558 (2003)
Loving v Virginia 338 U.S. 1 (1967)
Mabo v Queensland (No. 2) (1992) 175 CLR 1
Madzimbamuto v Lardner-Burke [1969] 1 AC 645
Members of the Yorta Yorta Aboriginal Community v Victoria (2002) 214 CLR 422
McCloy v New South Wales (2015) 257 CLR 178
McDonald v Cain [1953] VR 411
McGinty v Western Australia (1996) 186 CLR 40
McGrain v Daugherty 273 US 135 (1927)
Minister for Home Affairs and Another v Fourie and Another 2006 (1) SA 542 (CC)
Minister for Immigration and Citizenship v Haneef (2007) 234 ALR 606
New State Ice Company v Liebmann 285 US 262 (1932).
New Zealand Maori Council v Attorney-General [1987] 1 NZLR 641 (CA)
Nixon v Administrator of General Services 433 US 425 (1977)
NTEU v Commonwealth (2001) 111 FCR 583
Obergefell v Hodges 576 U.S. ___ (2015)
Olmstead v United States 277 U.S. 438 (1928)
Onus v Alcoa of Australia Ltd (1981) 149 CLR 27
Plaintiff M68/2015 v Minister for Immigration and Border Protection (2016) 257 CLR 42
Planned Parenthood of Southeastern Pennsylvania v Casey 505 U.S. 833 (1992)
Queensland v Commonwealth (Second Territorial Senators Case) (1977) 1329 CLR 585
R v Ndhlovu 1968 (4) SA 515 (RAD)
R v Oakes [1986] 1 S.C.R. 103

R v Richards; Ex parte Firzpatrick and Browne (1955) 92 CLR 157
R v Somerset CC, ex p. Fewings [1995] 1 All ER 513
Re Amendment of the Constitution of Canada (1981) 125 DLR (3d) 1
Re Wooley; Ex parte Applicants M276/2003 (2004) 225 CLR 1
Roach v Electoral Commissioner (2007) 233 CLR 162
Roe v Wade 410 U.S. 113 (1973)
S v Makwanyane 1995 (3) SA 391 (CC)
S v Williams 1995 (3) SA 632 (CC)
Sankey v Whitlam (1978) 142 CLR 1
Senate Select Committee on Presidential Campaign Activities v Nixon 498 F.2d 725 (D.C. Cir. 1974)
Skinner v. State of Oklahoma, ex rel. Williamson 316 U.S. 535 (1942)
Soobramoney v Minister of Health, Kwa-Zulu Natal 1997 (12) BCLR 1696 (CC)
Tajjour v New South Wales (2014) 313 ALR 221
United States v A T & T 521 F.2d 384 (D.C. Cir 1976) and 567 F. 2d 121 (D.C. Cir 1977)
United States v Burr 25 Fed. Cas. 187 (1807)
United States v Nixon 418 US 683 (1974)
United States v Wheeler 435 U.S. 313 (1978)
United States Tobacco Co v Minister for Consumer Affairs (1988) 20 FCR 520
Victoria v Commonwealth (PMA Case) (1975) 134 CLR 81
Victoria v Commonwealth and Hayden (1975) 134 CLR 388
Walker v New South Wales (1994) 82 CLR 45
Western Australia v Commonwealth (First Territorial Senators Case) (1975) 134 CLR 201

Chapter 1
Public Disillusionment with Politics in Australia

Abstract This chapter examines why there is growing disillusionment with politicians and, by extension, with the political system, in Australia. Drawing on examples from the past 20 years, it illustrates how diminishing respect for the rule of law, political corruption, poor standards of personal behaviour and failure of leadership have affected people's confidence in the system of government. It also examines how the dominance of Australian politics by the two major political blocs, Coalition and Labor, has enabled this to happen. The chapter also argues that voters should recognise that the causes of their discontent with how politics is conducted lie in the rules of the system – that is, in the Constitution – and that therefore the solution lies in constitutional reform. The chapter also discusses impediments to constitutional reform – principally conservatism born of fear of changing a mechanism that most people do not understand, along with self-interested misrepresentation of the implications of reform by politicians. The chapter encourages people to think boldly, without fear and with regard to the experience of other countries in analysing what is wrong with the Constitution and how it might be improved.

1.1 Disillusionment with Politicians

Australians have a poor view of their politicians. Survey results indicate a profound dissatisfaction with the political class. A 2015 survey by the Swinburne Leadership Institute found that 59% of respondents viewed politicians as untrustworthy (the highest percentage for untrustworthiness recorded across a range of leadership groups).[1] Politicians were also considered less competent than any other leadership group, ranking equal last with trade union leaders in caring more about the short term than the long term. A 2018 study conducted by the Australian National University showed that only 26% of voters thought that politicians could be trusted, while 72% believed that those in government looked only after themselves.[2] The survey also found that 52% of respondents felt that politicians were out of touch with the concerns of ordinary people. A 2018 survey conducted by the Museum of

[1] Wilson and Fein (2015).

[2] Cameron and McAllister (2018).

B. Harris, *Constitutional Reform as a Remedy for Political Disenchantment in Australia*, https://doi.org/10.1007/978-981-15-3599-4_1

Australian Democracy and the University of Canberra found that only 23% of Australians trusted ministers and members of parliament (the lowest level of trust when compared to medical practitioners, judges, businesspeople, trade unionists and journalists), that only 31% trusted the federal government and that 61% believed that politicians have low standards of honesty and integrity.[3] These survey results are unsurprising because, as this chapter will show, voters have reason to be aggrieved by the behaviour of their elected representatives.

Perhaps nothing so inflames disdain for the governing class as the spectacle of politicians engaging in misconduct but suffering no adverse consequences. Despite the claim by politicians that they are accountable to parliament – and ultimately to the people – the public is confronted with what seems to be a never-ending stream of scandals. 'Accountability' has become a buzz-word devoid of meaning. This chapter focuses on different types of misconduct that have occurred over recent decades in order to demonstrate that Australians' disenchantment with their politicians is justified. The catalogue of malfeasance appears long, but it is important to gain an appreciation of just how low is the calibre of our politicians. Space requires that its focus be limited, so I have chosen the past two decades as a reasonable period to examine. Examples of misbehaviour are drawn from across party lines – no party has a monopoly of either virtue or vice, although it should also be noted that, as the Coalition has been in power for all but six of the past 23 years, its representatives feature more numerously, simply because they have had more opportunity to engage in wrongdoing. These problems are systemic in that their roots lie in the way politics is conducted. How politics is conducted in in turn determined by the constitutional system. That is why constitutional reform is key to ensuring that these problems are addressed.

The chapter addresses a number of key areas which have given rise to popular dissatisfaction with politicians and political processes – diminishing respect for the rule of law, dishonesty, poor standards of inter-personal behaviour, poor leadership and frequent governmental instability. The chapter also discusses how public disquiet over these issues has undermined confidence in the system of government itself and why the first step towards addressing them lies in overcoming attitudinal obstacles to constitutional reform.

1.2 Diminishing Respect for the Rule of Law

Although 'the rule of law' is lauded by lawyers, politicians and the general public, there is limited understanding of what it means. This is in part due to the fact that the concept is nebulous and has been given a range of definitions.[4]

---

[3] Stoker, Evans and Halupka (2018, pp. 21–2).

[4] For an interesting recent discussion of the rule of law see Laws (2017).

According to the narrowest definition, the rule of law means that government operates by law rather than by arbitrary will, that law is made by a defined process, that it is ascertainable, that it applies to everyone equally without prejudice and that it is enforceable by independent courts. As was stated extra-judicially by Lord Bingham of Cornhill, former Lord Chief Justice of England and Wales[5]

> The core of the existing principle is, I suggest, that all persons and authorities within the state, whether public or private, should be bound by and entitled to the benefit of laws publicly and prospectively promulgated and publicly administered in the courts.

Even this minimalist definition makes the rule of law a powerful concept in that it demands that the government itself, like any other person, be subject to the law.

Broader definitions go beyond these mere procedural requirements and impose obligations relating to the *content* of the law, requiring that that the law be consistent with human rights and that governments comply with international law.[6] This approach, which has long been accepted in jurisdictions which have bills of rights, and is increasingly accepted even in countries such as the United Kingdom which do not, adds an entirely new dimension to the rule of law, acknowledging that effective restraint on state power requires that law must conform to some external standard of justice.

Related to the rule of law is due process, which relates to the manner in which the law is applied. Key requirements of due process are that any deprivation of rights by the state must ultimately be subject to review by the courts, that the law must protect the right to legal advice and that judicial processes must be conducted in a procedurally fair manner. In the United States due process has been expanded even further, and it is now accepted as a general principle there that wherever the *effect* of the application of law on a particular group is less favourable than on other groups, the law breaches the constitutional right to due process and is therefore invalid.

In Australia there has been an observable diminution in respect both for the rule of law and for due process over the past two decades. No single event has had more of an impact on the relationship between the governors and the governed in Australia than the 9/11 attack in the United States, which led to a marked change in how state power is applied in our country. This is evidenced not only by the large volume of anti-terrorist legislation that has been enacted but, more significantly for purposes of this chapter, by the attitude and demeanour of those in power – in particular their willingness to express disdain for, and act contrary to, what were assumed to be the constraints imposed by the rule of law and the norms of a free society. This attitudinal change has impacted on areas as diverse as foreign policy, race relations, civil liberties and the plight of refugees, but has as a common thread a world-view that anything is justifiable in the name of protecting the country from external risks (some of which are real, some are not) and that all other considerations should be subordinated to that objective. Most of these measures were enacted during periods

[5] Bingham (2007, p. 69).

[6] Bingham (2007, pp. 69–84).

when the Coalition was in power. However long-standing bipartisanship on national security, coupled with a fear of being seen as 'soft' in this area, has had the consequence that Labor has not discharged the proper role of an opposition in this area and did nothing to wind back the securocratic state when it was itself in power. It has been left to a few backbenchers and minor party MPs to sound the alert over policies inimical to the rule of law. A number of events illustrate how the rule of law and due process have been undermined:

The attitudinal shift to the rule of law was first brought home to Australians by the case of David Hicks, an Australian citizen who was captured by American forces in Afghanistan and then taken to the Guantanamo Bay detention centre before being charged with engaging in activities in support of terrorism. The Howard government refused to ask the Americans to send Hicks home to Australia – a request the Americans would in all likelihood have acceded to, given that they agreed to send UK nationals home when requested by that country. The reason for this – frankly admitted by the government – was not because Hicks was guilty of a crime, but rather because he was *not* guilty of any crime under Australian law.[7] Hicks suffered prolonged assault and torture and more than 5 years of imprisonment before pleading guilty to a charge in order to bring his detention to an end.[8] The guilty plea and the conviction were subsequently overturned on the ground that the charge was invalid because it related to acts that were not offences at the time they were committed,[9] and because the process by which the plea was obtained was unlawful in that it was made involuntarily.[10] This latter ground was the result of the application of the fundamental legal principle that inculpatory statements are inadmissible if obtained by duress, and that prolonged detention without trial itself constitutes duress. Fear of never being released works as a powerful stimulus to an accused to confess to crimes – even if they are innocent, which is of course why we have statutory requirements that suspects must be charged and tried within defined time periods. The Australian government's conduct in condoning Hick's treatment not only displayed contempt for international human rights law in general and due process in particular, but also threw into doubt the sincerity of Australia's claim that its fight against terrorism was motivated by a desire to defend liberal values.

Another example of government indifference to the fate of Australian citizens was provided by the Mamdouh Habib. Habib, a dual Egyptian and Australian citizen, was arrested in Pakistan in 2001 and questioned by Pakistani intelligence officers and by the CIA. The CIA subsequently moved him between Egypt and Afghanistan before imprisoning him at Guatanamo Bay. At each location he was subjected to torture. Habib stated that his torture in Egypt was witnessed by Australian officials.[11] After being held at Guantanamo for three years, Habib was

[7] Coorey and Banham (2007).

[8] Hicks (2010).

[9] *Hamdan v United States* 696 F.3d 1328 (DC Cir, 2012).

[10] *Hicks v United States of America* CMCR 13-004 18 February 2015.

[11] Habib and Collingwood (2008, pp. 107, 121, 127–8).

released without charge. On his return to Australia, Habib sued the Australian government for complicity in his torture. The government resisted his claim for six years, but then reached an out of court settlement with him three days after the publication of a statement by an Egyptian intelligence officer confirming the identity of an Australian intelligence officer who had witnessed the torture.[12]

The next significant case was that of Dr Mohamed Haneef, who was arrested in 2007 and held for 12 days before being charged with providing support for a terrorist organisation. He was released on bail but immediately put into immigration detention when the Minister for Immigration and Citizenship, Kevin Andrews cancelled his visa on character grounds. Ten days later the Commonwealth Director of Public Prosecutions dropped the criminal case against Haneef, admitting that it had been an error to bring the charges, but the minister refused to reinstate the visa. Haneef took legal action seeking review of the revocation. The Federal Court found that the minister had acted unlawfully in that he had incorrectly applied the character test contained in the legislation, emphasising in its judgment the importance of governmental compliance with the rule of law.[13] The minister unsuccessfully appealed to the Full Court of the Federal Court, which confirmed the re-instatement of Haneef's visa.[14]

The Haneef affair was the subject of an inquiry conducted by former New South Wales Supreme Court Justice Michael Clarke.[15] The case raised a number of concerns for the rule of law including the prolonged detention prior to the laying of charges (which was made possible by anti-terrorism provisions contained in ss 23CB and 23D of the *Crimes Act 1914* (Cth) and the laying of charges when there was insufficient evidence to support them. However, the most concerning aspect of the case was the possibility that public power was being used for political ends.[16] The government was trailing in opinion polls in advance of a general election, and the appearance of being tough on terrorism would play to its political advantage. Evidence presented to the Clarke inquiry revealed that the AFP had concluded that there was insufficient evidence to charge Haneef[17] several days *before* charges were laid, that ASIO had informed the AFP that their agency had no intelligence suggesting Haneef's involvement in terrorism[18] and that the Commonwealth prosecutor considering the case had determined that there was insufficient evidence to lay charges.[19] The fact charges were nevertheless laid obviously indicates that they were laid under political direction.

---

[12] O'Brien (2011).

[13] *Haneef v Minister for Immigration and Citizenship* (2007) 242 ALR 290.

[14] *Minister for Immigration and Citizenship v Haneef* (2007) 234 ALR 606. 634.

[15] Clarke (2008).

[16] For a comprehensive discussion of the case, and in particular its political aspects, see Head (2009).

[17] Head (2009, pp. 108–9).

[18] Head (2009, p. 108).

[19] Head (2009, p. 109).

So far as the visa was concerned, the Clarke inquiry found that its cancellation and the placing of Haneef into Immigration Detention to prevent his being released after he was granted bail, was 'mystifying,' particularly in relation to its timing.[20] Despite all of this, the inquiry found that there was no evidence of a political motive behind the laying of charges or the cancellation of the visa.[21] However this finding was reached without Clarke being able to access key cabinet documents relating to the case.[22] In other words, the deliberations of very forum in which political discussions would have taken place were placed off-limits. Furthermore, Clarke lacked the power to subpoena cabinet members, including the former Prime Minister and Attorney-General, whom the evidence disclosed had been involved in multiple discussions about the case, and these ministers refused to make statements under oath or to be questioned by Haneef's legal representatives.[23] The conclusion one must reach, therefore, is that the inquiry's findings that there was no political motivation for the laying of charges or for the cancellation of the visa were unsustainable. The implications of the Haneef affair for the rule of law are obvious, not only in relation to the conduct of the Howard government, but also of the Rudd government, whose decision it was not give the inquiry the power to compel witnesses to give evidence.[24]

The treatment of asylum-seekers by successive governments – Coalition and Labor – has been found to be incompatible with various aspects of the rule of law. Violations of the rule of law begin with denial of due process when asylum-seekers are first encountered by Australian authorities. In 2012 the Gillard government introduced so-called 'enhanced screening' under which an immigration officer determines whether a person is lodging a claim for asylum. The problem with this procedure is that refugees are not advised that they have a right to claim asylum or that they have a right to legal representation – even if it would be possible to access legal advice, which is unlikely, particularly in cases where screening takes place at sea.[25] The implications of this practice for due process are obvious. Even more serious were reports in 2014 that navy personnel had burned the hands of refugees on a boat exhaust. These were dismissed by then Immigration Minister Scott Morrison as 'allegations' (ignoring the fact that of course every investigation of wrongdoing begins with an allegation) and were never investigated by agencies other than ones with a direct interest in the outcome. This was despite detailed corroborating evidence from several witnesses coming to light which contradicted self-exclupatory findings by the departments of Defence and of Customs and Border Protection.[26] Even more serious was the suspected failure of Australian authorities to come to the rescue of a vessel – SIEV X – in 2001, which resulted in the drowning of 353

[20] Clarke (2008, p. viii).
[21] Clarke (2008, p. 227).
[22] Head (2009, p. 104).
[23] Head (2009, p. 105).
[24] Head (2009, p. 105).
[25] Evershead, Farrell and Laughland (2014).
[26] Bachelard (2014).

asylum-seekers, which occurred during the tenure of the Howard government and which the Rudd government failed to investigate despite having previously promised to do so.[27]

The policy of mandatory detention is itself a breach of due process, made possible by the fact that the constitution does not include express protection for the right to personal liberty. The High Court has held that the doctrine of separation of powers in Chapter III of the constitution prohibits parliament from vesting in the executive a power to deprive a citizen of liberty without ultimate oversight by a court.[28] However, this due process right is significantly limited in that the court has held that its protections do not apply to categories of so-called 'non-punitive' detention – that is, detention which occurs outside the realms of criminal law, examples of which include detention for public health purposes and immigration detention.[29] Importantly, the court has also held that the list of circumstances in which non-punitive detention may be authorised is not closed.[30] Because non-punitive detention stands outside the protection afforded to people suspected of having committed a crime, a person can be detained by the executive without bringing them before the courts. Furthermore, the High Court has held that the duration of detention is not subject to the constraint of reasonableness – indeed it can be indefinite[31] – and has also held that detention does not become punitive even if its conditions are inhumane.[32] The bizarre consequence of this is that a person who is detained because they are suspected of having committed a crime is in an infinitely better position than a person who is detained for non-criminal reasons. The effect of this have been felt only in the case of non-citizens and of people in off-shore detention, but in Australia as well, where a 2007 report by the Commonwealth Ombudsman found that 247 citizens and lawful residents had been unlawfully detained under the *Migration Act 1958* (Cth).[33]

The off-shore detention regime has been particularly problematic from a due process perspective. In 2016 the High Court held that Australia had the power to transfer asylum-seekers to Nauru for detention and that people detained there were not, in law, detained by Australia, despite the obvious fact that Australia was the instigator and financier of the detention.[34] In 2015 the Australian Human Rights Commission released a report which found that the treatment of child

[27] Hutton (2011).

[28] *Chu Kheng Lim v Minister for Immigration, Local Government and Ethnic Affairs* (1992) 176 CLR 1, 27–29.

[29] *Chu Kheng Lim v Minister for Immigration, Local Government and Ethnic Affairs* (1992) 176 CLR 1, 32.

[30] *Kruger v Commonwealth* (1997) 190 CLR 1, 164.

[31] *Al-Kateb v Godwin* (2004) 219 CLR 562, 651 and *Re Wooley; Ex parte Applicants M276/2003* (2004) 225 CLR 1, 77.

[32] *Behrooz v Secretary, Department of Immigration and Multicultural and Indigenous Affairs* (2004) 219 CLR 486, 499.

[33] Commonwealth Ombudsman (2007).

[34] *Plaintiff M68/2015 v Minister for Immigration and Border Protection* (2016) 257 CLR 42.

asylum-seekers breached Australia's international human rights obligations.[35] The government's response was defiance rather than contrition, and the Human Rights Commissioner, Professor Jillian Triggs, was subject to bullying tactics by government senators – one of whom, Senator Ian McDonald, had not even read the report[36] – when she appeared before a parliamentary committee. Even the act of affording refugees legal representation has attracted the ire of the government. In 2017 Minister for Immigration and Border Protection Peter Dutton said that it was 'un-Australian' for lawyers to represent refugees – an attitude towards due process which is wholly inconsistent with the rule of law.[37] The United Nations has condemned the detention regime on several occasions, most recently describing it as arbitrary and open-ended.[38] In late 2018 Medecins Sans Frontieres issued a report stating that the psychological harm inflicted on detainees was akin to torture.[39]

Disrespect for the rule of law has also been manifested within Australia's borders in particular in the government's attitude to race. The most alarming instance of this was 'Operation Fortitude', in which the Immigration Department ordered Border Force officers to patrol the streets of Melbourne to check the migration status of 'any individual [they might] cross paths with'.[40] How the officers were to ascertain whom to question was not made explicit, but the operation raised the obvious suggestion of racial profiling, and was abandoned after protesters intervened on the streets of Melbourne to bring it to a halt. The Immigration Department published a ham-fisted explanation to the effect that the document announcing the operation had been 'clumsily worded', unconvincing to anyone who had read what was, in fact, a clearly worded document authorised both by the Border Force commander and by the Border Force Assistant Secretary for Communications and Media, and which had (twice) been sent to the minister's office.[41]

The racism reflected in Operation Fortitude was covert, in the sense that it was presumed that in the absence of expressed criteria that would be used to determine who would be challenged to prove lawful residence in Australia, appearance – that is, race – would have been the obvious marker which would have invited official attention. But there have also been overt statements which indicate that in the minds of some – and in that of Immigration Minister Peter Dutton in particular – 'Australianess' was synonymous with whiteness. This became evident in 2016, when Dutton said that the Fraser government had made a mistake by allowing Lebanese migrants to settle in Australia, because two-thirds of the people who had been charged with terrorist offences were 'from second and third generation

---

[35] Australian Human Rights Commission (2014).

[36] Chalmers (2015).

[37] Hall (2017).

[38] Ben Doherty (2018).

[39] Metherell (2018).

[40] Mills, Hasham and Willingham (2015).

[41] Taylor (2015).

Lebanese-Muslim background.'[42] This of course meant that they were Australians, rather than Lebanese, but the statement indicates a mindset that some migrants can never really become 'real' Australians. This attitude is deplorable not only because it is racist but because it is also dangerous: Australia undoubtedly faces a threat from terrorists motivated by Islamic extremism. Strategies for countering terrorism are heavily dependant on maintaining the co-operation of communities that might be targeted by terrorist recruiters, both in order to diminish the likelihood that extremist messages will fall on receptive ears and in order to maintain the flow of intelligence from the target community. It follows that statements which alienate ethnic or religious groups undermine anti-terrorist operations – and indeed make terrorism more likely.

These statements by Dutton reflected the same attitude to the rule of law as evinced by fellow ministers Greg Hunt, Alan Tudge and Michael Sukkar, who were forced to apologise to judges of the Victorian Court of Appeal in order to avoid being charge with contempt after saying that the judges were 'hard left activists' and the court itself an 'ideological experiment.'[43] The same attitude was also reflected by Prime Minister Scott Morrison, who brushed aside concerns that a plan to deprive convicted terrorists of citizenship would breach international law if it rendered them stateless by saying 'what I do is press on and just get it done.'[44] This exemplifies a cavalier attitude toward the law, as though law is a bothersome impediment to the government, which should be absolved from its legal obligations just so that it can 'get things done'.

The reason why these instances of disregard for the rule of law are significant, is that they show that governments cannot be trusted to act lawfully. But they are also significant not only for what they reveal about the attitude of the government but also because they are deliberate: Being *seen* to have contempt for restraint on government power is part of a strategy designed to appeal to a conservative political constituency which resists social change, resents what it sees as propitiation of ethnic minorities and refugees, and which is therefore content to see state power expanded in order to 'deal with' such groups, even at the expense of individual liberty. Yet tolerance that conservative elements in Australian society have for the abridgement of the rule of law is both paradoxical and dangerous. The paradox lies in the fact that members of this constituency would object to ideologies – which they would perceive as leftist – involving an increase in the power of the state vis-à-vis the individual, and would consider such policies a threat to their own freedom. Yet they tolerate such policies when directed against marginal groups because they cannot imagine themselves as being members of such groups. The danger lies in the fact that once state power is unleashed, it becomes impossible to control, and policies inimical to the rule of law initially directed against the few are soon directed against the many.

---

[42] Anderson (2016b).

[43] Wahlquist (2017).

[44] Calcutt (2018b).

1.3 Political Corruption

To say that the public considers politicians to be dishonest is a truism and the stock in trade of comedians, but political dishonesty in its various manifestations has become a significant problem in the mind of the Australian public. A 2018 survey by Transparency International Australia indicated that 85% of respondents believed that federal politicians were corrupt, while 56% had personally witnessed or suspected favouritism by a politician ore an official in exchange for donations or support.[45]

Particularly corrosive to the public interest is favouritism in the exercise of power. The most recent example of this was provided by the 2018 au pair scandal, which arose from the revelation that Immigration Minister Peter Dutton had intervened to grant visas to two au pairs who were about to be deported. One au pair, who was going to work for a relative of a major donor to the Liberal party, admitted that she planned to breach the conditions of her visa, yet the minister overruled departmental advice that she should be deported.[46] The au pair saga also illustrates how insubstantial is the convention, common to all countries with a Westminster system of government, that misleading parliament is one of the misdeeds for which a minister should resign. When the au pair scandal broke, Dutton made a categorical statement to parliament that he did not know the people for whom the au pairs worked, but it subsequently transpired that one of them worked for a former colleague of his from his days in the Queensland Police Service.[47] There then ensued a semantic dance over the meaning of the word 'know', and whether it could be said that one did not know a person merely because one had not had contact with them for some time. Although a Senate committee found that Dutton had misled parliament, he did not resign and was indeed given public support by the Prime Minister.[48]

Unfortunately, instances of ministers retaining their jobs despite having misled parliament are not uncommon. Significant examples in the recent past include Foreign Affairs Minister Alexander Downer telling parliament that Asian countries had not raised with him the withdrawal of an Australian aid programme whereas corresponded revealed that they had,[49] Aged Care minister Bronwyn Bishop telling parliament that checks on nursing homes were 'continuing' whereas in fact they had

---

[45] Transparency International Australia (2018).

[46] Probyn and Jennett (2018).

[47] Crowe (2018).

[48] Senate Legal and Constitutional Affairs Committee (2018).

[49] Murdoch (1996).

not even begun,[50] Defence Minister Robert Hill stating that the government was unaware of the abuse of prisoners in Iraq even though the Department of Defence had had knowledge of the events for several weeks,[51] the notorious Children Overboard scandal which involved Prime Minister Howard, Defence Minister Peter Reith and Immigration Minister Phillip Ruddock all maintaining that asylum-seekers had thrown children overboard despite having been informed by the navy that that had not happened,[52] John Howard's three denials to parliament that he had had discussions about ethanol subsidies with a businessman, subsequently found to be untrue,[53] Veterans' Affairs Minister De-Anne Kelly giving parliament incorrect information about the date on which she had approved a grant because on the date she had actually authorised the grant it fell outside her ministerial responsibilities,[54] Foreign Minister Alexander Downer[55] and Trade Minister Mark Vaile[56] telling parliament that they were unaware that the Australian Wheat Board had been breaking sanctions on Iraq whereas they had been aware of these activities six years previously, Employment Minister Michaelia Cash, telling a Senate committee five times that neither she nor her staff had been involved in tipping off the media about an AFP search of the offices of the AWU, whereas in fact one of her advisers leaked the location and timing of the raid to the media,[57] and Attorney-General George Brandis telling the Senate that he had consulted the Solicitor-General over a new process for providing legal advice by the latter whereas in fact he had not.[58] Special mention is warranted of the government's dishonest justification of Australia's participation in second Iraq War,[59] which was based on misrepresentation by both Alexander Downer and John Howard of what intelligence agencies said was the level of threat posed by suspected Iraqi weapons of mass destruction.[60] Taking a country into an unjustifiable war obviously ranks as one of the greatest evils a government can engage in, and the dishonesty was compounded by a subsequent inquiry the terms of reference of which were framed so as to omit any investigation of what the government knew at the time.[61]

Why do these instances of misleading parliament not lead to ministerial resignations? The reason is that the conventions which governed politics a generation ago – think of the Profumo scandal in the United Kingdom – are no longer followed.

---

[50] Wright (2000).

[51] Colvin (2004).

[52] Allard (2004).

[53] Seccombe (2003).

[54] Maher (2004).

[55] Rudd (2017, pp. 415–16).

[56] Hart (2006).

[57] Seccombe (2017).

[58] Senate Legal and Constitutional Affairs Committee (2016).

[59] Swieringa (2013).

[60] Rudd (2017, pp. 305–15).

[61] Rudd (2017, p. 420).

Nowadays a government's first instinct is to try to ride out a scandal even if it involves the supposed cardinal offence of misleading parliament and, unfortunately, such efforts are usually successful.[62] The calculation is nowadays political rather than ethical, and whether a minister resigns depends on whether the government thinks it will suffer more embarrassment by retaining the minister than by submitting to pressure and firing him.

Yet another form of political corruption is pork-barrelling. In Australia, pork-barrelling has become particularly evident in the allocation of Community Development Grants, the overwhelming bulk of which governments distribute to marginal seats,[63] giving them funding per capita which is grossly disproportionate to that allocated to other parts of the country.[64] Sometimes pork-barrelling occurs on a far grander scale, the most notorious example being the decision by Minister of Agriculture, Barnaby Joyce, to relocate the Australian Pesticides and Veterinary Medicines Authority from Canberra to Armidale in his own electorate of New England. The decision was found to be unjustifiable when subject to a cost-benefit analysis (which the government resisted releasing)[65] and which pointed an economic loss of $200 million arising from the cost of the move, the cost of recruiting new staff to replace those unwilling to move, reduced capacity due to disruption and loss of income to the pesticides and veterinary industries due to delays that would occur in determining product approval applications.[66] Sometimes pork barrelling – or more accurately, attempted pork-barrelling – occurs even before the food is in the trough, as happened in the run-up to the 2019 election, when Environment minister Melissa Price announced the awarding of grants before the grants application process had commenced.[67]

More recently, a report by the Commonwealth Auditor-General[68] found that 43% of successful applications for money from a $ 100 million sports grant fund distributed by then Sports Minister Bridget McKenzie in the run-up to the 2029 election were ineligible under the programme rules,[69] and that funds were allocated to projects on the basis of which electorate they fell into, rather than in accordance with the relative merit of projects as identified by Sport Australia, the body whose role it was to assess applications. The Minister's office conducted what the report referred to as its own 'parallel assessment process'[70] based on political criteria rather than on merit, resulting in 61% of grants being awarded to projects which fell below the threshold set by Sport Australia as being deserving of funding. The political basis

[62] Seccombe (2003).

[63] Bagshaw (2019).

[64] Bagshaw and Baird (2018).

[65] Vidot (2016).

[66] Donaldson (2016).

[67] Hasham (2019).

[68] Australian National Audit Office (2020).

[69] Karp (2020).

[70] Australian National Audit Office (2020, para 3.20).

upon which grants were awarded also led to what the report termed a 'distribution bias':[71] 41% of the grants went to 47 marginal seats or other seats being targeted by the government in the upcoming election, which meant that, on average, each of these seats received $ 872 000. By contrast, the remaining 59% of funds was distributed among the other 103 non-marginal seats, giving an average of $ 572 000 per seat.[72] The overall result was that funds were allocated to projects that were, on an objective basis, not deserving of funding, but which were located in seats that the government needed to retain or win in order to stay in office, whereas funds were denied to projects which would have been funded had money been allocated on the basis of merit. The sports grants scandal amounted to what an opposition Senator referred to as 'industrial-scale pork-barrelling.'[73]

Pork-barrelling is common enough, but it is difficult to find an example elsewhere in the world of what might be called 'negative pork-barrelling.' Yet such occurred in Australia in the wake of the 2013 election. This is demonstrated by the conduct of Liberal candidate Sophie Mirabella who, having been defeated in that election, let slip during her subsequent campaign in 2016 that, had she been re-elected in 2013, the government would have built a new hospital in her electorate.[74] Apart from being monumentally injudicious, the comment illustrated the extent to which politicians subordinate public needs to political interest.

These instances of the abuse of public power highlight the need for the creation of a federal anti-corruption commission, which 67% of respondents to the 2018 Transparency International Australia survey indicated support.[75] However the major parties have resisted calls for one for years. The effectiveness that such a commission would have in preventing pork-barrelling was revealed when none other than Barnaby Joyce said that if such a commission was ever to be established, ministerial decisions on grants for rural areas made contrary to departmental advice should be exempted from its scope – a position which combined both refreshing candour and an implicit admission of the partiality that pervades this area of government.[76] In 2018 the Morrison government announced that it would introduce legislation for the establishment of a commission, but the proposed scheme was criticised as embodying the type of commission that one would establish if one didn't want a commission: The body would not conduct hearings in public, would not be able to initiate investigations on its own motion and would have to satisfy the same standard required of criminal investigations before being able to act.[77] Former Victorian Supreme Court Judge Stephen Charles described it as 'a fraudulent nonsense, designed to protect ministers, parliamentarians and their aides from investigation

---

[71] Australian National Audit Office (2020, paras. 4.27–4.36).

[72] Tillett and McIlroy (2020).

[73] Snape (2020).

[74] Anderson (2016a).

[75] Transparency International Australia (2018).

[76] Koziol (2018).

[77] Witbourne (2018).

and exposure.'[78] It would, in effect, have been the Potemkin Village of corruption commissions.

Finally, the payment of political donations, although not itself a corrupt activity, is certainly conducive to corruption, for the obvious reason that donations may smooth the way for donors to obtain privileged access to ministers and/or exercises of discretion in their favour. The obvious prophylactic for this is disclosure, but our legislation in this area is exceedingly weak, and the major parties have been united in fighting tooth and nail against strengthening it. Only donations above $13 800 need be disclosed, there is no restriction of the number of donations that an individual or corporation may give (so it is possible to make multiple donations below the threshold) nor is there any ceiling on the amount that may be donated.[79] Furthermore, the time lag inherent in in the reporting schedule means that it can take up to 19 months donations to be disclosed. This becomes particularly significant in the case of donations made during an election campaign, because it can be months after an election that it becomes apparent who made donations to parties during the course of it. The Commonwealth regulatory system lags far behind that of the states, some of which require that donations be disclosed within seven days during an election. In 2018 the Coalition government and Labor united to defeat a proposal by the Greens for real-time disclosure of political donations at Commonwealth level and a lowering of the disclosure threshold to $1 000, which illustrates how the major parties share an interest in maintaining the opacity of the current system.[80]

Why are ministers are able to retain office despite blatant malfeasance and/or inefficiency? This is dealt with in detail in Chap. 7, but the essential reason is that while in theory ministers are responsible to parliament and hold office only so long as they retain the support of a majority of MPs, party discipline in Australia is so strong that it is inconceivable that a minister would lose the support of their own party simply because they had abused their powers or had made a serious error of judgement. Only if a government comes to the conclusion that it would suffer more political damage through the embarrassment of retaining a minister than by sacrificing him or her is that person ever asked to resign – in other words, whether a minister resigns or not depends more on the degree of public outrage than on the severity of the wrongdoing or incompetence. Unfortunately, the threshold of embarrassment seems so high in Australia as to be almost impossible to reach. Governments have proved remarkably thick-skinned when subject to criticism, and it is only rarely that ministers are forced to resign.

---

[78] O'Malley (2019).

[79] Chivers, Carmella, Wood, Danielle and Chivers, Kate (2018).

[80] Dalzell and Clarke (2018).

1.4 Poor Standards of Interpersonal Behaviour

Apart from engaging in abuse of power, Australian politicians display behaviours that alienate them from the general public, all the more so because party hierarchies prioritise power over civility, with the result that bad behaviour almost always goes unpunished. No doubt there would, among any group of randomly selected people, be a number whose behaviour was discreditable, but the proportion of MPs and senators who engage in harassment, bullying and boorishness is surely in excess of that which occurs in society as a whole. Because these occurrences are drip-fed into the public consciousness month by month with one scandal sinking from public view as the next occurs, there is a tendency to become inured to them. Therefore, although a comprehensive catalogue of instances would fill a book on its own, it is worthwhile to mention a number of the most memorable over the past two decades, so as to understand how, when viewed in aggregate, they illustrate the depths to which behaviour has sunk.

Some MPs seem to make a career out of bad behaviour – a notorious example of this was Wilson Tuckey, who not only attempted to pressure a State Police Minister to quash a traffic fine that Tuckey's son had incurred,[81] but also repeatedly engaged in disruptive behaviour in parliament, having been suspended from the House on 14 occasions.[82] The behaviour of Labor MP Belinda Neal was equally obnoxious, having famously said to Liberal MP Sophie Mirabella 'Evil thoughts will turn your baby into a demon' during a committee hearing.[83] Her behaviour outside parliament was no better, as evidenced by the public disturbance she created during a notorious public escapade at the Iguana Joe's nightclub in Newcastle, reportedly threatening the manager and pressuring one of her own staffers to into changing her account of the incident.[84] Sophie Mirabella garnered a reputation for personal offensiveness[85] as well as for misbehaviour in parliament, having been suspended five times in just 36 days.[86] Perhaps the low point in parliamentary conduct in recent times was the false accusation made under cover of parliamentary privilege by Senator Bill Heffernan, described by some as a person with a fixation about homosexuality,[87] that then High Court Justice Michael Kirby had solicited sex from prostitutes.[88] Subsequently, Heffernan commented on the fact that Prime Minister Julia Gillard had no children by stating that she was 'deliberately barren'[89] Labor MP Craig Thompson who was found to have misused a union credit card, *inter alia* to pay for

81 Lewis (2003).

82 Lundie (2013).

83 ABC News (2008a).

84 ABC News (2008b).

85 Kotsios (2013).

86 Dow (2011).

87 Gordon (2002).

88 Hudson and Gordon (2002).

89 Australian Associated Press (2007).

the services of prostitutes. Despite this, the governing Labor party refused to expel him from its caucus as that would have imperilled its slender majority. A similar lack of moral judgment was evident when the Labor government pressured the Speaker Harry Jenkins into resigning from the speakership (thereby gaining an additional vote on the floor of the House) and installed Peter Slipper, a renegade Queensland National who had had a falling out with his own party, in his place – despite the fact that Slipper was facing allegations of misuse of parliamentary travel entitlements. The government continued to support Slipper as Speaker even after he was accused of sexual harassment of a staffer.[90]

A feature of some politicians' conduct is the striking inconsistency between their public statements and their private behaviour. A prime example of this is provided by Barnaby Joyce. From an allegation of sexual harassment (leaked, and then inconclusively investigated, by the National Party),[91] to his self-confessed pursuit of women[92] (at odds with his campaign against marriage equality based on 'traditional family values,')[93] to his loss of leadership of the National Party after conducting an affair with a staffer (who was moved from job to job among the National Party parliamentary staff after the affair was disclosed)[94] he displayed both failed moral judgement and hypocrisy. In similar vein, fellow Nationals MP Andrew Broad was found to have used a 'sugar daddy' website to meet a woman in Hong Kong, having previously presented himself as a family man, and having insulted LGBTI people during the same-sex marriage debate.[95]

Particular vitriol on the part of politicians is reserved for those who expose errors on the part of a government or its MPs. A notable example was when Foreign Minister Julie Bishop lashed out at a New Zealand Labour MP who had asked a question in that country's parliament which had the effect of revealing that Barnaby Joyce was a New Zealand citizen. Bishop went so far as to say that she could not trust a New Zealand government in the wake of the affair[96] – a statement which revealed how desperate the government was to retain power, and how the supposed unique ANZAC relationship could so casually be sacrificed to political spite born of the embarrassment caused to the government by Joyce's carelessness.

The problem of bullying in parliament has become prominent of late. It transcends political boundaries. Peta Credlin, Tony Abbott's chief of staff, was notorious for bullying staff in the then Prime Minister's office and MPs.[97] Labor MP Emma Husar bullied her own staff, including by subjecting them to verbal abuse

[90] Maher (2012).

[91] Chan (2018).

[92] Halfpenny (2018).

[93] Ford (2014).

[94] Massola and Gartrell (2018).

[95] Shields (2018).

[96] Gartrell and Remeikis (2017).

[97] Piotrowski (2016) and Sava (2016, pp. 19–22, 54–5).

and requiring them to perform menial tasks unrelated to their official role.[98] The Liberal leadership challenge of 2018 was accompanied by a concerted campaign by supporters of the challenger to bully MPs into voting against Malcolm Turnbull.[99] Perhaps the most extraordinary sequel to this was a statement by Liberal Senator Concita Fierravanti-Wells, who denied that the Liberals had a bullying problem and who said that 'politics is a tough game and 'if you can't stand the heat get out of the kitchen.'[100] Similarly former Liberal Senator Helen Kroger that politics is 'a rough and tough game' and 'an environment which is not for everyone.'[101] Such statements are reprehensible because they cast the blame on the victims' supposed lack of toughness, rather than on those who use intimidation to obtain political advantage. The message that it sends is that the abandonment of the expectation of civil treatment is the expected – and acceptable – cost of a career in politics. This has the obvious consequence of deterring many public-spirited and talented people from entering public life.

Sometimes the behaviour of politicians reveals cruel arrogance, as when Tony Abbot, Mark Morrison and Peter Dutton laughed at the prospect of Pacific island nations being inundated by rising sea-levels,[102] an attitude echoed by Environment Minister Melissa Price's slur against Pacific nations when she said 'For the Pacific, it is always about the cash. I have my chequebook here. How much do you want?' to the former president of Kiribati.[103] More recently, Deputy Prime Minister Michael McCormack said that Pacific islanders whose countries faced inundation from rising seas caused by climate change because their citizens could come to Australia to pick fruit.[104] Yet despite their capacity to deliver insults, politicians have proved remarkably sensitive when they themselves face ridicule, and have not hesitated to use their power to shield themselves from embarrassment. The Liberal party in Victoria unsuccessfully attempted to get Twitter to delete a joke about then Assistant-Treasurer Kelly O'Dwyer, making a false copyright claim in the process. Immigration Minister Peter Dutton's staff asked journalists to take down a photograph published on-line on the ground that it was 'unflattering.'[105] Jobs Minister Michaelia Cash, embroiled in controversy after making sexist innuendos about opposition female staffers, was shielded from the press by a whiteboard as she walked through a corridor in parliament the following day.[106]

Some of the behaviour is objectionable not because it is morally discreditable but because it demonstrates profound stupidity – think of Kelly O'Dwyer accidentally

---

[98] Snow, Koziol and Smith (2018).

[99] Murphy (2018).

[100] Calcutt (2018a).

[101] Barbor (2018).

[102] Keany (2015).

[103] Conifer (2018).

[104] Smee (2019).

[105] Hunt (2016).

[106] Workman (2018).

voting against her own government,[107] Senator Eric Abetz's statement that abortion causes breast cancer,[108] Tony Abbott's opinion that global warming might be positive because 'more people die in cold snaps'[109] and Liberal MP Craig Kelly's statement that Russia's responsibility for downing of a MH17 should be 'slightly looked over' (sic) in the interests of improving relations with that country.[110]

The tenor of political discourse in Australia has become degraded. Certainly it seems uniquely obscene: Sexist cat-calls[111] and insults (the latter a particular vice of Liberal Democrat Senator David Leyonhjelm[112] and Liberal Senator Barry O'Sullivan[113]) are a feature of parliamentary debates in a way that does not occur in comparable parliamentary democracies. Even in the midst of heated debate in countries facing profound crises – think of the struggle in the United Kingdom between Margaret Thatcher and the union movement, or in South Africa between the government and the ANC – references were not made by politicians to their opponents' genitalia. Yet that was the level that political conflict descended to when Julia Gillard was subjected to obscene sexism.[114] Why is it that leaders of political parties have not only done nothing to raise standards but have actively contributed to their lowering? One needs only think of the contrast between Tony Abbott's exhortation to a 'kindler, gentler' parliament when he was trying to win the support of independent MPs following the indecisive 2010 election,[115] and the ensuing viciously rancorous 43rd parliament, notable for being the most disorderly on record, due in most part to disruptive behaviour engaged in by the Coalition.[116]

What is it about Australian politics that has caused it to become so debased, and has caused oratory to decline in inverse proportion to the rise in obscenity? Why is it that, instead of attracting the brightest and best, parliament has become the nation's emunctory? Is it simply the product of randomness that politics features a disproportionate number of obnoxious people, or is there something deeper at work which attracts power hungry people with limited intellects and even lower standard of behaviour? The reason why our political class is sunk in a morass of corruption, incompetence and boorishness is not just because of personalities involved: The problem is systemic and, I would suggest, stems from two fundamental defects, one ethical, the other constitutional.

The ethical defect is the attitude that the successful acquisition of power and its effective use are the chief criteria by which politicians should be judged, and that

[107] Keany (2016).

[108] Howden (2014).

[109] Bourke (2017).

[110] Crowe and Bourke (2018).

[111] Grattan (2011).

[112] Australian Associated Press (2018). See also Farr (2018).

[113] Worthington (2018).

[114] Gillard (2015, pp. 105–6).

[115] Hawley (2010).

[116] Lundie (2013).

moral failings belong either in a separate 'private' sphere or can be outweighed by effective political performance. The truth is that one cannot separate a person's moral calibre from other aspects of their lives, and it is naïve to think that lack of integrity in one area of a person's life does not act as a pointer to their behaviour in general. People who engage in bad behaviour are not just colourful 'characters', and to excuse them on that basis amounts to enabling. They are louts who substitute what they lack in intellect with abusive behaviour, poisoning the body politic in the process. We need to recognise that personal moral failings say something about the entirety of a person and, if sufficiently serious, should mark them as unfit for office – even if they are effective 'retail politicians'. So the reason why the bully and the vulgarian are unsuitable for office is because their behaviour demonstrates a defect in morality which will taint the political decisions they take. Such personality defects create a social risk because people who are ethically compromised in the way they conduct inter-personal relationships are also likely to make unethical decisions in the way they exercise public power. An additional resultant harm is the loss to society of the abilities of those who do not embark on a political career because they do not want to go through the experience of working with those who are poorly behaved. Political behaviour will improve only if the public demands it, and gives effect to that demand by taking both the personal and the political into account when deciding for whom to vote.

The other aspect of the political behaviour problem is constitutional, and more specifically relates to the electoral system. A feature of Australian politics frequently remarked on is the polarisation of politics to a far greater degree than in other parliamentary democracies. Voters are tired of politicians' relentless negativity towards their opponents, reflected in the attitude that that every suggestion by their own party is meritorious and every suggestion by the opposition is damnable. Logic tells us that this cannot be true – no single party can have a monopoly on wisdom, yet the confrontational, winner takes all style of politics in Australia encourages this approach while discouraging consensus-building. The critical fact to appreciate is that this style of politics is a direct product of the electoral system which, because it is based on single-member seats, inevitably leads to domination by two blocs and the denial significant parliamentary representation to smaller parties. These two blocs, spurred by undying hatred, fight over a prize which is all the more to be wished for because it does not have to be shared with anyone else. The electoral system thus not only enables combative to come to the fore, but actually rewards them. One could not imagine a system better designed to produce a conflict-ridden, bi-polar political structure which fosters poor standards of behaviour. As mentioned elsewhere in this book, the contrast in the tenor of politics could not be more different from Australia than it is in New Zealand, where that country's proportional electoral system creates a disincentive for parties to become eternal enemies and which rewards consensus politics. Another consequence of the domination of politics by two main blocs is that because it is extremely difficult – indeed almost impossible – to have a successful political career outside of one or other of them, our politicians are people who have had to cut their ethical cloth to fit the demands of either the Coalition or Labor, which means that many of them are therefore morally compromised from the outset of their careers.

The only way this will change is if voters themselves to come to the realisation that it is the constitutional system itself – and in particular the electoral system – which leads to the style of politics that we are burdened with, and that therefore only by adopting an electoral system which allows all points of view to be represented in parliament, which gives a multiplicity of parties the opportunity to participate in government and which rewards consensus that the current mould of politics will be broken. In short, if we change the electoral system, as is argued in Chap. 4, we will change the type of politician who achieves success and, by opening opportunities for that new breed of politician, we will create an environment which maximises the chance of an improvement in standards of political conduct.

1.5 Poor Leadership

One of the most significant shortcomings of the political class which causes great harm to the national interest, is the prioritisation of the acquisition and retention of power over all else, perhaps best illustrated by Tony Abbott's statement 'I would do anything for this job. The only thing I wouldn't do is sell my arse, but I'd have to give serious thought to it.' during negotiations with independent MPs after the 2010 election.[117] Of course, leadership is acquired through power and it would be naïve not to expect a desire for power to motivate leaders. Yet the mark of a true leader – as distinguished from the mere power-seeker – is the capacity to make decisions which are in the public interest, even if (or perhaps particularly if) those decisions put the leader him or herself at risk of losing power if they are unpopular. In other words, leadership sometimes involves telling voters what they don't want to hear. Unfortunately, there is a striking absence of willingness to do this in contemporary Australian politics. Contrasting examples which illustrate this point are provided by John Howard's adoption of the GST on the one hand and the approach to climate change by Tony Abbott, Malcolm Turnbull and Scott Morrison on the other.

In adopting the GST, Prime Minister Howard took a significant political risk which could have spelled electoral disaster for his government, yet the policy was undoubtedly necessary from an economic perspective in that it broadened the base of taxation while providing an opportunity to reduce income taxes. Most economists have subsequently called for the removal of exemptions and the raising of the rate of GST in the long-term interests of revenue stability.

By contrast, the failure to adopt a climate change policy which would enable Australia to transition from coal-dependence to renewables was motivated by a desire to retain power rather giving the electorate the uncomfortable news that the interests of the country – and of the world – required the prioritisation of long-term

[117] ABC News (2011).

environmental concerns over short-term concerns about energy prices. Instead of having the courage to deliver a difficult message about the future of energy over the next 10, 20 or 50 years, the focus of Liberal leaders in the second decade of the twenty-first century was on winning the next election, peddling slogans such as ‘Keep the lights on.’ This was irresponsible behaviour towards future generations, who would not look back fondly on predecessors who had sacrificed the environment in order to enjoy a few more years of cheap energy. Their motivations for their stance was also puzzling: Abbott made numerous different – and inconsistent – pronouncements on climate change,[118] and also appeared to be infected with an anti-science prejudice tinged with religious overtones.[119] Turnbull believed the science but was too afraid of the Liberal right wing to change the direction of policy. Morrison was nakedly populist in his approach, seeking to divert public attention away from climate change and towards the sole consideration of energy pricing. The overall result was the loss of years of opportunity to address an issue which is as urgent as it is important.

In the case of Labor too, leadership has been sorely lacking in recent times. Under Hawke and Keating, Labor took the enormously difficult and courageous steps of floating the Australian dollar and reducing import tariffs, despite fierce opposition from both business and unions. Equally significant and controversial were the introduction of compulsory superannuation and the privatisation the Commonwealth Bank and of Qantas. Keating’s prime-ministership was notable for its innovation and his willingness to initiate public debate on ‘big ideas’ which were of no immediate political benefit, such as the republic and Indigenous rights. Keating’s intellectual approach led to his being hated the right of Australian politics precisely because he showed up the intellectual inadequacies of the meat and potatoes men (and they are mostly men, as witness the fact that Tony Abbot’s cabinet contained only one woman, with Abbott himself serving as Minister for Women) who led the Coalition, and who, as conservatives, were opposed to any questioning of the fundamentals of society. Yet, despite its past history of policy innovation and supposedly being a party of social justice, Labor has, in recent years, been timorous in relation to reform – its long-standing opposition to marriage equality being a prime example. It also cravenly subordinated principle to self-interest on the issue of pokies regulation, which it abandoned in the face of opposition from the gaming and hospitality industry from which it receives significant political donations, and was swept along by populism in relation to the re-introduction of refugee detention.

In the current political climate in Australia, the idea of a politician acting out of principle at the cost of suffering political detriment would be considered bizarre by most career politicians. Winston Churchill’s famous decision to cross the floor and leave the Conservative party in favour of the Liberals in 1904 because of the former’s restriction of the rights of trade unions, its discriminatory attitude to Jewish migrants and its opposition of free trade, would be seen as absurd in contemporary

[118] O’Malley (2018).

[119] Middleton (2017).

Australia. That would be even more true of his self-exclusion from power during his 'wilderness years' of the 1930s, during which his rejection of appeasement with Nazi Germany alienated him from the political establishment. By contrast, today's politician submits to unthinking and slavishly subordination to the party line as the price of political advancement, and parrots stock phrases contained in daily briefing notes – often distributed in a ham-fisted manner, and thus embarrassingly discovered by the press, as on one memorable occasion when Coalition MPs were all told to say 'The government is functioning exceptionally well'[120] – rather than using their own voice to discuss political issues. It is no wonder that the increase in party discipline has been marked by a corresponding decline in oratory.

Australians have become tired of politicians' focus on the retention of power for its own sake to the detriment of policy development. They are also increasingly disillusioned with the major political parties, as is evidenced by the steady increase in support for minor parties (that is parties other than Labor, Liberal and National) and independents. This may in part be due to the generally better calibre of independent MPs as compared to those representing the major parties, as demonstrated by the careful and considered approach they take when considering issues – one need only contrast MPs such as Tony Windsor, Andrew Wilkie and Cathy McGowan, who considered each issue on its merits, with the ovine docility of MPs from the major parties, who rarely express an independent opinion. Perhaps the most excruciatingly embarrassing example of subordination to party discipline was provided by an interview with then Minister for Workplace Relations Bill Shorten, who said that he agreed a statement that had been made by Prime Minister Julia Gillard despite it being evident that he did not know what its content was.[121] In similar vein, Senator Penny Wong's obedience to party discipline was such that despite herself being gay, she expressed public support for Labor's then opposition to marriage equality.[122]

It is obvious that some who have attained leadership roles in recent times were temperamentally unfit to hold office. Kevin Rudd's famed fluency in Mandarin, which had been predicted as contributing to a positive relationship with China, was overshadowed by an obscenity-laced commentary on China's stance on global warming[123] and equally obscene attempt to record a message in Mandarin.[124] More damaging to him however was his legendary ungovernable temper[125] and disregard for staff[126] which made it impossible for people to work with him and which ultimately cost him his leadership.

---

[120] Massola (2015b).

[121] Sky News (2012). A video of the interview can be seen at https://www.youtube.com/watch?v=Kf4nlIEHfaU

[122] Abrahams (2010).

[123] Marr (2010).

[124] A video of this can be seen at https://www.youtube.com/watch?v=4RqAjMo19fs

[125] Gillard (2015, p. 42).

[126] Gillard (2015, pp. 16–17).

Tony Abbott was equally flawed, as had become evident from early in his career. As Minister for Health in the Howard government, he and members of his staff reportedly threatened pharmaceutical companies with negative repercussions if they marketed the RU486 abortion drug.[127] He also refused to meet terminally ill Bernie Banton, who was campaigning for funding for victims of mesothelioma, saying that Banton's attempt to meet him was 'a stunt' and impugned Banton's integrity saying that he was not 'pure of heart'.[128] An incident which revealed much about Abbott's own integrity occurred in an interview during the 2004 election campaign, when he was asked whether he had met Cardinal George Pell. After initially said he could not recall the meeting, Abbott was forced to admit that the meeting had occurred when the interviewer confronted him with the details of it.[129] This meant either that Abbott was lying or that his memory was so defective that he failed to recall a not insignificant event which had occurred just a few days before, which surely indicated that he was unfit for office, on grounds either of dishonesty or of incapacity. In his public statements he has offended women (suggesting that they were responsible for household ironing),[130] Indigenous people (saying that they should not be given support in order to enable them to live in traditional communities because it was a 'lifestyle choice')[131] and survivors of child abuse (saying that although he went to a Catholic school, no-one did anything to him perhaps because he was 'not good-looking enough').[132] Some of his behaviour was simply crass, as exemplified by his saying that a little bodily contact did no harm while being photographed surrounded by female netball players[133] and in his reference to the 'sex appeal' of a female election candidate.[134] Perhaps the nadir of his endorsement of sexism was his appearance at a political rally at which signs such as 'Ditch the witch' and 'Juliar – Bob Brown's Bitch' were on display.[135] His emotional instability was evidenced by a bizarre incident of silent head-wobbling rage during a television interview.[136] In office he made a threat to 'shirtfront' Vladimir Putin at the over the shooting down of MH17,[137] but instead regaled bemused world leaders at the G20 summit with a speech in which he bemoaned the difficulty of getting parliament to agree to the $7 Medicare co-payment.[138] His much-vaunted commitment to Christian beliefs was

[127] Cronin (2006).

[128] West (2007).

[129] Warne-Smith (2004). A video of the interview can be seen at https://www.youtube.com/watch?v=ZvYzLIywCiA

[130] Hausegger (2010).

[131] Bourke (2015).

[132] Doyle (2017).

[133] Munro (2013).

[134] Bourke (2013).

[135] Massola (2015a).

[136] Dick (2011). A video of Abbott's remarks and the subsequent television interview can be seen at https://www.youtube.com/watch?v=UUdPabnXUNA

[137] Massola and Cox (2014). .

[138] Taylor and Hurst (2014).

shown to be conditional – at least in relation to acceptance of refugees – when, in a speech to a conservative think-tank in the United Kingdom, he said that the Gospel injunction to love one's neighbour was leading Europe to catastrophe.[139]

How is it that politicians who engage in the types of behaviour discussed in this chapter meet with success? How is it that people such as Tony Abbott and Kevin Rudd, whose personalities made both of them so manifestly unsuited to any office, rise so far as to become Prime Minister? Surely people like this are not the best Australia has to offer? Again, as in the case of standards of political behaviour, I would argue that the solution lies in systemic reform, specifically in reform of the electoral system, in such a manner as to allow a wider range of voices – and thus a wider range of talents – to be brought into politics, a theme which is addressed in detail in Chap. 4.

1.6 Governmental Instability

A discussion of the state of politics in Australia would not be complete without some discussion of the public dissatisfaction generated as a result of the changes in Prime Minister as a result of internal party coups during the period 2010–2018, which saw Julia Gillard topple Kevin Rudd, Kevin Rudd topple Julia Gillard, Malcolm Turnbull topple Tony Abbott (having previously toppled Abbott as leader of the Liberal party when it was in opposition) and, after an abortive attempt by Peter Dutton to topple Malcolm Turnbull, Scott Morrison emerge as Turnbull's replacement. It must be recognised, however, that the power of the governing parliamentary party to change its leader – and thus who heads the government – is an inescapable feature of the Westminster system, under which it is parliament, and not the voters, who choose the Prime Minister. Many people lose sight of this fact because of references during election campaigns to 'the people choosing the Prime Minister'. Replacement of sitting Prime Ministers by their own parties has occurred in most countries in which the Westminster system operates, so Australia is by no means unique in this regard. However what does make Australia different is the frequency with which such events occur.

The repeated changes in leadership within the Liberal and Labor parties is not the product of some vice or ennui specific to those parties. Nor do these occurrences stem principally from the personalities involved (although, given the venom with which the protagonists treat each other, there is no doubt that personality plays a role). Rather they are the product of the electoral system which has led to the domination of Australian politics by a Labor – Coalition duopoly, led by parties who increasingly do not reflect the views of voters, evidence for which is provided by the fact that in the 2019 election 25% of voters gave their first preference votes to minor

[139] Baird (2015).

parties or independents.[140] This was despite the fact that, under our current electoral system, such votes are wasted in the sense that in the vast majority of electorates, votes become effective only once the voter indicates a preference for one or other of the major parties.

A system based on single-member electorates – particularly when the number of electorates is few relative to the voting population – inevitably leads to political domination by two major political blocs, whose success in gaining power depends upon maintaining unity at all costs. For this reason, both the Liberals and Labor are, in reality, not single parties but ramshackle coalitions. Menzies' creation of the so-called 'broad church' of Liberal party embracing both liberalism and conservatism was not so much a stroke of political genius as a cynical act bordering on a confidence trick, designed to paper over the differences between two profoundly incompatible ideologies – one prioritising individual liberty and a limited state, the other traditional institutions and a strong state – in order to exclude Labor from power. This alliance of convenience is also fundamentally unfair to voters, who do not know whether, by electing a Liberal government, they are electing a government that will be liberal, will be conservative – or may even be one in which there will be an ideological change mid-term if one wing of the party wrests power from the other, as happened when Malcolm Turnbull was toppled in 2018. The same is of course true of Labor, with its Byzantine factions of left, centre and right (and with sub-factions within factions) that bedevil every aspect of its operation, from candidate selection to cabinet formation.

It is precisely because the two largest parties are in reality uneasy alliances of incompatible ideological bedfellows that struggles become internalised within parties,[141] rather than playing out through political competition between a variety of parties, as would be the case if we had an electoral system which gave representation to parties which fairly reflected the range of diverse political opinions of voters. The internal coups that occurred during the 2010–2018 period usually occurred – or at least were justified by – the incumbent's decline in opinion polls. Yet, as was the case with the Rudd-Gillard-Rudd and the Turnbull-Abbot-Turnbull rotations, each new leader themselves suffered a decline in the polls, leading to a new leadership challenge. I would argue that the underlying reason for the unpopularity of successive leaders is not only related to the calibre of the leaders themselves, but is rather the fact that both the Liberals and Labor no longer have the loyalty of the voting public and that therefore, even if briefly buoyed up during a honeymoon period, whoever leads them is bound eventually to become unpopular. So it is the fact that neither of the major parties reflects the true sentiments of voters that is the underlying cause of the unpopularity which in turn leads leadership challenges. And the terrible conundrum faced by voters is this: Under our current electoral system, there are no potential governing parties other than Labor or the Coalition to whom they

[140] Results for various elections can be found on the Australian Electoral Commission website at https://results.aec.gov.au/

[141] For an analysis of intra-party factionalism and its impact on democracy see Warhurst (2018).

can turn, and so until the electoral system is changed in such a way as to break the Labor – Coalition duopoly, the voting public is doomed to play the role of a hapless ball, hit from one political bloc to the other in a never-ending game of political tennis.

In our single member electoral system, which gives only two players a chance of winning government, the avenue to power lies in maintaining the existence of a large party that preserves unity between a number of disparate factions. And it is because those parties are factionalised because they try to be too broad that Australia is politically unstable. This also explains why we cycled through six Prime Ministers in eight years. Contrast this with New Zealand, which has a system of proportional representation which gives many parties a realistic chance of achieving representation in parliament. Under such a system, party size does not matter because there is no electoral disadvantage in forming a small ideologically-cohesive party – such a party still has a realistic change of participating in government. Since its introduction in 1996, the New Zealand system has resulted in multi-party coalitions of remarkable stability – and, in contrast to Australia, has seen only three Prime Ministers in ten years. Angela Merkel, Chancellor of Germany, which has the same electoral system as New Zealand, has seen six Australian Prime Ministers during her 13 years as German Chancellor. The idea that an unfair electoral system such as ours is a necessary evil because it promotes governmental stability is therefore false, as the example of New Zealand (and of many other countries which use proportional systems) makes clear.

1.7 Lack of Confidence in the System of Government

Popular dislike and mistrust of politicians is hardly surprising, nor is it unique to Australia. The real significance of the survey results discussed at the start of this chapter lies in the fact that disenchantment with politicians is causing voters to become disillusioned with the system of government itself. In the wake of the 2016 federal election, when support for minor parties surged, Mark Triffitt, Politics lecturer at the University of Melbourne, observed that the election result 'highlighted that the dam wall of public dissatisfaction with the major parties and their disconnected way of "doing" democracy is near-to-bursting.'[142] The 2017 *Mapping Social Cohesion* report by the Scanlon Foundation found that 41% of respondents said that the current system of government either needed major change or should be completely replaced. [143] A 2018 Lowy Institute poll found that only 62% of respondents were of the view that democracy was preferable to any other form of government, while 23% agreed that non-democratic government might be preferable and 15% did not care what form of government we have.[144] A 2018 survey by the Museum of Democracy and the University of Canberra found that whereas 86% of voters were

[142] Triffitt (2016).

[143] Markus (2017).

[144] Oliver (2018).

satisfied with Australia's democracy in 2007, satisfaction had declined to 41% in 2018.[145]

Voters are obviously aware that something is wrong with the political system but struggle to articulate what the source of the problem is and what the remedy might be. A Fairfax survey,[146] in which respondents were asked to identify what they thought the flaws in the system of government were, elicited a wide range of responses, including compulsory voting, control of candidate selection by the major parties (made easier by the declining membership of parties), the adversarial nature and 'win at all cost' style of politics, an electoral system which favours a few major parties, politicians' lack of courage to make long-term and/or difficult decisions for fear of advantaging the opposition, the role of the media in encouraging short attention spans, the refusal of politicians to answer questions or admit error, the role of campaign donations in elections, growing social inequality and the operation of the federal system as problems.

As solutions, participants suggested reform of the electoral system, abolition of the states, limitations on the terms that politicians can serve, the establishment of a national anti-corruption agency, the encouragement of consensus politics, legislation by means of citizen-initiated referenda, abolition of political parties and the conscription of people to serve as parliamentarians. Some of these solutions are viable, some are not. Some are incompatible with a free society. Some are worthy aspirations rather than being actual solutions. Many respondents were able to articulate no more than a general dissatisfaction with the political system but not how it might be improved.

So Australians realise that something is wrong, but what is the remedy? Given that these popular discontents relate to how we are governed, the solution must obviously lie in changing the rulebook by which government is conducted – in other words, in changing the constitution.

1.8 Overcoming Impediments to Constitutional Reform

Constitutional reform would address the key sources of dissatisfaction with the political system: Electoral reform would ensure that all shades of opinion were heard in parliament and would break the duopoly currently enjoyed by Labor and the Coalition. The fact that any system embodying an element of proportionality (which is critical to fair representation of voters) would almost inevitably require coalition government would reward consensual rather than confrontational politics. An increase in the coercive powers of parliamentary committees so as to compel ministers to answer questions would enhance governmental accountability. The inclusion in the constitution of a bill of rights protecting more than just the few rights currently safeguarded would protect the individual from the excesses of state power. The abolition of the federal system would remove a source of wasteful

[145] Stoker, Evans Halupka, (2018, pp. 9, 21).

[146] Merrells (2018).

duplication and would mean that government resources were no longer allocated with reference to the wholly artificial entities which are the states. Codification in the constitution of the powers of the Governor-General – or of a President if Australia finally severed its link with its foreign monarch – would provide certainty and legal enforceability to the rules that govern crucial elements of the rules by which government operates. A broadening of the rules of standing, which determine who can initiate court action to enforce the constitution, would make for an engaged citizenry and would enhance government subjection to the law.

Unfortunately, most people have not been able to make the connection between the dissatisfaction they feel with the institutions of government and the need to reform of the rules by which those institutions operate. Indeed, the constitution is largely unexamined by those who are subject to it. Furthermore, notwithstanding the obvious deficiencies in the current constitution, arguing for constitutional reform is considered pointless, and even quixotic.

Part of this is a result of history – it is notorious that of 44 amendments proposed since 1901, only eight have been successful. Anyone proposing constitutional reform therefore invites the response that constitutional change is so difficult as to not be worth considering – which makes the prophecy that constitutional change is doomed to fail self-fulfilling.

Then there is the reflexive conservatism born out of ignorance.[147] The root cause of this lies in the poor standard of civics education in Australia (discussed in Chap. 12) which leaves people lacking the tools needed to debate constitutional matters. Although they may recognise that there are problems with the political system, their knowledge of the constitution is insufficient to enable them either to identify defects in it as the source of those problems or to understand how the problems could be remedied. For this reason, they instinctively vote 'No' when presented with the idea of constitutional change. It is of course understandable that people are afraid to meddle in a system they do not understand – but the solution is to become constitutionally literate, intellectually curious and attitudinally critical, rather than to be afraid of reform.

Shortcomings in the educational system can shoulder only part of the blame. The other contributing factors are complacency and indifference. Each of us needs to accept the civic responsibility of understanding how we are governed, yet here is a general disinterest and apathy about constitutional matters among many Australians. This is reflected in the 'If it ain't broke, don't fix it' mantra, the underlying assumption of which is invalid, given the fact that the constitution manifests flaws which are both obvious and significant. But even if there were no flaws in the constitution,

[147] See the bizarre defence of the electoral system in Sheppard (2018), whose author states that the electoral system is 'among the best in the world' (an astounding statement given the gross disproportionality of elections for the House of Representatives) because the Senate has semi-proportional representation (true only if one ignores the fact that the allocation of an equal number of seats to each State caused gross disproportionality) and because we have a 'stable and moderate party system', which leads to politics being 'fairly predictable' – which of course is the cause of the duopoly Australia lives under.

'not being broken' sets an insufficiently high standard for our most important legal document. Should not the aim be to have the best possible constitution, rather than one that meets a test of bare functionality? Good citizenship imposes an obligation on us to take an interest in, and engage with, constitutional matters, yet many people are happy to remain cocooned in the false belief that the constitution is of no relevance to them, unaware that it affects their everyday lives. The focus of Australian politics remains relentlessly on bread and butter issues such as interest rates and the cost the cost of energy. This is to some extent understandable, but it also has an element of pettiness and selfishness about it, because it demonstrates that many people are simply not interested in bigger and more important questions, such as thinking about what the role of the government vis-à-vis the individual should be. Unless people are willing to lift their gaze above the mundane, narrow perspective of their individual circumstances, our public institutions will never improve. To that extent, we have the sub-standard politicians we deserve.

Most disturbing of all – and undoubtedly the greatest impediment to reform – is the negative role played by politicians themselves, a product of their obvious self-interest in maintaining the status quo. Sometimes this takes the form of outright deceit. As an illustration of this, one can point to the repeated public pronouncements by the Howard government that it would not offer an apology in Parliament to Indigenous Australians, on the ground that to do that would be to expose the Commonwealth to legal claims for compensation. This was nonsense – the law of parliamentary privilege gives absolute legal immunity to anything said during the course of parliamentary proceedings. An apology in parliament simply could not have had the effect of making the government liable to pay compensation. Similarly, when the Rudd government created a committee to hold public consultations on the question of whether Australia should have a bill of rights, the terms of reference included a restriction that options canvassed by the committee 'should preserve the sovereignty of the Parliament' – in other words, should not suggest options which gave the courts the power to invalidate legislation or government actions which infringed a bill of rights. Anyone reading this clause without the benefit of knowing the Constitution would have assumed that the committee was being barred from proposing a model that would confer a radical new power on the courts. Yet the Commonwealth parliament is not 'sovereign', in that sense, and never has been. From the moment the Constitution came into force the courts have had the power to invalidate legislation passed by parliament – including legislation which infringes the four rights that the Constitution protects expressly, as well as others that it has subsequently been held to protect impliedly. The mandate given to the committee was misleading, because it suggested that the relationship between parliament and the courts was different from what it actually is.

On other occasions – the 1999 referendum on a republic being one example[148] – politicians have used the mantra 'If you don't know, vote No' as a means of blocking constitutional change. This tactic is reprehensible because it relies on emotion

[148] Political strategies adopted during the referendum are discussed in Williams (2000, pp. 492–8).

instead of rational debate and because it takes advantage of ignorance. Politicians have a moral obligation to explain their case to voters – and to educate them if need be. The 'If you don't know, vote no' manoeuvre avoids that, first because it shuts down debate and second because it inspires fear in the minds of voters as a means of avoiding the obligation to address the substantive issue at hand. Even more shameful is the fact that this approach exploits voter ignorance – in fact it provides a clear incentive to politicians who are opposed to constitutional change to keep voters in a state of constitutional illiteracy, because the less educated voters about constitutional matters, the more likely they are to vote against change. I had experience of this attitude when giving evidence before an inquiry by the Joint Standing Committee on Electoral Matters on the status of civics education in Australia in 2006.[149] My comments on the lack of public awareness of constitutional matters led to the following interchange with Senator Brandis (who later became Attorney-General):

Senator BRANDIS – When we talk about our system and the Constitution I do not think we should necessarily be teaching students – unless they are law students – about the particular provisions of the Constitution; what we should be teaching them about is democracy. It is in the high concept of democracy, rather than in the prosaic words of the Constitution, that we are going to capture people's imaginations.

Dr Harris – I agree that you have to inspire in the students an appreciation of democracy, but their next question will be: how is this theory implemented in Australia? The answer is: through the mechanism of the Constitution. Then they will ask: how does the Constitution work and does it actually deliver what you say it promises?

Senator BRANDIS – Do you think they do say that? Or do they – because, with all its limitations, I think we all have a sense that Australia is a pretty well-functioning democracy – merely accept that, without requiring the statutory verification of it?...........

Dr Harris – They do accept that, but they are unconcerned with the defects of it – for example, the idea that you can win a general election with significantly fewer popular votes than the opposition. They do not think that far ahead, unless you point it out to them, because the Constitution conceals that possibility.

Senator BRANDIS – I know that has happened a couple of times but that can happen in the most sophisticated democracy, can't it?

Dr Harris – The risk of it happening if you have proportional representation is very, very small. I was in New Zealand when they introduced the MMP system. At least you knew then that whatever government was formed had a majority of voters behind it. I think we should want our students and young people to ask those questions, and to say: 'This is a wonderful theory you are teaching us. Now show us how it works in the document.'

Senator BRANDIS – That is where I do not agree with you because, apart from teaching law students and perhaps politics students, I would not have thought

[149] Joint Standing Committee on Electoral Matters (2006).

you need to make the language of the document itself accessible to teach students, particularly secondary students, about the way Australian democracy works.
Dr Harris – But isn't it their Constitution?
Senator BRANDIS – I am not saying you should not, but I do not think you need to.

Surely a public representative should want all citizens – not just law students – to be as interested in, and as knowledgeable about, their constitution as possible, and for that constitution to be in the most accessible language possible? Lack of knowledge can operate only to the benefit of the powerful and to the disadvantage of the powerless.

Such proposals for reform as have been floated by governments have been self-serving. Examples of this were proposals by the Howard government to have 4-year terms for the House of Representatives[150] and to reduce the Senate's legislative powers,[151] both of which would have augmented the substantial dominance the constitution already gives to the majority party in the House of Representatives. Some commentators have advocated fixed-terms for the House of Representatives in order to deprive governments of the opportunity to choose the timing of elections in such a way as to give themselves a political advantage (although in fact, most federal governments run to very close to full term). Such a mechanism, an example of which is provided by the s 24B of the *Constitution Act 1902* (NSW), can however never really operate in a system based on the doctrine of parliamentary responsibility. As is contemplated by ss 24B(2) and (3), a government cannot remain in office if it loses the support of the house to which it is responsible or if the house rejects a money Bill. This means that a government that wants to call a general election before the expiry of its term can do so simply by voting itself out of office.[152] We need to recognise that constitutional reform is pointless unless it deals with the fundamental problems that afflict the constitution.

The reason for politicians' opposition to transformational constitutional reform is easy to understand: Most of the reforms mentioned earlier in this chapter, which are discussed in detail in subsequent chapters, would, by making government more representative, more accountable and more subject to restraint, operate to the detriment of the politicians who benefit from the maintenance of the status quo. It is because politicians have so much to lose that they will do whatever it takes to derail reform – and will, without compunction, exploit voters' fear of change. Public distrust of public institutions coupled with a lack of willingness to consider constitutional change creates a paradox in which current institutions are maintained to the benefit of the very politicians whom Australians distrust.

150 Jackman (2002).

151 Hudson (2002).

152 The same applies in the United Kingdom where, despite the fact that the *Fixed-term Parliaments Act 2011* (UK) mandates 5-year terms for the House of Commons, the system of responsible government requires that there be an exception, contained in s 2(3)(a) of the Act which requires an early election if there is a vote of no confidence in the government (which a government could of course initiate itself). Thus, despite the fact that elections had been held in 2015, the Act was unable to prevent an early election being called in 2017.

The solution, to put it bluntly, is for Australians either to stop whinging or start acting, and to find the courage to do what is necessary to address their discontents. Instead of being afraid of constitutional reform, we should embrace it and see in it an opportunity to re-frame our political system in a way which will restore faith in how government operates.

The object of this book is to show that many of the things that are cause for complaint are rooted in deficiencies in the constitution, and that therefore hope of restoration of confidence in our institutions lies in constitutional reform. But it would be mistaken to proceed on the basis that we should reform our institutions *in order to* make people feel satisfied. Reform of our institutions would certainly have that effect, because it would make our institutions more representative, more restrained in their dealings with the people and more subject to scrutiny. But the motivation for constitutional reform should not be just to 'make most people happy'. If it was, we would end up with a system as defective as the one we have now, in which majoritarian views would dominate to the detriment of fairness to the individual.

For this reason, a key theme of this book, explored in Chap. 2, is the identification of the *values* that should underpin a constitution, which is the preliminary question that must be settled long before drafting a constitution. The most important values to establish are those which govern the relationship between the individual and the state, because that is the key relationship ultimately underpinning the entire constitution. Only then would it be appropriate to move to the next stage – that of drafting the text of a constitution which gives effect to those values. The next chapter discusses the question of why values are important, and what fundamental value should underlie the constitution.

References

ABC News (2011) Abbott rejects sell-out claims. 28 August 2011

ABC News (2008a) Liberal MP demands apology over 'demon baby' comment. 30 May 2008

ABC News (2008b) Ex-Neal staffer 'crumbled' over Iguanas account – Melissa Batten says her original statement was shredded. 23 June 2008

Abrahams S (2010) Penny Wong labelled a hypocrite. Star Observer. 25 July 2010

Allard T (2014) Fresh holes in PM's account of children overboard. The Sydney Morning Herald. 17 August 2004

Anderson S (2016a) Sophie Mirabella's Wangaratta hospital claim a 'staggering revelation', Bill Shorten says. ABC News. 22 April 2016

Anderson S (2016b) Peter Dutton suggests Fraser government made mistake by resettling Lebanese refugees. ABC News. 22 November 2016

Australian Associated Press (2007) Fed: Gillard is not qualified to be leader: Heffernan. 1 May 2007

Australian Associated Press (2018) Leyonhjelm tells senator to 'stop shagging men' during women's safety debate. The Guardian. 28 June 2018

Australian Electoral Commission Official Election Results. https://resultsaecgovau/. Accessed 3 Oct 2018

Australian Human Rights Commission (2014) The forgotten children – National inquiry into children in immigration detention. https://www.humanrights.gov.au/sites/default/files/document/publication/forgotten_children_2014.pdf. Accessed 15 Oct 2019

Australian National Audit Office (2020) Award of Funding under the Community Sport Infrastructure Program. https://www.anao.gov.au/work/performance-audit/award-funding-under-the-community-sport-infrastructure-program. Accessed 25 February 2020

Bagshaw E (2019) Coalition accused of pork-barrelling grants in marginal seats. The Sydney Morning Herald. 10 March 2019.

Bagshaw E, Baird L (2018) The $1 billion cost of pork barrelling revealed. The Sydney Morning Herald. 20 January 2018

Baird J (2015) Love your neighbour: what Abbott gets wrong about the Gospel. ABC News. 29 October 2015

Barbor L. 'Rough and tough game': Liberal Party women deny bullying problem. ABC News. 30 August 2018

Bingham (2007) The rule of law. Cambridge Law J 66:67–85

Bachelard M (2014). Witness details burns claims. The Sydney Morning Herald. 7 February 2014

Bourke L (2013) Tony Abbott highlights Liberal candidate Fiona Scott's 'sex appeal' during campaign event. ABC News. 14 August 2013

Bourke L. 'Lifestyle choice': Tony Abbott stands by controversial comments despite indigenous leader backlash. Sydney Morning Herald. 11 March 2015

Bourke L. Tony Abbott says climate change 'could be beneficial' because people die in the cold. The Sydney Morning Herald. 10 October 2017

Calcutt L (2018a) Liberal senator Connie Fierravanti-Wells offers advice for women in politics. Nine News. 18 September 2018

Calcutt L (2018b) Scott Morrison wants new terror laws in place by end of year. Nine News. 23 November 2018

Cameron S, McAllister I (2018) Australian election study interactive data. https://australianelectionstudyorg/interactive-charts/. Accessed 2 Oct 2019

Chalmers M (2015) Ian Macdonald: great at sexism, not so good at reading and writing. New Matilda. 25 February 2015

Chan G (2018) Barnaby Joyce sexual harassment allegation: Catherine Marriott speaks out. The Guardian. 18 September 2018

Chivers C, Danielle W, Kate C (2018) Time for the federal government to catch up on political donations reform. The Conversation. 14 August 2018

Clarke J (2008) Report of the inquiry into the case of Dr Mohamed Haneef. Attorney General's Department, Canberra

Colvin M (2004) Hill abuse statement a 'whitewash.' ABC News. 16 June 2004

Commonwealth Ombudsman (2007) Lessons for public administration – ombudsman investigation of referred immigration cases. Commonwealth Ombudsman, Canberra http://www.ombudsman.gov.au/__data/assets/pdf_file/0018/26244/investigation_2007_11.pdf. Accessed 15 Oct 2019

Conifer D (2018) Environment Minister Melissa Price accused of dinner-time slur against Pacific Island nations. ABC News. 17 October 2018

Coorey P, Cynthia Banham C (2007) PM tells the party: I could free Hicks – but won't. The Sydney Morning Herald. 7 February 2007

Cronin D (2006) Abbott linked to 'threat' over RU-486 use. Canberra Times. 1 June 2006

Crowe D (2018) Peter Dutton au pair decision helped former Queensland Police colleague. The Sydney Morning Herald. 30 August 2018

Crowe D, Bourke L (2018) Liberal MP Craig Kelly angers colleagues over MH17 remarks. The Sydney Morning Herald. 18 July 2018

Dalzell S, Clarke M (2018) Labor, Coalition unite to reject legislative changes which would make political donations more transparent. ABC News. 15 November 2018

Dick T (2018) Silence speaks louder than words in this story. The Sydney Morning Herald. 10 February 2011

Doherty B (2018) Australia is reported to UN human rights council over illegal detention of asylum seekers. The Guardian. 15 September 2018

Donaldson D (2016) Robbing Canberra to pay Armidale: cost analysis doesn't support 'national interest.' The Mandarin. 28 November 2016
Dow A (2011) Sophie kicked out, yet again. The Border Mail. 27 August 2011
Doyle E (2017) 'Is he making light of this issue?': Chris Hemsworth takes a swipe at Tony Abbott for shocking gaffe where former PM described himself as being not 'good-looking enough' to be a victim of child abuse. The Daily Mail. 10 October 2017
Evershead N, Farrell P, Laughland O (2014) 'In' or 'out': what we know about 'enhanced screening' of asylum seekers. The Guardian. 3 July 2014
Farr M (2018) Senator David Leyonhjelm's long history of slurs', News.com.au. 3 July 2018. https://www.news.com.au/finance/work/at-work/senator-david-leyonhjelms-long-history-of-slurs/news-story/482528128f7c684b0af5be39246c0add. Accessed 15 Oct 2019
Ford C (2014) Barnaby Joyce does not understand marriage. The Sydney Morning Herald. 7 February 2014
Gartrell A, Remeikis A (2017) Julie Bishop says she could not trust a New Zealand Labour government after Barnaby fiasco. The Sydney Morning Herald. 15 August 2017
Gillard J (2015) My story. Random House, Sydney
Gordon M (2002) On the prowl. The Age. 16 March 2002
Grattan M (2011) Catcall sparks parliamentary gender row. The Sydney Morning Herald. 2 June 2011
Habib M, Collingwood J (2008) My story: the tale of a terrorist who wasn't. Scribe Publications, Carlton North
Halfpenny K (2018) 'I acknowledge there were issues': Barnaby Joyce tells some, not all, in new book. The New Daily. 8 August 2018
Hall B (2017) Lawyers representing asylum seekers are 'un-Australian': Peter Dutton. The Sydney Morning Herald. 28 August 2017
Hart C (2006) Vaile warned six years ago. The Australian. 2 March 2006
Hasham N (2019) Liberals announce environment grants before applications open. The Canberra Times. 4 April 2019
Hausegger V (2010) Beware the iron fist. The Canberra Times. 13 February 2010
Hawley S (2010) The powerful three. ABC Radio National – PM. 24 August 2010
Head M (2009) The Haneef inquiry: some unanswered questions. J Australasian Law Teachers Assoc 2:95–112
Hicks D (2010) Guantanamo: my journey. William Heinemann, North Sydney
Howden S (2014) Eric Abetz draws link between abortion and breast cancer before World Congress of Families. The Sydney Morning Herald. 7 August 2014
Hudson P (2002) Revealed: Libs push for Senate revamp. The Sunday Age. 14 April 2002
Hudson P, Gordon M (2002) Heffernan sacked after Kirby attack discredited. The Age. 19 March 2002
Hunt E (2016) Peter Dutton photo goes global after he demands it be deleted from internet. The Guardian. 4 May 2016
Hutton M (2011) SIEV X: ten years on the questions remain. ABC News. 17 October 2011
Jackman C. Howard backs four-year gap between polls. Sunday Telegraph 2. 14 April 2002
Joint Standing Committee on Electoral Matters (2006) Inquiry into Civics and Electoral Education. Transcript of proceedings. 11 August 2006. https://parlinfoaph.gov.au/parlInfo/search/display/displayw3p;db=COMMITTEES;id=committees%2Fcommjnt%2F9566%2F0004;query=Id%3A%22committees%2Fcommjnt%2F9566%2F0000%22. Accessed 15 Oct 2019
Laws J (2017) The rule of law: the presumption of liberty and justice. Judicial Rev 22:365–373
Karp P (2020) Sports rorts: almost half the projects funded were ineligible, audit office says. The Guardian. 13 February 2020
Keany F (2015) Dutton overheard joking about sea levels in pacific islands. ABC News. 11 September 2015
Keany F (2016) Kelly O'Dwyer accidentally endorses bill criticising Turnbull Government in procedural bungle. ABC News. 13 October 2016

Kotsios N (2013) Windsor gives Mirabella the 'nasty prize.' The Border Mail. 1 July 2013
Koziol M (2018) Nationals MPs rebel over government's integrity commission plans. The Sydney Morning Herald. 29 November 2018
Lewis S (2003) Tuckey tried to get son off fine. The Australian. 20 August 2003
Lundie R (2013) 'That's it, you're out': disorderly conduct in the House of Representatives from 1910 to 2013. Parliament of Australia, Canberra. https://www.aph.gov.au/About_Parliament/Parliamentary_Departments/Parliamentary_Library/pubs/rp/rp1617/DisorderlyConduct. Accessed 15 Oct 2019
Maher S (2004) Kelly faces growing pressure to quit. The Australian. 9 December 2004
Maher S (2012) Peter Slipper quits in sexism brawl after government support backfires. The Australian. 10 October 2012
Markus A (2017) Mapping social cohesion. The Scanlon Foundation. https://scanlonfoundation.org.au/archived-research/mapping-social-cohesion-survey-2017/. Accessed 15 Oct 2019
Marr D (2010) We need to talk about Kevin…Rudd, that is. The Sydney Morning Herald. 7 June 2010
Massola J (2015a) Julia Gillard on the moment that should have killed Tony Abbott's career. The Sydney Morning Herald. 23 June 2015
Massola J (2015b) Leaked talking points tell ministers to say 'our cabinet is functioning exceptionally well'. The Sydney Morning Herald. 19 August 2015
Massola J, Gartrell A (2018) PM's office says Vikki Campion jobs did not breach rules because she was not Barnaby Joyce's 'partner.' The Sydney Morning Herald. 12 February 2018
Massola J, Cox L (2014) Tony Abbott vows to 'shirtfront' Vladimir Putin over MH17 tragedy. The Sydney Morning Herald. 13 October 2014
Merrells N (2018) We asked if and how you thought Australia's democracy was broken This is what you said. Sydney Morning Herald. 3 April 2018
Metherell L (2018) Nauru mental health situation equivalent to 'victims of torture', Medecins Sans Frontieres says. ABC News. 3 December 2018
Middleton K (2017) Abbott looks to Pell on energy policy. The Saturday Paper. 14–20 October 2017
Mills T, Hasham N, Willingham R (2015) Border Force fiasco: operation Fortitude cancelled as protest shuts down Melbourne streets. The Age. 28 August 2015
Munro P (2013) 'Netball dad' Abbott at home among the young and sweaty. The Sydney Morning Herald. 29 August 2013
Murdoch, L (1996) Downer Stung by Asian Aid Admission. The Age. 25 June 1996
Murphy K (2018) Kelly O'Dwyer says MPs were bullied during spill, as senator vows to name names. The Guardian. 4 September 2018
O'Brien N (2011) Australians saw Habib tortured, says officer. The Sydney Morning Herald. 13 February 2011
O'Malley N (2018) Abbot's backbone is more rubber than steel say his opponents. Sydney Morning Herald. 22 August 2018
O'Malley N (2019) Coalition's anti-corruption body 'a sham', retired judge says. Sydney Morning Herald. 13 May 2019
Oliver A (2018) Lowy Institute Poll. https://www.lowyinstitute.org/publications/2018-lowy-institute-poll. Accessed 15 Oct 2015
Piotrowski D (2016) Peta Credlin 'bullied staff, damaged reputations and mocked the sacrifice of everyone': former top Tony Abbott staffer unleashes on his chief of staff. The Daily Mail. 7 March 2016
Probyn A, Jennett G (2018) Peter Dutton overruled Border Force advice when granting au pair's visa after AFL boss emailed his office. ABC News. 2 September 2018
Rudd K (2017) Not for the faint-hearted – a personal reflection on life, politics and purpose. Macmillan, Sydney
Sava S (2016) The road to ruin – how Tony Abbott and Peta Credlin destroyed their own government. Scribe, Brunswick
Seccombe M (2003) A different sort of truth. The Sydney Morning Herald. 16 August 2003
Seccombe M (2017) The true story of Michaelia Cash's union raids. The Saturday Paper. 4 November 2017

Senate Legal and Constitutional Affairs Committee (2016) Nature and scope of the consultations prior to the making of the Legal Services Amendment (Solicitor-General Opinions) Direction 2016. Commonwealth of Australia, Canberra. https://www.aph.gov.au/Parliamentary_Business/Committees/Senate/Legal_and_Constitutional_Affairs/SolicitorGeneralOpinion/Report. Accessed 15 Oct 2019

Senate Legal and Constitutional Affairs Committee (2018) Allegations concerning the inappropriate exercise of ministerial powers, with respect to the visa status of au pairs, and related matters, Commonwealth of Australia, Canberra. https://www.aph.gov.au/Parliamentary_Business/Committees/Senate/Legal_and_Constitutional_Affairs/AuPairs/Report. Accessed 15 Oct 2019

Sheppard J (2018) Australians don't trust politicians, but the pollies don't appear fussed. ABC News. 30 May 2018

Shields B. Andrew Broad built himself a pedestal, then fell off it. The Sydney Morning Herald. 17 December 2018

Sky News Agenda, 26 April 2012. https://wwwyoutubecom/watch?v=Kf4nlIEHfaU. Accessed 19 Oct 2019

Smee B (2019) Pacific islands will survive climate crisis because they 'pick our fruit', Australia's deputy PM says. The Guardian. 16 August 2019

Snape J (2020) Federal government targeted marginal seats in potentially illegal sports grants scheme, auditor-general reports. ABC News. 16 January 2020.

Snow D, Koziol M, Smith A (2018) 'New revelations about Emma Husar have grave implications for the party. The Sydney Morning Herald. 28 July 2018

Stoker G, Gerry, Evans M, Halupka M (2018) Democracy 2025 report no 1 – trust and democracy in Australia. Museum of Democracy/University of Canberra, Canberra

Swieringa, M (2013) Howard ignored advice and went to war in Iraq. The Sydney Morning Herald. 12 April 2013

Taylor L (2015) Border force announcement went to Peter Dutton's office twice before release. The Guardian. 30 August 2015

Taylor L, Hurst D (2014) G20: Tony Abbott 'whingeing' about domestic agenda on world stage. The Guardian. 15 November 2014

Tillett A, McIlroy T (2020) Why the sports grants scandal won't go away. Financial Review. 3 February 2020

Transparency International Australia (2018) Global Corruption Barometer Survey Results. http://transparency.org.au/september-2018/. Accessed 15 Oct 2019

Triffitt M (2016) Australia needs to lead again on democratic innovation. The Conversation. 26 August 2016

Vidot A (2016) Deputy PM blocks labor from accessing the cost-benefit analysis of moving the chemical regular from Canberra. ABC News. 19 October 2016

Wilson S, Fein J (2015) Leadership for the Greater Good Swinburne. http://apoorgau/system/files/54535/apo-nid54535-92856pdf. Accessed 2 Oct 2019

Wahlquist C (2017) Coalition ministers will not face contempt charges after court accepts apology. The Guardian. 23 June 2017

Warhurst J (2018) Party democracy myths and hypocrisy. The Canberra Times. 6 December 2018

Warne-Smith D (2004) Abbott admits Pell meeting after denial – Election 2004. The Australian. 1 October 2004

West A (2007) Abbott accuses asbestos fighter of political stunt. The Sydney Morning Herald. 31 October 2007

Williams G (2000) Why Australia kept the queen. Saskatchewan Law Rev 63:477–501

Witbourne M (2018) Ex-ICAC boss says Obeid would be a free man under Morrison's plan. The Canberra Times. 14 December 2018

Workman A (2018) Michaelia cash literally hid behind a whiteboard so people wouldn't take photos of her. Buzzfeed. 1 March 2018

Worthington B (2018) Conservative senators walk out as Greens leader slams their treatment of women. ABC News. 28 November 2018

Wright T (2000) By her own rules, Bishop should go. The Age. 8 March 2000

Chapter 2
A Question of Values

Abstract This chapter explains that before determining how to construct the mechanisms of government in a constitution, one first has to determine what value system should underpin the document. A constitution, like any law, is only so good as the ethical values that are its foundation. The chapter then examines the concepts of the rule of law and constitutionalism, before explaining that while broad discussion of values was conspicuous by its absence from the constitutional conventions of the 1890s, the Commonwealth Constitution nevertheless reflects by default the values of that time, which in jurisprudential terms are those of democratic positivism. In contrast to that, the chapter argues that a value-system based on human dignity, and in particular the ideas of Kant and Rawls, should underpin the constitution. These values form the framework of the remainder of the book.

2.1 Constitutionalism and the Rule of Law

There has been much talk from government ministers over recent years about 'Australian values'. Sometimes these values are so generic as to be meaningless – here one need think of 'mateship' which the Howard government wanted to include in a preamble to the constitution. In similar vein one can think of the frequently referred to concept of the 'fair go'. However, in the context of public law, values have a more substantive meaning.

In the case of constitutional law, the most basic value is that of constitutionalism, which means that the power of the state must be defined and limited by the law. The application of this principle was illustrated more than 200 years ago in the case of *Entick v Carrington*,[1] one of the most famous cases in English common law, in which the court held that merely because an action (in this case a search of a radical pamphleteer's house and possessions) was ordered by a government minister did not in itself make the action lawful. The court held that the government, just like anyone else, was subject to the law, and needed to point to legal authority which justified its trespass upon him.

---

[1] (1765) 19 St. Tr. 1030.

B. Harris, *Constitutional Reform as a Remedy for Political Disenchantment in Australia*, https://doi.org/10.1007/978-981-15-3599-4_2

The concept of the rule of law operates as a corollary to constitutionalism. As noted in Chap. 1, the rule of law is a very broad concept, but at its most basic it means that the law should be accessible, should not be applied arbitrarily and should be adjudicated by independent courts. Unless people can challenge unlawful actions by the government in the courts, and unless the government respects decisions of the courts, the definition and limitation of powers of the government by law are of no relevance.

But although constitutionalism and the rule of law are of fundamental importance, they are not in themselves sufficient to ensure a just society. The mere fact that the powers of government are defined by law and that those laws are adjudicated by independent courts says nothing about the *content* of the law. An unjust law which has been enacted according to correct legislative procedure, which is prepublished, which is applied equally to all and infractions of which are adjudicated by independent courts can still work great injustice. Therefore in order to ensure that laws generally, and the constitution in particular (as the law which authorises all other laws), are just, it is necessary to frame a system of values which the law should be built on. As noted in Chap. 1, there has been an increasing acknowledgement in some countries that adherence to the traditional idea of the rule of law is inadequate, and that the concept should be expanded so as to require adherence to some set of values external to the law.

To the extent that discussion on constitutional matters does take place in Australia, it is largely anti-theoretical, does not frequently involve any discussion of values, and is instead marked by a focus on pragmatics rather than on principle. So long as law is enacted according to proper procedure and achieves its objective, few people dwell on the question of whether the law corresponds with some notion of right or wrong, justice or injustice. This tendency reflects the English roots of Australia's political and legal culture, and in particular the fact that the common law grew not with reference to starting principles but rather through the haphazard development of a body of case-law containing rules governing particular circumstances. This is in contrast to legal systems based on Roman law, where legal codes state a general principle which is then expanded upon by subsidiary rules which provide for specific circumstances but which must all comply with the general principle. This is a subtle but important distinction. The political and legal institutions which the colonists had brought from the United Kingdom influenced them as they debated the constitutional arrangements under which federation would be formed. Absent from the constitutional Conventions held in the 1890s was philosophical debate on general principles of political theory or on the role of state vis-à-vis individual. The task before the delegates as they saw it was profoundly pragmatic: to hammer out a deal that would ensure that the six colonies (and, it was hoped, New Zealand) would unite into a single country. For that reason their focus was on matters such as customs, trade and the balance of power between the future Commonwealth and States.

Yet it would be a mistake to think that, because debate on values was absent from the Conventions, that the Commonwealth constitution is not founded on values. All constitutions embody values. Even if those values are not expressed, they exist nonetheless because in the absence of the formulation of a new set of values, the position which is impliedly accepted – what might be called the unarticulated premise – is that the prevailing values of society, and the power relationships they embody, will continue in existence. In that way, a failure to enunciate new values operates in favour of conservatism, as existing values operate by default. The values upon which nineteenth century British constitutionalism – which the colonists had inherited from the United Kingdom and assumed, unquestioningly, should underpin the Commonwealth constitution – embodied the theory of democratic positivism.

2.2 Democratic Positivism

To understand what is meant by 'democratic positivism', it is necessary to explore the difference between two important schools of legal philosophy. The first is positivism, which states that whether a government and the laws it enacts are legitimate depends solely on whether that government is effective in ensuring that its will is generally obeyed. For this reason, the legitimacy of a government is tested in accordance with what is called the doctrine of effectiveness. According to positivists, ethics are irrelevant to whether a law is valid. Whether a law is just or unjust is unimportant – identifying whether a law 'is' is the only important question, and whether it 'ought' to be a law is unimportant. It is also unimportant to positivists how the general obedience of the population is secured – be it through fear, mere acquiescence or voluntary agreement. Positivism is of obvious utility to governments which act unjustly, and was positivism which underlay the defence offered by the accused at the Nuremberg War Crimes Tribunal and other war crimes trials in the wake of World War II. The standard defence offered by the Nazi defendants of 'just following orders' reflected the mindset that, because orders were issued under the authority of rules promulgated by a regime that was effective in its control of its territory, those orders were binding on their subjects.

This is not to say that all who analyse law in positivist terms support tyranny. Some adopt a positivist approach because positivism is useful in a way that natural law (discussed below) is not, because positivism always allows one to identify whether a legal system is valid, simply by observing whether it is generally effective. Some positivists would also agree that a regime founded on democracy is preferable to one founded on dictatorship. However one needs to bear in mind that in order to be consistent with positivist doctrine that 'justice' and 'injustice' are irrelevant to the binding nature of law, such statements of preference can be based only on pragmatics – for example, that a democratic regime is likely to be more stable and prosperous than a dictatorship. If they are true to their philosophy, positivists cannot justify their preference for democracy by referring to concepts of 'right' and 'wrong', because such concepts are irrelevant to positivist theory. The flaw in positivism is therefore that because it is disjoined from ethics, a constitutional order founded upon it always carries the possibility of being unjust. Indeed, for democratic positivists, majoritarian approval of an unjust law provides absolution for any harm it may cause.

In contrast to positivism, natural law, which has its roots in the writings of Aristotle, is the theory that a laws is valid and worthy of being obeyed only if it is consistent with what is ethically correct. In other words, natural lawyers consider the positive law of a society – that is, the law of that society as it exists from time to time – as being subordinate to a 'higher law'. How the content of that 'higher law' is to be determined has occupied philosophers for more than 2500 years. Ancient and medieval concepts of natural law were theistic – natural law was considered to be divinely ordained. However, during the Enlightenment, philosophers argued that fundamental values of justice could be determined by the use of reason. The cornerstone of this argument, as expressed by the German philosopher Immanuel Kant, was that human dignity means that all people are equal and that therefore no person has the right to use another for their own ends.[2] From this it follows that each individual is entitled to personal autonomy and self-realisation and, conversely, is entitled not to be interfered with by their fellow citizens. The implication of this for the legal system according to the ideas of subsequent Enlightenment thinkers during the period of the French and American revolutions, is that individuals are entitled to the protection of such fundamental rights as are necessary for them to live life autonomously – examples being the rights to life, liberty, free expression, religion *et cetera*. The reasoning underlying Kant's argument, and those of modern twentieth century theorists on justice, is explored in greater detail later. Here it is important only to understand that, in contrast to positivism, natural law theory asserts that a law which is incompatible with human dignity is invalid and ought not to be obeyed. This was the basis on which prosecutors at Nuremberg argued that Nazi acts which amounted to crimes against humanity (a term which is rooted in natural law theory) should be punished even if their acts had been allowed – and indeed mandated – by German law as it stood at the time.

What is the relevance of these theories to an analysis of constitution-making in Australia as it took place at the end of the nineteenth century? As noted above, participants in the Conventions did not debate philosophical questions such as whether the constitution they were drafting was consistent with rights theories. Their minds were firmly concentrated on crafting a political compromise which would be sufficiently palatable to all six colonies as to ensure that they would agree to the constitution that was drafted. The focus of the debates was therefore issues such as the allocation of power between the future Commonwealth and state governments and on matters of finance and trade. The consequence of this was that the theory underlying British constitutionalism became the theory underlying Australia's new constitution – that of positivism, where the law was seen as unconstrained by supra-legal values and as being developed according to the practical needs to the time as determined by a majority of voters rather than in conformity with any over-arching ethical values.

As matters stood in nineteenth century, the key elements of British constitutionalism were an hereditary monarchy, with executive power wielded by a government

[2] For a concise explanation of Kant's theory see Robertson (2009 p. 37).

responsible to a Parliament elected on a restricted franchise. Parliament was not subject to any restrictions on how it might legislate. The concept of the 'rule of law' was also important, and offered a degree of protection for individual liberty, in that courts operated independently of the executive and in accordance with a degree of procedural fairness. However even such protection for individual liberty was offered by the rule of law were inherently susceptible to variation – parliament could, and did, legislate in such a way as to take away those liberties. Nowhere in the system was there a recognition that these institutions existed in the way that they did because it was thought that they *ought* to exist in that way. The system of constitutional monarchy had developed out of an interplay between forces of the crown and parliament in the seventeenth century, and was the result of a pragmatic political compromise reached at the end of a tumultuous period of civil war, not as the result of the implementation of any theory of justice. This is why it is accurate to describe the system as one of democratic positivism – it was democratic, but only because society had developed in a democratic manner, and there was no principle which could prevent anti-democratic measures being adopted nor any mechanism which restrained the legislative power of parliament to legislate in an unjust manner.

The absence of any theoretical basis to their inherited British institutions meant that when the Australian colonists debated their constitutional arrangements, they thought there to be nothing wrong in providing that the colonies (which would become states) should be allowed to keep in force laws which restricted the franchise based on gender, race and property-ownership. Nor did they consider there to be anything wrong in rejecting a proposal that the constitution should contain a right to due process, it being argued that since such a right could be read as requiring equality before the law, it would prevent the Commonwealth from discriminating against Asian and Indigenous people.[3] Such unabashed racism was permissible in a positivist environment.

What this discussion shows is that all constitutions embody values, and that those values must be settled before either engaging either in a critique of an existing constitution or in writing a new one. In other words, the text of a constitution the just a legal mechanism through which effect is given to underlying values, and a constitution is only as good as the values it reflects. To put this in a nutshell: There is no purpose in discussing what a constitution should contain unless one has first established a set of values to which the constitution should conform. Only then is it appropriate to go onto the next stage of discussing the textual mechanism by which the constitution will give effect to those values. Failure to establish values will lead to a result which will lack overall consistency and will be ethically bankrupt.

---

[3] *Official Record of the Debates of the Australasian constitutional Convention* (1898, pp. 668–85). The inclusion of a right to equal treatment before the law was rejected on the express grounds that the inclusion of such a right would have prevented the Commonwealth from discriminating against Asians and Indigenous people, see Robertson (2009, p. 59). See also Byrnes et al. (2009, pp. 24–6).

2.3 Constitutional Change in Australia

Unfortunately, discussion of values is conspicuous by its absence from debate on constitutional matters in Australia. This has been reflected many times in recent years. The example of the fate of the proposal to recognise the rights of Indigenous people in the Commonwealth Constitution serves to illustrate the point, as it was marked by a focus – particularly by both major political blocs – on what would be 'acceptable' to Australian voters, rather than on was is required by values, in particular the value of equality. In other words, the approach was the complete reverse of what it should have been: The practicalities of getting majority agreement – which had the effect of giving what was presumed to be the sentiment of the majority a veto, even before a referendum question had even been framed – was privileged over what was required by a values-based consideration of the issue. Instead of saying 'We can't establish an Indigenous advisory body or put a right to equality in the constitution because the majority of voters will never accept it' (as Malcolm Turnbull said, casting aside 5 years of work by proponents of Indigenous recognition and of consultations initiated by both Labor and Coalition governments), the country's political leadership should have had the courage to say 'The principle of Indigenous self-determination and of equality require us to change the constitution, so let's persuade the community of why they should support this'.

This is not to deny that winning public support for change – in particular for radical change – is difficult, and that the practicalities of achieving change have inevitably to be confronted, but any discussion of how to achieve change should occur only after discussing why change is needed and what form that change should take. The 'why' and 'what' logically come before the 'how'. The inversion of the correct order of questions of principle and of practicality is one of the chief contributing factors to the failure to achieve constitutional reform in Australia. Every proposal becomes bogged down in discussions of practicalities and of what voters, in their current state of mind, are presumed to be willing to accept, instead of first focussing on the objective to be achieved and then working out how to win public support for the achievement of that objective, and on how to change voters' minds where necessary. Furthermore, the initial focus on practicalities – which really means a focus on objections – is no accident: As will be noted in coming chapters, most of the necessary constitutional changes would have the effect of limiting the power of government. It follows that politicians have a vested interest in preserving the status quo and, therefore, in pointing to the (supposed) difficulties that make constitutional change impossible. We need a new approach which establishes values, works out what constitutional mechanisms would give effect to those values and then works out how to win support for the actualisation of such mechanisms.

2.4 Human Dignity

So what value or values should we refer to in analysing the constitution and in suggesting how it might be changed? As discussed earlier, one of the most important developments during the Enlightenment (building on the humanist theorists of the Renaissance) was the development of a new approach to ethics, one based on reason rather than on faith. Kant argued that each individual is entitled to dignity simply by virtue of being human. Although the term 'dignity' is used in a colloquial sense to mean 'importance' or 'pride', it has a different meaning in philosophy, that of 'self-worth' – in other words, the inherent value of the person as a person. Kant further held that if all people are equal, no person – or indeed group of people – has the right to impair the dignity of any other person. From this it follows that every individual is entitled to personal autonomy and the opportunity for self-realisation and, conversely, is entitled not to be interfered with by their fellow citizens. A crucial point to note here is that there is an obvious tension between government of any type – even democratic government – and individual autonomy. Enlightenment philosophers resolved this tension by saying that the legitimacy of government was underpinned by an implied agreement between the government and the people to the effect that government was entitled to govern only so long as it respected individual rights, failing which the people were entitled to rise in rebellion against it. The dignity of each person ought therefore to be the cornerstone of government, and required that there be limits to the circumstance in which one individual – or indeed a majority of individuals – could wield power over another. The implications of this theory for the protection of human rights is examined in Chap. 5.

The Enlightenment approach was thus founded on a clear choice between values: Society is either based on the idea that each person is presumed to be of equal status and to have the same rights as everyone else, or it is based on the law of the jungle, with the powerful dominating the weak, and that of these choices the first is preferred. But, to be devil's advocate for the moment, why is this necessarily so? For example, could one not argue that it is equally rational to order society according to the ideas of Friedrich Nietzche,[4] who argued that it is more efficient, and also more conducive to the survival of humankind, that society should *not* be based upon presumed equality, and that those who are endowed with strength and ability should rule – in other words, that human society should be ordered on the basis of the survival of the fittest? What is particularly rational about equality and respect for the dignity of the individual?

An elegant yet simple answer to this question is provided by the ideas of the twentieth century legal philosopher, John Rawls. Rawls sought to answer the question of whether there were any values that were truly universal in their application. He conceived the idea of what he called the 'original position' – a hypothetical exercise in which a random group of people would be invited into a room and asked to agree on a set of fundamental rules for a society that they would then live in once

[4] Nietzche (1887/1908).

they left the room.[5] The key constraint under which they worked, however, was that they were behind what Rawls called a 'veil of ignorance'.[6] In other words, they were not told what their condition would be in the new society – whether they would be man or woman, black or white, rich or poor, Muslim or Christian, heterosexual or homosexual, fully-abled or disabled *et cetera* – until after they had devised the fundamental rules.

Rawls concluded that in a situation where 'no one knows his place in society, his class position or social status; nor does he know his fortune in the distribution of natural assets and abilities, his intelligence and strength, and the like',[7] rational participants would agree on what he called the 'liberty principle', namely that each person should have the fullest degree of liberty as is consistent with everyone-else's equal liberty[8] and that social and economic opportunities should be arranged so as to be of greatest benefit to the least advantaged and so that there is equality of opportunity (the 'equality principle').[9]

The beauty of Rawls' theory lies in the fact that it appeals both to individualism (in that it protects freedom) and to altruism (in that it protects against disadvantage). What Rawls' theory shows is that, if stripped of prejudices arising from race, gender, religion *et cetera*, the rational person will choose to limit the power of the state so as to preserve a zone of personal autonomy for him or herself. Rawls' theory is also useful in that it serves to refute the argument that human rights theory is merely a Western construct that pays no respect to the values of other cultures: The point of Rawls theory is that it is neutral, grounded in common humanity and rationality.

This book is written from the perspective that the fundamental value that should underlie a constitution is the dignity of the individual. An implication of this is that, in analysing a constitution (or in formulating proposals for constitutional change), one should adopt a 'bottom-up' approach – in other words, an approach which takes the individual – not the institutions of government – as the basic building-block of the constitution, and which evaluates all questions with reference to the balance of power between the individual and the state. This is in marked contrast to the 'top-down' approach, adopted by the drafters of the Commonwealth Constitution, for whom the basic building blocks were the States and who addressed each issue with an eye to determining how each issue would affect the balance of power between the States and the Commonwealth, rather than on how it would impact on the individual. Each of the chapters in this book analyses a particular aspect of the constitution, assuming the equal dignity of the individual as being the fundamental value in accordance with which the constitution ought to be designed.

---

[5] Rawls (1972, pp. 17–22).

[6] Rawls (1972, pp. 136–42).

[7] Rawls (1972, p. 137).

[8] Rawls (1972, p. 60).

[9] Rawls (1972, pp. 60, 303).

References

Byrnes A, McKinnon G, Charlesworth H (2009) Bills of rights in Australia – history, politics and law. University of New South Wales Press, Sydney

Nietzche F (1887/1908) Zur Genealogie der Moral: Eine Streitschrift/Ecce homo: Wie man wird, was man ist. English edition: Kaufmann, W (1986). Vintage, New York

Official Record of the Debates of the Australasian Constitutional Convention (1898) Volume IV. Melbourne 8 February 1898

Rawls J (1972) A theory of justice. Clarendon Press, Oxford

Robertson G (2009) The statute of liberty: how Australians can take Back their rights. Random House, Melbourne

Chapter 3
Our Current Constitution

Abstract If you have an understanding of our constitution, you might pass over this chapter, but for readers who feel they need to find out how our institutions of government function before going on to the discussion of how they could be improved, this chapter will provide you with what you need to know.

3.1 Settlement and Australian Independence

The starting point for an understanding of Australian constitutional law is the Constitution itself.[1] Many people are surprised to discover that the Commonwealth Constitution is part of a statute, the *Commonwealth of Australia Constitution Act 1900* (UK), enacted by the United Kingdom Parliament. To understand why this is, we need to understand how the United Kingdom obtained the power to legislate for Australia.

Britain succeeded in asserting its power over Australia simply by occupying it. Although under current international law that act would be viewed as unlawful, the unfortunate reality is that from the perspective of eighteenth century Europeans, occupation and colonisation were not considered unlawful. But what of the perspective of Indigenous people? They would obviously have considered that dispossession was wrong. Many continue to argue that the taking of sovereignty by the British Crown, as well as all subsequent legal developments which depend on it – including the foundation of the Commonwealth – are invalid. The problem with this argument, appealing as it may be to one's sense of justice, is that because Britain succeeded in establishing its authority throughout Australia, taking power away from Indigenous peoples in the process, it led to a result in which, unless one recognises the validity of British sovereignty, one would have to conclude that no-one has sovereignty over Australia – neither the Indigenous sovereignty which, as a matter of historical fact, was supplanted (as evidenced by the fact that it is no longer effective) nor the Crown.

[1] For overviews of the Constitution see Joseph and Castan (2019) and Blackshield and Williams (2018).

B. Harris, *Constitutional Reform as a Remedy for Political Disenchantment in Australia*, https://doi.org/10.1007/978-981-15-3599-4_3

In addressing the problem of whether a legal order is valid – or 'legitimate' – legal theorists apply the theories of Hans Kelsen, who said that the legitimacy of a regime is tested by observing whether it is generally effective. This test has frequently used by courts in different countries to decide whether laws made by governments which came to power through coups or revolutions – that is, not in accordance with those countries' constitutions – were valid.[2] In such circumstances, where the previous regime has been overthrown, the new regime has succeeded in making its authority effective and there is no authority in the country other than the new regime, the courts have recognised the legitimacy of the new regime and the consequent validity of its legislation in order to avoid a legal vacuum. In so doing, the courts recognise that the very success of an unlawful act transforms it into a lawful one. Although this principle may seem harsh, and indeed as rewarding wrongdoing, it has been applied in numerous countries where the issue of whether the legal systems established by colonial authorities was valid. Kelsen's theory also states that all legal systems are founded on force, and that if one traces history back far enough one finds that all regimes are ultimately founded upon a taking of power that is recognised as lawful simply because it was effective. Just as the British Crown took sovereignty over Australia in 1788, the authority of preceding monarchs in the United Kingdom changed hands unlawfully three times over the previous 500 years (in 1485, 1649 and 1689) and many times in the centuries before that, yet legislation enacted by those monarchs was recognised as valid. In Australia, the High Court has affirmed the incontestability of the taking of sovereignty by the Crown.[3] Indeed, one cannot imagine it doing otherwise, as the validity of the entire legal system, including the existence of the High Court, logically depends upon the effectiveness of Britain's acquisition of sovereignty.

Colonisation had the consequence that English law became the law of Australia. This was because under the law as it stood in the eighteenth century, if a power successfully took possession of territory that was uninhabited, and which therefore lacked a legal system, the law of the occupying power became the law of that territory. This was called the doctrine of settlement, and was contrasted with the doctrine of conquest, which stated that if a power took possession of a territory that was inhabited, the law of the conquered people remained in force until changed by the occupying power. How was it, then, that English law became applicable in Australia, given that it was obviously inhabited by its Indigenous peoples, and why did Indigenous law not therefore continue in force? The answer is that by 'inhabited,' eighteenth century lawyers and governments meant 'inhabited by people who have legal institutions that are recognisable to us'. Since the Indigenous people in Australia appeared – erroneously – to the British not to live in communities governed by legal rules, the legal assumption upon which colonisation was based in this country was that of settlement rather than occupation. Courts in Australia have

---

[2] See, for example, the decision by the Rhodesian court in *R v Ndhlovu* 1968 (4) SA 515 (RAD).

[3] *Coe v Commonwealth (No 2)* (1993) 118 ALR 193 and *Walker v New South Wales* (1994) 82 CLR 45.

upheld the principle that the acquisition of sovereignty by the Crown made English law applicable upon colonisation, as well as the corollary that loss of sovereignty by Indigenous people meant that even if it is now recognised that Indigenous law, it was over-ridden by English law and ceased to have effect.

The six colonies that were created by Britain at various stages during the nineteenth century all had their own constitutions, which were Acts of the United Kingdom Parliament. During the course of the century many colonial politicians came to the view that the unification of the colonies would be beneficial both economically (because it would mean the removal of tariff barriers that colonies had erected against each other's products) and militarily (because a united country would better be able to defend itself against any external threat). This led to a series of inter-colonial constitutional conventions during the 1890s, at which representatives of the colonies debated what form a new Australian constitution might take. As we know, they agreed on a federal system, and the Constitution was enacted by the United Kingdom Parliament in 1900, coming into force on 1 January 1901. What we now know as the Constitution forms a schedule in s 9 of the *Commonwealth of Australia Constitution Act 1900* (UK).

As a colony, the Commonwealth of Australia remained subject to the power of the United Kingdom to enact legislation for it, just as the United Kingdom had had the power to legislate for the six separate colonies before they federated. However, Britain never actually used that power, and in 1926 recognised a convention (by which is meant a practice that is regarded as binding, even though it is purely political in nature and not legally enforceable) that, although it had the legal power to legislate for Australia and five other constitutionally-advanced colonies known as 'Dominions', it would refrain from doing so without their consent. That principle was subsequently enacted into law when the United Kingdom Parliament passed the *Statute of Westminster Act 1931* (UK), which stated that the United Kingdom would not enact laws applicable to any of the Dominions, unless asked to do so by the Dominion itself. The Dominions were given the option of deciding when to make the Statute of Westminster applicable to them, and Australia chose to do so in 1942. The power of the United Kingdom to legislate for Australia was finally removed by the *Australia Act 1986* (UK), which provides that the United Kingdom no longer has the power to legislate for Australia, even at Australia's request. Therefore one can say that although Australia has had de facto independence from Britain since 1926, its formal independence was achieved in 1986.

3.2 Federalism

Although the six Australian colonies were eager to create a single country, the colonies with smaller populations were concerned that their interests would be disregarded if representation in the new federal Parliament was based purely on population. The price they were able to exact for their agreement to the new constitution was that it embody a federal system. The key feature of a federal system is that, in contrast to a unitary system, where the constitution gives all law-making power to the central government which may delegate part of that power to provinces or states and may take that power back, a federal constitution confers some power on the central (or federal) parliament and some on state or provincial parliaments, and also provides that that distribution of powers cannot be altered by either the central government or the state or provincial voters acting alone – both levels of government, or their voters, have to agree to amendments.

The Commonwealth Constitution is federal in nature because of the way it distributes legislative power between the Commonwealth and the states. Delegates to the constitutional conventions agreed that the Constitution should confer power on the federal parliament to legislate on certain defined matters, with the states retaining what is called 'plenary' power – that is, the power to legislate on any matter whatsoever, so long as their laws did not clash with those of the Commonwealth. State legislative power was expressly preserved by s 107 of the Constitution. By adopting this scheme, the delegates hoped to create a federation with a limited central government, with the bulk of power reserved to the states. Most of the legislative powers of the Commonwealth parliament are found in s 51 of the Constitution, which lists 39 matters on which the Commonwealth parliament may legislate.[4] Commonwealth legislation is valid only if it relates to one of the powers contained in the Constitution. If the Commonwealth enacts legislation falling within one of its powers, and that legislation clashes with state legislation, then under s 109 of the Constitution, the state legislation is over-ridden to the extent of the inconsistency.

Although the Constitution was drafted on the assumption that, by defining the legislative powers of the Commonwealth parliament its powers would be limited, the balance between the Commonwealth and the states has been affected by the way in which the Commonwealth's legislative powers have been interpreted by the courts. Interpretation of statutes is a necessary function of courts all over the world, because language can be ambiguous. Statutes can also be ambiguous because words can differ in relation to what scope they cover. This type of ambiguity is particularly relevant to the Constitution, because where, for example, the Constitution gives the Commonwealth Parliament the power to legislate with respect to 'corporations', does this mean that the Commonwealth Parliament can enact laws regulating how corporations are formed? Or what corporations do? Or what others do that has an effect on corporations? Or on the working conditions of people employed by corporations? Just what does the concept of 'corporations' encompass? All these issues had to be determined by the courts in order to obtain certainty as to what the

[4]To mention just the most important, these powers include those to legislate on inter-State and overseas trade and commerce (s 51(i)), taxation (s 51(ii)), marriage (s 51(xxi)), corporations (s 51(xx)), immigration (s 51(xxvii)) and external affairs (s 51(xxix)). In addition to these there are a few other matters that the Commonwealth can legislate on by virtue of other powers conferred by other sections, relating to Commonwealth places (that is, physical areas owned by the Commonwealth government) and the Commonwealth public service (s 52), the imposition of customs and excise duties (s 90), defence (s 114), coinage (s 115) and the Territories (s 122).

Constitution means. Uncertainty can also arise when the meaning of words changes over time. For example, where the Constitution gives the Commonwealth the power to legislate on 'postal, telegraphic, telephonic and other like services', the courts had to decide whether that included the power to legislate on radio and television, modes of communication which were unknown in 1901. Similarly, prior to the legalisation of same-sex marriage, people debated whether the Commonwealth's power to legislate on 'marriage' included the power to enact a law permitting same-sex marriage. The concept of 'marriage' would certainly not have included same-sex marriage in 1901, but the issue that came before the courts in 2013 was whether it should be interpreted more broadly – a question which the High Court ultimately answered in the affirmative.[5] From these examples one can see that judicial interpretation is not only permissible but is indeed necessary, because without it there would be many instances in which the Constitution would not be able to function.

Constitutional interpretation has an impact on the federal balance because of the way the Constitution distributes power between the Commonwealth and the states. Of the legislative powers given to the Commonwealth, only a few (relating to Commonwealth places, the Commonwealth public service, duties of customs and excise, defence and coinage) are exclusive powers of the Commonwealth which state parliaments can never legislate on. All the others can still be legislated on by the states, and so are called concurrent powers. It is only if the Commonwealth has legislated on one of its areas of competence and the Commonwealth legislation is inconsistent with state legislation, that the state legislation is over-ridden under s 109. The relationship can be illustrated by the following diagram (Fig. 3.1).

The outermost oval (A) represents all the topics upon which it might conceivably be possible to legislate. Because the states have plenary legislative power, they are able to legislate on all these topics. A sub-set of those topics are those contained within the second oval (B), which represents the topics upon which the Commonwealth parliament may legislate. A sub-set of those (C) represents the topics which are within the exclusive legislative competence of the Commonwealth, and which the states can therefore not legislate on. It is important to note that whereas the states can never legislate on topics falling within (C), they can legislate on topics falling within (B), but if the Commonwealth has chosen to legislate on one of those topics, and the Commonwealth legislation is inconsistent with the state legislation, the state legislation will be invalid under s 109.

The reason why interpretation of the Commonwealth's legislative powers affects the federal balance is because the more broadly the courts interpret the scope of what is included within those legislative topics, the more likely it is that Commonwealth Acts will clash with state legislation, resulting in the latter being over-ridden. During the first few years of the federation, the High Court interpreted the Commonwealth's legislative powers restrictively, which had the obvious consequence of limiting the circumstances in which clashes occurred with state

[5] *Commonwealth v Australian Capital Territory (Marriage Equality Case)* (2013) 250 CLR 441.

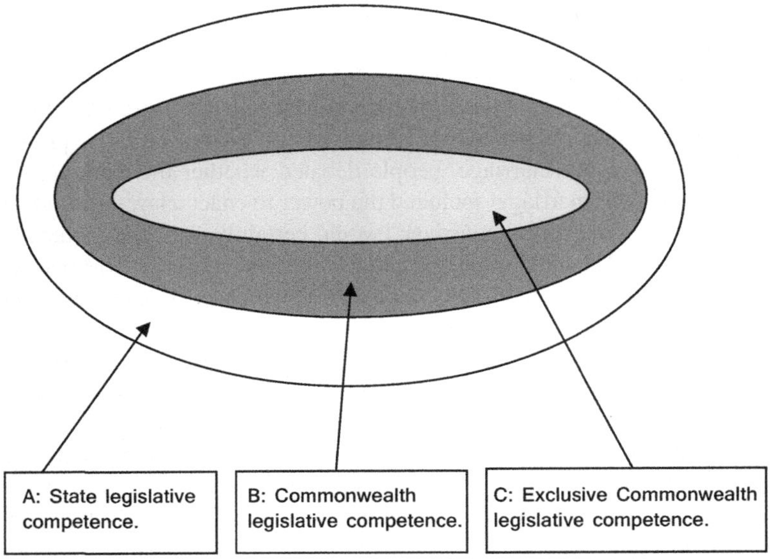

Fig. 3.1 Distribution of commonwealth and state legislative powers. (Reproduced, with permission, from Harris 2009)

legislation. However, after World War I, by when it had become apparent that the modern nation state needed a strong central government, the court changed its approach and in *Amalgamated Society of Engineers v Adelaide Steamship Company Ltd*[6] (commonly referred to as 'the *Engineers* case') adopted the approach of giving a broad interpretation to the Commonwealth's powers, which has meant that the potential for over-ride of state laws has increased. The need to ascertain which level of government has power to legislate on a particular matter means that the federal system imposes significant burdens on government because of administrative and legal costs and because of the complex negotiations that have to take place between the Commonwealth and state governments so as to avoid disputes arising between them.

The federal nature of the Constitution is also reflected in the requirements for constitutional amendment: After a proposed amendment has been agreed to by Parliament, it must receive the approval of a majority of voters nationwide, along with a majority of voters in a majority (that is four) states. In addition, if an amendment would affect the boundaries of any states or their representation in Parliament, those states would have to be among those whose voters approved the amendments. Of the 44 referenda held since 1901, only eight have succeeded in overcoming the 'double majority' hurdle.

[6](1920) 28 CLR 129.

3.3 The Branches of Government and Partial Separation of Powers

The Commonwealth Constitution created three branches of government – the legislative branch, consisting of parliament, which makes statute law; the executive, consisting of ministers who head the government departments and all the public servants who work in those departments, which applies the law; and the judicial branch, consisting of the courts and the judges who staff them, which decides disputes.

The idea of separation of powers according to these three functions was a product of the eighteenth century Enlightenment, an era of revolution when political philosophers discussed what type of government should replace the absolute monarchies that ruled most countries in Europe. The French philosopher, Montesquieu, said that avoidance of tyranny required that each of these functions be dealt with by a separate branch, that no branch should be able to interfere in the operation of the others, and that no individual should hold office in more than one branch simultaneously.[7] However, although our Constitution identifies the three branches of government, Montesquieu's theory of separation of powers does not apply absolutely in Australia. There are two reasons for this:

The first is that the Constitution, like those of so many other former British colonies, embodies the doctrine of responsible government (also often referred to as 'the parliamentary system' or 'the Westminster system') where the executive government – that is, the Prime Minister and ministers – is formed from among the members of whichever party or coalition has the support of a majority of members of the House of Representatives, and holds office only so long as that that majority is retained. Thus, winning a House of Representatives election is key to gaining control of the executive. Furthermore, s 64 of the Constitution requires that ministers be members of Parliament, or become members within 3 months of appointment. These rules obviously infringe the doctrine of separation of powers because the upper echelons of the executive (the cabinet ministers who head the government departments) depend on the support of another branch (Parliament) to stay in power, and because cabinet ministers are members of both the legislative and executive branches simultaneously.

The second way in which the doctrine of separation of powers is infringed is that Parliament often delegates its legislative powers to people or bodies that form part of the executive. So Acts of parliament frequently give the Governor-General, a cabinet minister or a statutory authority the power to make detailed laws known as regulations. There is a good reason for this: Parliament simply does not have the time to make detailed laws such as what drugs are registered under the PBS, or what forms need to be filled in when applying for a Centrelink benefit, so those matters are left to the executive to put into legislative form in regulations – which must of course comply with the delegation contained in the enabling Act, and which parliament can always overturn.

---

[7] Montesquieu (1748).

Although the legislative and executive branches are linked in the ways outlined above, separation of powers does exist in so far as the judicial branch is concerned. Chapter III of the Constitution confers the Commonwealth's judicial power on the High Court and any other courts that Parliament might create (which currently are the Federal Court, the Family Court and the Federal Circuit Court), and has been interpreted as meaning that only courts may exercise judicial functions (that is, may decide legal disputes) and, conversely, that courts cannot engage in non-judicial functions. The Constitution also protects judicial independence. Judges are appointed by the Governor-General in Council (which, as is discussed below, means the Governor-General acting on the advice of the cabinet) and, once appointed, cannot be removed except by majorities of both houses of Parliament on grounds of misbehaviour or incapacity, and cannot have their salaries reduced.

3.4 The Structure of the Federal Parliament

Parliament consists of three elements: the House of Representatives, the Senate and the Queen. The composition of the houses was a key subject of negotiation at the constitutional conventions leading to the formation of the federation. The colonies with smaller populations were concerned that their interests might be disregarded or over-ridden by a federal parliament dominated by New South Wales and Victoria. The compromise that was reached was that while seats in the House of Representatives would be allocated to states in proportion to their populations (although each state would always be entitled to a minimum of five), each state would have an equal number of seats in the Senate, irrespective of population. Furthermore, the smaller states insisted that the Senate should have equal power to the House of Representatives, including even the power to block the budget. This created the potential – which became reality during the constitutional crisis of 1975 – that a government (which, by definition has a majority in the House of Representatives) would be unable to function if its taxation and expenditure legislation was blocked by the Senate. This structural problem remains unresolved.

3.5 The House of Representatives

Seats in the House of Representatives each return a single-member of Parliament. The boundaries between electorates are drawn by the Australian Electoral Commission, paying attention to factors such as population and geography and ensuring that the number of voters in each electorate does not vary by more than 3.5% above or below the average enrolment in electorates in the particular State or Territory. Elections for the House of Representatives are held every 3 years, although the Prime Minister may ask the Governor-General to dissolve Parliament and call an election at any time during that 3 year period. Parties nominate candidates to fight seats for them at the election. This usually involves a process of pre-selection conducted in accordance with the internal rules of the party concerned. People may also stand without affiliation to a political party, in which case they are referred to as Independents. Elections for the House of Representatives are conducted according to the alternative vote system. This means that each voter is given a ballot paper in which they order candidates in their electorate in order of preference. To gain election, a candidate must obtain votes equal to 50% + 1 of the votes cast in the electorate. If no candidate obtains that amount when the first preferences are counted, the least popular candidate is eliminated and his or her votes are distributed according to their voters' second preferences. This process continues until a candidate eventually gains a majority of votes.

Like any country that operates a system based on single-member electorates, Australia has become dominated by two major political blocs – Labor and the Liberal-National Coalition – which alternate in power. This is because under a single-member electorate system, it is not how many votes a party has, but rather the critical factor of where they are that determines its electoral success, and the inevitable mathematical consequence of this is that two major parties will dominate the process. This has two major negative consequences: The first is that parties that have significant support nationwide, but without concentrations of support within particular electorates, will find themselves without any representation in the House of Representatives. The second is that it is quite possible – indeed not uncommon – for the vagaries of electorate boundaries to allow a party to obtain a majority of seats in the House of Representatives with a minority of the popular vote.

3.6 The Senate

The Senate consists of 12 Senators for each state and two for the ACT and the Northern Territory. Senators serve 6-year terms, with an election for half the Senators in each state (but all the senators for the territories) being held every 3 years, on a date coinciding with elections for the House of Representatives. Unlike in the case of elections for the House of Representatives where each state is divided into electorates, each state or territory functions as a single electorate for Senate elections. This means that it is easier for minor parties to secure Senate seats than it is for them to win seats in the House of Representatives, because winning a Senate seat can be won by obtaining 1/6 + 1 of the votes cast in that state. Senate elections are conducted using the Single Transferrable Vote system. Voters indicate an ordered preference between candidates, with the candidate with the lowest number of votes being eliminated at each round of voting until six candidates have been elected.

3.7 The Passage of Legislation

The passage of legislation through parliament involves the introduction of a Bill into either house (although legislation imposing a tax or allocating expenditure must originate in the House of Representatives). During its passage through a house, a Bill may be referred to a committee for consideration, at which time members of the public have the opportunity to make submissions. After being passed by one house, a Bill must then be passed by the other. After passage through both houses, the Bill is sent to the Governor-General for assent. Although s 58 explicitly states that the Governor-General shall 'according to his discretion' decide whether to give assent, convention requires that the Governor-General always give royal assent to legislation. The idea of conventions has already been touched on briefly, and is explained in more detail in the next section of this chapter, which deals with the executive.

3.8 Legislative Committees

Both the House of Representatives and the Senate have standing committees (that is, committees with permanent existence) which are allocated responsibility over particular legislative areas. Standing committees also perform the task of scrutinising the way the government administers the departments falling within the various portfolios. Apart from standing committees, committees are often established conduct hearings into matters of specific matters of public concern. It is up to each house to establish committees, and it is most commonly the Senate, where opposition parties rather than the government usually have a majority, that establishes committees to investigate possible government misconduct – a good example of this being the committee established to investigate the Children Overboard affair in 2002.

In theory the doctrine of executive answerability to Parliament, upon which responsible government is based, requires ministers and public servants to attend committees when asked to do so, and to answer questions put to them. However, in practice they often refuse to comply. Such non-compliance has never been challenged before the courts. The reason for this is that both the major blocs (Labor and Coalition), which alternate in government, have a vested interest in not having the question of the scope of the power parliamentary committees come before the courts, in case the courts were to find (as would be likely) that ministers can be compelled to answer questions and be punished if they do not. Since the support of one or other of the major parties would be required for a house of parliament to bring an action before the courts, the question remains unresolved, and the reality is that the scrutiny power of committees is very weak.

Although, as stated above, elections for the House of Representatives usually produce a majority for one of the two major blocs, the same is not true of the Senate, where minor parties usually hold the balance of power. This can lead to conflict between the houses. Conflicts are usually resolved by negotiation between the government and opposition parties in the Senate. However, if disagreement between the houses cannot be resolved, s 57 of the Constitution states that if a Bill that has been passed by the House of Representatives and rejected by the Senate on two occasions 3 months apart, the Governor-General (acting on the advice of the Prime Minister) can dissolve both houses of Parliament and call what is called a double-dissolution election, which means that an election is held for the House of representatives and the whole Senate (not just half the Senate as is usually the case). After that election, if the Bill that was in dispute between the houses is passed by the House of representatives and again rejected by the Senate, a joint sitting, at which all the members of both houses vote together on the Bill, is called. Whether the Bill passes that joint sitting or not determines whether it becomes an Act. Calling a double-dissolution election is always risky, as the government that was trying to get the legislation through the Senate may not be re-elected, or it may find that even if it does retain power, it cannot get the legislation through a joint sitting. There have been only seven double-dissolution elections since 1901, and only after one was a joint sitting needed to get legislation passed.

3.9 The Executive and the Operation of Conventions

At the apex of the executive branch of government is the Queen. Section 61 states that executive power is vested in the Queen and is exercised on her behalf by the Governor-General. Numerous other sections of the Constitution vest powers in the Governor-General. However, this does not mean that the Governor-General actually exercises these powers on his or her own initiative: It is crucial to appreciate that what the Constitution says in this regard and what happens in practice are very different. This is because of the operation of what are known as constitutional conventions – rules of constitutional practice which are regarded as binding by everyone participating in the system, even though they are not law. We have already met a constitutional convention which came into existence in the United Kingdom after World War I, and which was acknowledged in 1926, that Britain regarded itself under an obligation not to enact laws for the Dominions unless requested to do so by a Dominion, even though the United Kingdom certainly retained that power as a matter of law. That particular convention did ultimately become a law when the United Kingdom Parliament enacted the *Statute of Westminster Act 1931* (UK), but most conventions continue to operate as unenforceable rules of practice, rather than as enforceable rules of law. Conventions are an oddity and an anomaly, and lead to much confusion among people who are not versed in constitutional law. In Chap. 10, I argue that these rules should be transformed into law, so that the text of the Constitution matches how it works. But for the moment we need to understand how some of the major conventions came into existence and what their content is.

Our constitutional conventions come from the United Kingdom where, during the seventeenth and eighteenth centuries, there was a gradual shift in power from the monarch to parliament. Instead of the monarch choosing his or her own advisors to run what we would think of today as being the government departments, it came to be accepted that although the monarch was still the formal holder of executive power, that power would be exercised on the monarch's behalf by ministers who would be appointed by the monarch because they were able to command a majority in the House of Commons. This was the idea that lay behind a constitutional monarchy: Parliament controls the executive, because minsters rely for their appointment on the fact that they have the support of parliament. This constitutional arrangement is also referred to as 'responsible government', because the government is responsible to parliament in the sense that if a majority of MPs no longer support the government, the ministers must resign. The monarch's role thus became purely formal – some might even say peripheral – because instead of taking governmental decisions his or herself, the monarch did as advised by the ministers. The important thing to note, however, is that this change was achieved without a change to the law – the legal position remained that the monarch ruled the country, even though he or she acknowledged the rule that it was the ministers who exercised real power and that who was entitled to form the ministry depended on who had a majority in the House of Commons. Those non-legal rules are what we call conventions, and they are important because they were imported into Australia when colonial parliaments were established here.

The existence of the conventions of responsible government was assumed when the Commonwealth Constitution was drafted, and crucial aspects of the Constitution operate in accordance with them. All the powers which the Constitution gives to the Governor-General are regulated by convention: Where the Constitution gives powers to the Governor-General, this is understood as being subject to the convention that the Governor-General acts on the advice of the cabinet or relevant minister. Thus, the exercise of executive power in s 61 is subject to the convention that in reality it is the Prime Minister and cabinet who run the government, and advise the Governor-General on the exercise of his or her powers. Similarly, the apparently unqualified discretion conferred on the Governor-General by s 64 to appoint ministers is subject to the convention that the Governor-General appoints a Prime Minister who is able to command a majority in the House of Representatives, and then takes that person's advice on whom to appoint as ministers in charge of the government departments. As a final example one can refer to the fact that although s 58 of the Constitution explicitly confers on the Governor-General the power to assent to Bills and to reject Bills 'according to his own discretion', that has always been subject to the convention that the Governor-General will always assent to Bills passed by the two houses.

Apart from the powers that the Governor-General exercises on advice, there are a handful of powers – the so-called 'reserve' powers – that the Governor-General exercises him or her-self. The most important of these are the power to appoint and dismiss a Prime Minister, which are matters on which the Governor-General can obviously not take advice from a Prime Minister. However, although the

Governor-General does not exercise these powers on anyone's advice, their exercise is still subject to conventions which are designed to ensure that executive power is vested in the hands of a government which has the support of Parliament. In the case of appointment of a Prime Minister, the Governor-General must appoint the leader of whichever party or coalition has the support of the House of Representatives. So far as dismissal is concerned, if a Prime Minister has lost majority support and refuses either to ask the Governor-General to dissolve parliament and call an election, or to resign so as to allow someone who does have a majority to be appointed as Prime Minister, the Governor-General may dismiss the Prime Minister. The dismissal power was used in controversial circumstances in 1975 during the Whitlam – Kerr dispute, and this is discussed in Chap. 10.

3.10 The Formation of Government

Once a Prime Minister has been appointed, he or she advises the Governor-General on whom to appoint as ministers. The formal collective name for the Prime Minister and ministers is the Executive Council, which is the formal body that advises the Governor-General. However, far more important is the cabinet – which is the body of selected ministers who the Prime Minister chooses as his or her inner circle of policy advisers. Members of the cabinet are often referred to as 'front-benchers', because cabinet members sit on the front benches in parliament, as distinct from those members of a party's parliamentarians who are not ministers, and are referred to as 'back-benchers'. The collective name for all a party's parliamentarians is the caucus. In theory, the doctrine of responsible government means that the cabinet needs to retain the support of the caucus for its policies – and to stay in office. However, the reality is that party discipline is so strong that the senior members of the caucus – that is, the cabinet ministers – are able to dominate the back bench MPs, and can use the threat of disendorsement by the party at the next election as a lever to ensure that all MPs support the party line. The doctrine of responsible government also means that, in theory, government ministers must answer questions put to them in parliament, and that they and public servants must attend and answer questions put to them by parliamentary committees. However, as was discussed above, ministers regularly defy requests by committees to give evidence and often instruct public servants not to do so. How the doctrine of responsible government could be made to work as it is supposed to is discussed in Chap. 7.

The function of government ministers is to head the government department(s) falling within the portfolios (areas of administrative and policy responsibility) assigned to them by the Prime Minister. In exercising their powers, the ministers rely heavily on the public servants who work in the departments, and to whom legislation often allows ministers to delegate their powers – for example, it would be impossible for the Minister for Immigration to give personal consideration to every visa application made by people wanting to visit Australia, so legislation allows the Minister to delegate that function to officials within the department.

3.11 The Judicial Branch

The function of the judicial branch is to decide disputes and, where necessary as part of that process, to interpret the Constitution and other legislation. In the absence of legislation, the courts decide cases by applying and, where necessary developing, rules of the common law – the body of law derived from cases decided over the centuries by judges in England and subsequently in Australia. It is important to recognise that the courts are, in a sense, passive actors in the legal system – they cannot take the initiative in giving rulings, they must wait for litigants to approach them with a dispute. On the other hand, it is also crucial to understand that it is the courts, first and foremost, upon which we depend to defend the rule of law – that is, to ensure that the government is restrained by law by giving remedies when laws are broken. It is only the courts that can provide a check on the government, the most powerful institution the individual comes into contact with. It is the capacity of the courts, through the orders they give, to provide the individual with a mechanism for the vindication of their rights, which is the foundation of the rule of law. Both the other branches – parliament and the executive – are creatures of politics, where decisions are ultimately taken on political grounds. It is the apolitical nature of the courts, staffed by judges who need appeal to no constituency or interest group, and who make decisions on a purely legal basis unaffected by bias founded on personal interest or party allegiance, which sets them apart from the other two branches. We have already seen in the discussion of the doctrine of separation of powers how rules about judicial security of tenure and the prohibition on the reduction in salary of judges protect the independence of the judiciary. In addition, the Constitution has been interpreted as embodying functional separation between the judicial branch and the other two branches. This means that only the courts, and not parliament or the executive can perform judicial functions (that is, decide disputes and give binding declarations of what the law is), and also that the courts cannot perform non-judicial functions (such as making law or formulating policy).

The only court created by the Constitution is the High Court. However, the Constitution does allow Parliament to create other courts do deal with cases arising under federal law – a practical necessity, given that it would be impossible for one court to hear all federal cases. Parliament has used this power to create the Federal Court and the Family Court and, under them, the Federal Circuit Court. All these courts and their judges are protected by the principles of judicial independence and separation of powers discussed above. The jurisdiction of the Federal Court, Family Court and Federal Circuit Court are defined by legislation. The jurisdiction of the High Court is defined by the Constitution. This is important – the drafters of the Constitution realised that if they did not put the power of the nation's highest court out of the reach of parliament, there would be a risk that parliament would try to diminish or completely exclude the jurisdiction of the court to hear cases brought against the government, which would have had devastating consequences for the rule of law.

The High Court has two types of jurisdiction: original (to hear cases for the first time) and appellate (to hear cases on appeal from another court). It is rare for cases to commence in the High Court, but does occur, particularly in cases involving the validity of Commonwealth legislation. Because all organs of government must comply with the Constitution, the High Court has the power to declare invalid Acts of Parliament or actions by the executive which are unconstitutional. Another very important part of the High Court's original jurisdiction is that conferred by s 75(v), which gives the court the power to hear cases where a person affected by a decision of a Commonwealth government officer (which could be a minister or a public servant) seeks judicial review of that decision. Judicial review is a process whereby a court determines whether a decision has been taken in accordance within the limits of the law that conferred the power to make the decision, and that the decision-maker acted in accordance with fair processes. This provides individuals with an important weapon to challenge wrongful government decisions.

The appellate jurisdiction of the High Court gives it the authority to hear appeals from the Federal Court and the Family Court (which themselves hear appeals from the Federal Circuit Court). But not only does the High Court serve as the ultimate court of appeal on cases arising under Commonwealth law, it also serves as the final appeal court for matters arising under state law. This is because once a litigant has taken a case through their state's court system, they can take that case on final appeal to the High Court. So the High Court is truly the ultimate court for both levels of the federal system, because it is the ultimate court of appeal that decides principles of law for the Commonwealth and the states.

3.12 Individual Rights

Although the Constitution is the only law capable of restraining the power of the state vis-à-vis the individual (because the Constitution is the only law that can restrict the power of parliament and the executive), our Constitution offers scant protection for individual rights and places few restrictions on the law-making powers of parliament. In failing to provide adequate protection for rights, Australia is rare among democracies. Only a few rights are protected: the right to compensation when property is compulsorily acquired by the Commonwealth from a state or from an individual (s 51(xxxi)), to jury trial for certain Commonwealth offences (s 80), to freedom of religion (s 116), not to be discriminated against on grounds of residence in another State (s 117) and to freedom of inter-State trade, commerce and intercourse (s 92). This rather unusual collection of rights reflects the specific matters that were of concern to drafters of the Constitution in the 1890s, but the list is obviously deficient in so far as it does not protect fundamental rights such as freedom from arbitrary arrest, freedom from arbitrary search and seizure, the right to vote, freedom of expression, the right not to be discriminated against and the right to privacy, to name but a few. Nevertheless, the fact that the Constitution does protect rights, and that the courts can declare legislation which is inconsistent with those rights to be constitutionally invalid, illustrates an important principle: That the Constitution serves to protect the individual from the power of the state and that the judiciary is the branch from which the individual can obtain a remedy. The inclusion of a full Bill of Rights into the Australian Constitution would therefore increase the scope of the judiciary's capacity to protect the individual from the state, but would not give a new type of power to the courts.

Apart from the rights that are expressly mentioned in the Constitution, the courts have also held that certain rights are implied by the text of the document, even though they are not expressly mentioned in it. This may seem strange to people not familiar with the law, but it is not uncommon for the courts, when interpreting contracts or legislation, to find that there were unstated assumptions underlying the document, without which it would not achieve the objective it was designed for. The High Court has implied two important rights into the Commonwealth Constitution: freedom to engage in communication about political matters, and a right to vote. Both these rights were implied because sections 7 and 24 of the Constitution state that the Senate and House of Representatives respectively must be 'directly chosen by the people'. The High Court held that direct choice by the people cannot be achieved unless people have the vote and unless they are able to engage in political discussion in order to make an informed choice at the polls. The implication of rights into the Constitution is less satisfactory than express inclusion, but it is obvious why the High Court came to the conclusion that it did, given that the Constitution creates a representative democracy.

References

Harris B (2009) Constitutional law guidebook, 2nd edn. Oxford University Press, South Melbourne

Joseph S, Castan M (2019) Federal constitutional law – a contemporary view, 5th edn. Lawbook Co, Pyrmont

Montesquieu C (1748) L'Esprit des Lois. English edition: Nugent, T (1949). Hafner, New York

Williams G, Brennan S, Lynch A (2018) Blackshield and Williams Australian Constitutional Law and Theory – commentary and materials, 7th edn. The Federation Press, Annandale

Chapter 4
Democracy

Abstract The chapter begins by discussing what the term 'democracy' means, and emphasises that the extent to which a constitution embodies democracy is a matter of degree, and depends on how representative the electoral system is. It then discusses the current electoral system for the House of Representatives and how, because it is based on single member electorates, it produces results which inevitably fail to reflect the political sentiment of voters, and can even lead to a government winning power with a minority of votes. It then discusses how the criteria of overall representivity and the need to have identifiable local representatives need to be balanced in designing a new electoral system, and explains how the Single Transferrable Vote system, currently used for the Senate and for upper houses at state level, as well as in other countries, would provide the best balance between these two factors. The chapter rebuts the argument that because electoral systems with a proportional element inevitably lead to coalition government are inherently unstable, drawing on research from a wide range of countries. The chapter concludes with an analysis of the likely effect on Australian politics of electoral reform, and argues that, as in New Zealand, a more representative parliament it would lead to a more consensual and less confrontational style of politics.

4.1 Defining Democracy

What is a democracy? Is Australia a democracy? The answer to this question may self-evidently in the affirmative, but more detailed consideration gives a qualified answer.

Before discussing the specifics of democracy as it operates in Australia, we need to explore what 'democracy' is and what it is not. A key point to understand is that democracy is not itself a value. It is a process by which laws are made. In this, it is no different from monarchy, autocracy or oligarchy. Whether democracy is preferable as compared to other systems depends on which values one applies. If one adopted efficiency as the value against which governmental systems should be evaluated, it is by no means certain that democracy would be preferred – an arguable case could, for example, be made for the proposition that an oligarchy whose members were selected on the basis of proven ability and experience in administration might provide optimal stability and prosperity for its citizens. The same might even

B. Harris, *Constitutional Reform as a Remedy for Political Disenchantment in Australia*, https://doi.org/10.1007/978-981-15-3599-4_4

be said of a benevolent dictatorship. However, if one takes human dignity as the touchstone against which one evaluates governmental institutions, then it is obvious that democracy is qualitatively different from other systems because it is the only system which allocates political power to each person. In other words, democracy is preferable not because of any practical benefit inherent in democracy itself – some would argue that democracy can be disorganised, fractious and slow in comparison with authoritarian systems of government – but because democracy serves a value external to itself, that of human dignity.

If one accepts that democracy is to be preferred because human dignity requires that equal power should be allocated to each individual, it follows that whether a system is, in fact, democratic can be determined only by discovering the extent to which it satisfies that requirement. Furthermore, it is crucial to understand that for a system to be truly said to 'allocate power to each individual equally', it must do so both in form – in other words, it must be conducted in accordance with procedures which give voters a genuine opportunity to choose between different points of view in a procedurally-fair process – and in fact – in other words, it must result in each individual voter having an equal *impact* on the political process. The reason why it is necessary to emphasise this is because many governments are described – or describe themselves – as 'democratic', without actually being so.

To take some examples: If 'democracy' is defined simply as the act of casting a vote, then North Korea is a democracy, despite the fact that, given that it is a one-party state, elections there are a foregone conclusion. Obviously then, something more than just casting a vote must be required before a system can be described as genuinely democratic.

What if, in contrast to North Korea, other parties were permitted to field candidates? Would that be enough to make a system truly democratic? The answer here is in the negative. This is illustrated, for example, by Russia, where although there is notionally freedom to form political parties and for their members to stand for election, in reality politically-motivated charges and procedurally-deficient trials often lead to candidates being prohibited from standing, there are irregularities in the actual conduct of elections and government control over the media means that voters are not able to access a full range of views. So in light of this one can add another requirement that must be fulfilled for a system to be considered democratic – not only must there be voting, but there must be freedom for candidates reflecting a variety of views to stand for election, fair election procedures and free access to the media.

So, what if one had a system where multiple parties were permitted to contest elections and where there were fairly conducted elections and a free press? Would that be sufficient? Here again, the answer must be 'no': In several countries during the colonial era, South Africa and Rhodesia being good examples, black voters were put on a separate voters' rolls where they elected MPs to a number of seats that was tiny in comparison to the number of seats to which their proportion of the population would have entitled them. Nominally-speaking, these voters, like white voters, had a vote, but their votes were of miniscule effect. This example illustrates that the mere ability to cast a vote is insufficient to mark an electoral system as being democratic.

To be truly democratic, a system must ensure that every vote must, as far as is practicable, have an equal impact on the composition of parliament. What is meant by 'as far as practicable' is what is achievable given the realities of geography, electorate size and the competing objectives of the electoral system – an issue which is discussed in detail below.

The examples above show that whether a system is democratic in the sense of conferring equal political power on each individual, is a matter of degree rather than of absolutes. One could arrange voting systems along a continuum, from least to most democratic, depending on the extent to which they were consistent with that fundamental principle. The key question is whether, taking into account every circumstance which can affect the power actually wielded by each voter, equality of impact is achieved.

4.2 The Australian Electoral System

How then does Australia compare? Although under our system people have freedom to form political parties, voters are presented with a choice of views and there is media freedom, the system suffers from significant deficiencies. The example which best illustrates this, because it is the most notorious, was that which operated in Queensland during the Bjelke-Petersen era, when blatant gerrymandering led to rural areas (where voters predominantly supported the ruling National Party) being allocated far more seats than their inhabitants entitled them to, as compared to urban areas which were allocated far fewer seats. A measure of how gross the disparity was is provided by the fact that rural electorates might have only 6000 voters while urban ones had 36,000.[1] That system patently did not give equal political power to each voter, because a vote in a rural electorate had far greater impact on the outcome of an election than did one in an urban electorate.

Electoral boundaries were changed as a result of legislative changes by the Goss government. The law now requires that the number of voters within electoral boundaries vary by no more than 10% above or below the average.[2] Yet, that is not the end of the story. In the 2012 Queensland elections, the Liberal-National party obtained 50% of the popular vote but an astounding 88% of the seats in Parliament, whereas the Labor party obtained 27% of the vote but only 8% of the seats. These results teach a far more important lesson than does what happened during the Bjelke-Petersen era, because they show that each person's vote clearly did not have an impact on the composition of parliament, despite the equalisation in the number of voters in each electorate. This is because in any system based on geographical electorates, it is the wholly arbitrary factor of where electoral boundaries are drawn (no

[1] Rudd (2017 p. 133).

[2] Section 45 of the *Electoral Act 1992* (Qld).

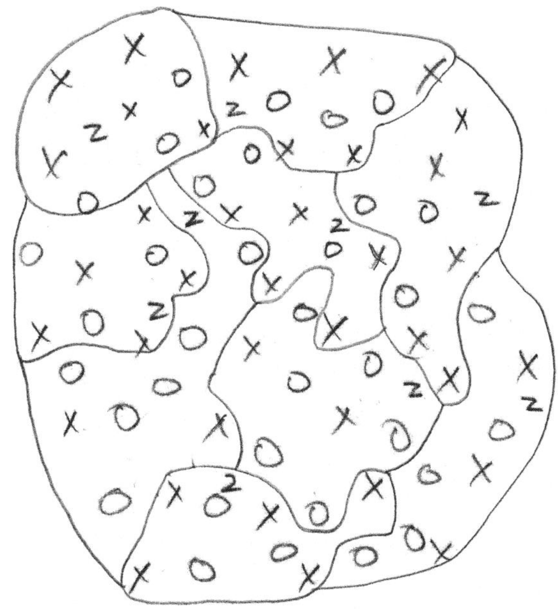

Fig. 4.1 Electoral boundaries

	Votes	Seats
	X: 37	X: 6
	O: 35	O: 3
	Z: 9	Z: 0
TOTAL	91	9

matter how equal their populations may be) which determines whether an individual's vote has any impact on the composition of the legislature.

Exactly how electoral boundaries either diminish or enhance the effect of votes and can lead to distorted results is demonstrated in Figs. 4.1 and 4.2 which, for ease of explanation, demonstrate on a small scale the operation of the system which is used on the large in state and federal elections:

The diagrams suppose a country with a nine-seat parliament and nine voters in each electorate. It is crucial to note that in each diagram *the number of votes* won by each party X, O and Z remains exactly the same, as does the *physical location* of their voters. The only difference lies in how the electoral boundaries are drawn. The diagrams show that, irrespective of how the boundaries are drawn, party Z wins none of the nine seats, even though its nine out of 81votes would, on a proportional basis, entitle it to a seat. The problem faced by party Z is that because its supporters are widely spread, there is no single electorate in which it has a majority. What is also striking is how a change in electoral boundaries causes a *reversal* in the fortunes of parties X and O: In Fig. 4.1, party X wins a clear majority of seats – and

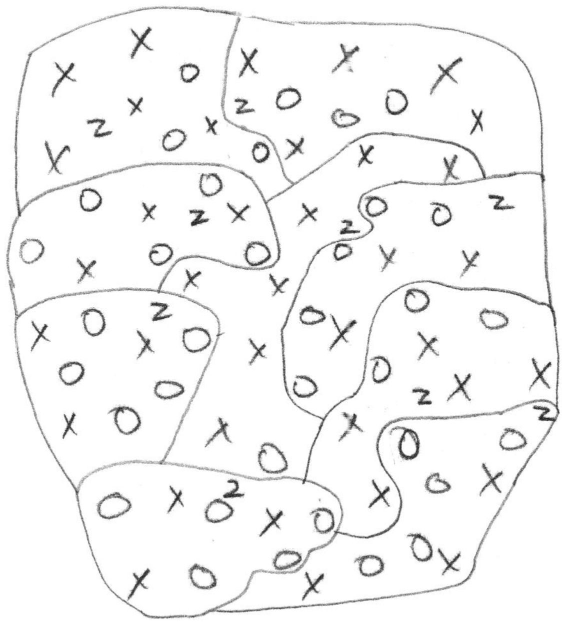

Fig. 4.2 Alternative electoral boundaries

	Votes	Seats
	X: 37	X: 4
	O: 35	O: 5
	Z: 7	Z: 0
TOTAL	91	9

would therefore form government – even though its vote is less than the combined votes of parties O and Z. But in Fig. 4.2, party X wins a smaller number of seats than does party O, even though party X has more votes. Furthermore, party O would form government, even though its vote is less than parties X and Z combined, and is less even than that of party X on its own. In other words, the critical factor that determines the outcome of elections is not how much support a party has, but rather the accident of where its supporters happen to be located. A more arbitrary electoral system is difficult to imagine.

The pernicious effects of an electoral system based on geographic electorates extends beyond the fact that whether a person's vote has any impact on the composition of the legislature depends on where that voter is relative to electoral boundaries. This tendency is magnified if, as is the case at federal level, the size of parliament is small relative to the number of voters. The system also has the consequence that parties receive a different percentage of seats to the nationwide percentage of votes cast for them, frequently allows a party to win government without obtaining a majority of votes and sometimes even leads to a party winning a majority of seats

Table 4.1 Election results 2019 federal election

	Percentage of first preference votes.	House of representatives seats won.	True seat entitlement in proportion to nationwide share of first preference votes.
Australian Labor Party	33.34	68	50
Liberal	27.99	44	42
The Greens	10.4	1	16
Liberal National Party	8.67	23	13
The Nationals	4.51	10	7

with fewer votes than the major opposition party. A survey of results in a federal elections reveal the magnitude of the problem[3].

In the 2019 federal election, the results (excluding those of parties and independents) were as follows (Table 4.1).

The electoral system clearly gave an enormous advantage to the two major political blocs constituted by the Australian Labor Party and the Coalition (Liberal/Liberal National/National). The Labor party's 68 seats significantly exceeded its notional entitlement of 50. Similarly, the Coalition's 77 seats (Liberals, plus Liberal Nationals and Nationals) were substantially in excess of its notional entitlement of 62. By contrast, the electoral system was extraordinarily unfair to Greens voters, who are represented by just one seat as compared to their proportional entitlement of 16.

It is important to note that it makes no difference that elections in Australia are conducted using the preferential vote system – all that does is allow supporters of minor parties to express an initial preference for the party they really support, before being forced (if they want their vote to have any effect on the outcome of the election in their electorate) to vote for one of the major parties that actually has a chance of winning the seat. Put simply, preference voting in single-member electorates is a sop to make voters believe that their voices have been heard, whereas in reality, in the vast majority of electorates it is only when they make a choice between Labor and the Coalition that their votes have any impact.

Furthermore, because it is the location, rather than the number, of voters that a party obtains that is critical to its electoral success, parties put most effort into campaigning in marginal seats. The influence of the marginals is dramatic. This was particularly so in the 2007 election: While 12,930,814 votes were cast, the outcome was effectively decided by just 8772 voters in 11 electorates[4] who, if they had given their first preferences to the Coalition instead of to Labor, would have handed victory to the former – and this in an election which, the allocation of seats in Parliament

[3] All results are taken from the Australian Electoral Commission website http://www.aec.gov.au

[4] These electorates were: Bass, Bennelong, Braddon, Corangamite, Cowan, Deakin, Flynn, Hasluck, Roberston, Swan and Solomon.

Table 4.2 Federal election results 1990 and 1998

Year	Party	Nationwide percentage of first preference votes.	Percentage of house of representatives seats won.
1990	Labor	39.4%	52.7%
	Coalition	43.4%	46.7%
1998	Labor	40.1%	45.2%
	Coalition	39.1%	54%

(83 to Labor and 65 to the Coalition) gave the appearance of a Labor landslide. In 2010 the margin was even closer – 13,131,667 votes were cast, but had only 2175 voters in two electorates[5] voted for the Coalition instead of Labor (and had the Greens and independents made the same decisions as to who to support in government), the Coalition would have won power.

How can an electoral system be considered fair when the winning of government depends upon the geographical location of a tiny number of voters? Most voters naively believe that because they fill in a ballot paper every 3 years they control power in the country whereas for many of them their vote has no impact whatsoever on the composition of parliament. Indeed, it is only swing voters in marginal seats who truly determine the outcome of an election: Voters for any of the losing parties in an electorate have no impact on the composition of parliament – and the number of wasted votes will amount to 49.9% of the total in closely fought electorates. Also wasted are votes for the winning party in an electorate which were surplus to what it needed to win.

Distortions of this type are characteristic of every election. But what is even more disturbing from the perspective of democratic principles are the results from elections in which a government won power after obtaining fewer votes than the opposition. Take, for example, the elections held in 1990 and 1998 (Table 4.2).

What is striking about these results is that clearly the 'wrong' party won both elections, in that the victor (that is, the party which obtained a majority in the House of Representatives) was *less* popular in terms of nationwide share of the first preference vote than the vanquished. This is by no means a rare occurrence: Governments also came to power with fewer votes than were won by the opposition in 1954, 1961 and 1969.

Another consequence of the current electoral system is that one can say with certainty that the government that will replace the current Coalition one will be a Labor one, and that the government which will replace that one will be a Coalition one, and so on, *ad infinitum*. In a true democracy, one should not be able to make such predictions, and the fact that one can in Australia demonstrates that we live under a duopoly, not a democracy. This is because of the inescapable mathematical truth that an election in a single member electorate will always be reduced to a

[5] The electorates of LaTrobe and McEwen.

choice between two – and only two – candidates, which in turn means that parliament as a whole will be dominated by two parties.

This, I would suggest, is a key reason why voters are becoming resentful of, and disengaged from, the political system. A reflection of this is the fact that an ever-increasing number of voters are expressing their frustration with the major parties by directing their first preference votes to parties other than Labor or the Coalition: In the 2007 election 14.5% of first preference votes went to minor parties or independents.[6] This increased to 18.2% in 2010, 21% in 2013, 27% in 2016 and 25% in 2019 – and this is despite the fact that a first preference vote cast other than for one of the major parties amounts, in most instances, to no more than a gesture to be made before having to make a reluctant choice between parties that can actually win a seat but with which the voter may have no affinity at all. The fact that the electoral system leads to votes in favour of minor parties and independents as effectively being wasted – a fact which the major parties exploit during election campaigns[7] – is deleterious to the democratic process, because it means that, in its practical operation, the system is not neutral as between parties. It also means that *the system itself*, and not just voters' political sentiment, determines how votes are cast. This is surely not consistent with democratic principle.

The dominance by two major blocs, which is the inevitable consequence of our electoral system, has a pernicious effect on politics, apart from its obvious unfairness to voters. The very phrase 'two sides of politics' points to an underlying assumption that the diverse political views of Australians can and/or should, be reduced to a choice between Labor or the Coalition. The reality of course is that there is a wide range of ideological positions within Australian society – in other words, there are many 'sides', and each deserves and equal opportunity to be represented in parliament.

The electoral system also has a narrowing effect on political talent. An aspirant politician has little, if any, chance of success outside the two major parties. The system thus actively works against independently-minded politicians, and in favour of *apparatchiks* who are willing to surrender their judgement to a party machine. Is there any wonder that the system produces compliant yes-men and women, and that Australians are disillusioned with politicians and disinterested in becoming involved in politics? This has led to a decline in membership of political parties, which has served to accelerate the very trend that produced it – the decreasing pool of ordinary party members has made it increasingly easier for a relatively small number of party machine operators to dominate the candidate selection process, with the result that ever more mediocre, beholden and compliant candidates are selected. In short, parliament is not the place where either a deep thinking – or a free thinking – person is likely to have a successful career. The two-party system has the effect of squashing individual initiative, and party bosses know that their dominance is unchallengeable,

[6]That is to parties other than the Liberals, Labor and the various manifestations of the Nationals (Liberal Nationals, Nationals and Country Liberals). The calculation ignores informal votes.

[7]Rhiannon (2016).

because there is no future for an MP outside the fold of one of the two major blocs. The other side of this bargain is that that so long as MPs follow party discipline, the party will stand behind them, irrespective of the behavioural shortcomings.

So, in answer to the question posed at the beginning of this chapter of whether Australia is a democracy, it would be correct to say 'to some extent'. To define democracy merely as the freedom to cast a vote is to reduce the concept to mere formalism. The unfairness to individual voters of the current election system and the resultant distortions it produces are different only in degree from the unfairness caused by the unequal and racially-discriminatory voters' rolls that existed in South Africa and Rhodesia and the electorates of varying population size in Queensland during the Bjelke-Petersen era. Whether the denial of equal voting power derives from disproportionate allocation of voters to seats or from the arbitrary effect of the placement of electoral boundaries, the effect is the same. It is impossible for a system based on single-member electorates to comply with the requirement that equal political power – which, to mean anything, must mean the capacity to have equal political impact – be conferred on each voter.

4.3 Designing a New Electoral System

A democratic system cannot be said to be working unless every voter can, to the extent that is reasonable practicable, vote for party they truly support (and, crucially, for that party to have a chance of getting into parliament) rather than be forced to vote for whichever if the major parties they least dislike in order for their vote to count.

The root cause of this problem is that, as it stands, the Commonwealth Constitution defines no standard with which electoral legislation must comply, other than to state that members of the House of Representatives must be 'directly chosen by the people'.[8] Apart from that and mandating how seats in the Senate and the House of Representatives are allocated to states, the Constitution leaves the framing of electoral law to parliament, and the system we have today is that contained in the *Commonwealth of Australia Electoral Act 1918* (Cth). Despite this lack of specificity in the Constitution, the validity of the electoral system has twice been challenged (on both occasions unsuccessfully) by litigants in the High Court, although on narrower grounds than that as a geographically-based system it is inherently unfair.

In the first of these, *Attorney General (Cth); Ex rel McKinlay v Commonwealth*,[9] a challenge was launched against a provision in the Act permitting a 10% deviation in voter population between electorates. The court rejected the challenge on the basis that the Constitution does not mandate a particular electoral system other than

[8] See sections 7 and 24 respectively of the Commonwealth Constitution.

[9] (1975) 135 CLR 1.

by using the phrase 'directly chosen by the people', and that the system embodied in the Act provided for a direct choice by the people. However, some of the justices stated that, at some point (which they did not define) and electoral system might become so unequal in its treatment of voters as to no longer comply with the mandate of direct election by the people.

The second case, *McGinty v Western Australia*,[10] was as the result of a challenge to provisions in the *Electoral Distribution Act 1947* (WA) which worked in such a way as to lead to a situation where electorates in metropolitan Perth had an average of 23,000 electors (plus or minus 15%) while rural electorates had an average of 12,000 electors (plus or minus 15%). Although this case related to state law, what the Court had to say is of relevance to the federal level, because the state and Commonwealth Constitutions all embody the same system of representative government. The court rejected the challenge, holding that, just as in the case of the Commonwealth Constitution, the Constitution of Western Australia did not mandate any particular electoral system, and that the degree of variation between electorates was permissible in a system of representative government (the phrase used by the court to refer to democracy). This was despite the obvious fact that the disparities in Western Australia echoed those for which Queensland had been notorious. Members of the court did however re-affirm what had been stated in *McKinlay* to the effect that an electoral system could be so disproportionate in its treatment of voters as not to be consistent with representative government, and some also said that an electoral system which restricted the vote on grounds of race, gender or property ownership would not be permissible.

However, the problem with these decisions is that although in both cases justices of the High Court said that – at some point – an electoral system could be so disproportionate in its treatment of voters as to no longer be considered to be consistent with democracy, they did not produce any overarching theory to justify that statement or explain how disproportionate an electoral system would have to be before it reached that point. More importantly than that however, they did not frame criteria which should be referred to in determining whether or not an electoral system was consistent with democracy. This is the critical question which needs to be addressed, and answering it requires one to identify what the purpose, or purposes, of democracy are, because only once that is done is it possible to determine which electoral system best serves those purposes. So what are those purposes?

In its original direct form in Ancient Greece, democracy was 'rule by the people' in the truest sense of that term, because all citizens were members of the assembly (the *ekklesia*), and this obviously meant that the law-making body reflected the diversity of views among citizens with complete accuracy. However, in a representative democracy, where the citizen is not directly involved in law-making, and thus relies on an electoral system to ensure that his or her views are represented by those who are members of the legislative body, conformity to the principle of rule by the people requires that the electoral system should operate in such a way as to reflect,

---

[10](1996) 186 CLR 40.

with as little distortion as possible, the same diversity of views as would be reflected in a legislature elected under system of direct democracy. The data provided earlier in this chapter demonstrates that our current electoral system manifestly fails to do this.

If accurate reflection of the will of the voters was the sole purpose of the system of representative democracy, then legislative compliance with that constitutional mandate would be relatively easy, and could be achieved by means of a system of pure proportional representation. Under this system, which operates in Israel for example, there are no electorates. Instead voters vote for parties which have submitted ordered lists of candidates to the electoral authorities. Each party receives seats in proportion to the number of votes it obtained nationwide.

However representative democracy serves an additional purpose, which is to provide voters with control over who their representatives are, and identifiable representatives to whom they can take their concerns. A system of pure proportional representation would not serve that purpose, as under such a system the country is effectively one large electorate, with MPs representing voters of no particular locality. Furthermore, because the election of candidates is determined by their positioning on lists generated by parties, voters have no way of controlling the identity of their representatives or of voting out representatives they do not want.

Thus the electoral system serves two purposes in a democracy, and these purposes, while both important, are in tension. Furthermore, an electoral system which best serves one purpose will fail in relation to the other: Pure proportional representation, which best reflects the popular will, fails to provide identifiable representatives to electors and also does not enable voters to control the identity of their representatives. By contrast, the single-member electorate system we currently have, fails to reflect voter sentiment, but does provide voters with identifiable local representatives who voters can vote out of office. There is therefore no perfect electoral system. One has to balance the two objectives in such a way as to achieve the greatest degree of proportionality while ensuring sufficiently close identification of representatives with a community of voters. The question is which, of the enormous array of possible systems[11] would achieve that end.

4.4 The Single Transferrable Vote System

In doing so, we would not need to look far. The multi-member electorate Single Transferrable Vote (STV) already used in the legislative houses that provide government in the ACT and Tasmania, as well as in the Senate and all state upper houses,

[11] For a concise explanation of various electoral systems and their respective advantages and disadvantages see the ACE Project Electoral Knowledge Network website (http://aceproject.org/ace-en/topics/es/default). A detailed comparative analysis of electoral systems is provided by Farrell (2001).

barring Tasmania,[12] satisfies the objectives of proportionality and the provision of identifiable representatives to voters. STV is also used in the houses that form government in the Republic of Ireland and Malta. Although technically not a proportional system (because MPs are elected from geographical constituencies rather than from lists) STV can produce highly proportional results, depending on how many seats are allocated to each electorate.

Under STV,[13] the country is divided into a number of large electorates, each returning more than one member. Parties may nominate as many candidates for each electorate as there are seats to be filled. Voters receive a ballot paper on which all the parties' candidates are listed, and then indicate ordered preferences between them. The number of votes required for a candidate to be elected (referred to as the 'quota') is the total number of votes cast in the particular electorate, divided by the number of seats plus one, plus one vote. So, for example, if 10,000 votes were cast in a 4-seat electorate, the quota would be (10,000/5) + 1 = 2001 votes. If a candidate reaches the quota after the count of first-preference votes, he or she is declared elected. Any votes a candidate receives in excess of what they required to be elected are redistributed among the remaining candidates – the calculation is complex, but the objective is to ensure that if, for example, candidate A needed 14,000 votes to be elected and obtained 15,000 votes, the 1000 surplus votes are distributed among the remaining candidates in the same proportions that all voters for candidate A indicated their preferences. The process of distributing preferences goes on in successive rounds of counting of preferences. If no remaining candidate reaches the quota after redistribution of the preferences of the most recently elected candidate, the candidate who received the fewest votes in that round of counting is eliminated and his or her second preferences are transferred to the remaining candidates. The process continues until all seats in the electorate are filled.

The advantage of STV is that as well as being able to produce highly proportionate results between parties,[14] all members of the legislature are identifiable with a specific electorate, and that unlike in systems which rely on party lists, voters rather than parties have ultimate control over whether each candidate is elected. This is true even as between candidates of the same party because, unlike in the case of single-member electorates where supporters of a party have to accept whoever that party selects as its candidate, in multi-member electorates voters can express a preference as to which of a party's candidates they prefer. An important condition for the effectiveness of the system is that there should be no option of 'above the line' voting where voters only vote for a party and allow that party to determine the distribution of their preferences. Voters should be required to vote for individual candidates. This would not only mean that voters would have to evaluate individual candidates on their merits (even where those candidates are from the same party)

[12] For a survey of Australian electoral systems see Bennett and Lundie (2007).

[13] For an explanation of how STV works which is both entertaining and clear see http://www.youtube.com/watch?v=ZA6xT0a5kgg

[14] For an analysis of the proportionality of various voting systems see Farrell and McAllister (2004) and Catt et al. (1992).

but would also reduce the malign effect of 'preference whisperers' – political operatives who negotiate preference distribution deals with other parties in order to maximise their party's haul of seats. Furthermore, preferential voting should be optional – in other words, a voter should be able to express as many or as few preferences they wish up to the number of seats available in the electorate. This too would limit the effect of preference deals and would also reduce the likelihood of candidates with very small numbers of first preference votes being elected.

If STV was adopted, the most important issue to determine would be the number of members returned by each multi-member electorate (referred to by psephologists as the 'district magnitude'), because greater the number of MPs returned by each electorate, the more proportional the outcome of elections, and the lower the likelihood that a government can be elected without securing a majority of votes nationwide.[15] This is because the number of seats per electorate affects the quota that a candidate needs to reach in order to be elected: In a five-member electorate, the quota is 16.7% of the total number of votes, plus 1 vote. Thus a party that had, for example, 15% support nationwide, but no sufficient concentration of voters in any particular electorate, would not obtain representation in parliament. In a seven-member electorate, the quota is 12.5% of the voters cast, plus 1 vote. In a nine-member electorate, the quota would be 10% of the votes cast, plus 1 vote. (The reason why odd numbers of seats are preferred is that this minimises the chances of results ending up with ties in the allocation of votes to candidates).[16]

The critical question here is how to balance the representivity of the system against the degree of contact voters have with their representatives: The greater the number of members allocated to each electorate, the lower the threshold required for election and therefore the more representative the results. However against this must be weighed the fact that the greater the number of members, the larger the geographical area of the electorates. Is the selection of five, seven or nine-member electorates (or indeed electorates returning any other number of members) inevitably arbitrary? I would argue that the way out of this conundrum is to focus on the issue raised at the start of this chapter – namely that a key defect in the current electoral system is the fact that it not infrequently produces such disproportionality between votes and seats as to enable a party with a minority of votes nationwide to win an election. To put it positively, a basic test of the fairness of the electoral system is that it should lead to government by parties which in combination have the support of at least 50% of the voters. It follows that a reasonable standard to set for a new electoral system would be that it should provide for whatever minimum number of seats per electorate will reduce to a minimum the likelihood of a government without majority support winning power. Ensuring that each electorate has the minimum number of seats that would be needed to achieve that objective will ensure that voter contact with representatives is maximised and the geographical size of seats is minimised. The question is: Where does the mathematical cut-off point in

[15] See the discussion in Farrell (1997, Chap. 7).

[16] See the discussion at http://aceproject.org/ace-en/topics/es/esd/esd02/default

the number of seats per electorate lie in order to eliminate the problem of governments being formed without having gained a majority of votes?

In Ireland, which uses a mix of three, four and five member electorates, 18 elections have been held since STV was introduced,[17] and governments have won a majority of seats with fewer than a majority of votes in only two of them.[18] In Malta, which uses five-seat electorates,[19] governments have won power without achieving a majority of votes six times[20] in 23 elections. The experience of Tasmania[21] is particularly informative, because it had seven-seat electorates between 1959 and 1986, during which period eight elections were held and no government won power with less than a majority of votes. But after 1989, when the number of seats per electorate was reduced to five, governments were twice able to win power with a minority of votes in the eight elections held since that change came into effect.[22]

These results indicate that a system based on five-member electorates carries a significant risk that a government can win power with a minority of votes, whereas adopting a seven-member per electorate system would, based on the data from Tasmania between 1959 and 1986, make it very difficult for a government winning a majority of seats with a minority of votes. In a seven-seat electorate, the quota would be 12.5% plus one vote. This would give a reasonable opportunity for voters who support minor parties to ensure that they obtain representation in Parliament.

Would having seven-member electorates enable MPs to maintain a sufficient degree of connection with their voters and to service them adequately? In answering this question, one has to have regard to the level of representation currently afforded to voters in Australia, having regard both to population and geography.

First, as matters currently stand, s 24 of the Constitution bases the composition of the House of Representatives on a system of allocation of seats to states. This produces disproportionality in representation, because although seats are allocated to states in proportion to their population, this is subject to the exception that each state has a minimum of five seats, even if its population was to fall below what would entitle it to that level of representation. Given that, later in this book, I recommend the abolition of the federal system, the question of whether electorates cross state boundaries becomes academic. Nevertheless the point needs to be made that basing seat allocation on states as geographical entities rather than of the people

[17] Information on elections in Ireland is obtainable from the Department of Environment, Community and Local Government at http://www.environ.ie/en/LocalGovernment/Voting/. A convenient summary of election results since 1918 has been collated by Whyte (2007).

[18] In 1965 and 1969.

[19] See the discussion of Maltese election results on the University of Malta site at http://www.um.edu.mt/projects/maltaelections/elections/parliamentary

[20] In 1921, 1927, 1981, 1987, 1996 and 2008.

[21] Information on elections in Tasmania can be obtained from the Tasmanian Electoral Commission at http://www.tec.tas.gov.au/. A summary of Tasmanian election results since 1909 can be found at the Tasmanian Parliamentary Library site http://www.parliament.tas.gov.au/tpl/Elections/ahares.htm

[22] In 1982 and 1989.

living in them is a feature that needs to be abandoned if fair representation is to be achieved. The theory of states' interests has never been reflected in political reality. Members of both houses of parliament vote along party rather than state lines, and so the idea that states, as states, have an inherent entitlement to representation, makes no sense from a political perspective. Furthermore, there is no sound reason compatible with democratic theory as to why, for example, people who happen to live in a particular state should be entitled to a minimum number of seats while any other randomly selected group of the same number people elsewhere in Australia are not. The electoral system should be designed in such a way as to give the most accurate representation to individual voters, rather than to states as artificial constructs. Furthermore, even if seats were allocated to states strictly proportional to population (with no minimum entitlement), disproportionality would still arise, because the number of seats a state is entitled to is inevitably not a whole number, which means that the number has to be rounded up or down, which in turn means that voters in some states will be under-represented whilst voters in others will be over-represented.

Disproportionality also results under the current system from the fact that s 29 of the *Commonwealth of Australia Electoral Act 1918* (Cth) prohibits electorate boundaries from crossing state boundaries. This makes it difficult to ensure equality of voting population within each electorate from state to state. Having seven-member electorates would obviously mean having larger electorates than we do at the moment, and the system could not work if boundaries between seats were constrained by state boundaries rather than according to the distribution of voters throughout the country as a whole. However, this would not mean that geographical realities would not be relevant in the determination of electorate boundaries. In common with similar legislation in other countries, our legislation requires a number of factors to be taken into account in setting boundaries, including economic, social and regional interests, communication and travel considerations and the physical features of electorates.[23]

A final very important consideration to take into account in designing an electoral system is the fact that the ratio between voters and elected representatives is significantly higher in Australia than in comparable democracies: In the 2019 federal elections, there were on average 109,092 registered voters in each of the House of Representatives' 151 seats. This compares to 72,847 registered voters per seat in the United Kingdom in 2017, and 27,483 voters per seat in New Zealand in 2017.[24] In other words, Australian voters are significantly under-represented at Commonwealth level in comparison to voters in the United Kingdom and New Zealand. This is one of the reasons why the Labour-Coalition duopoly is so

[23] Section 66(3)(b) of the *Commonwealth Electoral Act 1918* (Cth).

[24] It should also be noted that the smallness of the House of Representatives relative to Australia's population has served to accentuate the distorting effect of the single-member electorate system, because the fewer the number of seats, the greater the effect of the placement of boundaries, the more difficult it is for minor parties to secure representation and the greater the dominance of two major parties.

strong – the smaller the parliament, the easier it is mathematically for two major parties to become dominant.

So, if one was to balance proportionality, geography and the ratio between MPs and voters, what would be a fair electoral system for Australia?

First, as to proportionality of results, although STV is not a proportional representation system (because all MPs are elected in electorates rather than from party lists), its *effect* is increasingly proportional as the number of seats per electorate increases. As the discussion earlier in this chapter shows, having seven-seat electorates would ensure a high degree of proportionality because in such electorates, the quota (12.5% of the votes +1 vote) would be sufficiently low to enable a party which was able to obtain just over 1/8 of the votes in an electorate to secure representation. No longer would supporters of parties with, for example, 20% of the votes in an electorate, be forced ultimately to vote for an MP from one of the major parties for their votes to have any effect on the outcome. This would also mean that the number of wasted votes (votes that have no effect on the outcome) would, at most, be just under 1/8 of the total number cast. Contrast this with the fact that, in a single-member electorate, it is possible for 49.9% of the votes not to affect the composition of parliament.

Having seven-member electorates would also satisfy the requirement that governments should not be able to be performed without obtaining a majority of votes nationwide. The data from Tasmania during the period between 1959 and 1986 demonstrates that under a seven-member per electorate system the relationship between votes won by parties and their share of seats in Parliament would be such that it would be almost impossible for parties which formed government not to represent a majority of voters.

The next question to ask is how many seven-member electorates there should be. This is where considerations of geography and the ratio between MPs and voters become important. Geographical realities, as well as the distribution of population within Australia mean that in a seven-member per electorate system, there would have to be a sufficient number of electorates whose boundaries enabled MPs to provide adequate service their constituents. One relevant point of geography is that Tasmania is an island and must therefore form an electorate of its own. Another is that since each electorate would elect seven members, the overall number of MPs would have to be increased so that electorates did not become impossibly large – although note that, within the electorates, the task of servicing voters would be shared by seven representatives and, because each electorate would have representatives from a number of parties, voters would be able to take their concerns to an MP representing whichever party they thought would best represent their interests.

Although, as already discussed, a new electoral system should not be determined by state boundaries, the fact that Tasmania is an island requires that the bounds of an electorate should be confined within its area, as servicing of voters by MPs would obviously be extremely difficult if the boundaries of an electorate extended to the mainland. Because the number of MPs in Tasmania would be fixed at seven, and because the number of voters in each electorate would be equal, the number of electorates would vary over time depending on population movements. Currently the

Tasmania has a population of 520,000. If its voters were represented by seven MPs, then the total number of MPs required to represent the entire population of Australia on a proportional basis would be 331. Since each electorate would return seven members, the number of electorates currently required to arrive at a total number of MPs closest to that figure would be 47, giving a total of 47 × 7 = 329 MPs. Having 329 MPs would also address the current under-representation of voters in Australia. Based on 2019 enrolment figures, 329 MPs would give an average of 50,069 voters per MP, a number about half way between the averages in the United Kingdom and New Zealand, and a marked improvement on the current ratio of 109,092 voters per MP.

An increase in the number of members of the House of Representatives would no doubt be controversial in an era of increasing resentment of politicians, and would doubtless be fixed upon by the major parties as an argument against reform. Precisely the same tactic was used by the major parties in New Zealand during the referendum on electoral reform in 1993, an aspect of which involved an increase in the number of MPs. As in that case, the rebuttal is simple – given that the choice would be between a small parliament and one that is elected fairly, which would be preferable? It would be paradoxical if disenchantment with politicians and with the political system was to lead Australian voters to oppose an expansion in the number of MPs as a necessary element of the adoption of an overwhelmingly fairer electoral system, a political consequence of which would include the breaking of the Coalition-Labor duopoly which is the source of much of that dissatisfaction.

4.5 Coalitions and Governmental Stability

Because it is extremely rare for a single party to obtain the support of more than 50% of the voters, it is almost inevitable that an elections conducted under STV would produce a results where no party was able to form government on its own. This means that coalition governments would be the norm. There is no doubt that, if electoral reform was to become a live issue in Australia, the major parties, who would see their chance of governing on their own disappear forever, would argue that coalition governments are inherently unstable, and that the status quo should therefore be preserved. This was the tenor of debate in New Zealand, where the major parties, having made the tactical mistake of committing themselves to a referendum on electoral reform,[25] fought hard to prevent the 'Yes' campaign from

[25] In an attempt to gain an advantage over the National party in the 1987 elections, the Labour party promised to hold a referendum on electoral reform, however Labour Prime Minister David Lange subsequently reneged on the promise, saying that if electoral reform was designed to achieve fairness, he wanted nothing to do with it, because he had entered politics to 'slaughter' the opposition rather than to be fair to them. In order to capitalise on public disapproval of Labour's *volte face*, the National party made a commitment in the 1990 campaign to what, in retrospect, turned out to be the grievous political mistake (from its perspective) of holding a referendum on electoral reform, which led to the adoption of proportional representation in 1993.

succeeding. However, when put to the test, it becomes apparent that the argument that coalition governments are inherently unstable is not supported by the evidence.

The first problem with the instability argument is that it elevates considerations of practicality – and ill-founded ones at that – above the principle that that each citizen should enjoy equal voting power. Making stability rather than fairness the ultimate political value is the hallmark of authoritarianism. Whatever inconvenience or delay might be caused by the need to form coalitions (and, as is demonstrated in the next paragraph, the evidence does not justify the claims that a more proportional system would have a negative effect on government formation) cannot justify the injustices caused by the current electoral system. The onus of justification should be on supporters the current position to advance an argument defending a system in which whether a vote has an impact on the composition of parliament depends entirely on the arbitrary factor of the positioning of electoral boundaries. As demonstrated above, the current system also fails what must surely be the most basic test of democracy, which is whether the government formed as a result of an election represents a majority of voters. As previously indicated, governments won power in 1954, 1961, 1969, 1990 and 1998 after obtaining fewer first-preference votes than the opposition. Under an STV system using seven-seat electorates, it would be almost impossible for the parties forming government not to represent a majority of voters.

Second, even leaving aside matters of principle, data on the effect of electoral systems on governmental stability do not support the contention that systems that lead to coalition government are inherently unstable. In the most comprehensive available study,[26] a tabulated ranking of countries listing their electoral systems and durability of governments indicated that whereas some countries (for example, the United Kingdom and Jamaica) using disproportionate single-member constituency systems produce long-lived governments, other countries using the same system (such as India and Papua-New Guinea) are afflicted with severe governmental instability. Conversely, while some countries using proportional representation (such as Italy and Israel) are prone to instability, others (such as Switzerland and Austria) have governments that are more stable than those in the United Kingdom. Another interesting statistic is that while there have been the same number of elections in Germany since 1949 as in the United Kingdom (19 in each country) overall German politics has been more stable, with eight Chancellors compared to 14 Prime Ministers in the United Kingdom, despite that the former uses a highly proportional system and the latter single-member electorates.

Moving closer to home, New Zealand, which uses a system of proportional representation, has had three Prime Ministers in the last 10 years, whereas Australia has had five. In other words, the data fails to show any causative relationship between coalition government and governmental instability. This result is not surprising – it simply reflects the fact that a whole range of factors, including economic

---

[26] Farrell (2001, pp. 194–6).

conditions, ethnic composition and national character affect the politics of a country – and thus how stable its governments are. Furthermore, an important issue frequently left out of consideration when discussing the stability of coalition governments is the fact that, contrary to the idea that internal disputes are likely to cause coalition governments to fracture, coalition partners have a powerful incentive to ensure that internal disputes are contained and that their government endures, as voters are likely to punish parties who put self-interest ahead of governmental stability by bringing the government down. In other words, there are both centripetal and centrifugal forces at work in a coalition, and it is wrong to assume that simply because coalition governments contain two or more partners they are inevitably unstable.

Perhaps the most powerful point that can be made against those who argue that coalition government is unstable is to point to the fact that here in Australia, coalitions have held power for 59 (in other words, half) of the 118 years the Commonwealth has been in existence. Of that period, 42 years are accounted for by three very long periods of Liberal/Country Party or Liberal/National Party coalitions, from 1949–1972, 1975–1983 and 1996–2007. Thus, for refutation of the idea that coalitions are inherently unstable one need look further than our own back yard. Of course, as one of the two major political blocs which dominate Australian politics, the Coalition would be in the forefront of opposition to electoral reform, given that it, along with Labor, would suffer the most if it were to occur. But the question should be put to them of why they should assume that a coalition between parties other than the Liberals and Nationals would be any less stable than theirs has been?

The next objection is that because coalition governments are formed as a result of post-election negotiations between parties, voters do not choose the government. This objection is based on a misunderstanding of how the system of parliamentary government works. It is fundamentally erroneous, when discussing a system of parliamentary government such as ours, to say that the voters 'elect a government'. Voters elect a parliament, and parliament elects a government. This rule of the constitution has been lost sight of precisely because, in a two party system, voters know that one or other of the main parties will win a majority in parliament and will therefore form government. They therefore erroneously believe that the purpose of the election is to choose a government. However, it is vital to grasp that the two processes – election of the legislature, and formation of the executive government – are separate and distinct, that the voters participate only in the first part of the process and that after that, who forms government depends on the balance of power between parties in parliament, not on any decision by the voters. This is in distinction to the system in the United States, for example, where voters do elect the government by electing a President who then forms a cabinet without reference to Congress.

This distinction between elections and formation of government would be obvious to us if we consider 17th and eighteenth-century Britain, when the system of parliamentary government was developed, long before the era when politics was dominated by two major parties. The critical constitutional outcome of the victory of parliament over the monarchy during two wars in seventeenth century England (the Civil War between parliament and Charles I from 1642–1651, and the Glorious Revolution against James II in 1688) was that the monarch would govern with the consent of parliament. The practical implication of this, which gradually became established during the eighteenth century, was that after parliament had assembled, the monarch would choose as leader of the government (formally the First Lord of the Treasury, an office which became known as that of Prime Minister in 1721) whoever could command the support of parliament, rather than simply whoever he or she favoured. However no-one knew, until parliament assembled, where the balance of power lay between members of the loose, nascent political parties (Whigs and Tories) and the large number of non-aligned MPs. No-one voting in elections in the eighteenth century thought that they were 'electing a government'. The government emerged from the interplay of factions in parliament.

It was only well into the second half of the nineteenth century, when party discipline had hardened to the extent that, as is still true in both the United Kingdom and Australia, there is no role for small groupings of MPs or independents, that one could predict who would win government by observing which of the two main political parties had won the election. The consequences of that two-party dominance has been that voters no longer see elections and government-formation as the discrete events that they are – everyone simply assumes that the purpose of elections is to choose a government, whereas adherence to the system of parliamentary government properly understood requires an acceptance that it is parliament, not the voters, who choose the government. Confusion over this issue became particularly evident in the aftermath of the 2010 federal election, which produced a result in which neither the Coalition nor Labor had an absolute majority. During the days that followed, each of the major parties claimed on various grounds (having a greater number of seats than the other or having a larger share of the popular vote than the other) that they should be regarded as having been 'elected as government' by the voters. From a legal point of view, the ultimate determination of who would form government depended on who could demonstrate that a majority of MPs was willing to support one or other party – that is, choose someone who had the confidence of the House. The role of the voters in the process had long since expired and was, from a constitutional perspective, irrelevant, even though from the perspective of fairness one would argue that it was whichever grouping of parties and independents had obtained the largest number of votes nationwide, rather than the largest number of seats, who deserved to win government. Interestingly, however, amidst all their posturing, neither Labor nor the Coalition argued that we should adopt an electoral system which would deliver power to whoever had the most votes – which indicates how much the two major blocs benefit from the current system.

Once one understands how the parliamentary system of responsible government works, it becomes apparent that there would be nothing odd at all about having a multiplicity of parties negotiate to determine who should form government. In fact, that was the norm during the 18th and early nineteenth centuries – and one would be hard pressed to say that Britain, at the height of its international military and economic dominance, was badly governed because of it. Such a process is also the norm in other democracies which have parliamentary government in combination with proportional representation: The voters elect the legislature and then the parties in the legislature determine who will govern.

One could end the argument about government being formed by deals between parties by saying that that is what the system anticipates, and that it is only the fact that the electoral system produces distorted results, and a resultant dominance by two major parties, that gives the illusion that voters are electing the government. Such a response would be correct as a matter of law, but it would be unlikely to defuse the suspicion that opponents of proportional representation would be able to engender among voters who are unaware of these constitutional rules. Therefore, one also has to address the argument on political, and not just legal, grounds.

So, does the process of government-formation by political parties after an election conducted under proportional representation mean that the voters do not have control over who forms government and cannot hold it accountable? The answer to these questions is 'No', for the following reasons: It is very common for voters to know which parties will go into coalition, and with whom, long before election day in countries with fair electoral systems – in other words, the inter-party negotiation is as likely to occur before the election as after. Thus in many elections, voters will know ahead of time which parties are likely to go into coalition with which, and to factor that into their choice as to who to vote for.

Most importantly however, the reason why it is untrue to say that proportional representation and resultant coalitions do not give voters control over who governs is that, unlike in the case of the current system, a government formed as the result of an election where the yield of seats for parties correlates with their share of the votes will represent a majority of voters, because the parties forming the coalition will, in combination, represent more than 50% of the voters. As the results in Tasmania between 1959 and 1986 demonstrate, it is virtually impossible under a seven-member electorate system for a government to be formed with less than 50% of the popular vote, yet as the election results discussed at the start of this chapter demonstrate, that is a not uncommon, and obviously unjust, occurrence under the single-member electorate system. How could one say that a system which gives power to a government which a majority of voters do *not* want gives voters less control over the formation of government than a system which ensures that a government represents a majority of voters?

The final objection raised against coalition governments is that that voters cannot hold coalition governments to account in the same way as they can single-party governments, because coalition parties can blame their coalition partners for the compromises they have had to make in order to secure a coalition agreement and for failures of government performance. This is spurious for a number of reasons: First, it ignores the fact that Australia voters historically appear to have no difficulty in determining accountability between coalition partners, given the compromises that are made between the Liberal and National partners of the Coalition. Second, it must be recognised that parties in a coalition government are judged on the totality of their performance – including on the compromises they make. In other words, it is untrue to say that parties are able to deflect responsibility to coalition partners for compromises, because the very fact of having compromised on a key policy carries the substantial risk of punishment at the next election. Parties therefore do not have *carte blanche* to betray voters, nor does the fact that they are in a coalition provide them with immunity from the need to be accountable to voters – the deals they make become part and parcel of their record, and voters can and do hold them accountable accordingly.

4.6 Electoral Reform and Australian Politics

What effect might electoral reform have on politics in Australia? This is a difficult question to answer. Under the current system, a vote for a party other than Labor or the Coalition is of no effect except in that handful of electorates where minor parties or independents have managed to secure election, usually because of specific local factors.[27] Furthermore, because a ballot will not be counted unless the voter has indicated a preference for all candidates,[28] a voter is ultimately forced to express a preference for either of the two major parties which will ultimately win the seat for their vote to have any effect at all. In other words, as stated earlier, we live in a pseudo-democracy – or, more accurately, in a duopoly. In reaction to this there has been an increasing trend for voters to delay the inevitable and to give their first preference vote to candidates from other than the two major parties. Clearly many voters are not being heard. I would suggest that the following consequences would be likely to ensue from reform of the electoral system:

First, voter behaviour would be very different. Many more voters would vote for minor parties in circumstances where those parties had a realistic chance of success. Voters would no longer be reduced to choosing between which of the two major blocs should form government. Instead they would choose which party from among many they would prefer to be a *participant* in government. One would therefore expect that parties other than the Coalition and Labor would receive far more than the 25% of votes they obtained in 2019.

Second, because more parties would secure representation, electoral reform would shatter the duopoly so long enjoyed by Labor and the Coalition. The wider variety of parties achieving representation would also mean that a far broader range of talents would be reflected in Parliament. No longer would aspirant politicians have to sell their souls to either Labor or the Coalition in order to make a career in politics. It surely cannot be that the politicians we currently have – whose

[27] The 2019 elections saw the election of six minor party and independent MPs: Zalie Steggall who defeated former Prime Minister Tony Abbott who faced a wave of unpopularity in his electorate; Rebekah Sharkie who drew on a personal following in Adelaide; Helen Haines, who succeeded Cathy McGowan, an independent who had previously taken the seat from Sophie Mirabella whose personality had alienated her electorate; Andrew Wilkie, who had become prominent as a whistle-blower; Bob Katter, whose family had long dominate politics in his electorate and Adam Bandt who won a Melbourne inner-city electorate for the Greens.

[28] Sections 240 and 268 of the *Commonwealth Electoral Act 1918* (Cth).

behavioural shortcomings were illustrated in Chap. 1 – represent the best that this country has to offer. There is no doubt that we can do better. A reform of the system would attract a new type of politician – those who are independent thinkers, unwilling to conform to the intellectual straightjackets represented by Labor and the Coalition.

Third, the need to form coalitions would lead to a more consensual type of politics, in contrast to the relentless negativity that infects current political discourse. Observers have often remarked on the difference in tenor in politics in true multiparty systems, such as those in New Zealand and Germany. In Germany, consensus-based politics has become the norm since World War II, and at various times coalitions have been formed between various combinations of the right-leaning CDU/CSU, the centrist FDP, the left-leaning SPD and the Greens. Switzerland presents a particularly interesting picture, because despite being a country of linguistic diversity, it has developed a system of consensus-based politics in which government is conducted by a perpetual coalition, within which the allocation of posts varies according to the strength of parties in the legislature. Such a degree of co-operation is currently unimaginable in Australia – yet if the Swiss can operate a system based on consensus, why could we not do so? In a milieu where today's opponent may be tomorrow's coalition partner, there will be less of a tendency to adopt a scorched earth policy during elections and during day to day political debate. The creation of an environment in which it was in their own interests for parties to work with each other would lead to more civil, harmonious and respectful political discourse. Furthermore, in a true multiparty system, there would be nothing for a political party to gain by taking the passive-aggressive stance of saying that they would refuse to enter into a coalition. Willingness to enter into a coalition would be the only road to power, and a party which refused to act co-operatively with others would simply be excluding itself from government.

The fourth consequence of an opening up of the system to a multiplicity of parties is that there would be an increase of democratisation *within* parties. Currently the Liberal, National and Labor machines exercise tremendous power over individual MPs because, in the absence of a viable political career outside the main parties, the threat of disendorsement constitutes a potent disincentive against MPs defying the party line. However, in an environment where it was possible for disenchanted MPs to either join one of a range of parties in which they might have a reasonable chance of continuing their political careers, party leaderships would have to loosen the reins of party discipline and adopt a far more consultative approach toward their back benchers. It would no longer be possible to subject MPs to a party whip to the same extent as now, and MPs would assert the right to vote their own minds in a way that they cannot under the current system.

Fifthly, electoral reform would lead to the fracturing of existing political parties and the emergence of new ones. Currently, the factional differences within Labor and the Coalition are kept in check by the imperative of maintaining unity in order to win power. However in an environment where the major parties would not be able to govern on their own, a key justification for maintaining internal unity would be removed. This would in all likelihood see a dissolution of the unhappy marriage between liberals and conservatives that is the Liberal Party, resulting in split into two separate parties. The Nationals/LNP would perhaps amalgamate with the conservative wing of the former Liberal party. Labor's factionalism, barely controlled even under the current electoral system, would finally sunder the party, probably leading to the formation of a left-leaning economically-interventionist party, and a centrist, market-friendly, socially liberal party. That centrist party might then join with the liberal faction of the former Liberal Party, resulting in the creation of a broad party similar in ideological position to the former Australian Democrats. There would also likely be a far right party combining Hansonites, Katter's Australian Party and other right-wing elements. The Greens would carry on as usual, perhaps incorporating some members from the old Labor left. In that scenario, Australian voters would have a choice between at least five parties with a realistic prospect of achieving parliamentary representation, reflecting conservative, liberal centrist, left wing, right-wing nationalist and green interests. Other parties might emerge to capture parts of the political spectrum, which would further broaden the range of available choices. Any of these parties would have a realistic chance of participating in government, and no party would enjoy the built-in advantage that the current electoral system confers on Labor and the Coalition.

Finally – and this may seem paradoxical – a new electoral system would be likely to enhance rather than diminish political stability. As stated in the previous paragraph, the Liberal and Labor parties are, in reality, coalitions – and uneasy ones at that, as evidenced by the intra-party bloodletting and rapid change in leaders in the decade since 2009. When a voter votes for the Liberal party, for example, they are really voting for an entity which contains two parties with fundamentally incompatible ideologies – liberal and conservative – whose antagonism towards each other has been reflected in leadership coups. But the marriage between these two wings endures because the political cost of dissolving it is too high. Therefore, what we have is a political party which, instead of breaking into two separate parties offering quite different policies to voters, maintains a façade of unity which leaves voters never quite sure which wing of the party they are voting for is (or will become) dominant. The same dynamic applies to the right/centre/left factions within the Labor party. Under the current electoral system, voters are therefore forced to vote for inherently unstable entities which, in reality, conceal separate parties. The splitting of these major blocs into their natural components would, for the first time, give voters the opportunity to choose between those separate component parties. In addition, because the new parties would be ideologically cohesive, their leadership would be more stable and coups would therefore become far less frequent. I would also argue that governments made up of whatever combination of parties might form a coalition would be more stable than the unhappy unions that are the Labor and Liberal parties. This is because those parties would have to maintain inter-party consensus and leadership stability in order to remain in power, in contrast to the current situation where the Coalition and Labor can retain power despite indulging in internal coups which have led to a revolving-door in leadership. One would also expect that the passage of legislation would become far easier than it is at the moment when it has to be negotiated piece-meal with cross-benchers in the Senate:

Negotiations for the formation of a coalition government would take place on a single occasion before the government was formed and would result in a single agreement addressing all aspects of its proposed legislative programme.

Electoral reform would effect a sea-change in Australian democracy. No longer would it be a case of voters who are dissatisfied with two major blocs reluctantly having to choose the lesser of two evils, or of voting on the basis that they should throw the current crowd out to 'give the other crowd a chance'. They would be able to exercise a real choice and see representatives holding their particular views gain representation in a Parliament which accurately reflected popular sentiment. It is probably true to say that this is the constitutional reform that would beget all the others, because only once the duopoly of the major parties is broken will we have a realistic chance of effecting the many other reforms we need.

References

ACE Project Electoral Knowledge Network. http://aceproject.org/ace-en/topics/es/default. Accessed 4 Oct 2019

Australian Electoral Commission. Official election results. https://results aec.gov.au/ Accessed 3 Oct 2018

Bennett, S and Lundie R (2007) Australian electoral systems. Research Paper No 5, Parliamentary Library. Parliament of Australia, Canberra

Catt H, Harris P, Roberts N (1992) Voter's choice: electoral change in New Zealand? Dunmore Press, Palmerston North

Department of Environment, Community and Local Government, Government of Ireland. http://www.environ.ie/en/LocalGovernment/Voting/ Accessed 4 Oct 2009

Farrell D (1997) Comparing electoral systems. Prentice Hall, London

Farrell D (2001) Electoral systems: a comparative introduction. St Martin's Press, New York

Farrell, D and McAllister, I (2004) Voter satisfaction and electoral systems: does preferential voting in candidate-centred systems make a difference? Center for the study of democracy, UC Urvine. http://www.escholarship.org/uc/item/4c51z9mt?display=all#page-10 Accessed 15 Oct 2019

Rhiannon, R (2016) The major party myth that stops people voting for the greens. New Matilda 21 June 2016

Rudd K (2017) Not for the faint-hearted – a personal reflection on life, politics and purpose. Macmillan, Sydney

Tasmanian Electoral Commission. http://www.tec.tas.gov.au. Accessed 4 Oct 2019

Tasmanian Parliamentary Library. House of assembly. Election results 1909–2014 http://www.parliament.tas.gov.au/tpl/Elections/ahares.htm. Accessed 4 Oct 2019

University of Malta. Malta elections. http://www.um.edu.mt/projects/maltaelections/elections/parliamentary Accessed 4 Oct 2019

Whyte, D (2007) Dail elections. http://www.ark.ac.uk/elections/gdala.htm Accessed 4 Oct 2019

Chapter 5
What Are ‘Rights’ and Where Do They Come from?

Abstract This chapter begins by discussing the difference between constitutional rights and other types of rights and then analyses the theory underlying human rights, arguing that human dignity is the source of all rights. It argues that unrestricted majoritarianism is incompatible with human dignity, and points to the inconsistency in the fact that the constitution currently protects some rights but not others. The chapter addresses the balance of power between the courts and parliament and refutes a number of arguments that have been made against having a full bill of rights in the constitution.

5.1 What Are Rights?

A fundamental problem that affects discussion of rights is that the term ‘rights’ is used in several different ways by the law. Someone who has entered into a contract to buy a car has a personal right to have the car delivered to them. A person who owns property has a bundle of real rights in relation to it, including the right to use it, to allocate rights over it to others (for example by lending it to a third party or by pledging it as security for a money borrowed from a third party), to sell it or to destroy it. An example of another type of right is where an Act confers a right on a person to be brought before a court within a prescribed period when they have been arrested. What these different rights have in common is that they can be over-ridden: Because parliament can over-ride the common law, it could enact legislation which had the effect of changing the rights of car-buyers or of property-owners. Parliament could also change the Act relating to the rights of arrested persons by either increasing or decreasing the duration for which they can be held without being brought before a court or, as was noted in the discussion on the rule of law in Chap. 1, could even provide for the detention of people without authorisation by a court. In other words, all such common-law and statutory ‘rights’ are inherently vulnerable to amendment or extinguishment by the state through its exercise of its law-making power. Furthermore, even if parliament was to act beneficially towards rights – in other words, was to confirm their existence in legislation – such rights would themselves be vulnerable to extinguishment because what parliament has enacted it can always later repeal.

B. Harris, *Constitutional Reform as a Remedy for Political Disenchantment in Australia*, https://doi.org/10.1007/978-981-15-3599-4_5

In this chapter the term 'right' has a completely different meaning. It refers a right contained in a constitution which confers a liberty or an entitlement on a person, and which may either restricts what the state can do to a person, or may require that the state do certain things for a person. These rights are different from the rights described above because, being in the constitution, they cannot be abrogated in the same way as other types of rights – indeed a law abrogating the rights would itself be unconstitutional.

5.2 The Theoretical Basis of Constitutional Rights

The question of whether to have a bill of rights, and what form it should take, is at its root philosophical, not legal. The starting point for this question should be a determination of the proper relationship between the power of the state on the one hand and the inherent dignity of the individual on the other. Does the dignity of the individual entitle him or her to a degree of protection for their autonomy even in the face of the general will, or are individual 'rights' simply the playthings of passing political majorities? What limits on the power of the state are mandated by respect for individual autonomy?[1] It is only after these questions have been addressed – and a theory of rights arrived at as a result – that one can then sensibly discuss constitutional design. It is only after the theoretical question has been answered that the implications of that theory for issues such as the allocation of powers between the courts on the one hand and the legislature and the executive on the other can be determined. In Australia, however, for the most part debate takes place in a normative vacuum without reference to fundamental rights theories. The focus is on utilitarian considerations in which primacy is given to the democratic will[2] without consideration of the incompatibility of that approach with human dignity, which requires that a real and effective limit be placed on the power of the state vis-à-vis the individual, which in turn is achievable only if the individual can vindicate constitutionally-protected rights before the courts.[3]

In Chap. 1 we noted that modern conceptions of the rule of law require not only that the law be made in accordance with correct procedure, be ascertainable and be equally applicable to the state and to its subjects, but also that it be consistent with human rights. But *why* should human rights be protected? Here it is necessary to expand upon the discussion of values contained in Chap. 2.

The foundation of rights is the concept of dignity. Dignity is a term which is alien to Australian legal language. To the extent that people think of it they consider it

---

[1] For a discussion of dignity as the foundation of rights see Rotenstreich (1983), Lasswell and McDougal (1943), and Lasswell and McDougal (1971).

[2] For examples of this approach see Moens (1994), Brennan (1998), and Craven (2004, pp. 181–8). By contrast, an eloquent presentation of the case for legislative subordination to a Bill of Rights is provided by former Deputy Chief Justice of South Africa, Dikgang Moseneke (2016).

[3] McDougal (1974).

analogous to pride. But that is not what dignity means in the legal sense. In Roman law, dignity meant a person's sense of self-worth. That concept was built upon by Enlightenment thinkers such as Immanuel Kant, and it is their ideas which form the basis of modern human rights theory. At its most basic, Kant's theory was that if one accepts that every person is of equal worth it follows that each person ought to have equal autonomy and that no-one should be able to interfere with the autonomy of another, as that would amount to the subordination of one person to another and thus the denial of that person's equal worth. The alternative to this (if one rejects the idea that every person is of equal worth) is a world in which dignity is not respected and where the weak are subject to the power of the strong. Kant's theory gives primacy to human dignity as the supreme value and presents an choice between, on the one hand, a system where each person is of equal dignity and where there are rules to ensure that that dignity is protected and, on the other, a system in which there is no restraint on what one person may do to another.

Although Kant's theory provides a useful overarching theory for rights, it does not directly answer the question of *why* human dignity should be protected. A belief in human dignity is not in itself sufficient to persuade some people, who might see no reason why a society founded on dignity is to be preferred to one founded on the arbitrary exercise of power. So what is needed is some argument – based on reason rather than belief – which explains why dignity ought to be respected. Here is where the theories of John Rawls, are useful, because they provide a reason-based methodology for determining what the basic rules of a society should be, and because they lead to the conclusion that rational people would chose rules under which dignity or, as Rawls referred to it, justice, is protected.

To re-cap what was said in Chap. 2, Rawls' methodology involves imagining a group of people who are given the job of framing basic societal rules behind a 'veil of ignorance' – in other words in a situation where they are unaware of what their identity or status will be in the society for which the rules are being created. In this situation, because a person would not know what race, gender, (dis)ablity, religion, wealth, legal position or other attributes they would have, they would approach rule-making in such a way as to ensure fairness for everyone, irrespective of their characteristics or life circumstances. Rawls' conclusion was that rational people would therefore choose to limit the power of the state so as to preserve a zone of personal autonomy for themselves and that they would formulate two fundamental rules: that each person should have the fullest degree of liberty as is consistent with everyone-else's equal liberty (what he referred to as the 'liberty principle')[4] and that social and economic opportunities should be arranged so as to be of greatest benefit to the least advantaged (the 'equality principle').[5] By placing participants behind the veil of ignorance, Rawls' theory strikes a balance between freedom and restraint, in that while participants would naturally want a system which maximised their scope to act as they pleased, they would also want to ensure that they would be protected

[4] McDougal (1974, p. 60).

[5] McDougal (1974, pp. 60, 303).

against the excessive exercise of individual freedom by others (hence the balanced framing of the liberty principle), and would also want to ensure that, whatever the vagaries of life, they would be ensured some degree of basic equality (hence the equality principle). Rawls' theory is also useful in that it serves to refute the argument that human rights theory is merely a Western construct: The point of the theory is that it is neutral, grounded in common humanity and rationality.

What implications do these ideas have for constitutional law? Both Kant's theory of dignity and Rawls' idea of liberty require that the power of the state be limited so as to preserve a zone of autonomy for the individual. Kant's theories were given effect by other Enlightenment figures, including those who drafted constitutions in the wake of the American and French revolutions and who included provisions in those constitutions recognising that individuals are entitled to the protection of such fundamental rights as are necessary for them to live life autonomously. Rawls too asserted that legal respect for human rights was needed in order to limit the power of the state.[6] Practically speaking, the implementation of these theories also required that, apart from recognising rights, a constitution should provide some mechanism which enables disputes between the individual and the state over the extent of that autonomy to be resolved and which provides people with a remedy where unlawful infringement of rights has occurred.

It is obvious that effective control of the power of the state to limit autonomy can be achieved only if its law-making capacity is restricted. Since that capacity comes from the constitution, it follows that the only way to limit state power is by including provisions in the constitution which restrict the power of the state to enact legislation which limits individual autonomy. The constitution also needs a mechanism for deciding disputes over the parameters of autonomy. This is what a bill of rights does. It specifies the rights – such as the rights to personal liberty, free speech, equality, privacy *et cetera* – which collectively comprise the various aspects of autonomy, and limits the power of the state to abrogate those rights. It also empowers the courts to decide disputes between the individual and the state, and to provide remedies such as the invalidation of legislation, orders requiring the government either to cease or to perform some action, or financial damages to compensate for breaches of rights.

Here it is critically important to understand the relationship between the overarching idea of dignity and the specific rights which it implies. Respect for human dignity gives rise to the obligation to protect autonomy. Autonomy encompasses the full range of human activities, of which specific rights are the component elements. It follows that all those rights ultimately depend for their justification on the overarching theory of human dignity. If one poses the question as to why one should protect free speech, for example, the answer is that engaging in free speech is an aspect of individual autonomy and that if the state was to abrogate a person's free speech, that would therefore amount to an impairment of the that person's entitlement to equal dignity. The answer would be the same if one posed that

[6] Rawls (1999, p. 80).

question in relation to any other right. The protection of any right one would care to mention thus ultimately serves human dignity. Conversely, human dignity requires that all rights be given equal protection. There is no logically defensible justification for protecting some rights and not others. This is often referred to as the concept of the 'indivisibility' of rights – that because all rights are based on human dignity, one cannot pick and choose which rights to protect. No right is to be preferred above any other, and all rights are entitled to protection. This principle is of particular relevance to Australia, where a handful rights are granted constitutional protection while many others are not – an issue which is further explored later in this chapter. The fact that human dignity is an entitlement of all human beings also forms the basis for the 'universality' of rights – in other words, that all people, irrespective of nationality or culture, are entitled to their protection. Furthermore, the fact that rights are an inherent entitlement of being human means that their recognition should not dependant upon at the will of voter majorities and should not have to be begged for by those entitled to them – they are an inherent entitlement of being human, which is why many same-sex couples in Australia found the need to ask for their rights to be recognised during the 2017 marriage equality plebiscite demeaning. As was held by the United States Supreme Court in *Obergefell v Hodges*[7] (the decision in which the court ruled that prohibitions on same-sex marriage in that country were unconstitutional) the theory underpinning the Bill of Rights in that country is that freedom to exercise fundamental rights should not be contingent on democratic process[8] and that '[a]n individual can invoke a right to constitutional protection when he or she is harmed, even if the broader public disagrees and even if the legislature refuses to act', because 'fundamental rights may not be submitted to a vote; they depend on the outcome of no elections.'[9]

Effective protection rights requires that the courts be able to grant remedies when disputes arise over the abrogation of rights. In particular it requires that courts be empowered to declare state conduct (be it in the form of legislation or executive action) unconstitutional if it infringes rights. It is that feature, referred to as 'justiciability,' which makes a bill of rights effective. In the absence of a mechanism allowing the enforcement of rights, a mere listing of rights in the constitution is futile.

In concluding this section, it is instructive to consider the example of Germany where, in light of bitter historical experience, human dignity has been made the supreme constitutional value. Article 1 of the Constitution expressly provides that human dignity is inviolable and must be respected and protected by the state, and the Constitution then specifies a wide range of enforceable rights. Article 20(4) provides an express right to resist threats to the constitutional order (obviously including the rights provisions) if no other remedy is available – a clear repudiation

---

[7] 576 U.S. ___ (2015).

[8] 576 U.S. ___ (2015), 23–6.

[9] 576 U.S. ___ (2015), 24.

of the argument raised at the Nuremberg trials that gave supremacy to obedience to the law that infringed human rights. The German Constitution thus clearly signals that the state – even one founded on democratic government – should be subordinate to human dignity rather than the dignity of the individual being subject to the unrestricted power of the state.

5.3 Human Rights and Democracy

Undoubtedly the most common objection raised to the inclusion in the constitution of a full bill of rights is that it is anti-democratic in that it places a restraint upon the popular will as expressed through parliament. Because this objection is so fundamental, it is addressed before other objections, which are dealt with later in this chapter. Those who reject having a justiciable bill of rights in the constitution do so on the basis that they do not was 'unelected judges' over-ruling the will of parliament. Yet this glib response conceals a profound misunderstanding both of the nature of rights and of who the parties to a dispute over rights are.

At the start of this chapter I discussed the theoretical basis of rights, how all rights derive from human dignity and how therefore no right can be preferred above others. Among the political rights implied by dignity is the right of each person to equal participation in law-making (this was the basis for the argument in favour of electoral reform in Chap. 4). The reason why people should have a right to political participation – in other words, a right to vote – is because human dignity mandates that each person should enjoy equal political power with their fellow citizens. Therefore, a society is democratic because freedoms are respected – it is not free because it is democratic. In the absence of a commitment to human dignity there is no practical reason why people should have a right to vote. A case could be made for benign dictatorship or enlightened oligarchy as a better form of government than democracy – if 'better' is defined as more efficient. But such forms of government are incompatible with human dignity because they deny each individual the right to an equal share of political power. The supposed dichotomy between democracy and protection of human rights is therefore false, as is the idea that the constitutional protection of human rights is somehow anti-democratic, because the right to vote and to live under a democratic government can, like every other right, itself be justified on a principled basis only by reference to human dignity.

Democratic elections for a representative law-making body are the vehicle for giving effect to the right to vote, and the enactment of statutes by parliament is the culmination of an aggregate exercise of that political right over their fellow citizens by individual voters. Thus parliament is not the real actor – it is just an intermediary giving effect to the will of the voters who ultimately affect the rights of their fellow human beings through the statutes enacted by parliament. Voting amounts to an exercise of one right by people which has consequences for other rights of their fellow citizens. But since this political right is just one right among many which, like all rights, is ultimately traceable back to human dignity, and bearing in mind that respect for dignity mandates that all rights be protected, it follows that the exercise of this political right is no more worthy than other rights, and therefore cannot be left unrestrained. It has to be exercised with due regard for other rights. Having a justiciable bill of rights in a constitution ensures that this democratic right is balanced against all the others. Viewed in this light, one can see the falsity in the argument that having a bill of rights imposes an unjustifiable restriction on the legislative power of parliament. In truth a bill of rights is necessary to ensure that a balance is struck between the political rights of people to make laws affecting their fellow citizens on the one hand and the many other – equally important – rights of those fellow citizens on the other. It is one thing for a majority of one's fellow citizens to enact a law setting speed limits, quite another to enact a law authorising detention for six weeks before having to be brought before a court.

The origin of the undue pre-eminence given to the democratic will by opponents of a bill of rights is puzzling, but it may be a problem of lack of imagination, coupled with a lack of empathy. It is a truism to say that the dominant view expressed in debate will be the view of the dominant – that is, majority – group. That inevitably means that it is not the voice of the member of the ethnic minority, the person under arrest, the person who is gay, the person wishing to express unpopular views or the person who is detained while mentally ill. Most of us, who do not belong to these groups, cannot imagine doing so, and therefore do not concern ourselves about their legal position – and it is this lack of imagination that breeds lack of empathy. Those who reject a bill of rights reflect either a striking lack of empathy for their fellow citizens confronted with the power of the state, or else a naïve belief that they can trust the state not to impair their own rights and therefore will never need to have recourse to a bill of rights themselves. This is why Rawls' theory of the veil of ignorance is so powerful a tool in providing a justification for the protection of rights. It not only provides an objective method of discovering what the requirements of human dignity are, but also uniquely combines altruism (in that it requires a person to imagine themselves being in disadvantaged circumstances) and self-interest (because it requires one to imagine what freedoms one would want to exercise ones-self).

Another weakness of majoritarian philosophy is that if pursued to its logical conclusion, it leads to results which even its proponents would find unacceptable. For example, if asked whether laws providing for torture or for imprisonment without trial should be permitted, most opponents of a bill of rights would say that such laws would go 'too far' and ought never to be enacted. Yet as soon as one says that a law goes 'too far,' one is implicitly conceding that law must be subject to control by some external ethical value and that what the majority thinks is right cannot be the touchstone what is permissible. Consistency would then require that whatever ethical value is relied on would have to be applied to all laws, not just some of them. Furthermore, if one accepts the ethical principle that the majority should not have untrammelled power to remove the rights of the minority, one has to accept the corollary that the only institutional mechanism capable of restraining the legislative capacity of parliament is a bill of rights enforced by the courts.

The argument that the constitutional protection of rights constitutes an unwarranted subordination of parliament to the judiciary is also invalid, because it misidentifies the participants in disputes over rights. When an individual goes to court to challenge the validity of an Act of parliament on the grounds that it infringes their rights, parliament (or, more usually, whoever is enforcing the law enacted by parliament) is only a defendant in the institutional sense. We need to look behind parliament and see that the ultimate defendant is the rest of society on whose behalf parliament passed the Act. The plaintiff is, therefore, contesting the right of his or her fellow citizens to enact the law on the ground that the law constitutes an unwarranted limitation on his or her rights. The courts are not a party to the contest at all – their role is to provide the forum to determine whether the plaintiff's case is valid. It is therefore false to characterise adjudication over constitutional rights as a conflict between parliament and the courts – in reality it is a conflict between one citizen and the rest of society, in which the plaintiff seeks to defend his or her exercise of whatever right an Act has infringed against the consequences of the rest of society's exercise of its political right to make that Act.

It is also important to understand the difference between democratic decision-making and judicial decision-making. At elections, voters cast their ballots in pursuit of self-interest. Once elected, politicians make self-interested decisions in relation to what policies to pursue and what laws to enact in furtherance of their parties' interests and in order to retain power – which they do by keeping a majority of voters happy. Thus one can see that in this process, both voters and politicians act out of self-interest – which is entirely legitimate. Democratic decision-making is therefore well-suited to furthering the interests of majorities, but it is supremely ill-equipped to look after the interests of minorities or individuals, whose interests may be of no consequence either to voter majorities or the politicians elected by them. Yet this is not well understood in Australia. Typical of Australian views of democracy is this statement by Menzies[10]:

> There is a basic difference between the American system of government and the system of 'responsible government' which exists both in Great Britain and Australia...With us a Minister is not just a nominee of the head of the Government. He is and must be a member of Parliament, elected as such, and answerable to Members of Parliament at every sitting...Should a minister do something that is thought to violate fundamental human freedom he can be promptly brought to account in Parliament.

This is glib and it is also a fantasy. As we will see in Chap. 7, the executive is not subject to effective control by Parliament – in fact the strength of the party system and the way the rules of parliamentary privilege operate serve to make the government a virtual elective dictatorship. More fundamentally, however, Menzies' argument, which is re-stated in various forms by current opponents of a bill of rights, ignores the fact that it is parliament itself that poses the principal threat to fundamental rights. After all, the government holds power by virtue of the fact that it has

[10] Menzies (1967, p. 54). See also Byrnes et al. (2009, pp. 34–5, 54–9).

a majority in parliament, and it is parliament that enacts legislation that can, and does, infringe human rights, which the executive government then implements.

The fact that a law has been agreed to by a majority in a society is not an irrefutable argument for its validity. Consider the example of South Africa under apartheid: During the apartheid era, the South African parliament, for which only the white population (which amounted to 20% of the total) could vote, enacted racially-discriminatory legislation which determined where the remaining 80% of the population could live, work, go to school and even whom they could marry or have sexual relations with. This racist legislation was supported by a range of other Acts which infringed civil liberties and suppressed dissent. South Africa was rightly condemned on the ground that this legislation infringed numerous fundamental rights. But was apartheid objectively wrong or wrong only because it was implemented by a minority against a majority? What if whites had amounted to 51% of the population? Would those same racist laws have then been unobjectionable because they were supported by a majority? In other words, were the laws inherently wrong, or were they wrong only because they did not enjoy the support of a majority of South Africans? Obviously, the answer is such laws were inherently wrong because of the unjust *effect* they had on those subject to them – an effect on its victims which would have been equally unjust, irrespective of whether they constituted 80% or 49% of the population. In other words, it is the content of the law, not how many people support it that determines whether it is just or unjust. Although a law made in a democracy may be less likely to infringe human rights than one made by an absolute monarch – if only because democratic law-making involves debate during which human rights considerations can be ventilated – it is the *content* of the law, not the manner by which it is made, that ultimately determines whether it is just or unjust, because it is entirely possible for an absolute monarch to make a just law and for a democratic majority to make a profoundly unjust one.

Democratic tyranny is no better than one-man tyranny and a law which is unjust in its consequences is not cured of its unjustness merely because it is approved of by a majority. To say otherwise would mean that the implementation of the will of 51% of the population justifies denying human dignity to the other 49%. Typical of that attitude was Tony Abbott's exhortation to voters during the 2017 marriage equality plebiscite 'And I say to you if you don't like same-sex marriage, vote no,'[11] a statement which revealed a lack of understanding of the need to place a limit on the effect which the 'likes' of voters have on the freedom of their fellow citizens to make intimate life choices. As was stated by Sachs J in his judgment in *Minister for Home Affairs and Another v Fourie and Another*,[12] in which the prohibition on same-sex marriage was declared unconstitutional in South Africa

> The antiquity of prejudice is no reason for its survival. All were based on apparently self-evident biological and social facts; all were once sanctioned by religion and imposed by law, the first two are today regarded with total disdain, and the third with varying degrees of

[11] Hunter (2017).

[12] 2006 (1) SA 542 (CC), 554–5.

> denial, shame or embarrassment. Similarly, the fact that the law today embodies conventional majoritarian views in no way mitigates its discriminatory impact. It is precisely those groups that cannot count on popular support and strong representation in the legislature that have a claim to vindicate their fundamental rights through application of the Bill of Rights.

The idea that the ultimate value of a society ought to be the will of the majority only has to be stated for it to become obvious that it could not be the foundation of an ethical state, as witness the fate of minorities such as African Americans in the United States, Catholics in Northern Ireland and Ainu people in Japan, to name but a few who have been denied civil liberties by democratically-elected governments. But having said that it is important to recognise that the reason why human rights should be respected is not only – or even principally – in order to protect minority groups, rather in order to protect the smallest minority – the individual – whose entitlement to human dignity is worthy of defence, even against the will of the rest of society. So the inescapable conclusion is that there has to be a way, other than crude majoritarianism, of determining whether a law is consistent with human dignity, and the only possible mechanism for that is to have a bill of rights applied by courts which can grant to plaintiffs the remedy of invalidating legislation which is inconsistent with the bill of rights.

Such ethical considerations are rarely, if ever, form part of debate on human rights in Australia. The relentless focus is on pragmatics and on satisfying the will of the majority. The problem here is that a pragmatic case can be made for a host of policies that are inimical to human dignity. For example, in many countries it was commonly argued that denying access to contraceptives was a necessary and useful measure directed towards reducing promiscuity. Whether the underlying hypothesis is correct as a matter of behavioural science is neither here nor there – the fact is that legislation to that effect was enacted by democratically-elected legislatures in several countries and yet was obviously inimical to the right of individuals to govern intimate aspects of their lives. Therefore even if the underlying hypothesis was correct, such laws should be unconstitutional, as indeed they were found to be in the United States in the famous case of *Griswold v Connecticut*,[13] in which the Supreme court struck down a statute which prevented people from using contraceptives. The protection of human dignity necessarily requires that there be limits on the legislative power of parliament, otherwise the extent of human dignity would expand or contract depending on passing whims of electoral majorities. If the only limits to what laws could be passed were the ambition of politicians and the prejudices of electoral majorities, there would in reality be no limits at all.

In concluding this section, it is important to discuss the role of the judiciary in enforcing a bill of rights. As Geoffrey Robertson states,[14] a bill of rights

> …means justice for people whose particular plight would ever be noticed by Parliament, or prove interesting enough to be raised by newspapers or a constituency MP. Far from undermining democracy by shifting power to unelected judges, it shifts power back to unelected

[13] 381 U.S. 479 (1965).

[14] Robertson (2009, p. 8).

citizens: democracy from its inception has relied on judges ('unelected' precisely so they can be independent of party politics) to protect the rights of citizens against governments that abuse power.

Robertson's argument also highlights not only that democratic majorities take decisions that are incompatible with individual rights, but also that democratic processes by their nature fail to provide an adequate and timely remedy when human rights are breached. In a society without a bill of rights, the only course open to victims whose rights are being infringed by an unjust law is to try to get the law changed at the next election. Yet it is absurd to think that this constitutes an effective remedy. A person who has been wrongfully detained, or who has been denied the right to express themselves, or who has been prohibited from exercising their religious freedom needs an immediate remedy – they cannot wait for three years for the law to be changed. Furthermore, elections being what they are, one would have to be naïve to imagine that the breach of the rights of any particular individual would feature in the election campaign, that a political party would take up their cause to have the law changed and that a change would successfully be navigated through Parliament.

By contrast, a bill of rights provides minorities and individuals with a mechanism that they can use to protect themselves in cases where democratic decision-making leads to results which are inimical to human dignity. The difference between democratic decision-making and judicial decision-making is that, in contrast to voters and politicians, when judges make decisions they are required by oath to do so neutrally – that is, completely *disinterestedly* – without reference to what is popular or to the interplay of party political forces and solely with regard to the preservation of human dignity. This was well put by Albie Sachs, former Justice of the South African Constitutional court who wrote[15]:

> But judges did know about human dignity, about oppression and about the things that reduced the status of the human being to a status below that which a democratic society would regard as tolerable. Efficiency may well be one of the great principles of government, and the utilitarian principle of producing the greatest good for the greatest number might well be the starting off point…But the qualitative element, based on respect for the dignity of every one of us, should never be left out. This is where the vision of the judiciary, institutionally tunnelled in the direction of respect for human dignity, comes into its own. And the principled balancing the courts do is quite different from the compromises worked out in political life.

He further wrote that[16]:

> My view is that…it is actually an advantage for judges not to be accountable to the electorate. We have a constitutional duty to defend deep core values which are part of emerging world jurisprudence, and which relate directly to evolving constitutional notions in our own country. This makes me sharply aware of the manner in which the Constitution connects the maintenance of judicial independence and the protection of human dignity. The very notion of entrenching rights is to provide a basic framework of constitutional regard for every

[15] Sachs (2008, p. 171).

[16] Sachs (2008, pp. 212–13).

> human being. It is not the duty of the courts to side with one section of society against another, however powerful or weak. Nor may they permit purely personal opinions on political, social and moral questions to hold sway. Of course judges have opinions, frequently strong ones, but any influence these opinions may have, needs to be refracted through the prism of judicial reasoning. And it is the Constitution itself which makes it incumbent on judges to continue to see to it that basic respect for the dignity of every person is maintained at all times. This is why we have fundamental rights.

It is therefore precisely because judges are unelected, and therefore neither beholden to any interest group nor acting in pursuit of power, that their decisions are as objective as is humanly possible. It is their neutrality that is the courts' greatest strength – it is not a weakness. In interpreting a bill of rights and deciding whether a statute or government conduct impermissibly infringes that bill of rights, judges make decisions through the application of legal principle, not political policy. Yet many people do not understand this, as exemplified by former New South Wales Premier Bob Carr who, arguing against a bill of rights, wrote of the judicial role as follows[17]:

> It's all easy to imagine a charter when we imagine every judge as a Michael Kirby. But you might one day have a combination of conservative government and conservative judiciary....Conservative judges would make out of a Charter of Rights what they wanted.

Carr, it should be noted, subsequently lobbied Kevin Rudd to reject a bill of rights by recruiting two of the most conservative figures in Australia to assist him: Archbishop Peter Jensen and Archbishop George Pell.[18] Carr's line of thinking misapprehends the judicial role and is influenced by observation of the United States, where the role of the President in nominating federal justices, and the Senate in confirming them, has led to overt politicisation of the judicial appointments process. Indeed, the process used in the United States is among the worst one could imagine. This is why it is crucial that it be designed in such a way as to eliminate the operation of political factors and ensures that appointees have the broadest possible background and experience. This issue is addressed in detail in Chap. 11, where a process that which would restrict the government's role in appointing judges to that of choosing from candidates nominated by a widely-drawn interview panel is suggested. Of more concern, however, is Carr's view that the question of whether to have a bill of rights should be decided on the basis of a political calculation as to whether the judiciary would be likely to produce decisions which accorded with one's ideological position. This reflects a misunderstanding of the role of the courts as a branch of government and of the doctrine of constitutionalism, which requires acceptance of judicial decisions irrespective of whether they work to the advantage or disadvantage of any particular point of view. It also reflects a failure to understand the effect of the judicial oath, which requires office-holders to do justice without fear or favour – which is a thing of real meaning to judges, not some formulaic utterance. If we had a bill of rights, every case would have a result which doubtless

---

[17] Carr (2018, p. 264).

[18] Carr (2018, p. 265).

satisfied some and disappointed others – and that is as it should be. And if judges were selected in the manner suggested in Chap. 11, those decisions would not be the product of a 'conservative' or of a 'liberal' judiciary, because the apolitical nature of the process would eliminate appointments on an ideological basis.

5.4 Human Rights Protection in Australia

The legal status of rights in Australia can best be described as a hotchpotch, with protection afforded to only a handful of rights, some of which are protected against depredation by both the Commonwealth and by the states, others of which are protected only against infringement by the Commonwealth.

Before discussing statutory and constitutional provisions relating to rights, it is necessary to address what are sometimes referred to as 'common law' rights. The common law is a body of legal principles developed by judges as they decided cases over the centuries. A decision in a case would constitute a rule of law which, under the doctrine of precedent, would then be applied to litigants in any subsequent cases where the essential facts were similar. Common law pre-dates statute law – indeed, there was no statute law until the first parliaments were called in the thirteenth century. But even in the centuries after parliaments began enacting legislation, significant areas of the law were – and still are – governed by the common law in counties which derive their legal system from England. The common law protects individual autonomy in that one of its general principles is that a person may do anything that the law does not prohibit.[19] Furthermore, the common law protects rights that are found in human rights documents – procedural rights which ensure a fair trial being a good example. However, the fundamental weakness of the common law is the fact that it can be over-ridden by inconsistent legislation, and so if a parliament enacts a statute containing a different rule to that contained in the common law, the common law is abrogated and the law as contained in the statute must thereafter be followed. In that sense then, common law 'rights' are not real rights in the sense of constitutional rights as explained at the start of this chapter, because they provide the individual with no protection from a parliament bent on removing those rights.

Also of limited usefulness are the statutory charters of rights that have been enacted by Victoria and the ACT. Although these charters are laudable in that they list fundamental rights that are usually found in a bill of rights, both the *Human Rights Act 2004* (ACT) and the *Charter of Human Rights and Responsibilities Act 2006* (Vic) are ordinary statutes which, like any other statute, can be repealed or amended without any special constitutional procedure. Furthermore, although both Acts require that other legislation must be interpreted consistently with the human rights Acts if possible,[20] they also explicitly state that if other legislation is found to

[19] *R v Somerset CC, ex p. Fewings* [1995] 1 All ER 513, 524.

[20] ACT s 30, Vic s 32(1).

be inconsistent with the human rights Act, such a finding does not affect the validity of that other legislation which must still be applied.[21] So these two Acts are not true bills of rights because they are not protected from amendment and because they are not justiciable.

So far as the Commonwealth Constitution is concerned, the question of what rights ought to be protected in a future federal constitution was debated at the Conventions held in the 1890s. The debates are notable for the absence of any discussion of human rights theory or broad questions of what ought to be the relationship between the individual and the state. Delegates ultimately agreed on the inclusion of only five express rights in the Constitution, not as the implementation of any theory but rather as a pragmatic response to particular political controversies that had to be settled in order to get all the colonies to agree to federation. Thus s 51(xxxi) (requiring just terms compensation for the acquisition of property), s 117 (requiring equal treatment of residents of different States) and s 92 (protecting freedom of inter-State trade, commerce and intercourse) all obviously addressed apprehended abuses of Commonwealth powers by the states or by the states vis-à-vis each other. The prohibition of religious discrimination in s 116 reflected a concern that sectarian tensions not influence law-making by the Commonwealth, there being a social division between Catholics and Protestants in Australia at the time.[22] Only the s 80 requirement of jury trials for indictable Commonwealth offences is conceivably identifiable as a provision protecting fundamental rights, yet it can easily be circumvented simply by the Commonwealth parliament classifying offences as summary rather than indictable. The aspect of the Constitutional Conventions of the 1890s which is most revealing of attitudes to rights was the debate over the question as to whether a right to due process should be included in the Constitution. That proposal was rejected for the morally discreditable reason that would prevent racially discriminatory legislation being enacted against Indigenous people and Asians.[23]

In the wake of World War II, and in particular following the revelations of war crimes and crimes against humanity committed by the Axis powers, the international community responded by drafting the *Universal Declaration of Human Rights*, which was adopted by the United Nations General Assembly on 10 December 1948 (a date thereafter commemorated as Human Rights Day). Australian Attorney-General and Foreign Minister H. V. Evatt played a key part in the drafting process in his role as President of the General Assembly. Key principles underlying the Declaration were those of the universality of rights and their supremacy over state sovereignty. This meant that the inherent dignity of people entitled them to protection of human rights irrespective of who they were and notwithstanding what the law of any particular government might say. Apart from their obvious roots in the

[21] ACT s 32(3)(a) and s 40B(2), Vic s 32(3)(a) and s 38(2).

[22] Ely (1976, pp. 19–20, 130).

[23] *Official Record of the Debates of the Australasian Constitutional Convention*, Melbourne, 8 February 1898, 665–6 (Sir John Forrest). See also Robertson (2009, p. 7).

philosophies discussed earlier in this chapter, these principles owed their origin at least in part to what had transpired at the war crimes trials at the end of the war. Although there was no doubt that, in accordance with the generally-accepted doctrine of positivism (discussed in Chap. 2) the Nazi government was the lawful government of Germany at the time its servants committed crimes against humanity against its own citizens and citizens of other countries, the Nuremberg War Crimes Tribunal rejected the defence that obedience to the law excused acts contrary to fundamental principles of humanity.[24] The same approach was subsequently adopted by German courts, which held invalid Nazi laws which authorised breaches of fundamental rights.[25] These courts operated on the basis that the dignity of the human being set limits on the law-making capacity of the state and that state sovereignty was subordinate to supra-legal values. It was those values that were given concrete form by the Declaration. Subsequently the United Nations adopted the 1966 *International Covenant on Civil and Political Rights* (ICCPR) and the 1966 *International Covenant on Economic, Social and Cultural Rights* (ICESCR), which amplify the rights stated in the Universal Declaration but which (unlike the Declaration), have the status of treaties at international law, imposing a duty on signatories to give effect to their content.

Unfortunately, despite Australia's involvement in the drafting of the Declaration and the Covenants, Australia failed to enact these document into domestic law so that they could be enforced in the courts. The Menzies government elected in 1949 rejected the idea of a domestic Bill of Rights, among other reasons because it might lead to litigation by Indigenous Australians contesting the discrimination to which they were subject – notably the same ground upon which the idea of a right to due process had been rejected at the Constitutional Conventions. This is why to this day, although a signatory to the ICCPR and the ICESR, Australia has yet to enact these documents into domestic law.

The only progress that has been made in constitutional rights-protection has been by judicial interpretation of various provisions in the constitution which, on the face of them, do not appear to confer rights but which the courts have said impliedly do so. Thus in *Australian Capital Television v Commonwealth (No 2),*[26] the High Court held that because sections 7 and 24 of the Constitution, which relate to elections for the Senate and House of Representatives respectively, embody representative government, and because representative government requires freedom to exchange political views for it to function, the Constitution impliedly protects the right to engage in political communication. In *Chu Kheng Lim v Minister for Immigration, Local Government and Ethnic Affairs*,[27] the court held that the doctrine of separation of powers contained in Chapter III of the Constitution implied a right to due

[24] For a comprehensive discussion of the Nuremberg Trials see Office of the United States Chief Counsel for the Prosecution of Axis Criminality (1946).

[25] The German cases which found that Nazi laws were invalid are discussed in Fuller (1957–1958) and in Mertens (2003).

[26] (1992) 177 CLR 106.

[27] (1992) 176 CLR 1.

process when a person is deprived of liberty although, as discussed in Chap. 1, the right does not apply in all instances. Finally, in *Roach v Electoral Commissioner*,[28] the High Court again relied upon the doctrine of representative government to find that the Constitution protected an implied right to vote. Although these are welcome developments, the ability of the courts to 'find' rights in the Constitution is limited by what can be implied from the text, and that means that the full range of rights protected by international human rights documents cannot be constitutionalised.

There seems to be an attitude of exceptionalism at play in Australia, as though the fact that we are a democracy exempts us from the obligation to enact into domestic law the international human rights conventions we have signed. Yet one will search in vain for a footnote to these documents stating 'These rights do not apply to democracies'. As explained earlier in this chapter, rights are founded on universality – that they protect everyone, everywhere – and on the inherent right of every person to that protection, irrespective of the will of political majorities.

Subsequent Australian governments have maintained opposition to the inclusion of a bill of rights into the constitution, and have been openly hostile to the United Nations when it has criticised human rights breaches. Some ministerial statements have, unfortunately, echoed what used to be said of the United Nations by South African politicians during the apartheid era.

Several unsuccessful attempts have been made to insert new rights into the Constitution. In 1944 a proposal to make the s 116 protection for freedom of religion applicable to the states and to incorporate freedom of expression in the Constitution failed. In 1988, following on the recommendation by the Constitutional Commission that a new chapter be inserted into the Constitution protecting a wide range of rights,[29] the government responded with a proposal limited to expanding the s 116 right to religious freedom and the s 51(xxxi) requirement for just terms compensation when property is acquired so as to make them applicable to the states, and incorporating in the Constitution an express right to vote and a requirement that all electorates have an equal number of voters. Both proposals were defeated.

In 2008 the Rudd government established the National Human Rights Consultation (NHRC) to hold public consultations on the question of whether Australia should have a bill of rights.[30] The terms of reference included a restriction that options canvassed by the committee 'should preserve the sovereignty of the Parliament' – in other words, should not suggest the inclusion in the Constitution of new rights which would restrict the legislative power of parliament. Anyone reading this clause – and in particular the word 'preserve' – without the benefit of knowing the Constitution would assume that the courts currently do not have the power to invalidate laws enacted by parliament and that therefore a recommendation to give them such a power would have amounted to a departure from current constitutional arrangements. Yet, as we have seen in Chap. 3, the courts have had that power since

[28] (2007) 233 CLR 162.

[29] Constitutional Commission (1988, Vol 1, p. 476).

[30] Attorney General's Department (2009). The report is available at http://apo.org.au/node/19288

the Constitution came into force. The mandate given to the committee was therefore misleading, because it suggested that the relationship between parliament and the courts was different from what it actually is.

Hobbled as it was by its terms of reference, the NHRC ultimately recommended that the Commonwealth enact a Human Rights Act that would be similar to the type used in the ACT and Victoria. In so doing, the NHRC was influenced by the public polling done as part of the consultation process. Among the questions put to respondents was one in which they were asked to express support or disagreement for a range of measures to protect human rights: Parliament paying attention to human rights when enacting laws, government paying attention to human rights when developing policies, increased human rights education, a non-binding statement of human rights issued by the government and, finally, 'an enacted human rights law'. Among these options, 57% of respondents either supported or strongly supported the enactment of a human rights law. Crucially, however, because a justiciable bill of rights was off-limits to the NHRC, and because the respondents were not asked to express a preference as between different types of human rights law, one simply does not know what level of support for that option would have been. The NHRC ought to have taken the lead in educating, rather than just being shaped by, public opinion, which it could have done by explaining the different types of human rights document and the constitutional status of each. In the end, the government decided not to adopt even the mild recommendation proffered by the NHRC, and instead enacted the *Human Rights (Parliamentary Scrutiny) Act 2011* (Cth) which requires only that a Parliamentary Joint Committee on Human Rights examine legislation and report to both houses of Parliament on the compatibility of the legislation with the international human rights documents Australia has ratified, and that anyone introducing Acts to parliament or promulgating delegated legislation must similarly report to parliament on its compatibility with those documents. The Act expressly states that a finding of incompatibility does not affect the validity of the legislation concerned.

Politically speaking, human rights have become playthings in partisan debates in which consideration of the philosophical theories underlying rights has been notably absent. Both the right and the left of Australian politics have rejected additional protection for rights, motivated by a shared self-interest in not allowing the power of government to be curbed, and in the process have adopted positions which are logically unsustainable and internally inconsistent.

Conservative voices have been selective both in the rights they are willing to defend and the circumstances in which they should apply. Despite stating that it believes in 'the inalienable rights and freedoms of all peoples,'[31] the Liberal party has consistently opposed the broadening of constitutional rights. This is bizarre given that maximisation of individual liberty and minimisation of the power of the state has been the cornerstone of liberal political philosophy since the eighteenth century. In a surprising statement in view of his former position as Human Rights

[31] The Liberal Party website is at https://www.liberal.org.au/our-beliefs

Commissioner, Liberal MP Tim Wilson said that a bill of rights was 'inconsistent with socially conservative values.'[32] Protection even of a right as fundamental as racial equality was rejected by Tony Abbott who, in the course of debate on the constitutional position of Indigenous people, opposed the inclusion of a such a right in the Constitution, stating that he rejected the inclusion of a 'one-clause bill of rights'[33] which would lead to legislation being subject to 'second-guessing by non-elected judges.'[34] This comment not only indicates a failure to understand the nature of fundamental rights but also shows that Australia has moved little beyond the attitude to race and rights evident at the Constitutional Conventions of the 1890s, when a right to due process was rejected on the ground that it could lead to constitutional challenge of discriminatory legislation.

Interestingly, however, conservatives have not taken their aversion to a broadening of constitutional rights to its logical conclusion, which would be to call for the removal from the Constitution of such rights as it does protect. Indeed they have vigorously defend selected rights which are consistent with their world-view. A key example is freedom of religion, in relation to which Prime Minister Mark Morrison said 'Religious freedom – it doesn't get more serious than that when it comes to liberties. If you don't have the freedom to believe in your own faith, then what is liberty?'[35] – a comment which begs the question as to why freedom of religion should be prioritised over rights such as freedom of the person, freedom from torture or the right to a fair trial. Similarly, conservatives have been supportive of the implied constitutional freedom to political communication – although here again inconsistency has been apparent, in that whereas they have rejected the idea that racial vilification should be prohibited they have been prepared to limit that freedom when its exercise was thought inimical to other aspects of the conservative agenda, as in the case of legislation which forbade medical practitioners from reporting on the conditions of detainees in immigration detention.[36] The same selective attitude towards rights has been evinced by conservative commentators such as Janet Albrechtsen, who rejects the idea of a bill of rights on the grounds that it is an anti-democratic restraint on parliament[37] while nevertheless arguing that s 18C of the *Racial Discrimination Act 1975* (Cth) – a restraint enacted by parliament – unjustly infringes freedom of expression.[38] The same is true of academics such as Greg Craven, who vociferously opposes a bill of rights[39] and yet expresses support for constitutional protection of freedom of religion.[40] At the heart of the attitudes of

[32] Elton-Pymm (2018).

[33] Williams (2014).

[34] Henderson (2015).

[35] Australian Broadcasting Corporation (2018).

[36] Hall (2016).

[37] See for example Albrechtsen (2001, 2003, 2004, 2007).

[38] Brull (2016).

[39] Craven (2004, pp. 181–8).

[40] Craven (2018).

political conservatives lies a failure to understand that because all rights derive from human dignity, all are entitled to equal protection, and that there is no theory which can justify the protection of some rights but not others. The fact that the Constitution protects some rights and not others is therefore a mark of internal inconsistency.

The political left has been no more supportive of rights. Despite supposedly being a party of social justice, Labor has not moved to enhance rights protection when in office – indeed former Labor Premier of New South Wales, Bob Carr, has been in the forefront of opposition to a bill of rights.[41] Even commentators with a progressive reputation, such as Fr Frank Brennan, rejected the inclusion of a right not to be subject to discrimination on grounds of race or ethnicity, proposed for inclusion in a new section (s 116A) of the Constitution by the Joint Select Committee on Constitutional Recognition of Aboriginal and Torres Strait Islander Peoples in 2015.[42] Because his arguments illustrate much of what is wrong with debate on rights in Australia, it is worthwhile analysing them in detail:

The grounds of Brennan's opposition were numerous – invidiousness in protecting only Indigenous people from racial discrimination,[43] invidiousness in not prohibiting discrimination on other grounds or of protecting other rights,[44] difficulties in interpreting such a non-discrimination right particularly if it included an affirmative action provision,[45] the inability of the public to understand an affirmative action clause,[46] public opposition to the conferral of power on an 'unelected judiciary'[47] and potential opposition by such interest groups as National Farmers' Federation, the Minerals Council and the Business Council of Australia.[48] These arguments fail to prioritise the principle of inherent entitlement to dignity which I would argue imposes a moral duty on proponents of human rights to overcome difficulties rather than surrender to them.

The anti-discrimination provision contained in the proposed s 116A would have prohibited racial discrimination against all Australians, not only against Indigenous people. Of course it would be preferable to adopt a full bill of rights which prohibited discrimination on a wide range of grounds – but that is no reason to argue against the progressive embedding of specific rights in the Constitution or to require Indigenous people, who have been waiting for more than 200 years for constitutional protection against racism, to wait still longer. As to difficulties in interpretation, if courts in other jurisdictions have been able to interpret a right to non-discrimination in tandem with affirmative action provisions, why should that be

---

[41] Australian Broadcasting Corporation (2008).

[42] Joint Select Committee on Constitutional Recognition of Aboriginal and Torres Strait Islander Peoples. (2015, p. 89).

[43] Brennan (2015, pp. 6–7).

[44] Brennan (2015, pp. 6–7).

[45] Brennan (2015, pp. 220, 244–7).

[46] Brennan (2015, p. 270).

[47] Brennan (2015, p. 271).

[48] Australian Broadcasting Corporation (2015). A recording of the interview can be heard at http://mpegmedia.abc.net.au/rn/podcast/2015/05/bst_20150519_0806.mp3

beyond the wit of courts in Australia? Any change to statute law requires interpretation, and in this respect constitutional interpretation is neither more nor less difficult. If uncertainty over the effect of a change was accepted as a general objection to constitutional reform, then reform would never occur and, remembering that the issue is one of fundamental principle, saying that it would be 'too difficult' to interpret a new right is to trivialise what is at stake. So far as public misunderstanding of, and apprehension in relation to, proposed reform is concerned, surely the remedy here is to apply every effort to convincing the public of the nobility of the cause – as was done during the 1967 referendum – and to muster arguments to assuage their doubts? The argument relating to the conferral of power on an 'unelected judiciary' has been addressed earlier in this chapter and ignores the fact that since its inception, the Constitution has empowered the courts to invalidate legislation inconsistent with such rights as it protects. Finally, so far as opposition from commercial groups are concerned, even assuming that these interest groups had the audacity to come out publically against a right to non-discrimination, what of it? Are the contours of constitutional rights to be determined by economically powerful groups? Should they have a veto on fundamental freedoms? Ought we not publically challenge such views rather than defer to them?

We are left in the bizarre position that while the Constitution protects the rather esoteric right not to be discriminated against on the grounds of which state one resides in, it does not protect a range of fundamental rights that are obvious incidents of human dignity, such as the right to equality, the right not to be subject to inhumane treatment, the right to privacy, the right to liberty of the person and the right to due process. This is why true respect for dignity requires the inclusion in the constitution of a full bill of rights along with remedies that the courts can apply in cases where they are infringed.

5.5 Other Objections to a Bill of Rights

Apart from the view that a justiciable bill of rights is anti-democratic already addressed, several other objections to a bill of rights are frequently advanced, and it is necessary to consider those before discussing what a bill of rights should contain. Some of these objections are substantive. Others are trivial – which has not prevented them from exploitation by those opposed to a bill of rights.

To start with the trivial, a commonly advanced view is because the Second Amendment to the United States Constitution protects the right to bear arms, an Australian bill of rights would necessarily include that right, which would in turn lead to the high levels of gun crime that are experienced in the United States. In contrast to other rights such as freedom of religion, freedom of expression and liberty of the person et cetera, which were ultimately founded on dignity, the inclusion of the Second Amendment was a purely pragmatic reaction to specific political circumstances, namely the attempt by British authorities to confiscate arms during the revolution.[49] No-one argues that the right to bear arms is a component of human dignity, and none of the contemporary human rights documents based on human dignity includes it. Therefore there is no reason why such a right would appear in an Australian bill of rights. Those raising the existence of the Second Amendment in the United States as a reason for not having a bill of rights in Australia do so mischievously and without advancing a rational – as opposed to sensationalist – basis for apprehending that such a right would be included.

The second commonly advanced objection is the 'lawyers picnic' argument, according to which the inclusion of a bill of rights in the constitution would lead to frequent litigation of which lawyers would be the principal beneficiaries. While this argument might be dismissed as testimony to the continued force of a Shakespearian aversion to lawyers,[50] it has attracted support from across the political spectrum, which is perhaps indicative of the fact that, irrespective of their political hue, governments would prefer not to be subject to the limitations imposed by a Bill of Rights. Thus, in response to a call by former Prime Minister Malcolm Fraser for a Bill of Rights, John Howard said[51]

> If you have a Bill of Rights, you open up a whole new opportunity for court cases because people say their rights have been infringed, [and] they go to court to get redress.

The first thing that strikes one about this statement is its sense of outrage that people might dare to assert their rights against the government. More important however is the fact that its unspoken premise – that the activities of the legal profession and enforcement of a bill of rights are a social evil – are incompatible with the rule of law. This animus against lawyers is puzzling. Since no-one argues that a person who has been injured in a road accident, or who has been defamed or who has had their property destroyed should not avail of the services of a lawyer to obtain a remedy from the courts, why should a person be any less entitled to sue the government when it acts unlawfully by infringing their rights, and why should it be any less legitimate for lawyers to represent them? In fact, surely such litigation should be applauded as a benefit to society in that it compels the government to comply with the law? This is particularly the case in an era of declining government respect for the rule of law, as illustrated by Immigration Minister Peter Dutton's view that it was 'un-Australian' for lawyers acting on behalf of refugees to challenge the lawfulness of governmental action.[52] Any law – not just a bill of rights – should be met with court action if it is breached. That is the price we pay for a society ruled by law. No doubt if modern opponents of a Bill of Rights had been at Runnymeade in 1215 they would have whispered in King John's ear 'Don't sign Magna Carta your Majesty, you will create a lawyer's picnic'.

---

[49] Kopel (2012).

[50] 'The first thing we do, let's kill all the lawyers,' *Henry VI Part 2*, Act IV, Scene 2.

[51] Peake (2000). The argument was also made by Bob Carr, Labor Premier of New South Wales in his submission to the New South Wales parliamentary inquiry into whether the state should have a bill of rights – see Parliament of New South Wales (2001, para. 6.50–2).

[52] Hall (2017).

Leaving aside the fact that human rights litigation fosters respect for constitutionalism, the underlying hypothesis of the 'lawyers' picnic' argument – that a bill of rights would lead to a deluge of litigation – would be true only if there was widespread infringements of rights. In other words, how many human rights cases there were would lie in the hands of the government itself – the fewer the number of breaches of human rights, the fewer the number of cases. Commentators in jurisdictions which have bills of rights have noted the educative effect such documents have on the behaviour of governments – having the strictures imposed by a bill of rights in mind leads to more careful decision-making so as to avoid legal challenges being brought. In other words, if a government is careful to ensure that rights were respected, cases against it will fail – moreover, as in any other area of law, the bringing of non-meritorious cases would be deterred by the prospect of costs being awarded against the plaintiffs. One therefore suspects that the real source of the 'lawyers' picnic' argument is a fear on the part of those making it (in particular politicians) that a bill of rights would prevent governments from acting in ways that are at odds with fundamental rights – which is of course demonstrates all the more clearly why we need the protection which a bill of rights affords.

In contrast to the previous argument that because rights are infringed the courts will be clogged by people seeking to vindicate them, the next objection is that rights are in fact never infringed and so we do not need a bill of rights. Curiously, the fact that the previous argument and this one are mutually inconsistent has not prevented them from sometimes being raised by the same people. The idea that rights are not infringed does not stand up to scrutiny. To take a recent very public example, Operation Fortitude, discussed in Chap. 1, which would have seen Border Force officers stopping members of the public in Melbourne and requiring them to prove lawful residence – presumably on the basis of racial profiling – would obviously have infringed the right to liberty of the person as well as the right to equality had it not been stopped by a mass public protest.[53] Indeed the extent to which the right to liberty of the person and the right to due process are infringed in Australia is illustrated by the fact that a 2007 report by the Commonwealth Ombudsman found that because migration legislation makes it possible for a person to be detained without being brought before the courts, 247 citizens and lawful residents had being unlawfully detained by the Commonwealth.[54] However the scope of breaches of human rights extends far beyond migration law. Most people are unaware that there are a wide range of statutes, Commonwealth and state, which remove fundamental rights. These include provisions which cast on the accused the burden of disproving elements of criminal liability thus removing the presumption of innocence, provisions removing the right to silence, thereby making it an offence for a person not to answer questions even at peril of self-incrimination, and provisions denying people the right to natural justice, thereby removing their entitlement to seek judicial review of the actions of government officials when those officials act contrary to

[53] Mills et al. (2015).

[54] Commonwealth Ombudsman (2007). This is also discussed in Chap. 2.

law. In its 2018 report, the Institute for Public Affairs identified no less than 358 statutory provisions (and this only at Commonwealth level) which infringed these rights. Similarly, in a report on rights and freedoms published in 2016,[55] the Australian Law Reform Commission found numerous examples of Commonwealth legislation (the terms of reference did not extend to state and Territory law) which infringed a range of rights including freedom of expression, freedom of association, the right to the presumption of innocence, the privilege against self-incrimination, freedom of movement and the right to a fair trial – and this was without considering a number of other freedoms which are protected by international human rights documents but which were excluded from the scope of the Commission's inquiry.

Of course, many people comfort themselves with the belief that they will never be accused of a crime, never be unfairly arrested and will never be required to make a statement which could incriminate them (something that they could be compelled to do even by something as mundane as legislation governing corporations)[56] and never be in the position of being unable to challenge a governmental decision adverse to them. This naïve attitude is akin to saying 'There hasn't ever been a fire in my neighbourhood, so I'm not going to bother getting fire insurance'. The fact is that none of us can predict when the vagaries of life might put us in the position of having our rights infringed, and it is precisely to provide one with a weapon to combat the power of the state on such occasions that one needs a bill of rights.

The next argument against a bill of rights is that if one defines certain rights in the constitution, one runs the risk that such rights as are not mentioned will no longer exist. The problem with this argument is its implicit assumption about the current status of rights-protection in Australia. The argument rests upon a misunderstanding of a rule of statutory interpretation expressed in the maxim *expressio unius est exclusuio alterius* (mention of one means the exclusion of others). An example of the operation of this maxim would be that if a statute said that 'Trucks and cars may be driven on the freeway,' it would be interpreted as meaning that other forms of transport, such as motorcycles and bicycles, were impliedly prohibited. But the operation of the maxim depends upon the existence of a class of things that would otherwise be included if nothing was stated at all. Apart from the few rights which are expressly mentioned in the Constitution or which have been implied from it, Australian law does not protect rights in the sense that it is used in this chapter – namely constitutional rights against which legislation and government action may be tested. So-called 'common law rights' and rights conferred by statute are not constitutional rights because they can always be over-ridden by legislation. Therefore, as long as those few rights that are currently protected in the constitution were included in a bill of rights, the listing of new rights in the constitution could not possibly be interpreted as meaning that protection was removed from

[55] Australian Law Reform Commission (2016).

[56] Under s 19 of the *Australian Securities and Investments Commission Act 2001* (Cth), when ASIC is investigating a corporation's affairs it may compel a person to answer questions subject to criminal prosecution if they fail to do so, and s 68 of the Act expressly states that the right against self-incrimination is not an excuse for failing to answer questions.

other constitutional rights, because no other constitutional rights exist under Australian law. In other words, one cannot exclude what doesn't exist in the first place. The very purpose of including a full bill of rights in the constitution would be to *expand* the range of rights that are afforded protection, and that would be its undoubted effect.

If there was a concern that any common law or statutory 'rights' might be omitted from the coverage of a bill of rights – which would be highly unlikely given the comprehensive nature of the UDHR, the ICCPR and the ICESR upon which an Australian bill of rights would be based – that concern could be addressed by including in a bill of rights a provision such as appears in s 39(3) of the South African Constitution, which provides as follows:

> The Bill of Rights does not deny the existence of any other rights or freedoms that are recognised or conferred by common law, customary law or legislation, to the extent that they are consistent with the Bill.

That would ensure that any such rights, although not of constitutional status, would continue in existence.

The final argument to consider is that a bill of rights would be ineffective. This is often based on simplistic arguments such as that by Bob Carr, former Premier of New South Wales, who wrote as follows[57]:

> 'Some people argue our liberties aren't complete without a Bill of Rights,' I remember McCallum [Carr's political science professor] saying across a canyon of fifty years. 'But America has had a Bill of Rights for 160 years and Negroes were denied the right to vote for much of that time. Stalin's Soviet Constitution of 1936 conferred a lot of human rights, none of which meant anything.' This clicked a light bulb. I've been a sceptic about Bills of Rights ever since. History teaches us there is, in fact, no guarantee they work.

However Carr's analysis of his road to Damascus experience was based on poor logical foundations, because the argument he presents is analogous to saying because some drugs are of limited efficacy, all medicines are useless. How a bill of rights operates depends what is in it – and, as importantly, what is omitted. Racial discrimination flourished in the United Sates for many decades because the text of the bill of rights did not expressly provide that it applied to state governments. This meant that the use of the bill of rights to challenge racial discrimination had to await the Supreme Court's decision in *Brown v Board of Education of Topeka*,[58] in which it was held that the due process clause not only guaranteed equal treatment as between races by the federal government but was impliedly binding on the states. So that argument does not support the contention that all bills of rights are ineffective, rather it is a lesson in ensuring that a bill of rights provides comprehensive coverage in its application. Certainly modern bills of rights expressly state that they apply to all organs of government.[59] The argument based on the Soviet constitution of 1936 (a standard hoary chestnut of those opposed to a bill of rights, often

[57] Carr (2018, p. 263).

[58] 347 U.S. 483 (1954).

[59] See for example s 8(1) of the South African Bill of Rights.

accompanied by arguments that because the Weimar republic had a bill of rights and yet the Nazis came to power, all bills of rights are useless) not only misreads history but is also dangerous to constitutionalism. The reason why these regimes committed the atrocities they did was because they had no respect for the law in general, not just for bills of rights. Any government can act unconstitutionally if it sets its mind to it – in which case all law becomes irrelevant. But saying that a bill of rights is of no use because a government may not obey its constraints logically implies that constitutions as a whole are of no use because they too are equally vulnerable to over-ride by a tyrannical government. So, if pursued to its logical conclusion, the 'Stalin bill of rights' argument begs the question as to why there should be rules limiting government at all and why we should not just revert to the pre-Magna Carta era, where the word of the monarch was law. One has only to voice this argument to realise that at best it is facile, and at worst could be used to justify the abrogation of the constitutional order. One either debates the question of a bill of rights accepting that the doctrine of constitutionalism applies, in which case there is no doubt that a bill of rights adds to the quantum of human freedom or, if one goes beyond the parameters of constitutionalism, one has to concede that all constitutional law – not just a bill of rights – is useless.

References

Albrechtsen J (2001) Judges there to serve the law, not make it. The Sydney Morning Herald. 9 Apr 2001

Albrechtsen J (2003) Human rights plea a scam for con artists. The Australian. 5 Nov 2003

Albrechtsen J (2004) Wary of a world where high priests hold sway. The Australian. 30 June 2004

Albrechtsen J (2007) Conservatives must join charter of rights discussions. The Australian. 5 Dec 2007

Attorney General's Department (2009) National human rights consultation report. Commonwealth Government, Canberra. https://apo.org.au/node/19288. Accessed 15 Oct 2019

Australian Broadcasting Corporation (2008) Carr steadfast in opposition to human rights bill. The World Today. 10 Dec 2008

Australian Broadcasting Corporation (2015) Radio national breakfast. 19 May 2015 http://mpeg-media.abc.net.au/rn/podcast/2015/05/bst_20150519_0806.mp3. Accessed 15 Oct 2019

Australian Broadcasting Corporation (2018) 7.30 report. 11 Sept 2018

Australian Law Reform Commission (2016) Traditional rights and freedoms – encroachment by commonwealth laws. Australian Law Reform Commission, Brisbane. https://www.alrc.gov.au/inquiries/freedoms. Accessed 15 Oct 2019

Brennan F (1998) Legislating liberty? a bill of rights for Australia. University of Queensland Press, St Lucia

Brennan F (2015) No small change: the road to recognition for indigenous Australia. University of Queensland Press, St Lucia

Brull M (2016) Hypocrisy has a new name, and it's Janet Albrechtsen. New Matilda. 15 Feb 2016

Byrnes A, McKinnon G, Charlesworth H (2009) Bills of rights in Australia – history, politics and law. University of New South Wales Press, Sydney

Carr B (2018) Run for your life. Melbourne University Press, Melbourne

Commonwealth Ombudsman (2007) Lessons for public administration – Ombudsman investigation of referred immigration cases. Commonwealth Ombudsman, Canberra.

https://www.ombudsman.gov.au/__data/assets/pdf_file/0018/26244/investigation_2007_11.pdf. Accessed 15 Oct 2019
Constitutional Commission (1988) Final report of the Constitutional Commission, vol 1. Australian Government Publication Service, Canberra
Craven G (2004) Conversations with the constitution: not just a piece of paper. University of New South Wales Press, Sydney
Craven G (2018) Deliver us from hostility to freedom of faith. The Australian. 12 Oct 2018
Elton-Pymm J (2018) Ruddock's religious freedom report handed to Malcolm Turnbull. SBS News. 18 May 2018
Ely R (1976) Unto God and Caesar: religious issues in the emerging commonwealth. Melbourne University Press, Melbourne
Fuller L (1957–1958) Positivism and fidelity to law – a reply to Professor Hart (1957–58). Harvard Law Rev 71:630–672
Hall B (2016) 'A huge win for doctors': Turnbull government backs down on gag laws for doctors on Nauru and Manus. The Sydney Morning Herald. 20 Oct 2016
Hall B (2017) Lawyers representing asylum seekers are 'un-Australian': Peter Dutton. The Sydney Morning Herald. 28 Aug 2017
Henderson A (2015) Government renews reservations about race discrimination ban in constitution ahead of indigenous recognition summit. ABC News. 4 July 2015 http://www.abc.net.au/news/2015-07-04/government-renews-reservations-about-racediscrimination-ban/6594726. Accessed 15 Oct 2019
Hunter F (2017) Marriage plebiscite: Tony Abbott urges a 'no' vote to reject political correctness and protect religious freedom. The Sydney Morning Herald. 9 Aug 2017
Joint Select Committee on Constitutional Recognition of Aboriginal and Torres Strait Islander Peoples, Parliament of Australia, Final Report (2015) 89
Kopel D (2012) The American revolution against British Gun Control. Admin Regul Law News 37:4–7
Lasswell H, McDougal M (1943) Legal education and public policy: professional training in the public interest. Yale Law J 52:203–295
Lasswell H, McDougal M (1971) Criteria for a theory about law. South Calif Law Rev 44:362–394
Liberal Party – Our Beliefs. https://www.liberal.org.au/our-beliefs. Accessed 4 Oct 2019
McDougal M (1974) Human rights and world public order: principles of content and procedure for clarifying general community policies. V J Int Law 14:387–421
Menzies RG (1967) Central power in the Australian commonwealth. Cassell, London
Mertens T (2003) Nazism, legal positivism and Radbruch's thesis on statutory injustice. Law Critique 14(3):277–295
Mills T, Hasham N, Willingham R (2015) Border Force fiasco: operation Fortitude cancelled as protest shuts down Melbourne streets. The Age. 28 Aug 2015
Moens G (1994) The wrongs of a constitutionally entrenched bill of rights. In: Stephenson M, Turner C (eds) Australia, republic or monarchy?: legal and constitutional issues. University of Queensland Press, St Lucia
Moseneke D (2016) The balance between robust constitutionalism and the democratic process. In: Speech presented at the Seabrook Chambers Public Lecture, University of Melbourne, 16 June 2016. http://law.unimelb.edu.au/__data/assets/pdf_file/0012/1998183/Seabrook-Chambers-Lecture-2016-Justice-Moseneke.pdf. Accessed 15 Oct 2019
Office of the United States Chief Counsel for the Prosecution of Axis Criminality (1946) Nazi conspiracy and aggression. Government Publications Office, Washington
Official Record of the Debates of the Australasian Constitutional Convention (1898) Volume IV. Melbourne. 8 Feb 1898
Parliament of New South Wales (2001) Standing committee on law and justice. A NSW bill of rights. https://www.parliament.nsw.gov.au/lcdocs/inquiries/1737/A%20NSW%20Bill%20of%20Rights%20Report%20October%202001.pdf. Accessed 15 Oct 2019
Peake R (2000) PM rejects Fraser's call for rights bill. Canberra Times. 26 Aug 2000, 3

Rawls J (1999) The law of peoples. Harvard University Press, Cambridge
Robertson G (2009) The statute of liberty: how Australians can take back their rights. Random House, Melbourne
Rotenstreich N (1983) Man and his dignity. Magnes Press, Jerusalem
Sachs A (2008) The strange alchemy of life and law. Oxford University Press, Oxford
Williams G (2014) How would a referendum change Australia's racist laws? The Sydney Morning Herald. 22 Sept 2014

Chapter 6
What a Bill of Rights Should Contain

Abstract This chapter discusses how a bill of rights should be drafted, drawing on overseas examples, particularly the bill of rights contained in the South African constitution. It then discusses the difference between first, second and third generation rights and their enforceability. It explains how rights need to be balanced against each other, and the textual mechanisms by which this can be done, before giving a brief explanation of the content of each of the rights that should be protected.

6.1 Generations of Rights

Before discussing the specific rights that would be protected in an Australian bill of rights, it is necessary to examine the distinction that is drawn between different types of rights, often referred to as first, second and third generation rights.

First generation rights, commonly referred to as civil and political rights, were the earliest type of right accorded constitutional protection. They were acknowledged in eighteenth century human rights documents, such as the Bill of Rights in the United States and in the Declaration of the Rights of Man and of the Citizen promulgated during the French Revolution. In modern times they are reflected in the ICCPR. They include such traditional rights as the right to life, freedom of the person, the right to equality, the right to a fair trial, the right not to be subject to inhumane treatment, the right to vote, the right to privacy, freedom of religion, freedom of movement and freedom of expression. Such rights were said to impose essentially negative obligations on the state, in the sense that respect for them can be achieved by the state refraining from interfering with a person's personal liberty, exercise of religion, free speech et cetera. Although that may be true as a general statement, it cannot be taken as absolute, because sometimes these first generation rights do impose positive obligations on the state. For example, to be effective, the right to a fair trial requires that the state pay for legal representation to those who cannot afford it, while the right not to be subject to inhuman treatment obviously requires that the state allocate sufficient resources to ensure minimum standards of care of prisoners.

Second generation rights are referred to as socio-economic rights. They were included in international human rights documents – most importantly in the

B. Harris, *Constitutional Reform as a Remedy for Political Disenchantment in Australia*, https://doi.org/10.1007/978-981-15-3599-4_6

ICESR – from the 1960s at the instance of socialist and third-world countries, although they had been presaged by Franklin Roosevelt in his inclusion of 'freedom from want' in his formulation of fundamental rights in 1941, and his reference to the need for a 'second bill of rights,' protecting socio-economic rights, in 1944. The principle underlying socio-economic rights is that full respect for human dignity requires more than the protection of civil and political rights and must include the protection of rights to material wellbeing, such as rights to health, housing, education and welfare, without which the freedom to exercise first-generation rights is illusory.

Third generation rights, often referred to as communal rights, received recognition in the second half of the twentieth century. They include rights such as to a clean environment, to the preservation of cultural heritage and the rights of Indigenous people to self-determination. The feature which distinguishes them from first and second generation rights is that, in general, they protect the distinct communal interests of groups rather than individuals, although of course they also benefit the individuals which make up the groups.

In contrast to some (but not all) first generation rights, second and third generation rights cast a positive obligation on the state for their realisation. Interestingly, although protection of such generation rights is usually seen as more radical than protection of civil and political rights, a significant number of respondents to the Australian government's National Human Rights Consultation expressed support for the inclusion of socio-economic rights if human rights were given statutory protection.[1]

An important issue that would need to be addressed if second and third generation rights were included in a bill of rights is that their realisation is contingent on government resources. Whether a government is able to provide public health, housing, education and welfare at a sufficient level to satisfy the needy will obviously depend on a variety of changing factors, such as the wealth of the country, the economic conditions it faces from time to time and spending priorities dictated by those conditions. In recognition of this, drafters of the South African Constitution, which protects a range of second[2] and third[3] generation rights, qualified the obligations imposed by such rights so as to provide that the state should 'take reasonable legislative and other measures, within its available resources, to achieve the progressive realisation' of such rights.

An example of how that qualification has been interpreted by the courts is provided by *Government of the Republic of South Africa v Gootboom,*[4] a case concerning a claim to housing by people living under plastic sheeting in a field, who said that the failure of the state to provide them with shelter amounted to a breach of the

[1] National Human Rights Consultation (2009, pp. 78–82, 96).

[2] These are housing (s 26), health care, food, water and social security (s 27), the social rights of children (s 28) and education (s 29).

[3] These include the right to a health environment (s 24), the right to language (s 30) and the rights of cultural, religious and linguistic communities (Is 31).

[4] 2000 (11) BCLR 1169 (CC).

Constitution. The Constitutional Court held that held that the constitutional requirement to take 'reasonable steps' gave the government a degree of leeway: There might be a wide range of possible steps that could be taken and it was not for the court to say which of these might be the best. So long as the steps that are taken are reasonable, the Constitutional guarantee will have been complied with. The fact that the government had begun implementing a coherent national plan to provide housing amounted to such reasonable steps. However, the evidence also showed that the plan did not adequately cater for the short term needs of those most desperately in need of assistance. For this reason the court found that the respondent's rights had been breached, and ordered that the state devise, fund, implement and supervise, a programme to provide measures to assist those in desperate need.

It should be noted that the court did not make an order that the particular respondent be provided with immediate relief, rather it ordered that the state implement a general plan for the benefit of all similarly situated people, which would be assessed against the criterion of reasonableness in the light of available resources. The *Grootboom* case therefore shows that there is little reason to fear that the recognition of socio-economic rights will lead to judicial micro-management of government spending – so long as a government can show that it is acting within the bounds of reasonableness in light of the resource constraints and the competing demands it faces, its spending decisions will not be able to be challenged, nor will particular individuals be able to claim immediate provision of public services from the state, so long as an overall plan is being implemented – indeed the satisfaction of any particular claim might itself cause socio-economic injustice if there are other claimants whose needs are even more pressing, and to whom the state ought therefore give preference to in the orderly implementation of its plan.

The idea of courts determining the bounds of reasonableness under legislation which may impose a financial obligation is familiar in Australia. Anti-discrimination statutes enacted by the Commonwealth and the states recognize that in the case of some rights – disability rights being an example – compliance may require the expenditure of resources, which the party against whom the claim has been brought may not have. Thus s 35(1) of the *Anti-Discrimination Act 1991* (Qld) states that discrimination on grounds of disability is not unlawful where the person discriminated against would require special services, and it would impose 'unjustifiable hardship' on the party which has allegedly engaged in discrimination to provide such services. Section 5 of the Act states that whether 'unjustifiable hardship' exists will be determined by having reference to factors including the costs of supplying the services and the number of people who would benefit or be disadvantaged, the financial position of the discriminating party, the disruption the supply of services would cause and, in general, 'the nature of any benefit or detriment to all people concerned'. There is therefore no reason why, if a developing country like South Africa can include second and third generation rights in its constitution, an Australian bill of rights should not extend protection to them as well, subject to the caveat that the government's obligations are limited to taking such steps as are reasonable in the light of competing claims on its resources.

6.2 Limitation of Rights

It is obvious that rights are not absolute and that it limits may need to be imposed on their exercise. To take the most extreme example, it may be necessary for a police officer to take the life of a citizen in order for the officer to protect him or herself or someone-else. The right to freedom of expression may be limited by a law prohibiting incitement to crime. One could think of countless other instances where rights may be limited in furtherance of competing social interests. This means that, as a necessary corollary of a bill of rights, the law must contain a test that can be used to determine whether limitations on rights are constitutional.

In some countries, there is no express test in the constitution, and so it has been necessary for the courts to develop one. Such is the case in Australia where the question of how to balance constitutionally-protected rights against other interests was first addressed by the High Court in 1943 in *Adelaide Company of Jehovah's Witnesses v Commonwealth*,[5] a case in which legislation gave the Governor-General (obviously acting on the advice of the government) the power to declare associations prejudicial to the defence of the Commonwealth, to dissolve them and to confiscate their property. The legislation had been used against the Jehovah's Witnesses, who were pacifists and preached against involvement in the war. They challenged the validity of the law on the basis that it infringed their right to free exercise of religion, protected by s 116 of the Constitution. The court made important statements relating to the interpretation of s 116, reasoning which is applicable to the interpretation of constitutional rights provisions in general. Noting that no right is absolute, Starke J held that s 116 permitted such limitations on the right as were 'reasonably necessary for the protection of the community and in the interests of social order.'[6] This dictum was important, because it constituted an early explicit reference by the court to a test requiring the balancing of constitutional freedoms against other important societal interests – referred to in later cases as the 'proportionality' test – in order to determine whether a limitation on a right was reasonable.

The application of a reasonableness test is therefore nothing new for our legal system, nor does it involve the courts exceeding their customary bounds. Apart from constitutional law, courts have applied a reasonableness test for centuries across many areas of the law, such as in the law of torts, where liability in negligence depends on whether a person has shown reasonable care, in criminal law when a court has to decide whether a person who raises a plea of self-defence used reasonable force to ward off an assailant, or in administrative law when a court has to decide whether a government official exercising a statutory power did so reasonably. So when courts apply a test of reasonableness to determine whether to declare legislation invalid because it infringes constitutionally-protected rights – a power they have always had under the Constitution – they perform a function which is a long-standing part of the judicial role. In passing one can say that this illustrates

[5] (1943) 67 CLR 116.

[6] (1943) 67 CLR 116, 155.

why parliament is no better positioned to attempt to address the question of how to balance rights when they compete with each other than it is to determine what conduct is negligent under the law of torts. Such cases are always depend on the facts of specific cases, and the importance of competing interests, and are therefore impossible to predict, much less determine, through a legislative process. This is why it is the courts, which make decisions on a case by case basis, are better able to determine cases involving competing constitutional rights, just as they do in determining torts cases.

Different versions of the proportionality test as it applies to constitutionally-protected rights have been developed by the High Court over recent decades.[7] The current formulation was established in *McCloy v New South Wales*,[8] in which the court stated that whether a limitation of a constitutional right is permissible depends upon the application of a three-stage test. The first stage involves an inquiry as to whether the law limiting the right is rationally connected to the legitimate purpose of the law. The second stage involves an inquiry as to whether the law limits the right to a greater extent that is necessary to achieve the legislative purpose. If there are other reasonably practicable ways which would have been equally effective in achieving that purpose but which would have had a less restrictive effect on the right, then the law will be found invalid. The practical implication of this is that when parliament enacts a law which has the effect of limiting rights, it must take care to do so in a manner which restricts rights as little as possible. The third stage involves an inquiry as to whether there is proportionality between the importance of the purpose to which the law is directed and the extent to which the law limits rights. This requires a balancing of the benefit conferred by the law against the negative effect it has on constitutional rights. This will obviously be a matter of degree – the greater the importance of the purpose served by the law, the greater the limitation of rights that will be found to be justified. Conversely, a law serving a purpose of relatively low importance will not warrant a significant limitation of rights.

Although the test in *McCloy* improved upon earlier tests (in particular by adding the requirement that a law limiting rights must do so to the least degree necessary to achieve the purpose of the law), ambiguity remains in relation to the first stage of the test, because although the majority in that case stated that, to be constitutional, a statute limiting rights must be rationally connected to 'the statute's legitimate purpose', it remains unclear as to how legitimacy of purpose is to be determined, because the court stated no criteria against which legitimacy should be tested. Here it would be useful to draw upon the Canadian proportionality test formulated in *R v Oakes*,[9] in which Dickson CJ held that a for provision limiting rights protected by the Canadian Charter of Rights and Freedoms to be constitutional.

[7] See *Australian Capital Television Pty Ltd v Commonwealth (No 2)* (1992) 177 CLR 106, *Lange v Australian Broadcasting Corporation* (1997) 189 CLR 520 and *Coleman v Power* (2004) 220 CLR 1.

[8] (2015) 257 CLR 178, 194–5.

[9] [1986] 1 S.C.R. 103, 138–40.

1. The law must serve a pressing and substantial objective.
2. The law must be proportional, which requires that

   (i) the law must be rationally connected to the objective
   (ii) the law must impair rights to the minimal extent possible and
   (iii) there must be proportionality between the impairment of rights and the objective served by the law.

Although this test is very similar to the one in *McCloy*, the first step of the *Oakes* test has the effect of requiring that, for a law limiting rights to be constitutional, it must serve a purpose that is sufficiently important to warrant limitation of rights. It therefore has the advantage over the test in *McCloy* of requiring the courts to consider what one might refer to as the 'weightiness' of the interest being served by the law.

A similar formulation is contained in s 36 of the South African Constitution, which provides as follows:

36. Limitation of Rights

1. The rights in the Bill of Rights may be limited only in terms of law of general application to the extent that the limitation is reasonable and justifiable in an open and democratic society based on human dignity, equality and freedom, taking into account all relevant factors, including

   the nature of the right;
   the importance of the purpose of the limitation;
   the nature and extent of the limitation;
   the relation between the limitation and its purpose; and
   less restrictive means to achieve the purpose

2. Except as provided in subsection (1) or in any other provision of the Constitution, no law may limit any right entrenched in the Bill of Rights.

This test goes further than the *Oakes* test in that while it requires that the courts consider the importance of the purpose of the limitation, they must consider that (along with the other four factors listed in s 36(1)) in light of what is justifiable in 'an open and democratic society based on human dignity, equality and freedom.' Apart from that, the factors listed in s 36(1) coincide with those listed in *Oakes*.

If Australia had a bill of rights, certainty as to the test to be applied when determining the constitutionality of laws limiting rights would be enhanced if, instead of relying on the *McCloy* test, a more detailed test similar to that used in Canada and South Africa was included in the constitution. Such a test is included in the model constitution that appears in the Appendix.

6.3 The Content of a Bill of Rights

What rights should be included in an Australian bill of rights? A comprehensive examination of this question would fill a book on its own, but in general most modern bills of rights are modelled on the Universal Declaration of Human Rights, the ICCPR and the ICESR, that were drafted in the wake of World War II. As discussed earlier in this chapter, the idea underlying these international human rights documents is the inherent equality and dignity of the individual, and his or her entitlement to self-realisation. In order to give effect to that idea, the documents were drafted in such a way as to express the rights in as general a manner as possible, covering core aspects of the human condition. The rights they protect are universal and timeless. The argument that a bill of rights runs the risk of becoming divorced from contemporary realty is unconvincing – one cannot plausibly maintain that fundamental rights such as freedom of the person, freedom of religion, freedom of expression, freedom from torture et cetera, would become redundant. To adopt a Rawlsian perspective, they are rights which a rational person would always want to have protected.

Most modern bills of rights are based on the international charters. Of particular note are the Canadian Charter of Rights and Freedoms and the Bill of Rights contained in the South African Constitution, which reflect the content of international human rights documents as well as advances in thinking about human rights since World War II. The bill of rights contained in the model constitution at the end of this book is similar to those two documents.

Although space does not allow a full discourse on every right, it is useful to give a brief explanation of the content of each right.

6.3.1 The Right to Life

The need to protect the right to life is self-evident as it is the prerequisite for the enjoyment of all other rights. However, as with all other rights, there will be instances where even this right is over-ridden by legislation protecting countervailing interests – an example being the one given earlier, where a police officer shoots a suspect in circumstances where that is reasonably necessary to protect the life of another.

6.3.2 *Freedom of the Person and Associated Procedural Rights*

The right to personal liberty is not only inherently important, but is also important because it is the prerequisite for the exercise of most other rights – for example, freedom of movement, association and communication are wholly contingent on a person being at liberty. The rights to privacy, freedom of religion and freedom of expression may also either be curtailed or absolutely removed when a person is deprived of liberty. Therefore the idea that a person should be able to be detained by the government without the legality of that detention being challengeable before the courts is – or ought to be – anathema to anyone who believes in individual freedom and the rule of law.

The right to personal liberty comprises two separate and equally important aspects: a procedural right to have a court determine whether one's detention is authorised by law, and a substantive right to test the constitutional validity of the law authorising detention. In English law systems the roots of these rights lie in Articles 39 and 40 of Magna Carta. Article 39 provides:

> No free man is to be arrested, or imprisoned, or disseised, or outlawed, or exiled, or in any other way ruined, nor will we go against him or send against him, except by the lawful judgment of his peers or by the law of the land.

Article 40 provides:

> We will not sell, or deny, or delay right or justice to anyone.

In combination these Articles require that any deprivation of liberty be lawful or, to express it negatively, should not be arbitrary, as well as guaranteeing that persons deprived of liberty have a right to access the courts. In the centuries after Magna Carta, the courts and parliament progressively developed, and gave statutory protection to, the writ of *habeas corpus* as a method of enforcing these rights. The writ can be sought either by the person detained or by someone acting on their behalf, by which they petition the court for an order that the detained person should be brought before the court where the lawfulness of their detention can be tested.

Magna Carta strongly influenced the drafters of the Bill of Rights in the United States, where the Fourth Amendment prohibits unreasonable search and seizure of persons and property and requires proof of 'probable cause' (that is proof of reasonable suspicion of an offence) before a person may be arrested.[10] In addition, the Fifth and Fourteenth Amendments provide that no person shall be 'deprived of life, liberty, or property, without due process of law.' The 'due process of law' requirement has provided the foundation for a range of procedural rights, most importantly the requirement that detained persons have a constitutional right to approach the courts to challenge the lawfulness of their detention by applying for *habeas corpus*, which is also protected by Article 1, Section 9 of the Constitution.[11]

---

[10] *Atwater v City of Lago Vista* 532 U.S. 318 (2001).

[11] For a recent application of this doctrine see *Boumediene v Bush* 553 U.S. 723 (2008) in which the Supreme Court upheld the right of foreign combatants held at Guantanamo Bay to petition the courts for *habeas corpus*.

The position is different in Australia. It was an irony that in the week of the 800th anniversary of Magna Carta in 2015, the principal concern of the government was the drafting of legislation to allow the government to deprive a person of citizenship without needing to go to court to prove why that deprivation of rights was justified – the very antithesis of due process promised by Article 39.[12] In Australia, the right to personal liberty rests on unstable foundations. The extent of a person's rights upon arrest and at trial is at the mercy of Commonwealth, state and territory legislatures, as there are no express constitutional protections against legislation which unreasonably intrudes upon those rights. The only exception to this is the rule in *Chu Kheng Lim v Minister for Immigration, Local Government and Ethnic Affairs*,[13] in which the High Court held that the doctrine of separation of powers contained in Chap. 3 of the Constitution implies that the legality of detention be under the ultimate oversight of the courts. However that rule does not apply in cases of so-called 'non-punitive' detention and, as was held in *Al-Kateb v Godwin*,[14] in such circumstances it lies within the legislative power of parliament to enact legislation which provides for detention of unlimited duration. The fact that people can be detained without court authorisation led to the unlawful detention of 247 citizens and lawful residents in the early 2000s.[15]

A bill of rights must protect the right to liberty in all circumstances. As was argued in Chap. 1, the concept of 'non-punitive detention' is an oxymoron. All detention is punitive from the perspective of the person detained, irrespective of whether it is imposed as a penalty for a crime or for some other reason. Indeed deprivation of liberty is arguably more offensive to human rights when it is non-punitive than when it is punitive. Assuming that the right to personal liberty was included in a bill of rights, key issue in determining whether a law (be it common law or statute) was unconstitutional would be whether it struck a reasonable balance between the right to personal liberty and whatever social interest(s) the law served. Here is also important to note that a constitutional challenge to a law limiting a right can be brought against the law as written or against the law as applied. In the former case, the plaintiff alleges that the law on the face of it is unconstitutional, and if the challenge is successful, the law is declared invalid in its entirety. In the latter case, the plaintiff alleges that while the law is facially valid, the circumstances in which it was applied were unconstitutional. A good example of circumstances where the latter would apply is provided by Operation Fortitude, discussed earlier in this chapter, where Border Force officers were instructed to patrol the streets of the Melbourne CBD and to stop people to demand that they prove their residence status. Even if the statutory provision under which they were operating was valid, the fact that the power it conferred was being applied on an arbitrary basis – that is, on the basis of people's appearance – would lead a court to declare that its use in that manner was

---

[12] Eleanor Hall (2015).

[13] (1992) 176 CLR 1.

[14] (2004) 219 CLR 562.

[15] Commonwealth Ombudsman (2007).

constitutionally invalid. By contrast, if the power was used to detain a person about whom an officer had reasonable suspicion based on specific information about that person, the exercise of the power would be found to be constitutional.

A bill of rights should also protect the due process rights (alternatively referred to as procedural rights) which support the right to individual liberty, starting with the right of a person who has been detained to be brought before a court where they can contest the validity of the detention and where the state should bear the burden of proving that the detention was reasonable in the circumstances. Such procedural rights should also include the right of people to be informed of their legal rights upon detention, the right to silence, the right to be presumed innocent, the right to legal advice (including the right to state-funded legal advice where people cannot afford their own lawyer) and the right to a trial before an open and impartial court at which they can challenge evidence brought against them. Finally there are a number of prohibitions which are important to individual liberty and should therefore be included in a bill of rights, such as a prohibition against unreasonable search and seizure, a prohibition against retrospective criminal law, and a prohibition against trying a person twice for the same offence.

6.3.3 Freedom of Movement

Freedom of movement is a necessary corollary to the right to individual liberty. Although the right to individual liberty protects the individual against being placed under detention by the state, it could be rendered nugatory if the state could enact legislation confining a person to a particular geographical area. Such legislation would, except for physical restraint by officers of the state, achieve the same object as detention. A bill of rights ought therefore to provide explicit protection for freedom of movement.

6.3.4 The Right Not to Be Subject to Inhumane Treatment or Punishment

An obvious and essential aspect of human dignity is the entitlement never to be treated as less than human. The risk of de-humanising treatment at the hands of the state is at its maximum when a person becomes subject to its coercive powers as a result of detention, imprisonment or sentencing, because in these circumstances the person's autonomy is at best severely limited and in some cases is completely removed. In such circumstances, people are dependent on the state for their physical and mental wellbeing, and because of this, the duty of care owed to them by the state increases in direct proportion to the degree to which their freedom has been removed.

The right not to be subject to inhumane treatment is multi-dimensional. At the most basic level, it encompasses the right of detainees and prisoners to receive adequate food, shelter and clothing. It also imposes on the state the obligation to maintain the physical and mental health of those subject to its coercive power, a duty which has obvious implications for the conditions under which detainees and prisoners are kept. Most importantly, however, respect for the right requires the state not to engage in torture, a practice which is viewed with abhorrence, although that did not prevent two Australian academics from arguing in favour of it as a measure to be taken in the so-called 'War on Terror',[16] a view which it is gratifying to note was firmly rebuffed by others.[17] I would argue that given the especially dehumanising nature of torture, the constitution ought specifically to prohibit it.

So far as inhumane punishment is concerned, the most pertinent recent case law comes from South Africa, where s 12(1)(e) of the Constitution protects people from being 'treated or punished in a cruel, inhuman or degrading way'. In *S v Makwanyane*,[18] the very first decision by the Constitutional Court after the new constitution came into force, the Court held that the death penalty annihilated human dignity and was inherently depersonalising, cruel, inhuman and degrading. Similar reasoning was adopted in *S v Williams,*[19] where the court ruled that corporal punishment was unconstitutional. I would argue that although the death penalty has not been used in Australia since 1967, it, as well as corporal punishment ought to be specifically proscribed by the constitution as punishments which are inhumane.

6.3.5 Freedom of Expression

At the outset it is important to distinguish the broad right to freedom of expression from the narrow freedom of political communication which exists in Australia. The former, which is a standard inclusion in bills of rights around the world, protects all types of expression, including artistic expression, the right to engage in peaceful protest and what might be called the 'passive' dimension of freedom of expression, which is the right of an audience to receive information from those engaging in expression.

In Australia however, the narrowly-drawn implied freedom of political communication applies only to communications which, in the rather stilted language of the High Court, are necessary for the 'maintenance of the constitutionally-prescribed system of representative and responsible government'[20] – in other words, it applies only to communications relating to debate on political and governmental matters.

[16] Bagaric and Clarke (2005).

[17] See Manderson (2008, pp. 27–43) and Allen (2005, p. 216).

[18] 1995 (3) SA 391 (CC).

[19] 1995 (3) SA 632 (CC).

[20] *Lange v Australian Broadcasting Corporation* (1997) 189 CLR 520, 567.

In framing the freedom, the High Court drew a distinction between 'rights' and 'immunities,' holding that the implied freedom does not confer a 'right' on individuals but rather an 'immunity' from laws which unreasonably limit the freedom. Although the distinction echoes the famous matrix of legal relationships formulated by the American legal philosopher Wesley Hohfeld, its use by the High Court in implied freedom cases is mystifying, first because the court did not engage in any Hohfeldian analysis as a justification for the distinction (indeed, did not even mention Hohfeld in any of the implied freedom cases), and secondly because its effect weakens the scope of the freedom. An example of how this happens is provided by *John Fairfax Publications Pty Ltd v Ryde Local Court*.[21] In this case the court rejected the argument that it was a breach of the implied freedom to deny a journalist access to a court record, which the applicant argued was necessary in order to enable it to comment on the administration of justice, an issue which relates to the operation of one of the branches of government. The court held that since the implied freedom only confers an immunity from laws which restrict political communication and does not confer a positive right to engage in communication (or, as in this case, to obtain access to documents) the freedom had not been breached.

Effective protection of freedom of expression requires that a bill of rights contain a broadly-stated provision which protects all types of expression – not just that related to politics – and which also extends to the right to receive information.

6.3.6 *The Right to Vote and Other Political Rights*

The ethical justification for democratic government is that it serves human dignity, specifically the requirement that each person should exercise equal political power. Therefore to be truly democratic, a constitution must ensure that each adult enjoys such rights as are necessary to achieve that objective. First, and most obvious, is the right to vote – but, as discussed in Chap. 4, this right embraces more than just the formality of being able to cast a vote. An effective exercise of this right requires that, as far as is reasonably practicable, each vote have equal *effect* on the composition of the legislature, because if it does not the voting system fails to serve the value of equal political rights for every citizen. This requirement of equal effect would be expressly stated in those sections of the constitution dealing with the electoral system, but it should also be included in the formulation of the right to vote which appears in the bill of rights. The bill of rights should also protect the right to stand for public office, as well as the right to engage in peaceful protest, both of which are important political rights.

---

[21] (2005) 62 NSWLR 512.

6.3.7 *Freedom of Association*

In *Tajjour v New South Wales*[22] the High Court rejected the argument that a free-standing right to freedom of association was, like freedom of political communication, a necessary implication of the system of representative government. Nevertheless it is obvious that in the absence of freedom of association, the exercise of freedom of expression as well as rights of political engagement become difficult – and in some circumstances impossible – to exercise effectively. Curtailment of the right to associate has been a hallmark of oppressive regimes, an example of which is provided by South Africa during the apartheid era, where the government imposed 'banning' orders on people prohibiting them from being in the company of more than one other person. Freedom of association is also important as the foundation for the right of people to form unions and civil society organisations.

6.3.8 *Freedom of Religion*

Freedom of religion is one of the few rights protected by the Commonwealth constitution, although it is subject to the anomaly that it binds on the Commonwealth and not the states, which are left free to restrict religious freedom. Given that the constitution proposed in this book is unitary rather than federal, that distinction would be redundant, but the fact that it exists under the current constitution serves to illustrate how inconsistent rights protection in Australia currently is. Freedom of religion comprises a number of different aspects: the right to practise religion, along with prohibitions against the establishment of religion and legally-mandated religious observance.

6.3.9 *The Right to Property*

The right to own property and to receive fair compensation when it is expropriated by the state is an important economic right. Like freedom of religion, it too applies only to the Commonwealth and not to the states. Furthermore, as currently framed, the right protects people only against the *acquisition* of property and – although the issue has never been tested in the courts – might not entitle them to compensation if property is destroyed. A re-formulated right ought therefore to state that the right to compensation arises if property is either acquired or destroyed by the state.

---

[22] (2014) 313 ALR 221.

6.3.10 Right to Information

The ability to access to government information is currently regulated by the *Freedom of Information Act 1982* (Cth). Although the governing principle of the Act is that the public have a right to access government information, a swathe of exemptions prevents access to certain categories of information. Furthermore, even where government claims of exemption are ultimately unsuccessful, the processes mandated by the Act often enable ministers to oppose FOI applications for months, which raises the question as to the legitimacy of the government spending public money in order to deny people access to information about an institution which is meant to be their servant rather than their master. Among the most notorious examples of government resistance to FOI applications are Treasurer Peter Costello's objection to the release of information about the effects of bracket creep on taxes on the grounds that release of the information would 'lead to confusion' and would 'not make a valuable contribution to the public debate,'[23] and the months it took to obtain access to the cost-benefit analysis of the move of the Australian Pesticides and Veterinary Medicines Authority from Canberra to Armidale.[24] If a right to access government information was included in a bill of rights, the constitutionality of the exemptions and procedures would be open to challenge. This would result in a far better balance being struck between the right of the public to access information and justifiable limitations of that right. The constitutionalisation of freedom of information would also bolster freedom of expression, as the right to receive information is an obvious corollary of freedom to express it.

6.3.11 Administrative Justice

Although constitutional theorists may find cases in which courts are called upon to determine the validity of legislation the primary and most interesting manifestation of the tension between individual rights and the power of the state, in reality most conflicts of that type occur as a result of the quotidian exercise of administrative power by government officials. For this reason, it is important that the constitution protects the right to administrative justice, and in particular the right to judicial review of administrative decisions. Although s 75(v) of the Constitution confers on the High Court the jurisdiction to review the actions of Commonwealth officers and to grant certain remedies, the section has been narrowly interpreted and is not taken to confer jurisdiction to engage in broad *ultra vires* review – that is, substantive review on grounds of unreasonableness. It is also the case that legislation can expressly exclude common law review on grounds of unreasonableness. A new constitutional right to judicial review ought therefore be drafted in such a way as to

[23] Finn (2007).

[24] Vidot (2016).

specify that administrative decisions are reviewable both on procedural and substantive grounds.

6.3.12 Privacy

The term 'privacy' is used in two very different senses in the law. The first of these relates to interests which are recognised by the law of torts, infringement of which can be remedied by an action for damages. In the United States the common law has been developed over the past 120 years to allow plaintiffs to sue for a number of different types of invasion of privacy. Such a right does not exist in Australia, and in *Australian Broadcasting Corporation v Lenah Game Meats Pty Ltd*[25] the High Court declined to accept the argument that it should create a common law action for invasion of privacy, albeit leaving open the possibility that such a tort might be developed in future. The only protection afforded to privacy under Australian law is that given by the *Privacy Act 1988* (Cth) and parallel state statutes, which regulates the circumstances in which Commonwealth agencies and certain businesses may collect, store and grant access to personal information.

The other, completely different, meaning of the term 'privacy' relates to a constitutional right developed by the United States Supreme Court, which has held that because the Fifth and Fourteenth Amendments to the Constitution prohibit deprivation of liberty without 'due process of law,' and the Ninth Amendment states that the specification of certain rights in the constitution did not mean that other rights were denied, the constitution contains and implied right to 'privacy' in the sense of individual autonomy. The classic statement of this principle is found in the opinion of Brandis J in *Olmstead v United States*,[26] where he argued that the constitution protected 'the most comprehensive of rights and the right most valued by civilised men … the right to be let alone.' Subsequently, in *Meyer v Nebraska*, McReynolds J held that where the due process clause of the Fourteenth Amendment protects 'liberty' this

> … denotes not merely freedom from bodily restraint but also the right of the individual to contract, to engage in any of the common occupations of life, to acquire useful knowledge, to marry, establish a home and bring up children, to worship God according to the dictates of his own conscience, and generally enjoy those privileges long recognised at common law as essential to the orderly pursuit of happiness by free men.

In essence, what the court developed was a 'freedom to be free,' the general principle of which is that there is what the court in *Griswold v Connecticut*[27] referred to as a 'zone of privacy' – an area of decision-making in which the state is not permitted to interfere, unless it can demonstrate that any limitation of that freedom is

[25] 208 CLR 199 (2001).

[26] 277 U.S. 438 (1928).

[27] (1965) 281 US 479, 484 per Douglas J.

both necessary and narrowly tailored to serve a compelling governmental interest.[28] The right to privacy has subsequently been used to declare the unconstitutional the compulsory sterilisation of criminals,[29] anti-miscegenation statutes[30] as well as prohibitions on same-sex intercourse,[31] and to uphold the rights to access to contraceptives,[32] to termination of pregnancy[33] and to same-sex marriage.[34]

The general approach taken in these cases is that the more intimate the decision, the more likely it will be that legislation regulating it will be found unconstitutional. As was stated in *Planned Parenthood of Southeastern Pennsylvania v Casey*,[35] 'it is a promise of the Constitution that there is a realm of personal liberty which the government may not enter.'[36] The court held that its refusal to countenance governmental intervention in areas such as marriage, procreation contraception et cetera were based upon the principle that these were matters[37]

> ... involving the most intimate and personal choices a person may make in a lifetime, choices central to personal dignity and autonomy, [which are] essential to the liberty protected by the Fourteenth Amendment.

Similarly, Stevens J linked autonomy and dignity, holding that the ability to make such decisions 'is an element of basic human dignity' and that 'Part of the constitutional liberty to choose is the equal dignity to which each of us is entitled.'[38]

An Australian bill of rights ought to protect privacy in both senses in which that word is used. This should be done by including a right to information privacy which entitles people to constitutional protection against the government in relation to the collection, storage, verification and correction of data held about them. The bill of rights ought also to include a right to personal autonomy which would protect freedom in relation to intimate life decisions.

---

[28] *Griswold v Connecticut* 381 U.S. 479 (1965), 496–8, citing *Bates v Little Rock* 361 U.S. 516 (1960), 524. For a concise discussion of the development of the right to privacy see a Feinberg (1986, pp. 87–94).

[29] *Skinner v. State of Oklahoma, ex rel. Williamson* 316 U.S. 535 (1942).

[30] *Loving v Virginia* 338 U.S. 1 (1967).

[31] *Lawrence v Texas* 539 U.S. 558 (2003).

[32] *Griswold v Connecticut* 381 U.S. 479 (1965) and *Eisenstadt v Baird* 405 U.S. 438 (1972).

[33] *Roe v Wade* 410 U.S. 113 (1973).

[34] *Obergefell v Hodges* 576 U.S. ___ (2015).

[35] 505 U.S. 833 (1992).

[36] 505 U.S. 833 (1992), 847.

[37] 505 U.S. 833 (1992), 851.

[38] 505 U.S. 833 (1992), 920.

6.3.13 Equality

The right to equality protects people from being subject to arbitrary discrimination. Commonwealth and state anti-discrimination statutes prohibit discrimination on grounds such as race, sex, age, disability, pregnancy, breastfeeding, parental status, religious belief, political and union activity, family responsibilities, gender identity and sexuality.[39] Putting these grounds in the Constitution would mean that they were protected against legislative over-ride of the type which occurred when s 132 of the *Northern Territory National Emergency Response Act 2007* (Cth) over-rode the *Racial Discrimination Act 1975* (Cth), thereby depriving Indigenous people of many rights taken for granted by other Australians.[40]

In framing anti-discrimination provisions in a constitution it is necessary to incorporate some mechanism which will allow the state to enact legislation designed to provide redress for historic wrongs – sometimes referred to as positive discrimination or affirmative action. In the absence of such a provision, legislation designed to benefit one group would be found unconstitutional on the ground that it discriminated against groups who are not benefited. The right to equality should therefore be subject to the rider (similar to that contained in s 8 of the *Racial Discrimination Act 1975* (Cth)) that any law which redresses historical inequality should not be unconstitutional merely because it differentiates between different groups of people.

6.3.14 Socio-economic, Cultural and Environmental Rights

The principles underlying the socio-economic and communal rights were analysed in the discussion of generations of rights. Socio-economic (or second generation) rights typically protect rights such as those of access to water, food, shelter, medical care, welfare and education, while communal (or third generation) rights include rights of people to practise their culture and to a healthy environment. The protection of such rights is contingent on what resources are available to the state. That practical limitation needs to be taken into account in drafting the provisions protecting second and third generation rights. However, the mere fact that the realisation of these rights is resource-contingent does not render them insignificant – as the case law discussed earlier in this chapter shows, the inclusion of these rights in a constitution acts as a spur to the government to ensure that the allocation of such resources as it has at its disposal takes place on a fair basis.

Constitutional protection of such rights would be of particular benefit to Australia, given its unusual population distribution, with the vast majority of the population highly concentrated in urban areas and a much smaller population widely and remotely dispersed in rural areas. This creates a risk that the rural minority might

[39] This list is taken from s 7 of the *Anti-Discrimination Act 1991* (Qld).

[40] For a discussion of the intervention see Manderson (2009).

not receive the same level of service as do the urban majority. Constitutional protection of socio-economic rights would address that risk because, as the case law from overseas shows, it would be possible to challenge inequities in the allocation of funding. Of course many factors would be relevant in determining the reasonableness or other wise of a government's resource allocation, including overall costs and benefits, but the existence of a remedy that could be used to challenge unreasonable allocations would act as an inducement to governments to ensure that their decisions were fair. It would be fascinating to see what the impact of the justiciability of socio-economic rights would have the allocation of Infrastructure Grants which, as discussed in Chap. 1, is the subject of brazen pork-barrelling where grants are awarded to communities in marginal electorates rather than on the basis of need.

6.4 To Whom Should a Bill of Rights Apply?

Among the most complex questions pertaining to a bill of rights is whether it should apply only to state action – that is to legislation enacted by parliament and to conduct by the state – or whether it should also apply to non-state entities in their conduct towards each other.

So far in this chapter we have approached a bill of rights on the assumption that it acts only as a mechanism for restraining the state's exercise of power over individuals – often referred to by human rights theorists as 'vertical' application. However, since the 1950s, European theorists have developed a theory known as *drittwirkung*, in terms of which a bill of rights could also apply horizontally – that is to non-state actors in their dealings with each other.[41]

Part of the reason why discussion of this issue is complex is because of the relationship between statute law and common law. Confusion arises because it is easy to fall into the error of thinking that the state affects people exclusively through statute law and that therefore only conduct which takes place under statute law would be subject to a bill of rights and that because of that, relationships between individuals would not be affected by a bill of rights. This is incorrect. The state affects people's rights not only by enacting legislation, but also by exercising its inherent common law powers, and in either circumstance it would be subject to a bill of rights. Furthermore, so far as relations between individuals are concerned, although many of these are regulated by the common law (in particular by the law of contract) private interactions are also frequently regulated by legislation. An obvious example of this is anti-discrimination legislation which affect relationships between employers and employees. Such legislation would, like any other legislation, have to be consistent with a bill of rights. But challenges to such legislation have nothing to do with horizontality: The enactment of a statute to which

---

[41] For a comprehensive discussion of *drittwirkung*, its wide and narrow conceptions and its application in different jurisdictions see Chirwa (2006).

individuals are subject quintessentially involves the vertical relationship between the state and individuals.

True questions of horizontality arise only in the *absence* of any statutory provision regulating conduct between individuals. Examples of this might be where a shopping-mall owner prohibited someone from engaging in public protest on their property, or where a corporation imposed restrictions on what comments contractors (as distinct from an employees, who are almost always covered by anti-discrimination statutes) may make on matters of public concern, even if unrelated to the work they were contracted to do (the practice of sports bodies using 'disrepute' clauses to sanction players' public statements is an obvious example of this). In these instances, should rights under the law of property or of contract respectively be able to be used to limit freedom of expression? Or should such horizontal relationships be left unregulated by constitutional law?

Two distinct schools of thought have developed among students of *drittwirkung*: The first of these adopts a broad approach under which individuals would be able to sue each other directly for breaches of a bill of rights. Under the second and narrower approach, individuals would not be able to sue each other for breaches of the bill of rights, but the courts would be obliged to develop the law in conformity with it. This approach is consistent with the rule that the courts, like the other branches of government, would be subject to a bill of rights and that since one of the functions of the courts is to develop the common law, the courts would have to ensure that the common law conformed to the bill of rights. This second, indirect, form of *drittwirkung* is arguably more suited to a common law jurisdiction such as Australia than is the first, as it leaves the courts free to determine the circumstances in which rights will apply in private litigation through their long-standing incremental development of the common law. Something very close to this approach was adopted by the High Court in *Lange v Australian Broadcasting Corporation,*[42] in which, although without considering *drittwirkung*, the court held that the common law of defamation should be developed so as to be consistent with the implied freedom of political communication. On this basis I would argue that the question of the application of rights as between individuals would be impliedly (and satisfactorily) dealt with by the inclusion of a section which stated that the bill of rights applied to all branches of government, including the courts, and to all types of law, including the common law.

One other issue relating to the application of a bill of rights remains to be dealt with, and that is the question of extraterritoriality. There is a presumption in law that legislation (including a constitution) applies only within the jurisdiction which enacts it. However, it is possible for the legislation to expressly over-ride that presumption by stating that it applies with extra-territorial effect. This is not uncommon. One of the most famous examples of this is the *War Crimes Act 1945* (Cth), which was amended in 1988 so as to make it applicable to acts committed outside Australia, thereby making it possible to prosecute alleged war criminals for conduct

[42] (1997) 189 CLR 520.

they had engaged in in various parts of the world in World War II. Another example is provided by Division 272 of the Commonwealth *Criminal Code* which makes it an offence to commit sexual offences against children outside Australia. Given that the state engages in activities all over the world and that there is a need to ensure that when it does so it respects human dignity, it would be necessary to include in the constitution a provision which stated that the bill of rights applied with extraterritorial effect. If it did not there would be a risk that government agencies might breach human rights in the course of their operations overseas.

References

Allen R (2005) Torture, criminality and the war on terror. (2005) 30 Alternative Law Journal: 214–18

Attorney General's Department (2009) National human rights consultation report. Commonwealth Government, Canberra. https://apo.org.au/node/19288. Accessed 15 Oct 2019

Bagaric M, Clarke J (2005) Not enough official torture in the world? The circumstances in which torture is morally justifiable. (2005) 39 University of San Francisco Law Review: 581–616

Chirwa D (2006) The horizontal application of constitutional rights in a comparative perspective. (2006) 9 Law, Democracy and Development Journal: 21–48

Commonwealth Ombudsman (2007) Lessons for public administration – Ombudsman investigation of referred immigration cases. Commonwealth Ombudsman, Canberra. https://www.ombudsman.gov.au/__data/assets/pdf_file/0018/26244/investigation_2007_11.pdf. Accessed 15 Oct 2019

Feinberg J (1986) Harm to self. Oxford University Press, New York

Finn F (2007) An opportunity spurned: Michael McKinnon's case. (2007) 35 Federal Law Review: 297–313

Hall E (2015) What can Tony Abbott learn from the Magna Carta? Australian Broadcasting Corporation. The World Today. 15 June 2015

Manderson D (2008) Another modest proposal: in defence of the prohibition against torture. In: Gani M, Mathew P (eds) (2008) Fresh perspectives on the 'war on terror'. ANU Press, Canberra, pp 27–43

Manderson D (2009) Governor Arthur's proclamation: aboriginal people and the deferral of the rule of law. (2009) 29 Arena: 1–54

Vidot A (2016) Deputy PM blocks labor from accessing the cost-benefit analysis of moving the chemical regular from Canberra. ABC News. 19 October 2016

Chapter 7
Holding Government to Account

Abstract This chapter discusses how the doctrine of responsible government fails to operate in Australia because the rules of parliamentary privilege, coupled with the dominance of two major political blocs, ensures that the mechanisms which are theoretically available to parliament to ensure executive subordination to the legislature are never used. The chapter examines several instances of executive defiance of parliament and argues that the power of parliamentary committees to force members of the executive to answer questions need to be enhanced, drawing on the example of the United States where paradoxically, despite not having a system of responsible government, the executive is subject to the scrutiny of the legislature to a far greater degree in Australia. The chapter also discusses how the right of parliament to obtain information from the executive should be balanced against executive claims of public interest immunity. The chapter also argues that the method of choosing the Speaker of parliament needs to be reformed so as to ensure that the incumbent is genuinely independent.

7.1 Scrutiny of Government

A bill of rights would provide people with a means of challenging the validity of legislation and governmental action when their individual rights are infringed. However, adherence to constitutionalism – the doctrine that the power of the state should be dined and limited by law – obviously requires the legal system to do more than just remedy breaches of individual interests. The exercise of power by 'the government' – which in legal terms means the executive branch, consisting of ministers and public servants – affects all of society from day to day. For this reason it is important to have some method which enables continual monitoring the government's exercise of its powers. Unsurprisingly, inquiries set up by governments into their own conduct yield little of value. For example, both the inquiry into the circumstances in which Australia entered into the second Gulf war and that which investigated political interference in the treatment of Dr Haneef amounted to what might be termed Potempkin Village inquiries, with limited terms of reference (in the

B. Harris, *Constitutional Reform as a Remedy for Political Disenchantment in Australia*, https://doi.org/10.1007/978-981-15-3599-4_7

first instance)[1] or with access denied to critical documents and people (in the second).[2]

The idea that the government should be subject to scrutiny is an aspect of the doctrine of responsible government. This doctrine was discussed in Chap. 3. The essential rules of the doctrine are that that the government holds power only so long as it retains the support of a majority in Parliament and that in exercising its powers, the government is answerable to parliament. It is the second of these rules that we are concerned with in this chapter. These rules developed incrementally in England over the period spanning the sixteenth to eighteenth centuries and were part of the parliamentary system exported to the Australian colonies. Crucial as these rules are, their inherent weakness is that they are not embodied in legislation. As explained in Chap. 3, they are conventions, and so rely for their effectiveness on voluntary adherence by political actors, rather than on legal sanction. This means that the extent to which the government submits itself to scrutiny depends on prevailing political culture, which in Australia has unfortunately developed in a direction of executive disregard for parliament. This is in marked contrast to countries such as the United Kingdom and New Zealand, where ministerial behaviour is markedly more deferential to the legislature. In Australia there has also been a departure from the convention as it developed in the United Kingdom that ministers take responsibility for the actions of their staffers and the public servants within their departments. This principle is important because whereas staffers and public servants are not subject to the political judgment of electors, ministers are. Therefore ministers ought to accept responsibility for misconduct or maladministration – whether they were aware of it or not – and should not shift blame to staffers or public servants, as occurred, for example when a staffer in the office of Minister for Employment Michaelia Cash, was found to have tipped off the media about a police raid on the offices of the Australian Workers Union, despite Cash having told a Senate committee five times that neither she nor anyone in her office had done so.[3]

Provision of information is obviously central to the effectiveness of scrutiny of government. Without access to information, parliamentarians have no way of knowing how the government is exercising its powers or of calling the government to account in cases of inefficiency or wrongdoing. It follows that since the government controls all the information relating to its own activities, those seeking to hold the government to account rely on the government itself voluntarily to provide such information as is requested. Yet although the government must in theory provide answers to parliament in relation to how it (the government) exercises its powers, the reality is far different, and ministers and public servants (acting under ministerial direction) often refuse to provide answers to questions put by parliamentary committees. Perhaps even more disturbingly, there is no effective method of overcoming that refusal. The net result is that because the government decides what

[1] Rudd (2017, pp. 306, 334–5, 420).

[2] Head (2009).

[3] Seccombe (2017).

information it will give parliament, it is very easy for the government to avoid scrutiny by the legislature – which undermines a fundamental pillar of responsible government.

This chapter considers the constitutional mechanisms which should, in theory, provide accountability of government, why they fail to achieve that objective and how the Constitution could be reformed so as to provide for effective scrutiny of government by parliament.

7.2 Parliamentary Debate and the Role of the Speaker

The first and most obvious method of holding government to account is through parliamentary debates, and in particular through the process of question time, when MPs and Senators can ask questions of ministers. In this instance, by 'MPs and Senators' one really means opposition MPs and Senators, because parliamentary discipline is so rigid in Australia that it is unheard of for members of the governing party to express dissent from, or ask embarrassing questions of, their own ministers. This is in marked contrast to the United Kingdom, for example, where back-bench MPs frequently challenge government policy on the floor of parliament. Granted, opposition parliamentarians are entirely self-interested in their efforts to expose government inefficiency or wrongdoing, nevertheless their pursuit of the government has the potential to play an important role in subjecting the government to scrutiny.

How effective parliamentary debates are as a scrutiny mechanism depends on the fairness of the procedures under which they are conducted, and it is here that the role of the Speaker (in the House of Representatives) and the President (in the Senate) are important. Because it is in the House that the government is formed, it is the role of the Speaker which is of particular significance.

Unfortunately, the speakership of the House of Representatives has never enjoyed independence – in the sense of the freedom to act impartially without fear of removal by MPs – as does the Speaker of the House of Commons in the United Kingdom. To put it bluntly, the expectation in Australia is that the Speaker is expected to favour the governing party that used its parliamentary majority to elect him or her.

The willingness of the government to pressure the Speaker it elected to act favourably towards it has become increasingly apparent over the last few decades. In 1975, the Whitlam government used its majority on the floor of the House to over-rule a decision by the Speaker, Jim Cope, to put a motion to suspend a cabinet member for misbehaviour. Cope believed that it made his position untenable and resigned. Controversy also arose during the speakership of Billy Snedden, who narrowly survived in office when he attracted the anger of the government after refusing to put to the House a motion that then opposition leader Bob Hawke be named for calling Prime Minister Fraser a liar. Hopes that the office of Speaker might be de-politicised were raised when, during the 1996 election, then opposition leader John Howard pledged a future Coalition government to a system with a 'completely independent Speaker' within two years of coming to power.[4] Yet after its election, the Coalition government abandoned its promise, and indeed provided a stark illustration of the subservience of the office to the government of the day by forcing Speaker Bob Halverson to step down after becoming frustrated at his impartiality in enforcing discipline on both Coalition and Labor MPs,[5] and at the increased opportunity for scrutiny of the government arising from his practice of allowing opposition MPs to ask supplementary questions of government ministers when original answers were evasive.[6] Controversy over the role of the Speaker arose again in 2003 and 2004, when proposals for an independent speakership along the lines of that which exists in the UK, were floated by then Labor opposition leaders Simon Crean[7] and Mark Latham,[8] but were rejected by the then Coalition government.

Control of the speakership became particularly controversial after the 2010 election, when Labor won more seats than the Coalition but did not have a majority in the House, and Independents held the balance of power. Paradoxically, in these circumstances an exercise by the government of its usual power to elect a Speaker would have been politically detrimental to it, as traditionally the Speaker does not cast a vote in parliament (other than in the event of a tie), and so the election of a Labor Speaker would have deprived the government of a much-needed vote on the floor of the House. The period immediately after the election saw a flurry of negotiations between the major parties and Independents, the latter demanding parliamentary reform (including an independent speakership) as part of the price for their support. Both major parties initially agreed to a Speaker drawn from the governing party and a deputy from the opposition, with both being independent and abstaining from attending their party caucus.[9] However, within a few days the Coalition withdrew their agreement, with the result that Labor's Harry Jenkins remained Speaker. Some months later, in order to increase its vote on the floor of the House, the Labor government pressured Jenkins into resigning, and installed Peter Slipper, a renegade Queensland Liberal-National Party member, who had had a falling out with his own party, as Speaker.[10] However, Labor's blatantly political tactic had negative repercussions for it, as Slipper subsequently faced allegations of misuse of parliamentary entitlements and sexual harassment of a former staffer, ultimately resigning over a separate scandal involving sexist phone texts.

The Coalition election victory in 2013 saw the election of Bronwyn Bishop to the speakership. Even prior to taking office, hopes that she would act impartially were undermined by statements that in her view Labor bore the brunt of the blame

[4] Seccombe (1998).

[5] Henderson (1998).

[6] Armstrong (1998).

[7] Coorey (2002).

[8] Atkins (2004).

[9] Franklin (2010).

[10] The Slipper saga is discussed in Singleton et al. (2012, p. 154).

for low standards of behaviour in the previous parliament.[11] Yet the partisanship she displayed went beyond the wildest expectations even of a parliament accustomed to favouritism towards the government of the day: Of 400 suspensions from the chamber she ordered, 393 were directed toward the opposition and only seven against government members.[12] Her tenure eventually ended when public outrage over excessive expenditure of parliamentary entitlements caused the government sufficient embarrassment to ask her to step down.

The recent history of the speakership makes it clear that, irrespective of what they say, neither of the major parties has any genuine interest in an independent speakership. The office is treated as a spoil of government and a Speaker who dares to act independently of the government which elected him or her will find their career cut short. This subjection of the office to the party in government serves to diminish an important institution. Impartiality in the application of the rules of debate and of behaviour is critical to the proper functioning of parliament, and there is no doubt that the poor behaviour of MPs, instances of which were discussed in Chap. 1, are at least partly due to the fact that speakers shield misbehaving government MPs from censure.

The capture of the office by the party in government, and the consequent lack of impartiality exhibited by the Speaker in controlling the House, contributes to a feverish and ill-disciplined atmosphere, of which boorish conduct is an all too frequent feature. However, the Speaker's ability to control the House is constrained not only by vulnerability to government pressure, but also by the inadequacy of the disciplinary powers at their disposal. Under Standing Orders, the Speaker's power to exclude a member from the House for misbehaviour is limited to one hour.[13] Suspension for longer periods requires that the Speaker formally 'name' the member, which in turn requires that a motion be put to the house that the member be suspended.[14] Obviously when the named member is from the governing party, the government can simply refuse to support the motion, which is indeed what happened when Whitlam government MPs voted against the naming of one of their members in 1975, leading the Speaker to resign. The practical effect of the rules is that the Speaker is dependent on government MPs for the imposition of all but the mildest sanction.

Things are very different in the United Kingdom, where the convention of an independent speakership has been upheld since the 1840s. The convention originated when the Tory government led by Robert Peel refrained from using its Commons majority to vote out the Speaker elected under the preceding Liberal government.[15] Peel expressly stated that his purpose was to ensure that no party should seek advantage through the election of the Speaker and that the authority of

[11] Australian Broadcasting Corporation (2013).

[12] Malone (2016).

[13] Commonwealth of Australia, *House of Representatives Standing Orders*, (2015) SO 94(a).

[14] Commonwealth of Australia, *House of Representatives Standing Orders*, (2015) SO 94(d).

[15] Laundy (1964, pp. 22–5).

the speakership in maintaining order would be enhanced if the incumbent had been elected on the basis of the general good will of the House. Since then, sitting Speakers have been re-elected by each new Parliament until he or she decides to retire, irrespective of changes in government. By tradition, once a Speaker is elected, they sever links with their party and do not attend caucus meetings.[16] Furthermore, although the Speaker must, like any other MP, secure re-election to Parliament, they run as 'the Speaker seeking re-election', not as a member of a party, and the major parties by convention do not run candidates in their constituency — effectively meaning that the Speaker runs unopposed.[17] By de-politicising the speakership and ensuring that the Speaker does not feel vulnerable to replacement by the government, the House of Commons has ensured that the Speaker has the independence that necessary to enable him or her to act impartially as between government and opposition MPs.

There is a clear need to reform the office of Speaker in Australia so that it functions along the same lines as it does in the United Kingdom. One defect in the UK model is the unfairness that would arise towards the constituents who elected the Speaker if the office became apolitical and the Speaker was returned to Parliament uncontested at each election. A solution to this was proposed by Kevin Rozzoli who served as Speaker of the New South Wales Legislative assembly for seven years.[18]

Although writing about reform of a state parliament, Rozzoli's proposal could be applied to the Commonwealth. He proposed that once chosen by a secret ballot of MPs, the Speaker would then become a 'member at large', serving a notional electorate until retirement, while his or her actual seat would automatically be filled by a nominee of the party for which the Speaker had stood, and would be contested in the usual way at the next election. Therefore, although still an MP, the Speaker would cease to be the representative of their electorate or party, and would serve until retirement. As in the United Kingdom, the fact that the Speaker would no longer be a member of their party caucus would ensure that the Speaker was elevated above party politics. The nomination of a replacement in their electorate, and the contestation of that electorate as usual at the next election, would mean that the Speaker's constituents would not be deprived of current or future representation. Allowing the Speaker's party to nominate a replacement would also avoid the unfairness of requiring the party which had already won the seat to win a by-election.

Rozzoli's other key recommendation was that de-politicisation of the office would require that the Speaker should be able to be removed only by a two-thirds majority of Parliament — which in practical terms would mean only with the concurrence of both government and opposition. Although not included in Rozzoli's model, the same principle suggests that the Speaker should also be elected by a

---

[16] Laundy (1964, p. 7).

[17] Laundy (1964, pp. 108–15). The contrasts in this regard between the speakership in the UK and Australia are discussed in Ward (2012, pp. 180–1).

[18] Rozzoli (2006, pp. 194–201).

two-thirds majority. This would also ensure that whoever was chosen as Speaker enjoyed the support of both government and opposition, and would therefore be likely to be someone who both sides of politics were confident would be impartial in the exercise of their powers.

Finally, the Speaker's independent disciplinary powers should be increased – perhaps to allowing him or her to suspend an MP for up to seven days. The threat of such a punishment might have a significant positive effect on standards of behaviour in the House.

7.3 Parliamentary Privilege

Although parliamentary debates provide some opportunity for holding the government to account, it is parliamentary committees which – in theory at least – provide the most effective mechanism for parliament to scrutinise the executive, by questioning government ministers and public servants. An understanding of the scope of this power requires an examination of parliament's rules of internal government. This body of law consists of powers (to do certain things), immunities (freedom from external control) and privileges (rights which parliament alone enjoys). For convenience, these are often collectively referred to as 'parliamentary privilege'.

Although the English parliament developed internal procedures over many centuries, the principle that it could govern itself free from external interference was established during the struggle between the monarch and parliament, which led to two civil wars from 1642–49 and 1688–89. A number of issues divided the parties, including whether the monarch had the power to impose taxes without the consent of parliament as well as disputes over religious tolerance, but the essential underlying struggle was over which institution – crown or parliament – would be politically dominant. During the reign of Charles I, MPs who expressed disagreement with royal policies were frequently detained for what they had said in parliament, and some were even arrested in the chamber. When parliamentary forces ultimately defeated the forces of James II in 1689, parliament invited William and Mary to take the crown, but on terms which ensured that the monarch would from then on rule with the consent of parliament. This ultimately led to acceptance of the principle in the eighteenth century that the ministers chosen by the monarch could hold office only if they had the support of a majority in the House of Commons.

As part of the settlement of 1688, parliament enacted the *Bill of Rights Act*, which was not a bill of rights in the sense that that term was used in Chap. 5, but was rather an Act which regulated the future relationship between parliament and the crown. Remembering how MPs had been persecuted during the reign of Charles I, one of the key things parliament wanted to ensure was that there would be no interference in its operation by outsiders. The result was Article 9 of the Act which is still part of the law in the United Kingdom and which states 'That the freedom of speech and debates or proceedings in Parliament ought not to be impeached or questioned in any court or place out of Parliament.' The effect of this is that the courts were prohibited from inquiring into parliamentary proceedings or even from receiving as evidence anything that occurred as party of such proceedings. This makes MPs immune from civil suit (for example defamation actions) and from criminal prosecution for anything they might say or do during the course of parliamentary business.

When parliaments came to be established in the Australian colonies, they adopted the same powers and privileges which operated in the United Kingdom. The same was true when the Commonwealth was formed: Section 49 of the Commonwealth Constitution provides that the 'powers, privileges and immunities' of the House of Representatives and the Senate were the same as those of the House of Commons in the United Kingdom, subject to the Commonwealth parliament having the power to provide otherwise through legislation. Parliament used that power to enact the *Parliamentary Privileges Act 1988* (Cth), which changed some of the rules but which also confirmed that the crucial text appearing in Article 9 of the *Bill of Rights Act 1688* remained part of Australian law. This means that the houses of the Australian parliament continue to enjoy the same internal autonomy as originated in the United Kingdom.

There is no doubt that the free speech aspect of parliamentary privilege is critical to democracy, as it enables parliamentarians to engage in debate free from concern that they might be subject to legal sanction. Privilege applies not only to parliamentary debates but to all 'proceedings in parliament', which includes things said in, and communicated to, parliamentary committees, including by members of the public.

The rule that the courts are excluded from inquiring into what transpires during parliamentary proceedings is subject to qualifications: Section 16(5) of the *Parliamentary Privileges Act 1987* (Cth) states that the courts can inquire into parliamentary proceedings when determining whether s 57 of the Constitution (which governs the method of resolving conflicts between the House of Representatives and the Senate over legislation) or in interpreting the meaning statutes, which frequently requires the courts to look at parliamentary proceedings in order to discover the purpose underlying legislation. In addition, because the powers and privileges of parliament derive from the common law as supplemented by statute, their scope is able to be determined by the courts as part of their normal function of stating what the common law is and of interpreting statutes. Thus, as was stated by the High Court in *R v Richards; Ex parte Fitzpatrick and Browne*,[19] while it is up to the courts to determine whether conduct amounts to a breach of privilege, once the court has answered that in the affirmative, the effect of s 16 of the *Parliamentary Privileges Act 1988* (Cth) means that it is up to parliament to determine the consequences of a breach of that privilege.

---

[19] (1955) 92 CLR 157.

7.4 The Scrutiny Power of Parliamentary Committees

The most important mechanism parliament has to hold the government to account is the power of its committees to call upon ministers and public servants to answer questions. The power of the committees to do this – and to impose sanctions for non-compliance – derives from the law of parliamentary privilege.

Both the House of Representatives and the Senate have committees. There are also joint committees, which draw their membership from both houses. Parliamentary committees have a variety of roles. One is to give detailed consideration to legislation referred to them by their respective house. The House of Representatives has 17 standing committees – that is, committees with permanent existence – most of which scrutinise legislation falling within a particular area of government responsibility. The Senate has a similar system, although it divides the areas of responsibility among eight standing committees. Apart from standing committees, a house may establish a select committee to investigate a particular issue. These committees cease to exist once they have reported to the house that established them. Senate select committees often investigate politically controversial matters which the government, given its majority in the House of Representatives, would not establish a House committee to investigate – a prime example being the committee established by the Senate in 2002 to investigate whether children had been thrown overboard by refugees who were seeking to land at Christmas Island.

A particularly important role of Senate standing committees is to investigate how ministers and the public servants within their departments have conducted themselves. This occurs twice every year, when each standing committee acts in its 'Estimates' capacity (and is then often referred to as a 'Senate Estimates committee'). On these occasions each committee enquires into how the government has spent the money allocated to it by parliament for the portfolios falling under that particular committee's areas of responsibility. Because all government activity requires the expenditure of money, committees are able to range the scope of their inquiries at estimates hearings to include all aspects of government activity.[20] This gives committee members (and in particular, members of the opposition) the opportunity to question ministers and public servants on any matter pertaining to the operation of the departments for which they are responsible, and it is on these occasions that government inefficiency or wrongdoing can be exposed.

Obviously, the capacity of committees to investigate government activity depends for its effectiveness on the committees having the power to compel the government to provide information and to impose penalties in cases of non-compliance. The *Parliamentary Privileges Act 1987* (Cth) does not specify all types of conduct for which the houses of parliament can impose a penalty. Section 4 of the Act simply says that an offence against parliament is any conduct which interferes with the free exercise of the functions of parliament, its committees or its members. Section 7

[20] Evans (2004, p. 369). For a discussion of the role of Senate Estimates Committees see Parliament of Australia (2019) and Lynch (2001).

says that a house of parliament can impose a punishment of imprisonment for up to six months or a fine of $ 5000 in the case of natural persons, or of $ 25,000 in the case of corporations. Although the scope of s 4 has never been tested in the courts, there is authority at state level for the rule that a refusal by a member of the executive to provide evidence requested by parliament amounts to contempt and can be punished. In *Egan v Willis and Cahill*,[21] a case arising from New South Wales, in which the Treasurer, who was a member of the Legislative Council (the upper house of the New South Wales parliament) had refused to provide documents it requested, the High Court held that the Legislative Council enjoyed such privileges as were reasonably necessary to enable it to discharge its functions as a legislative chamber operating as part of a system of responsible government. These include the power to compel a minister who was a member of that chamber to produce documents requested by the chamber and to sanction him when he refused to comply. This case is important because it is not unreasonable to think that, were the High Court to decide a case relating to the powers of committees of the Commonwealth parliament to compel ministers to give evidence, it would reach the same decision as it did in the case arising under the New South Wales Constitution, since both it and the Commonwealth Constitution embody the system of responsible government.

The internal rules of the houses of the Commonwealth parliament have been drafted on the understanding that their committees enjoy these powers. Under its internal rules, the Senate has the power to issue a summons to compel witnesses to appear before its committees and to produce documents,[22] although usual practice is for an invitation to be sent to the person to attend, and for them to attend voluntarily.[23] Refusal by a witness either to attend or to answer questions amounts to a breach of parliamentary privilege,[24] and can be reported by the committee to the Senate as a whole which, if it finds that the refusal amounts to contempt, can impose the punishments provided for in s 7 of the *Parliamentary Privileges Act 1987* (Cth).[25] The same applies to committees of the House of Representatives. On the face of it then, it would appear that the committee system provides parliament with a powerful weapon to use in ensuring government accountability by questioning ministers and public servants. However, in practice, this is far from the case.

---

[21] (1996) 40 NSWLR 650.

[22] Evans (2004, pp. 30, 57, 377).

[23] Evans (2004, p. 378).

[24] Evans (2004, Appendix 2, Paras 12 and 13).

[25] Evans (2004, pp. 416–7, 423).

7.5 Executive Defiance of Parliament

Despite the ability of parliamentary committees to compel members of the executive to give evidence, ministers not uncommonly refuse to attend committees or answer questions when requested to do so. They also instruct public servants to do the same. A number of the most prominent examples of this from the past two decades include John Howard's refusal to allow political advisors employed in his office and in that of the then defence minister Peter Reith to appear at the inquiry into the Children Overboard affair,[26] the prohibition against a defence force officer appearing before the inquiry into what knowledge ADF personnel had of torture of Iraqi prisoners at Abu Ghreib,[27] and the prohibition against public servants appearing before the inquiry into the AWB scandal.[28] More recently, then Minister for Migration, Scott Morrison, refused to answer questions posed by a Senate committee on migration matters[29] and officials from the Department of Immigration and from Operation Sovereign Borders refused to answer a Senate committee question as to whether the government had paid people smugglers to return asylum-seekers to Indonesia.[30] These instances all related to matters which raised questions suggesting serious misconduct by the government, yet there are others that relate to more mundane matters, which itself indicates how common is governmental defiance of the legislature.

The habitual refusal of the executive to allow ministerial advisors and public servants to be questioned has led one commentator to express his frustration – and that of the voting public – in the following terms:[31]

> If all public servants were subject to legal or parliamentary scrutiny, neglectful ministers and their devoted servants alike would be constantly obliged to think about how their actions or inactions would be greeted by ordinary Australians….we need to remove the gag from the mouths of public servants appearing before Senate estimates hearings. In a healthy democracy there is no justification for reducing transparency: the culpable need to be held accountable.

Why then does practice diverge so strikingly from the law? If parliament has the power to ensure compliance by the executive, why does the executive succeed in defying the legislative branch, to the extent that Australia now lives under what one commentator referred to as 'a sort of elective monarchy'[32] where governments appear to be beyond scrutiny by parliament?

---

[26] Walters (2004).

[27] Kirk (2004).

[28] See Maiden (2006), Ross Peake (2006) Australian Broadcasting Corporation (2006).

[29] See Emma Griffiths (2013) and Zander (2014).

[30] Anderson (2016).

[31] Thompson (2006).

[32] Ryle et al. (2005).

There are three reasons for this:

The first is that the power to have that person sanctioned for contempt lies not in the hands of any individual committee member, nor even in the committee itself, but rather in the house as a whole. A committee which encounters an unco-operative witness must first refer the matter to the house's privileges committee for a determination as to whether the conduct amounts to a breach of privilege. That committee will then make a recommendation to its house. However, the house is not bound by the committee's report and will the ultimate decision on whether privilege has been breached and, if so, what penalty should be imposed.

The second, which follows on from the first, is that when an issue which places a minister at risk of sanction is referred to a house by its privileges committee, the result is unfortunately – and inevitably – determined along party lines, and so whether an MP or Senator will be found to have breached parliamentary privilege depends on which party has a majority in the relevant house, rather than on the merits of the case. This reveals the folly of vesting a quasi-judicial decision in a political body. As an example of this, one can cite an instance which occurred in 1999, when it was alleged that at the time of his nomination for election, government MP Warren Entsch had been a shareholder in a company which had contractual dealings with the Commonwealth and was therefore ineligible to be elected under s 44(v) of the Constitution, which prohibits anyone with a pecuniary interest in a Commonwealth contract from being elected. Instead of referring the matter to the High Court, the government used its majority to declare that Entsch had not breached the rules. In light of this it is unsurprising to learn that the House of Representatives – in which the government by definition has a majority – has never sanctioned a government MP, and therefore to understand that it is impossible to conceive of a government compelling one of its ministers to answer questions put to it by one of the House's committees. As Harry Evans, Clerk of the Senate said in a speech to the National Press Club in 2002:[33]

> Responsible government was a system which existed from the mid-19th century to the early 20th century, after which it disappeared. It involved a lower house of parliament with the ability to dismiss a government and appoint another between elections. This system has been replaced by one whereby the government of the day controls the lower house by a built-in, totally reliable and "rusted on" majority. Not only is the government not responsible to, that is, removable by, the lower house, but it is also not accountable to it. The government's control of the parliamentary processes means that it is never effectively called to account…

What then of the Senate? Given that the government usually does not have a majority in that house, surely if one of its committees referred to the house a refusal of a minister to answer questions, it would be likely that he or she would be found to be in contempt? Before answering this question, one should note that the possibility of the Senate taking action against a government minister arises only during those periods when the government does not have a majority in the Senate. When the government does have a majority, the Senate is no more likely than the House to

[33] Evans (2002).

create select committees into alleged government malfeasance or to use coercive powers against government ministers.

However – and this is the third reason why parliamentary scrutiny of the executive is ineffectual – even when the government does not have a majority in the Senate, the Labor-Coalition duopoly which dominates Australian politics works to ensure that a precedent of a government minister being punished for refusing to answer questions is never established. This was starkly illustrated in 2002, when the Senate was holding an inquiry into the Children Overboard affair. The critical issue in contention was at what stage information from defence personnel to the effect that children had not been thrown overboard by asylum-seekers was communicated to ministers in the then Coalition government, who were in the midst of an election campaign in which they alleged that the children had been thrown overboard. Peter Reith, who had been Minister of Defence at the time the events occurred, refused to give evidence before the Senate committee, and the cabinet ordered that his staffers not comply with the committee's requests to attend. At the time, the Coalition lacked a majority in the Senate, which meant that Labor, in conjunction with the minor parties, had sufficient numbers to compel Reith's attendance, and could have used their majority to impose a fine or imprisonment if the committee met with recalcitrance. The reason that did not happen was that despite the fact that the Australian Democrats and Greens supported such a step, Labor refrained from using its Senate votes to exercise the contempt powers. This demonstrates the political cynicism that afflicts what is the two-party system in Australia: As a party which might come to power in the future, Labor was unwilling to establish the precedent that ministers, advisors and public servants should be compellable witnesses before legislative committees. Collusion between the major political parties to obstruct parliamentary scrutiny of government constitutes a dark form of bipartisanship, one in which, despite their hatred for each other, Labor and the Coalition collude to undermine the fundamental principles upon which responsible government is – or should be – based.

The result is that never in the history of the Commonwealth has a minister who has refused to provide information to a parliamentary committee been subject to the penalties provided by the *Parliamentary Privileges Act 1988* (Cth). The most that ever occurs to unco-operative ministers is that a motion of censure (in other words, a formal slap on the wrist) is passed against them – a remedy which the major parties are happy to use because it causes political embarrassment to the government but which does not establish a precedent that would expose ministers to significant penalties such as suspension from the house, a fine or imprisonment for failing to attend or give evidence.

7.6 Reforming the Rules of Executive Accountability

There is an obvious a need to enhance the power of parliamentary committees to hold governments to account. The preceding discussion shows that the fundamental reason why there is no effective scrutiny of the executive is because breaches of parliamentary privilege can be punished only by a house and not by committees or by individual members. Effective scrutiny of the government will therefore be achieved only if the workings of the committee system are put beyond the capacity of political parties to block their operation. This means that there needs to be a change in the rules governing both the initiation and the adjudication of contempt proceedings in such a way as to put them on a legal, rather than political, foundation. To leave the law unchanged would be to allow the principle of executive accountability to remain hostage to the two major political blocs, who have a vested interest in ensuring that true accountability never becomes established.

I would therefore argue that the constitution should explicitly state that individual members of parliamentary committees should have the right to subpoena witnesses and require them to answer questions and, most importantly, that whether failure to do so amounts to contempt should be determined by the courts, rather than by the relevant house concerned.[34] These reforms would represent a major departure from current law, which leaves it to parliament's internal workings to determine whether breaches of privilege have occurred, and how they should be punished. The autonomy won by parliament in the seventeenth century was meant to strengthen its power relative to the executive, yet the rigid party system that developed during the twentieth century has led to executive dominance of parliament – the very reverse of what responsible government is meant to be. In other words, parliamentary privilege has had the paradoxical effect of undermining rather than strengthening scrutiny of government, to the extent that scrutiny now barely exists. Since the rationale for the law of parliamentary privilege is to serve the interests of responsible government (the line of reasoning which lay at the heart of the High Court decision in *Egan v Willis and Cahill*[35]), any reform that enhanced the power of parliament to hold the government to account would undoubtedly be positive. If MPs were able to approach the courts for assistance in getting answers from ministers would radically change the balance of power between parliament and the executive, restoring the former to its rightful supremacy over the latter.

[34] In 1994 Senator Kernot of the Australian Democrats introduced a Bill which would have made it a criminal offence, prosecutable in the Federal Court at the instance of a House of Parliament, to fail to comply with an order of a House or a committee. The Bill would also have empowered the court to order compliance with the legislature's request. The Bill provided for a public interest immunity defence, with the onus being on the accused to prove that the public interest in not complying outweighed the need for open parliamentary inquiries. Courts could conduct in camera hearings to determine whether the defence had been established. Unsurprisingly, the Bill was not proceeded with due to opposition by the major parties.

[35] (1996) 40 NSWLR 650.

7.7 Public Interest Immunity

The final important issue to consider is what limits should be placed on the power of parliamentary committees and the courts to compel ministers to provide information. Clearly there will be circumstances in which ministers should not be compelled to answer questions. This is so because of the principle of public interest immunity, which is a legal rule to that sometimes evidence which a person would otherwise be compelled to give should either not be disclosed or should be disclosed subject to certain conditions because there is some countervailing public interest that justifies it being kept out of the public domain. In a sequel to the case of *Egan v Willis*[36] discussed above, the court in *Egan v Chadwick*[37] held that the obligation of the executive to produce documents might, depending on the circumstances, be qualified by considerations of public interest immunity, and that there were circumstances where interests such as cabinet confidentiality would outweigh parliament's right to scrutinise the government. In other words, the court held that the operation of responsible government requires a balancing of interests: Although responsible government requires parliamentary scrutiny of the executive, the executive cannot discharge its role under the system without the freedom to deliberate on policy matters in private.

The existence of a public immunity exception to requests for information is acknowledged by parliament.[38] However, the scope of the immunity has never been tested in the courts. On the one occasion when a ministerial refusal to produce documents on such ground was referred to the Senate's privileges committee (in 1975),[39] the committee divided along party lines, with the majority government senators holding that the ministerial refusal was lawful – a prime example of the politicisation of questions which should be decided on their legal merits. In all other instances where the executive has refused to accede to Senate committee requests, the Senate has not pursued the matter. But while it is clear that the disclosure of some information would be harmful to the defence, foreign affairs, commercial or other interests of the country, the point is that whether information is, in fact, justifiably held back on grounds of public interest immunity is a legal, not political, question. However, as things stand, the government frequently raises public interest immunity when faced with questions by parliamentary committees, and since under current procedures such matters are not referred to the courts, the end result is that the government itself determines whether its own refusal to provide information is lawful. Many of the contentious instances in which governments defied parliamentary committees listed earlier in the chapter were ones in which the government claimed public interest immunity, yet in the absence of an impartial determination as to whether such claims were justified, parliamentarians and the public were left

[36] (1998) 195 CLR 424.

[37] (1999) 46 NSWLR 563.

[38] Evans (2004, pp. 643–4).

[39] Evans (2004, pp. 659–60).

wondering whether the claims were genuine or were rather raised in order to shield the government from embarrassment. Under current practice, there would be nothing to stop a government from declining on grounds of public immunity to answer a question as trite as how many paintings there are in the National Gallery of Australia – because there is no mechanism for determining whether such a claim is legally valid.

So, assuming that members of parliamentary committees were able to approach the courts to compel ministers to provide information to parliament, how should the courts address ministerial claims that public interest immunity justifies non-disclosure of that information? For an answer to that question, one can look to the United States where the principle of judicial determination of disputes between the legislature and the executive has long been acknowledged.

7.8 The Example of the United States

In the United States, congressional committees enjoy far greater powers to call cabinet members to account than does parliament in Australia. There is great irony in this, as one would think that the Australian system of responsible government, where the executive depends for its tenure on the support of the legislature, would provide for greater levels of legislative control over the executive than would be the case in the United States where, under the doctrine of separation of powers, the executive does not depend on legislative support to hold office and thus the doctrine of responsible government does not apply.

The right of Congress to subpoena witnesses and to punish them for failing to attend and answer questions is long established: In 1821 in the case of *Anderson v Dunn*,[40] the Supreme Court held that an investigative power was implicit in the legislative powers of Congress, and that a subpoena power was a necessary element of that investigative power. The leading case on this issue is now *McGrain v Daugherty*,[41] in which the Court affirmed that a power to investigate is 'an essential and appropriate auxiliary'[42] to the legislative power of Congress. The court also held that the investigative power of Congress can be exercised not only when considering specific legislation, but 'for legislative purposes',[43] which includes investigations of whether the executive branch is properly discharging its functions.[44] The significance of this case lay in the fact that the issue before the court was whether a Senate committee could subpoena witnesses and documents relating to the a decision by Attorney-General Harry M. Daugherty not to prosecute those involved in what was

[40] 19 US (6 Wheat.) 204 (1821).

[41] 273 US 135 (1927).

[42] 273 US 135 (1927), 174.

[43] 273 US 135 (1927), 177.

[44] 273 US 135 (1927), 177.

known as the Teapot Dome scandal, involving corruption in the awarding of drilling leases over federal land.[45] In answering this question in the affirmative, the Supreme Court confirmed that it is proper for the legislature to investigate the conduct of the executive, including members of the cabinet. This theory of legislative – executive relations was consistent with what had been enunciated by Woodrow Wilson in 1913 prior to his becoming President[46]:

> It is the proper duty of a representative body to look diligently into every affair of government and to talk much about what it sees.... Unless Congress have and use every means of acquainting itself with the acts and the disposition of the administrative agents of government, the country must be helpless to learn how it is being served ... and must remain in embarrassing, crippling ignorance of the very affairs which it is most important that it should understand and direct. The informing function of Congress should be preferred even to its legislative function.... The only really self-governing people is that people which discusses and interrogates its administration.

The principle of compellability of cabinet members is balanced by the doctrine of separation of powers, which prevents interference by one branch in the affairs of the other. This means that there are limits on the ability of Congress to compel disclosure of information from the executive and that the courts recognise that there are circumstances in which the public interest requires that the workings of the executive branch remain confidential. Much of the case law balancing Congress' right to know against the executive's right to confidentiality arose from the Watergate scandal, when Congress sought to use its subpoena powers to obtain evidence of wrongdoing by members of the Nixon administration. In *Senate Select Committee on Presidential Campaign Activities v Nixon*,[47] the Federal Court held that evidence would be compelled from the executive only where it was 'demonstrably critical' to the legislature's inquiry. Subsequently, in *United States v Nixon*,[48] the Supreme Court outlined in more detail the principles that determine the limits of executive privilege (the equivalent of public interest immunity in Australia).[49] The court held that the executive cannot be compelled to give information if the possibility that communications would be subject to disclosure would impair the confidentiality and candour of policy deliberations within the executive.[50] However, the court explicitly asserted that the executive's mere claim of privilege is not determinative – any case involving such a claim will be decided by the courts,[51] balancing the

---

[45] For a discussion of this case see Marshall (2004, pp. 792–7).

[46] Wilson (1913, p. 303).

[47] 498 F.2d 725 (D.C. Cir. 1974) 732–3.

[48] 418 US 683 (1974).

[49] Although this case involved the question of the extent to which executive privilege can serve to defeat a subpoena in which information or attendance of a witness is sought by the judicial branch (in other words, in court proceedings), what was held by the Supreme Court applies equally to cases where information is sought from the executive by the legislative branch. See Tribe (2000, p. 784).

[50] 418 US 683 (1974) 705, 708.

[51] 418 US 683 (1974), 703.

competing demands of the interest to be served by disclosing the information against the executive's claims to confidentiality.[52] The court held that claims of executive privilege will be particularly strong in relation to information relating to foreign affairs, diplomacy and national security,[53] but that even in a case where a claim of privilege is made based on state secrets, the executive must satisfy the court that such an issue is involved, if necessary by providing evidence to the court *in camera*.[54] The Supreme Court re-stated these rules on executive privilege in *Nixon v Administrator of General Services*,[55] in which it held that there was no blanket right to executive privilege,[56] and that a claim of privilege would succeed only where the executive could show that disclosure would significantly impair the executive branch's ability to achieve its constitutional function.[57] This line of cases thus demonstrates that the concept of executive privilege exists, but also that it is by no means a trump that will always defeat requests for information by the legislative branch.

It should not however be thought that, because the courts in the United States have the ultimate role in deciding inter-branch disputes, contests between the legislature and the executive are frequently the subject of litigation. Given that the legislature has the whip hand, the executive generally defers to it, knowing that there will be a political price to pay if it (the executive) tries to avoid scrutiny by claiming privilege.[58] In most cases, the two branches reach a compromise,[59] and it is a quite normal feature of the political process for members of the executive, including members of the cabinet, to appear voluntarily before public hearings of congressional committees[60] (as President Ford did, when requested to answer questions relating to his pardoning of President Nixon),[61] or for information to be provided to a committee in a closed session.[62] Disputes are thus almost always settled by negotiation between Congress and the administration.[63] The fact that the judicial branch is the ultimate determiner of the degree to which the executive is accountable to the legislature has not led to the courts being confronted with policy questions that they are incapable of deciding without becoming involved in party-political disputes – the case law that has been developed provides rules of sufficient precision to enable the courts to determine whether a claim of executive privilege is valid, irrespective

[52] 418 US 683 (1974), 711–12. See also *Senate Select Committee on Presidential Campaign Activities v Nixon* 498 F.2d 725 (D.C. Cir 1974) and *United States v A T & T* 521 F.2d 384 (D.C. Cir 1976) and 567 F. 2d 121 (D.C. Cir 1977).

[53] 418 US 683 (1974), 710–11.

[54] 418 US 683 (1974), 713–14.

[55] 433 US 425 (1977).

[56] 433 US 425 (1977), 446–7.

[57] 433 US 425 (1977), 443.

[58] On the political ramifications of claims of executive privilege see Louis Fisher (2002).

[59] Fisher (2002, p. 325).

[60] Fisher (2002, pp. 394–401).

[61] See Rozell (1994, p. 90).

[62] Rozell (1994, p. 150).

[63] Marshall (2004, pp. 806–08).

of the politics of the case before them. To repeat what was said at the start of this section, it is a matter of supreme irony that despite operating under a system of separation of powers, the legislative branch in the United States has far greater power to scrutinise the executive than is the case under our system of responsible government which supposedly subjects the executive to legislative control.

If courts in Australia were called upon to determine the validity of executive claims to immunity from disclosing information to parliament, they could draw upon the existing body of case law governing immunity in so far as it applies to every-day proceedings before the courts, as there is no reason why the same rules should not apply when determining the circumstances in which public interest immunity would entitle the executive to withhold evidence from the legislature. The leading case on this issue is *Sankey v Whitlam*,[64] in which the High Court held that public interest immunity is not absolute and that it is up to the courts to balance the need for confidentiality of government communications against the needs of justice in any given case.[65] The courts have applied the test in *Sankey v Whitlam* in a range of different circumstances, including whether information in the possession of ASIO can be introduced as evidence in court proceedings.[66]

The key point arising from these cases is that public interest immunity should not be conceived of as a trump to be waved in the face of parliament or the courts, permitting the executive to avoid scrutiny whenever it pleases. This is why the case law from the United States is particularly significant: The role it gives to the courts to balance the competing claims of legislative inquiry against executive confidentiality ensures that the executive is not judge in its own cause when questions of its amenability to legislative inquiry arise. As it will be recalled, a similar balancing was undertaken in *Egan v Chadwick*,[67] where it was held that cabinet confidentiality is an important element of responsible government, and that therefore documents revealing the deliberations of cabinet should be immune from disclosure to parliament. The outcome of the balancing process will depend upon the facts of each case, but one would expect that cases involving foreign affairs and national security would be ones in which some degree of deference would be shown to the executive once it proves its claim – during *in camera* proceedings if necessary. Similarly, discussions between members of the cabinet, and documents which were genuinely related to cabinet proceedings,[68] would also be likely to be immune from legislative inquiry. A court adjudicating such issues might find that information is wholly covered by executive privilege, or it might allow a parliamentary committee to receive

---

[64] (1978) 142 CLR 1.

[65] (1978) 142 CLR 1), 38–43.

[66] *Alister v The Queen* (1984) 154 CLR 404. See also *Commonwealth v Construction, Forestry, Mining and Energy Union* (2000) 171 ALR 379 and *NTEU v Commonwealth* (2001) 111 FCR 583.

[67] (1999) 46 NSWLR 563.

[68] Confidentiality would thus not apply to a document merely because it had been physically present during a cabinet meeting – for an example of trolley-loads of documents being wheeled into cabinet meetings simply in order for it to be said that they were 'cabinet documents' see Roberts (2006).

the evidence subject to conditions – for example that the evidence be presented *in camera* and without a record being kept, as sometimes happens in the United States.

7.9 Reviving Responsible Government

The doctrine of responsible government has ceased to operate in Australia. As shown in this chapter, the key factor which has led to this state of affairs is the way in which party discipline has become a feature in every jurisdiction which uses this model of government, but which is far more rigid in Australia than in other countries. In the United Kingdom, backbenchers frequently express public dissent from government policy and vote against it in parliament. In Australia, by contrast, independent thought and action of that type is so rare as to be newsworthy. The consequence is that whereas in theory the doctrine of responsible government requires that government should be subordinate to parliament, in practice it is the other way round: The front bench of the governing party or coalition uses party discipline to control the House of Representatives, which means that there is no likelihood whatsoever of the government permitting its own MPs to call it to account. When one adds to this the fact that parliamentary privilege bars recourse to the courts, one arrives at a position where the government, through its use of the majority it has in the house to which it is nominally responsible, becomes judge in its own cause: Every question – whether bad behaviour by an MP amounts to contempt of parliament, whether a minister should be required to answer questions put by a parliamentary committee, or even whether an MP was validly elected to parliament under the s 44 of the Constitution[69] – is ultimately determined along political lines by a majority vote, which the government is bound to win, rather than according to the merits of the issue. Giving a quasi-judicial adjudicatory powers to a legislative body inevitably leads to decisions being taken on a partisan basis rather than objectively and in accordance with the legal merits of the issue.

Ultimate control over executive accountability must be wrested away from politicised majorities. This is why a reformed constitution should confer on individual members of parliamentary committees the power to compel witnesses to give evidence and, subject to a defence of public interest immunity, should make non-compliance subject to sanction by the courts. In so doing, the power imbalance that exists between legislature and executive, would be reversed and would ensure that the government was truly responsible to the legislature – which is what our system is supposed to do.

[69] The issue of how cases involving ineligibility under s 44 are processed is discussed in Chap. 11.

References

Anderson S (2016) Senior officials refuse to answer questions on payments to people smugglers. ABC News. 5 Feb 2016
Armstrong G (1998) Damage control as speaker quits. The West Australian. 4 Mar 1998
Atkins D (2004) Proposal to have an impartial speaker. The Courier Mail. 19 Mar 2004
Australian Broadcasting Corporation (2006) Labor questions legality of Senate estimates gag. News On-line. 14 Feb 2006
Australian Broadcasting Corporation (2013) Bishop: Gillard's misogyny speech should not have been allowed. Radio National Breakfast. 17 September 2013. http://mpegmedia.abc.net.au/rn/podcast/2013/09/bst_20130917_0832.mp3. Accessed 17 Oct 2019
Coorey P (2002) Behaviour hits the bottom line. Adelaide Advertiser. 1 July 2002
Evans H (ed) (2004) Odgers' Australian Senate practice, 11th edn. Department of the Senate, Canberra
Evens H (2002) The Australian Parliament: time for reformation. Address to the National Press Club. 24 Apr 2002. https://australianpolitics.com/2002/04/24/harry-evans-parliamentary-reform-speech.html. Accessed 17 Oct 2019
Fisher L (2002) Congressional access to information: using legislative will and leverage. Duke Law J 52(2002):323–402
Franklin M (2010) Independents secure overhaul of parliament. The Australian. 7 Sept 2010
Griffiths E (2013) Immigration Minister Scott Morrison defies Senate order to release information about Operation Sovereign Borders. ABC News. 19 Nov 2013
Head M (2009) The Haneef inquiry: some unanswered questions. J Aust Law Teach Assoc 2:95–112
Henderson G (1998) PM's backflip on speaker reform. The Courier Mail. 9 Mar 1998
House of Representatives (2015) Standing orders. Commonwealth of Australia, Canberra
Kirk A (2004) ABC Television. The World Today. 1 June 2004
Laundy P (1964) The Office of Speaker. Cassell, London
Lynch A (2001) Called to account – in praise of the estimates process. Canberra Times. 2 Oct 2001
Maiden S (2006) Gag in Senate illegal, clerk warns. The Australian. 12 Apr 2006
Malone P (2016) Tony Smith as Speaker returns order to the Parliament. Sydney Morning Herald. 6 Feb 2016
Marshall W (2004) The limits on Congress's authority to investigate the president. Univ Ill Law Rev 781–825
Parliament of Australia (2019) Senate brief no 5 consideration of estimates by the Senate's legislation committees. https://www.aph.gov.au/About_Parliament/Senate/Powers_practice_n_procedures/Senate_Briefs/Brief05. Accessed 21 Oct 2019
Peake R (2006) Cover-up claim as officials gagged. Canberra Times. 14 Feb 2006
Roberts G (2006) To hell with the critics. The Australian. 26 Aug 2006
Rozell M (1994) Executive privilege: the dilemma of secrecy and democratic accountability. Johns Hopkins Press, Baltimore
Rozzoli K (2006) Gavel to Gavel: an insider's view of parliament. University of New South Wales Press, Sydney
Rudd K (2017) Not for the faint-hearted – a personal reflection on life, politics and purpose. Macmillan, Sydney
Ryle G, Pryor L, Metherell M (2005) Senate boss blasts PM's monarch. Sydney Morning Herald. 21 June 2005
Seccombe M (1998) Unlike Howard, at least Halvo was true to his word. Sydney Morning Herald. 4 Mar 1998
Seccombe M (2017) The true story of Michaelia Cash's union raids. The Saturday Paper. 4 Nov 2017
Singleton G, Aitkin D, Jinks B, Warhurst J (2012) Australian political institutions, 10th edn. Pearson, Frenchs Forest

Thompson K (2006) Public accountability non-existent in Howard Govt. The Canberra Times. 26 Sept 2006

Tribe L (2000) American constitutional law, volume One, 3rd edn. Foundation Press, St Paul

Walters P (2004) A fearless public servant. The Australian. 17 Aug 2004

Ward A (2012) Parliamentary Government in Australia. Australian Scholarly Publishing, North Melbourne

Wilson W (1913) Congressional Government; a study in American politics. Houghton Mifflin, Boston

Zander J (2014) As it happened: Scott Morrison fronts Senate committee over asylum seeker policies. ABC News. 31 Jan 2014

Chapter 8
Federalism and the Efficiency Deficit

Abstract Federalism is arguably the chief defining characteristic of the Constitution, yet there is widespread misunderstanding of what federalism is and how it differs from unitary systems. The chapter begins by defining what a federation is and how its chief effect is to limit the capacity of national government. The chapter then discusses the costs of federalism to the Australian economy before refuting the justifications commonly advanced for federalism in Australia. The chapter addresses the confusion that many participants in the debate over federalism have between levels and powers, and argues that a unitary system would give national government the capacity to delegate powers to rationally-based regional and local governments as circumstances dictate, rather than being shackled by a system which restricts the capacity of national government in arbitrary ways and which confers powers on states whose existence is not underpinned by any economic or geographical rationale.

8.1 The Origins of Australian Federalism

There is irony in the fact that the Commonwealth Constitution's most prominent feature – federalism – is also the source of its major dysfunction. Its effect is that of a monkey wrench in constitution which interferes in operation of government in sudden, unpredictable and purposeless ways.

That the drafters of the Constitution opted for a federal rather than a unitary system was inevitable in the political sense, given the rivalries and suspicion that existed between the colonies at the time the Constitution was debated. Their chief concern was to ensure that no colony should obtain an advantage over any other and that the power of a new national government over all of them should be restrained. Accordingly, the main focus of the Constitutional Conventions held between 1891 and 1898 was how the new Constitution would regulate the interaction of states with each other, and how power should be distributed between the states on the one hand and the future Commonwealth government on the other. Matters of trade and taxation in particular occupied a significant amount of time during the debates. The process of drafting a new constitution was thus overwhelmingly – perhaps one should say ruthlessly – pragmatic: As discussed in Chap. 2, Convention delegates spent little time discussing matters of principle, and none debating philosophical

B. Harris, *Constitutional Reform as a Remedy for Political Disenchantment in Australia*, https://doi.org/10.1007/978-981-15-3599-4_8

questions such as the relationship between state and the individual. Boiled down to its essentials, the key issue which exercised their minds was power – specifically the balance of power between the future states and Commonwealth – not questions involving values.

The choice between a federal and a unitary system can, sometimes, involve higher values. For example, in countries where ethnic groups live in geographically-defined areas, federalism can serve the right to self-determination by giving autonomy to those groups. But no question of values faced the drafters of the Commonwealth Constitution. The decision to adopt a federal system could not be labelled 'right' or 'wrong' in the ethical sense, and current supporters of federalism are unable to articulate any *moral* principle according to which that legislative authority over lighthouses (to choose an example from the Constitution) must be conferred on the Commonwealth while denying it authority over health, education or the environment (none of which it can legislate on).

The reality is that Australia became a federation through a combination of historical accident (that the United Kingdom, as the colonial power, had established several colonies in what became Australia rather than just one), and politics (that the existence of the separate colonies had given rise to vested political interests, which had to be accommodated if a new nation was to be formed). But had there been one colony rather than several, or had the colonial governments placed the common interest of the future country above their own sectional interests, Australia could have been a unitary state. These facts are frequently lost sight of – if indeed they are thought of at all – by defenders of federalism, some of whom operate on the assumption that the federal system was the inevitable, natural and only practical system that could have been adopted. Certainly, from a purely *political* point of view, and in the absence of a self-sacrificing altruistic approach by the colonial governments, federalism was inevitable, but it was not inevitable from a legal perspective. It would have been entirely possible to establish a unitary system. To put it in a nutshell: Australian federalism derives from the existence of wholly artificial historical entities and the political interests to which they gave rise. The result is that we have nine different legal systems and nine sets of government departments, collectively wielding authority over a population that is no larger than some of the major cities of the world.

8.2 What Is Federalism?

Before going any further, it is important to explain precisely what is meant by terms such as 'unitary' and 'federal' and, in particular, what the key features are of a federal system which sets it apart from a unitary one. Discussions on Australian federalism are often affected by confusion over this – confusion which, as we will see, is exploited by defenders of federalism who, in discussing overseas examples, sometimes label as federations countries which are not.

The difference between a unitary and a federal system relates to how a country's constitution distributes legislative power. In a unitary system – examples of which are provided by the United Kingdom and France – all original legislative power is vested in a central government. The term that is often used is that the legislature has 'plenary' power, which means that it is omnicompetent and can therefore legislate on any topic it pleases. Parliaments in unitary states can, and do, delegate legislative powers to sub-national units. In the United Kingdom, parliament has devolved law-making authority to assemblies in Wales, Scotland and Northern Ireland and to local authorities in England. Similarly, in France legislative authority is delegated to *departements*. But the key constitutional principle to bear in mind is that any delegated legislative authority can be taken back, and that the existence of delegated legislative authorities does not in any way impair the power of the national legislature.

A federal system is very different. The first characteristic of a federal system is that the constitution distributes legislative power between the central government and the sub-national units – in other words, it provides that both the national legislature and the sub-national units enjoy original legislative power. The second characteristic is that neither level of government acting on its own can disturb that balance – in other words, amendment of the constitution requires co-operation between both levels. The Commonwealth Constitution satisfies these rules by allocating certain legislative powers to the Commonwealth, leaving the rest to the states, and because amendments to the Constitution must be approved of by a majority of voters in the Commonwealth as a whole as well as by a majority of voters in a majority of states.

Appreciating what the essential elements of federalism are is a crucial first-step in understanding a discussion of whether Australia should retain its federal system. A common misconception is that we need federalism because a country the size of Australia could not be governed effectively by a single level of government. However the issue of federalism has nothing to do with *levels*, it has to do with *powers*, in particular what constitutional mechanism is used for the distribution of legislative powers to the different levels. As indicated by the examples of the United Kingdom and France, the fact that a country has a unitary constitutional system does not mean that it cannot have different levels of government. Indeed, there are very few countries in the world (most of them micro-countries such as Lichtenstein or Monaco) which have only one level of government, and almost all countries with unitary systems have at least two levels, each exercising legislative power over a defined geographical area, such as a province, state or local government area. The critical feature of a unitary system is therefore not the absence of different levels, but rather the fact that such legislative power as levels below the national government have are delegated to them by the national government and can be expanded, reduced or redistributed by the national government in accordance with what experience and the needs of the times require.

What sets Australia (and other true federations) apart from unitary states is that the Constitution prescribes the boundaries of the various levels of government and the powers of each. This necessarily involves restricting the topics over which the national government can legislate. This in turn makes government inefficient, because not only does one have to contend with multiple legal systems, but the inflexibility of the Constitution means that the distribution of legislative power between levels cannot be adjusted in the light of experience without going through the exceedingly difficult task of amending the Constitution. In other words, the essential feature of federalism is that the legislative authority of each level of government is cemented in for all time (or until the Constitution is changed, which in the case of Australia arguably means the same thing), rather than being able to be re-allocated in the best way needed to meet changing circumstances.

Another important feature of a federal constitution is that it has to have some rule for resolving clashes between statutes enacted by the national and sub-national units. In the case of the Commonwealth Constitution, s 109 states that state legislation will be invalid to the extent that it is inconsistent with Commonwealth legislation.

8.3 The Burden of Federalism

The existence of the federal system means that in every interaction between governments, and in every interaction between individuals and businesses on the one hand and the various levels of government on the other, several questions have to be asked in order to determine which component of the federation has jurisdiction over a particular matter: One has to ask which level of government can enact law relating to a particular activity, whether the provisions of the law clash with the law of another level and, if it does, whether all aspects of the law only some of them clash with the law of the other jurisdiction. Most people are probably unaware of this complex legal web that lies behind the operation of the federal system, how much federalism costs and why these cost arise, but the expense involved is no less real simply because it is opaque from the perspective of the average person.

First, as to how much federalism costs, in 2002 political economist Mark Drummond estimated that, at an absolute minimum, the existence of the federal system drained the Australian economy of $40 billion per year,[1] which was then the equivalent of 23% of the Commonwealth budget.[2] Adjusted for inflation,[3] that would amount to $ 58 billion today. Cast in individual terms, this meant that in 2002, federalism was costing every man, woman and child $ 2035 per annum which, adjusted for inflation, would be $ 2943 today.

There are a number of reasons why these costs are incurred. An obvious reason is duplication: Because Australia has nine jurisdictions (the Commonwealth, six

[1] Drummond (2007, p. 442).

[2] Australian Government Budget Archive (2002–2003).

[3] Calculated using the Reserve Bank of Australia's tool at https://www.rba.gov.au/calculator/annualDecimal.html

states and the two internal[4] territories of the ACT and the Northern Territory), there are nine departments of education, nine departments of health and nine departments of the environment et cetera – across all the various government portfolios – each administering different legislation and setting different policies. If there was a single, national education department administering one set of laws, the costs of delivering services would be much lower than it is now, both because of economies of scale and because the number of staff that would be required to administer a single set of laws, even in multiple sites throughout the country, would obviously be far less than is required by nine separate bureaucracies administering nine different sets of legislation.

Next are the costs incurred as a result of the administrative and legal burdens that federalism places on governments. Before a state parliament enacts legislation, it needs to ensure that the legislation is not inconsistent with that of the Commonwealth, otherwise the state legislation will be invalid under s 109. Matters are even more complex for the Commonwealth. Prior to introducing legislation into the Commonwealth parliament, the government has to ensure that it falls within one of the legislative powers of the Commonwealth. If the legislation lies outside those powers, the Commonwealth has to negotiate with the states to get them either to refer to the Commonwealth parliament the power to enact the legislation,[5] to pass parallel legislation through each of their legislatures,[6] to adopt as its own a uniform law enacted by one of them, or for the jurisdictions to enter into an inter-governmental agreement whereby the states undertake to comply with the Commonwealth's objective in exchange for a financial grant.[7] In addition, if the Commonwealth wishes to avoid a legislative patchwork, it has to ensure that it obtains the *unanimous* agreement of the states to one of these mechanisms. For example, while the strictness Australia's defamation law has led the country to being derided around the world,[8] the last time this area of the law was reformed it took two decades of abortive attempts before all the states could be persuaded to agree on a uniform law. This obviously makes further reform all the more unlikely. Sometimes agreement is never reached, as in the case of health care, which the Rudd unsuccessfully tried to bring under the aegis of the Commonwealth during the 2007–2010 period. All the costs incurred in deciding which level of government has power over a matter – as well as the time and costs involved in negotiation and litigation where that question is disputed – represent a lost opportunity to spend money on services delivered to the people of Australia.

---

[4] Australia's external Territories fall under the legislative authority of the Commonwealth.

[5] This is made possible by s 51(xxxvii) of the Constitution, which allows States Parliaments to refer (in reality confer) power on the Commonwealth Parliament to legislate on a topic that the Commonwealth does not have power over. This is the basis for the *Corporations Act 2001* (Cth).

[6] For example, the uniform *Defamation Act* enacted by all the States and Territories in 2005.

[7] There are numerous inter-governmental agreements governing a wide range of issues including health education and housing. They are frequently used by the Commonwealth as a means of attaching conditions to grants given to the States for specific purposes.

[8] Hutchinson and Eddie (2019).

Federalism even has the bizarre effect of even inhibiting the Commonwealth in giving money away. This is because the Commonwealth has no power to give grants directly to people. It has to rely on s 96 of the Constitution which, although it empowers the Commonwealth to give financial grants to the states on such terms as it sees fit, does not require the states to accept the money if they are unwilling to accept the conditions that are tied to the grant. If a grant is accepted, the movement of funds from Commonwealth to states to recipients obviously comes at cost that would not arise if the money was granted directly, because it has to pass through the intermediation of the state government with all the administrative costs that entails. Incidentally, it is the need to administer grants that it gives to states that is one of the reasons that the Commonwealth has departments administering health, education and many other portfolios covering matters in relation to which the Commonwealth parliament itself cannot enact legislation: Even though the Commonwealth does not have the capacity to legislate on those topics, it still needs departments in those areas to oversee state compliance with policies that the Commonwealth has formulated and which the states have to comply with as a condition of receiving Commonwealth grants.

Apart from costs to government, federalism imposes multiple costs on individuals, in terms both of money and inconvenience. Australians are a mobile population – 375,000 people migrated from one jurisdiction to another in 2016[9] – so these costs are significant in aggregate. As anyone who has migrated from one state or territory to another will know (and many people make several such moves during their lifetime), each move involves multiple costs arising from things such as stamp duty on property purchases, vehicle registration (which involves a fee for initial registration in the new jurisdiction, the costs of roadworthy testing and, usually, the loss of at least some of the registration fee previously paid on the vehicle in the state of origin) and obtaining a new driver's licence. A person who is engaged in a trade will need to obtain a licence to operate in the state they are moving to. People with school-age children will incur the inconvenience of them having to adapt to a new curriculum and a different high school examination system. People re-locating a business will have to learn how to comply with different environmental, employment and occupational health and safety codes – often incurring significant legal expense. The challenge for businesses operating in more than one state or territory are even greater, as they have to bear the financial burden of ensuring compliance with the law of multiple jurisdictions.

Finally, the existence of state governments has a distorting effect on the economy, the impact of which is most severely felt in relation to housing affordability – certainly one of the most pressing problems facing the average person. The reason for this has its roots in an objective that needed to be achieved in the formation of the federation was the elimination of tariffs between the colonies. In order to achieve this, s 90 of the Constitution gave to the Commonwealth the exclusive power of

---

[9] See data by the Australian Bureau of Statistics at http://stat.data.abs.gov.au/Index.aspx?DataSetCode=ABS_DEM_QIM

imposing duties of customs and excise, while s 92 prohibited the enactment of laws which interfere with inter-state trade and commerce. These undoubtedly necessary provisions have mean that the states are limited in the types of revenue they can raise. Section 90 prevents the states from imposing taxes on the production, sale or distribution of goods. The Commonwealth has *de facto* exclusive control over income taxes in that no state could afford the political consequences of imposing income tax on taxpayers on top of what they already pay to the Commonwealth. The consequence of this is that states and territories rely on Commonwealth grants for 47% of their expenditure because they have few sources of revenue of their own.[10] Some of these sources, such as business licence and vehicle registration fees, yield relatively small amounts. Mining royalties can yield significant amounts, but only in states with major mining operations. This leaves payroll tax, stamp duties and income from the sale of land. Payroll tax is surely one of the most bizarre taxes one could imagine, as it imposes a disincentive on employers hire employees. But it is stamp duty, which creates barriers to home ownership, population and downsizing, along with the high price of land drip-fed into the market by state governments,[11] which have the most deleterious effect because of the negative effect it has on housing affordability. This provides a clear example of a direct negative effect of federalism on ordinary people. Doing away with the states which rely on these sources of income would eliminate burdens currently borne by taxpayers and people struggling to either enter the housing market or to down-size. It would also open the way for a national government to replace lump-sum stamp duties with a land tax – a step long advocated by economists[12] – and would also open the way for the release of land at prices and in amounts designed to meet the country's housing needs, rather than at artificially high prices designed to prioritise financial support for the existence state and territory governments.

8.4 Refuting Arguments in Favour of Federalism

Despite the overwhelming evidence of the cost of federalism, proponents of the system argue that federations are, on average, more prosperous than unitary states. As an example of this, one can cite the defence of Australian federalism contained in a 2008 report written for the Council for the Australian Federation, whose members are all the state and territory Premiers and Chief Ministers, and which acts as a forum for them to discuss federal matters independently of the Commonwealth. The report, entitled *Federalist Paper I: Australia's Federal Future – Delivering Growth*

[10] For data on the amounts the Commonwealth gives to the States to aid the functions performed by the latter see Australian Government Budget Archive (2016–2017).

[11] See Mansillo (2013).

[12] See, for example, Australian Productivity Commission (2017, Chapter 4).

and Prosperity,[13] argued that over the previous 50 years, federations had delivered better economic performance and better government than unitary states.[14] One problem with the report was its imprecise use of the term 'federation.' As already explained, the key distinction between a unitary state and a federation (and the reason why federations are inherently inefficient) is that whereas in a unitary state the national government can legislate on any topic it chooses, in a federal system the constitution disables the national government from legislating on certain topics. The credibility of the report and its data analysis is therefore questionable given that it erroneously classified South Africa, one of the larger economies feeding into the data, as a federation, which it clearly is not given that its constitution confers on the national parliament the ultimate power to over-ride any law made by a provincial legislature.[15] Indeed, South Africa's Constitutional Court has explicitly stated that South Africa is not a federation and distinguished its constitutional arrangements from those countries which are.[16]

Far more problematic, however, was the flaw in logic underlying the report's assertion that the economic performance of federations was superior to that of unitary states: It is one thing to present data purportedly demonstrating that federations are more prosperous and better governed than unitary states, but a huge leap to say that it is *because* they are federations that those countries are more prosperous and better governed – a step which confuses correlation with causation. A host of social, political, ethnic, climatic, resource and geographical factors determine a country's prosperity, and report adduced no evidence to prove that, of all these factors, it was federalism that provided the key to economic prosperity. Given that the list of countries whose performance the report relied on included the United States, as well as Russia, Brazil, South Africa and Australia – which share the common characteristic of being among the most resource-rich countries in the world – it is wholly unsurprising that the report found then to have delivered higher than average growth as compared to other nations. So far as quality of government is concerned, the question arises as to whether Russia, Brazil and Venezuela, which are federations which are also notoriously corrupt or oppressive (or both) are that way because they are federations or are federations that just happen to be corrupt and / or oppressive? Conversely, are Canada and the United States well-governed because they are federations, or are they federations which happen to be well-governed? Which of these contradictory answers about the effect of federalism – corruption or good government – is correct? Posing these questions makes one realise the logical invalidity of sweeping claims about economic performance and good government as being the product of federalism when in fact they are the product of the interaction of multiple factors which have different impacts in different countries.

[13] Twomey and Withers (2007).

[14] Twomey and Withers (2007, p. 21).

[15] South Africa was not a federation in the 50 year period to which the report refers, nor indeed at any stage since its creation in 1910. Section 44 of its current constitution allows the national parliament to over-ride the laws of provincial legislatures.

[16] *Fose v Minister for Safety and Security* 1997 (3) SA 786 (CC).

Economic arguments aside, what advantages have supporters of federalism adduced as outweighing the enormous costs in time, money and effort that the system imposes on governments, businesses and individuals?

The first argument is that the framers of the constitution created a federation in order to protect the populations of the smaller states (by which is meant the states with smaller populations) from domination by the larger. A subsidiary to this argument is that without federalism, remote populations would be disregarded by Canberra. This argument is so frequently cited that it has attained the status of an article of faith. Yet, like many articles of faith, when exposed to rational analysis it discloses so flaws that are so numerous that it is difficult to decide which to address first. A good starting point is to challenge the underlying assumption that the population of a state such as South Australia, for example, is vulnerable to domination by voters in a state such as New South Wales, which has nearly five times its population. The problem with this argument is that it assumes that simply because a voter lives in South Australia, their vote is necessarily less influential than the vote of a person living in New South Wales and that they are therefore entitled to some sort of protection from voters in New South Wales. In a democracy all votes are of equal impact irrespective of where they are cast (or at least should be, assuming a fair electoral system). The hollowness of this argument is revealed if one considers what would happen if there were *no* states, and that therefore it was not possible to identify New South Wales voters and South Australian voters. What would happen then? The answer is that every vote would correctly be perceived to be the same as every other vote. In other words, it is only because the separate colonies existed before the Australian nation-state came into existence that people began (and have never stopped) thinking in geographical terms because of a false assumption that an Australian person who happens to be located within the boundaries of South Australia has different interests to those who find themselves in New South Wales. Yet the colonies and the states they became were, and are, completely artificial entities, and but for their existence, people would not have thought along state lines and how many seats each state had in parliament.

The argument that federalism is necessary in order to 'protect' the populations of the smaller states also assumes that voters in New South Wales are (at least potentially) antagonistic to voters in South Australia. That argument would make sense only if voters in New South Wales shared a common interest that was different to the interest shared by voters in South Australia. Yet that is patently not the case – in national elections, voters vote according to ideology, their economic interests, the environment, migration policy and a host of other issues too numerous to mention. A farmer in New South Wales has a rationally demonstrable commonality of interests with a farmer in South Australia – and conversely has no commonality of interests with a miner in New South Wales. Voters do not, and never have, voted for state-based parties. In contrast to there being a working class vote or an environmental vote, there is no 'New South Wales interest vote' or 'South Australia interest vote' represented by parties serving the interests of those states in parliament. Instead, Labor MPs from one state vote in the same way as do Labor MPs from any other. The idea that voters in each state have state-specific interests is chimerical, and that is why the entire 'small states versus big states' argument is irrational.

The negative effect of this line of thinking becomes apparent when one considers how it works significant injustice to voters. In the case of the House of Representatives, the fact that s 24 of the constitution allocates a minimum of five House of Representatives seats to each state irrespective of population means that the effect of every vote in the country is distorted by the over-representation of Tasmania which arises from the fact that its population would not be entitled to five seats if allocated pro rata to populations. In other words, each Tasmanian voter has a greater impact on the composition of parliament than does every other voter in the Commonwealth. Furthermore, even leaving aside the over-representation of voters in Tasmania, the allocation of seats among the remaining states is not truly relative to their populations because the constitution prohibits electoral boundaries from crossing state boundaries, which means that some states end up with more seats and others with fewer than their relative populations entitle them to. The distortion is even worse in so far as Senate representation is concerned. The fact that each state is entitled to an equal number of seats irrespective of population means that because the population of New South Wales is 13 times that of Tasmania, each Tasmanian voter has 13 times the influence on the composition of the Senate as compared to a voter in New South Wales. Thus the federal system works great injustice to voters, because the strength of their vote depends entirely on the arbitrary fact of which state they happen to live in.

Federalism also has nothing to do with the urban / rural divide. All states have densely populated urban areas and sparsely populated rural areas – there is no specifically rural state. The frequently made statement that federalism is of particular benefit to inhabitants of rural areas therefore does not make sense. More fundamentally, however, the idea that rural voters *should* be given power disproportionate to their numbers is at odds with the principle that should form the basis of an electoral system, namely that each voter should have equal impact on the composition of parliament. Of course it can validly be argued that because rural voters are in the minority, they are at risk of not receiving the same level of services as do voters in urban areas. However federalism does nothing to solve that. The solution to that problem lies in ensuring needs-based funding of government services. The most effective constitutional mechanism of ensuring that would be for the constitution to protect socio-economic rights that could be vindicated through the courts in instances where government expenditure was not rationally directed by need.

Another frequent justification for federalism is that it allows for diversity and inventiveness. Proponents of this argument often cite the famous statement by United States Supreme Court Justice Louis Brandeis[17] that federalism creates circumstances where 'a state may, if its citizens choose, serve as a laboratory; and try novel social and economic experiments without risk to the rest of the country'. Yet it would be idle to pretend that such a state of affairs exists in Australia. No state or

---

[17] *New State Ice Company v Liebmann* 285 US 262, 311 (1932).

territory has a reputation for doing things in a markedly better way than any of the others. Putting it bluntly, during the 119 years it has existed, Australian federalism simply has not produced an array of social laboratories, each drawing on the best the others have to offer, and thus the diversity argument is entirely unconvincing. But perhaps the most telling counter-argument to the one based on diversity is the fact that that argument is its own worst enemy, because the more diverse the laws of each sub-national unit in a federation, the greater the cost and inconvenience to people and businesses of having to comply with them.

The next argument is that by dividing legislative power between a national and regional governments, federalism protects liberty by preventing one party from controlling all governmental power, as would occur if all legislative power was vested in the national parliament. Leaving aside for the moment that an electoral system reformed in the manner advocated in Chap. 4 would make it virtually impossible for a single party to obtain a majority in the national parliament, this argument confuses the issue of distribution of powers between levels of government with the protection of individuals from tyrannical legislation by government at any level. Federalism has no effect whatsoever on *what* things governments can do to people, only on *which level of government* has the power to do them. Australia is a prime example of this, because state parliaments, unconstrained by a bill of rights, can limit freedoms as they please, and because the same applies to a significant extent to the Commonwealth, which is restrained by only a handful of rights. The mere *distribution* of powers between levels offers no protection for liberty – only a *restraint* on the extent to which governments may use their legislative powers to limit freedom can do that, and the only way of achieving that is by including a comprehensive bill of rights in the constitution. In short, whereas federalism restricts legislative power according to *topics*, a bill of rights restricts legislation in accordance to whether it complies with *values*. Federalism is neither a guarantor of liberty nor even necessarily a promoter of it, because federalism has nothing to say about the balance of power between the individual and government (however many levels of government there may be), which is the essential determinant of whether a society is free or not.

Another frequently cited argument is that a country the size of Australia cannot function without three levels of government. As a starting point, it is important to re-emphasise that the debate about federalism is not one about levels, it is to do with powers – so if the argument relates to the size of the country, the question to pose is: 'Does the size of Australia necessitate that the Constitution hinder the power of the national government in relation to the topics it can legislate on?' Or, the question might also be posed as follows: 'Is there a reason why Australia could not be properly governed unless there is a separate legislature for each of the geographical territories encompassed by the colonial boundaries that existed at the time of federation?' When cast in these terms, it becomes apparent that the burden on those seeking to justify federalism is first to demonstrate a rational basis for the state boundaries, then to demonstrate a rational ground for the existence of separate governments within those areas exercising legislative powers, and finally to demonstrate why the Commonwealth either should not or cannot exercise those powers.

The question of the existence of the states is easily disposed of. There is no rational ground for the particular configuration of their boundaries, because their existence was the result of a series of accidents of history, rather than any pre-planned scheme based on rational criteria. Had Australia been settled as a single colony rather than as six, the states would not exist at all. Conversely, had there been five, seven or ten colonies rather than six, there would be a correspondingly greater number of states. Former Prime Minister Bob Hawke described the states of Australia as a 'dangerous anachronism,' with the boundaries representing nothing more than 'the meanderings of British explorers some 150 years ago.'[18] It is therefore vain to argue that there is something significant about the states as entities which justifies their existence – the truth is that they are wholly artificial creations, born by accident rather than by design.

If the existence of the states as geographical entities is the result of arbitrary factors, so too is their existence as political entities. As already noted, given the lack of inter-colonial altruism at the Constitutional Conventions, it was inevitable, in the *political* sense, that Australia would become a federation – in other words, because it was contrary to the political self-interest of the colonial governments to agree to their own extinction, federalism was the only basis upon which the Commonwealth of Australia stood a chance of being formed. But that does not mean that it was a *practical* necessity that Australia should have become a federation rather than a unitary state.

The lack of substance underlying the argument that Australia is 'too big' for a unitary system and that the size of the individual colonies, and of Australia as a whole necessitated the continuation of the separate colonial / state governments becomes evident when, rather than uncritically accepting this assertion, one considers geographical realities and the actual capacity of governments to function: The distance between Perth and the furthest point of Western Australian territory, which its colonial government was evidently capable of administering in 1901, was 2300 km. This shows that distance was not the tyranny it is said to have been, because if it was possible in that era to govern an area 2300 km away, it would have been no more difficult to govern one 3600 km way (the distance between Canberra and the most distant part of Australia from it), unless one believes that there is some magical point between those two distances at which federation becomes imperative. The capacity of the Western Australian government to administer so large an area in 1901 is also telling when one considers that 2300 km is the same distance as that between the northernmost point in New South Wales and any point in that state and Victoria or South Australia – which suggests that New South Wales, Victoria and South Australia could also all have been administered as a single entity. The argument that the size of Australia necessitated federalism had no foundation in 1901. That is even more the case now, given the advances in transport and communications that have occurred over the past century.

[18] Australian Broadcasting Corporation (1979).

Furthermore, if, as even the most ardent federalist concedes, there is a need for a national government exercising at least some functions, how do they reconcile the apparent ability of the national government to exercise those functions with their argument that geography makes it incapable of exercising others? To take just a few examples from the list of legislative topics allocated to the Commonwealth by the Constitution, why is the Commonwealth capable of administering matters as complex as defence, the welfare system (with Centrelink offices in every corner of the country) as well as the operation of banks and corporations nationwide, and yet (according to federalists) is unable to administer health or education systems throughout the country? Surely the geographic size of Australia should have the same impact on the former as on the latter? Or, to pose the question differently, how is it that the Commonwealth is capable of administering such parochial matters as the positioning of lighthouses and the conduct of meteorological observations which are conferred on it by the Constitution, and yet not capable of administering environmental matters, over which the Constitution denies it authority? Geography did not in 1901, and does not now, render the national government incapable of conducting all necessary aspects of government, which means that the 'too big' for unitary government argument is without foundation.

Next, apart from the fact that there is no geographic or administrative rationale for federalism, the artificiality of Australian federalism is demonstrated by the fact that there is no community of interests served by the state governments. In contrast to those countries in the world where ethnic groups live in distinct geographic areas, and where federalism therefore serves the interest of ethnic self-determination, no such considerations operate in Australia. There is no distinctive political, social, economic or environmental interest shared by all the people living within the bounds of Western Australia, for example, that is exclusive to them and which differentiates them from everyone else living in Australia. Quite the contrary – whereas a miner in Western Australia, for example, has obvious shared political interests with a miner in Queensland, it is equally obvious that he or she has no shared political interests with a grazier in Western Australia. And if state boundaries were changed so that that miner's mine was no longer situated in Western Australia but rather in South Australia, it could not be pretended that his or her political interests would suddenly change so as to accord with those of everyone else in South Australia. In other words, federalism created (or rather, perpetuated) wholly artificial interests unrelated to human condition – namely the interests of the colonial, and subsequently state, politicians who had a stake in the continued existence of their various governments. The existence of these artificial interests is at odds with the reality that there is no such thing as Western Australian inflation or as the South Australian environment. Similarly, a Tasmanian suffering from diabetes has the same needs as a diabetic in Victoria and primary school student in the ACT has the same educational needs as one in Queensland. Human interests are national interests, and from this it follows that most interests should be addressed by a national government.

This artificiality of state boundaries is perhaps no more clearly exposed than during the annual dispute between the Commonwealth on the one hand and the states and territories on the other over the size of the annual grant from its GST revenues that the Commonwealth will give the states and territories. Every year the Commonwealth Grants Commission recommends how much money each state and territory should receive under a formula which is designed to ensure that each jurisdiction is able to provide the same services per capita its residents. The formula thus takes into effect things such as how widely distributed each state and territory's population is and how easy or difficult it is to deliver services to them. However, the Commission's recommendations are advisory only, and the Commonwealth may depart from them. This means that every year an argument occurs between the Commonwealth and the other jurisdictions over how much each should receive, and every year the arguments are the same. States with booming economies – which therefore contribute more to the Commonwealth's GST revenue than do less prosperous states – complain that they are 'losing' money to the less prosperous jurisdictions which end up receiving more from the Treasury (per capita) than their residents contribute to it. But the annual characterisation of some states as 'winners' and others as 'losers', which implies that each jurisdiction should receive from the Commonwealth as much money as its residents contribute (in which case of course the entire distribution process could be replaced simply by a refund to each state of the GST collected in it) masks the fact that whether a state or territory is a 'winner' or 'loser 'depends entirely on the happenstance of the operation of economic forces which do not respect state and territory boundaries. In other words, changes in the allocations of money to state and territory governments following the annual squabble between governments simply results in the Commonwealth trying to compensate for natural economic cycles in different states. How much each government ultimately gets cannot be characterised as being right or wrong, just or unjust, it is simply the result of the fact that in any geographic area with randomly drawn boundaries the economies of some regions will go up some will go down in accordance with economic forces. Thus during the period 2000–2008, when Western Australia was experiencing a mining boom, its government regularly complained that the grants system was unfair because the state was a net contributor to other jurisdictions, whereas in the period since 2008, it has argued that it is entitled to more revenue than it contributes because the state economy has contracted and it is unable to afford the services it previously could.

Of course, if the state and territory boundaries were differently drawn, there would be different political entities complaining that they were paying too much or receiving too little, which all goes to demonstrate that the entire system of Commonwealth grants is a product of the existence of the arbitrariness of state and territory boundaries. To express it another way, if, in the nineteenth century, instead of Australia being divided along territorial lines, the population had been divided into three political communities consisting of green, brown and blue-eyed people, and those communities' identities had been incorporated into the Constitution, then they would naturally have competed for grants, with each community being affected by the rise and fall in their circumstances from time to time, as is the case with the states now. The point is that those political identities based on eye-colour are as random as those that exist by virtue of the existence of the states. The only reason the annual grants-allocation dispute occurs is because every year economic forces have different effects on the areas we refer to as states and territories, but such arguments would arise in any system where lines were drawn across the country and people calculated which parts had generated more revenue and which parts had generated less – all of which is inconsequential if one understands that in any country, there are parts that are richer and parts that are poorer, that these change from time to time, and that the national interest obviously involves the allocation of funds 'taken' from the former and 'given' to the latter. It is only because we have state boundaries and can calculate which of these artificial parts (as arbitrarily drawn) are richer or poorer in any given year, and whose governments therefore complain of supposed inequities, that the concept of funding to states and territories has any meaning. The reality is that Australia has a national economy not eight separate economies, and that in the absence of federalism, government expenditure would simply involve the allocation of funds to projects, parts of the country and people as changing circumstances required, rather than requiring the propitiation of the governments of artificial sub-national units, whose electoral fortunes depend on 'winning' the battle over grants.

8.5 Confusion Between Levels and Powers

As indicated at the start of this chapter, in Australia the debate on federalism has been clouded by confusion between two separate questions – the question of how many levels of government there should be and the question of what powers the levels should have. The authors of *Federalist Paper I: Australia's Federal Future – Delivering Growth and Prosperity* cite the example of France, Italy and Spain, none of which are federations, as illustrating the benefits of federalism, arguing that those countries have found it beneficial to delegate power to sub-national units. But, if anything, these examples illustrate the *redundancy* of federalism in that they show that there is nothing to prevent a unitary state from delegating power to lower levels of government. In other words, it is critical to appreciate that both unitary and federal states can have different levels of government, but the difference between the systems is that whereas in a unitary system a national parliament has full legislative capacity, including the capacity to distribute legislative power to other levels of government and to change that distribution in light of experience and changing needs, in a federal system the legislative capacity of each level is limited by the constitution, and the constitution cannot be varied without the co-operation of the levels. Because the constitution in a federal system limits the topics on which the national government can legislate, the national government cannot address problems which, although national in their impact, do not fall within national legislative power as conferred by the constitution. Such problems can therefore be solved only after a laborious process – which may take years – of getting the other levels of government to co-operate in setting up a legislative scheme. Furthermore, because the a federal constitution actually prevents the national government from redistributing functions between it and sub-national units in light of experience, federations have a far diminished capacity to respond to the changing needs of the times – in contrast to unitary states such as France, Spain and Italy. This fettering of the power of the national government is the critical weakness of federation, and is one which defenders of federalism naturally avoid addressing, because no sensible argument can be presented to justify how putting shackles on the capacity of the national government can be conducive efficiency in terms of time, money and effort – an argument which reveals its weakness merely by being stated.

By setting the allocation of legislative capacity in concrete, a federal constitution denies the political system the flexibility it would have in a unitary state, in which the central parliament has plenary power and so can legislate on any topic it chooses and can allocate legislative capacity to sub-national units as required by changing circumstances. Since the allocation of powers to levels does not involve questions of moral principle and is rather a purely practical issue, it follows that practicality should determine the mechanism that should govern that allocation, and because it is obviously preferable to have flexibility rather than to have the allocation cemented into a constitution, it follows that, from a practical point of view, the unitary system is to be preferred because of its simplicity of operation, its efficiency and its capacity to respond to change. The reason why a unitary system confers these advantages stems from the fact that there would be a single legal system for the entire country, rather than the nine that we have in Australia. The importance of this is difficult to overstate: It is the fact that there are multiple legal systems and, most importantly, that there is no way of eliminating them short of changing the constitution, that is the key underlying cause of the inefficiency and waste that bedevil federal systems.

If we had a unitary system, parliament could create lower levels of government and decide which powers would be distributed to them. What principle should determine that distribution? Much is made by defenders of federalism of the idea of 'subsidiarity', which is the idea that the authority to manage issues should be conferred on the smallest and most immediate level of government capable of resolving them. However, there are three reasons why subsidiarity does not justify federalism: The first and most obvious is that maximised devolution to lower levels cannot be the sole determinant of how authority is distributed. Given free reign, subsidiarity could lead to the creation of an ever expanding number of units of government of ever decreasing size. Other key factors – in particular that of efficiency – also need to be balanced in the scale, because subsidiarity has the potential (which has unfortunately been realised in Australia) of leading to an enormous waste of time, effort and money.

The second reason why subsidiarity does not necessarily justify federalism is the rider to the subsidiarity principle – usually ignored by proponents of federalism – contained in the phrase 'capable of resolving them'. The fact is that in country as integrated as we have become since 1901, there are very few issues which are capable of being properly addressed at the sub-national level. Trade and commerce, health, education and environmental protection, to name but a handful of the areas of authority denied to the Commonwealth under the Constitution, are all issues calling for national uniformity rather than localised disparity. Indeed, I would argue that the guiding principle in the allocation of authority should be the *reverse* of subsidiarity – that in order to achieve efficiency and uniformity, and to lessen the burden imposed on human activity by multiple legal systems, authority to manage issues should be conferred on the *highest* level of government capable of exercising them, and that only where an issue is obviously one that affects *a specific community in distinction from others* (an important criterion which is discussed later on) should authority be devolved.

The third and final reason why subsidiarity does not justify federalism is because the devolution of authority to lower levels of government does not and should not require the removal from the national government of the capacity to decide the very question of to which authorities various functions should be devolved – which is what federal constitutions do.

As mentioned earlier, the fettering of the power of the national government is the key defect of the federal system and is the root cause of the inefficiencies in the system. Even the most ardent anti-federalist does not deny that powers may need to be devolved to lower levels of government where practicality and efficiency require. That is something that is done by national governments in unitary states all over the world. But it is a very different – and unnecessary – step to say that the way devolution is structured, and the topics that each level of government can legislate on, should be cemented into the constitution and thus be unchangeable except by constitutional amendment. Circumstances change all the time, and therefore so does what is the most administratively efficient way of addressing them. A distribution of powers between levels of government that is effective in one decade may be found not to be in the next. Unpredictability of events requires that a government must have the ability to respond quickly to the circumstances it faces – including, if necessary, by re-arranging the allocation of powers to levels of government. In other words, it is not just the idea that the allocation as it existed in 1901 is suitable today is absurd (although it certainly is) but that there is some benefit to be derived from denying the national government the power it needs to vary the distribution over time.

8.6 A New Model of Delegated Power

Assuming that Australia was a unitary state, and that parliament had the ability to create sub-national institutions and delegate powers to them, how should that task be done? Instead of working on the flawed assumption that drawing arbitrary lines on maps creates communities of interest for which governmental institutions must be created, a rational allocation of powers would be done first with reference to function and only then with reference to geography. The key question to ask would be: ‘Which issues so obviously affect specific communities in a way which is separate from how they affect other communities, and which therefore require that each community should be granted control over them?’ When framed in those terms, it becomes clear that there are relatively few issues that affect only specific populations as compared to the population as a whole to the extent that their management requires the establishment of subordinate governmental institutions. Whether that is necessary will always be a matter of practicality. Most services will be delivered most efficiently by a single national system. But obvious examples of matters which only affect discrete communities are those such as water supply, sewerage, refuse removal, planning approval and local transport – in other words, matters of a type that have long been under the control of local government.

As matters currently stand, local governments are creatures of the states. Such powers as they have to make local laws and to administer them derive from state legislation which delegates legislative and executive power to them. This role of conferring delegated power would fall to the Commonwealth if state governments were abolished. There would be no need to mention this power in the Constitution – it would simply be part of the plenary legislative power of the Commonwealth. Having said that, there would be no harm in referring to the fact that the Commonwealth could delegate powers to sub-national units in order to mark their significance under the new constitutional order.

Here it is worthwhile saying something about regional governments. Currently, local authorities vary enormously in size, from small council areas in densely populated cities to large shires in sparsely populated country areas. There may be merit in the Commonwealth creating larger, regional units in substitution for some local government areas. A survey conducted by Newspoll on behalf of Griffith University's Federalism Project in 2010[19] found that 42% of respondents favoured the creation of regional governments. Most people are more concerned about the quality of government services than which government delivers them, and for this reason, regional interests are often more important to them than state-based interests. For example, the residents of Queanbeyan in New South Wales, just across the border from the ACT, are more interested in the level of care that they will get from hospitals in Canberra, which are closer to them than any comparable facilities in New South Wales. Similarly, the inhabitants of Albury-Wodonga and the surrounding Border region have far greater community of interest with each other than they do with other areas of their own states. It may therefore be advantageous were the Commonwealth to delegate the power to make local laws to regional, or 'super-local' governments (often crossing what were formerly the boundaries between states), in cases where geography and economic factors indicate that that would be the best course to adopt.

Apart from the amalgamation of former local authorities into regional governments, another way of delegating authority could be for particular matters to be placed under the control of agencies operating under the joint control of several local governments. For example, a number of local governments might establish a joint agency for the co-ordinated the management of a common source of water. In all cases their existence, responsibilities and structure would be malleable according to the exigencies of the times.

The key point is that a system where the national government had the power to allocate functions (and, importantly, to re-allocate them in light of experience) to sub-national units in accordance with what is objectively necessary at the particular time

---

[19] Brown and Levy (2010, p. 10).

would be inherently flexible, and would make it possible to take into account the specific needs of specific parts of the country. The focus would always be on what practicality dictated: Function would drive form, in contrast to the current federal system where function is subordinated to the existence of the states and territories, with their arbitrarily-drawn boundaries which bear no relation to administrative reality.

A prime example of the way in which the existence of the states has compromised policy-making is provided by the ongoing disputes over the Murray-Darling Basin Authority, the purpose of which is to manage the Murray-Darling river system, including the key issue of water allocation. The Authority is charged with the implementation of the Murray-Darling Basin Plan, drafted after a tortuous series of negotiations between the Commonwealth, South Australia, Victoria, New South Wales, the ACT and Queensland, through whose territory the rivers flow. The plan is vulnerable because its existence depends on the continued willingness of the four states and the ACT to abide by it.[20] Far from being a triumph of federalism, the plan illustrates the absurdity of a system which makes the allocation of a natural resource contingent on whether artificial entities consider it to be in their interests to continue to co-operate in the arrangement. As any water scientist would tell you, there is no Queensland river, Victorian river or South Australian river – there is simply a river, which rolls on regardless of artificial claims which exist only because of the existence of political entities through whose artificially-bounded territories the river flows. If it were not for the existence of the states and territories whose governments argue over allocations in order to please their electorates, no-one would think of the river flow in terms of sectional interests. If we had a unitary system, there would be no need for the government to secure the agreement of governments representing arbitrary geographical areas – the river system would simply be administered in the interests of the nation as a whole. The same problem arises across a range of issues – energy supply being another good example – where economic realities require national solutions and where state boundaries are (or ought to be) irrelevant.

There is no doubt that there is significant public appetite for the abandonment of federalism, as has been borne out by a number of surveys. A survey conducted by Newspoll on behalf of Griffith University's Federalism Project in 2010 found that 39% of respondents wanted State governments abolished,[21] 42% favoured the creation of regional governments,[22] and that of the variety of possible options for the reconfiguration of Australian government, the most popular option, supported by 26% of those surveyed, was for Australia to be governed by a national government in combination with regional or local governments.[23] A particularly interesting

[20] Australian Broadcasting Corporation (2018).

[21] Brown and Levy (2010, p. 11).

[22] Brown and Levy (2010, p. 11).

[23] Brown and Levy (2010, p. 12). The options were: maintenance of the current status quo of federal, State and local governments; having federal and regional / local governments; having federal and States governments with the abolition of local government; have federal, State, regional and local governments; have no federal government (which begs the question of how Australia would function internationally!); have only federal government; or have more States.

finding was that most respondents (49% versus 44%) preferred that most decisions be taken by the highest level of government possible – in other words favoured the *opposite* of subsidiarity.[24] A subsequent survey by the Griffiths University Centre for Governance & Public Policy conducted in 2014 found that 71% of respondents favoured changing the current system (among whom there were differing preferences for the allocation of functions to national, regional and local governments).[25]

Even more significant however were the results of a Galaxy poll conducted on behalf of the public lobbying group Beyond Federation in 2013, which found that 78% of respondents favoured having a single set of laws for the country.[26] The importance of this result is that it focusses attention on the existence of multiple legal systems, which is the key source of the inefficiency of federalism. Interestingly, a follow-up poll conducted in 2014, found that 39% of those polled favoured abolition of the States, 31% were opposed and 30% were undecided. Those results raise an interesting question: Why, if 78% of respondents to the 2013 poll favoured a single set of laws did only 39% of the respondents in 2014 favour abolition of the states? Surely such a convincing majority in favour of a single legal system should have translated into support for abolition of federalism and its division of law-making authority between the Commonwealth and the states? It is unfortunate that the question about legal systems and the question about federalism were not asked in the same survey, but assuming the statistical validity of both sets of results, the inconsistency between the results suggests that there is a gap between what people want and their understanding of how the Constitution operates. In other words, there appears to be a failure to appreciate that there cannot be a single set of laws for the entire country in tandem with the existence of states wielding legislative power that cannot be over-ridden by the Commonwealth. To put it in a nutshell, having a single set of laws for the country cannot be achieved without the abolition of the federal system.

If we were writing the Constitution from new, would we divide Australia into states, each with its own legal system, and with a national government with limited capacity to govern a country which is obviously an economically integrated whole? If the answer to that is 'No', then why would we maintain such a system? The adoption of a unitary model would substitute a single legal system for the multiplicity currently in existence. Gone would be different sets of laws that individuals have to navigate when moving from one jurisdiction to another, and which businesses have to comply with as they operate in multiple jurisdictions. Gone too would be the waste of government time and resources currently absorbed in determining which level of government has the legislative capacity to address issues and in managing legal disputes which arise when there are inter-jurisdictional disputes on that point. Gone too would be the need for years of negotiations between jurisdictions in order to achieve uniformity in legislation throughout the country. We would instead have a system which was subject to a single legal system, which was efficient in its deployment of resources and which had the flexibility to enable the national

[24] Brown and Levy (2010, p. 9).

[25] Brown (2014, p. 15).

[26] Galaxy Research (2013).

government to delegate powers to local and regional governments according to the changing needs of the times.

Two final implications of de-federalisation need to be mentioned:

8.7 The Senate

The Senate was established as a 'states' house', and so de-federalisation and the consequent abolition of the states would render the Senate redundant. It is a notorious fact of Australian constitutional history that the Senate never discharged the role for which it was intended, because from its inception, Senators voted along party rather than state lines. Furthermore, the fact that each state receives equal representation in the Senate irrespective of population embeds gross distortion of voting power in the Constitution, because the weight of a person's vote depends on which state they live in, with the result that, on current figures, a vote in Tasmania has 13 times the effect of a vote cast in New South Wales. This is obviously incompatible with the voting system recommended in Chap. 4, which is based on electorates unconstrained by state boundaries and on the principle that, as far as practicable, each person's vote should have the same impact. Although the Senate has sometimes proved useful as a chamber in which ad hoc committees could be established to inquire into government misconduct, the adoption of the reforms recommended in Chap. 7 – in particular the imposition on members of the executive branch of a constitutional duty to answer questions put by committees – would enable committees of the House of Representatives to subject the government to far more scrutiny than the Senate can today. Finally, apart from being tied to the federal system, having a second chamber does not in itself confer any special benefit – there is no logical reason to think that having Bills debated by two groups of people rather than one improves law-making. Thus the loss of the Senate would have no negative effect on the way Australia is governed, because reforms advocated in this book, in particular having a House of Representatives elected according to a fair voting system and with committees having vastly increased powers of scrutiny, would provide far more effective oversight of governmental action than has ever been provided by the Senate.

8.8 Constitutional Amendment

The other change that would follow from the elimination of the states would be in relation to constitutional amendment. As discussed in Chap. 3, an amendment to the Constitution must be approved of by a majority of voters nationwide plus a majority in a majority of states. This is obviously anti-democratic, since the fact that where votes are cast partly determines the outcome of a referendum means that each voter does not have equal influence over whether an amendment succeeds or not. The elimination of the states would mean that constitutional amendments would be determined by a nationwide vote in which voters all had the same influence as each other. The question that would then arise is what majority should be needed to amend the constitution. Here I would argue that a distinction needs to be drawn between amendments affecting fundamental rights and other parts of the constitution. Given that, as discussed in Chap. 5, a bill of rights serves to protect the individual from majorities, it would be anomalous if the bill of rights could be amended by a simple majority. A very high majority – one that would make amendment extremely difficult to achieve – should therefore be required for amendments to the bill of rights. I would therefore suggest that whereas in general, a simple majority should suffice for amending the constitution, a 75% majority should be required for amendments to the bill of rights. However even this protection could be circumvented unless those parts of the constitution providing for the supremacy of the constitution as a source of law and its enforceability, along with the independence of the judiciary as well of course as the amendment mechanism itself, were not similarly protected. Therefore those parts of the constitution should also be amendable only by a 75% majority.

References

Australian Broadcasting Corporation (1979) The Boyer lectures. Bob Hawke. The resolution of conflict. https://www.abc.net.au/news/2019-06-13/bob-hawke-boyer/11207418. Accessed 21 Oct 2019

Australian Broadcasting Corporation (2018) Murray-Darling basin: NSW moves to withdraw from plan as SA urges Commonwealth action. ABC News. 15 February 2018

Australian Bureau of Statistics (2019) Interstate migration by states and territories of arrival and departure by sex. http://stat.data.abs.gov.au/Index.aspx?DataSetCode=ABS_DEM_QIM. Accessed 8 Oct 2019

Australian Government (2002–2003) Budget archive. https://archive.budget.gov.au/2002-03/index.htm. Accessed 8 Oct 2019

Australian Government (2016–2017) Budget archive. https://archive.budget.gov.au/2016-17/index.htm. Accessed 8 Oct 2019

Australian Productivity Commission (2017) Shifting the dial: 5 year productivity review. https://www.pc.gov.au/inquiries/completed/productivity-review/report. Accessed 8 Oct 2019

Brown A (2014) Australian constitutional values survey 2014. Griffith University, Nathan

Brown A, Levy R (2010) Australian constitutional values survey 2010. Griffith Law School, Gold Coast

Drummond M (2007) Costing constitutional change: estimates of the financial benefits of new states, regional governments, unification and related reforms. PhD Thesis, University of Canberra

Galaxy Research (2013) Australian laws study. http://members.webone.com.au/~markld/PubPol/GSR/Polls/Galaxy%20Australian%20Laws%20Study%20February%202013.pdf. Accessed 8 Oct 2019

Hutchinson S, Eddie R (2019) Defamation fears leave Turnbull's publisher in insurance lurch. The Age. 19 June 2019

Mansillo L (2013) Australian housing is too expensive. So why can't we talk about it? The Guardian. 24 July 2013

Reserve Bank of Australia – Inflation calculator. https://www.rba.gov.au/calculator/annualDecimal.html. Accessed 8 Oct 2019

Twomey A, Withers G (2007) Federalist paper I: Australia's federal future – delivering growth and prosperity. Council for the Australian Federation, Adelaide

Chapter 9
Indigenous People and the Constitution

Abstract This chapter begins by re-defining the debate on this topic, arguing that it is incorrect, and conducive to tokenism, to refer to the 'constitutional recognition' of Indigenous people, whereas what is at issue is the realisation of the constitutional rights of Indigenous people. The chapter discusses the recent inquiries into the constitutional position of Indigenous people before analysing the often-misunderstood concepts of 'sovereignty' and 'treaty.' The chapter proposes constitutional mechanisms that could be used to achieve Indigenous self-government and argues that this would be buttressed by the inclusion of rights to culture and to equality in the bill of rights. The chapter concludes by arguing that the creation of an Indigenous Voice to Parliament would not be inconsistent with representative government as some have argued.

9.1 Debate on Indigenous People and the Constitution

Perhaps nothing more powerfully illustrates Australia's outdated and ungenerous attitude to Indigenous peoples than the government's dismissive response to the 2017 Uluru Statement from the Heart issued by the Aboriginal and Torres Strait Islander National Constitutional Convention.[1] Prime Minster Turnbull's rejection of the key recommendation in the Statement – that an Indigenous voice to Parliament be enshrined in the Constitution – marked a depressing finale to a process which had dragged on for seven years and which manifested everything that is wrong about constitutional debate in Australia, including a focus on pragmatism rather than on values as well as the making of misleading statements about the constitutional implications of proposed reform. Coming a close second to Turnbull's rebuff in demonstrating disregard for Indigenous people was the hostile reaction from many public figures to the inclusion in the Constitution of a right not to be discriminated against on grounds of race.

Formal consideration of the constitutional position of Indigenous people began with the establishment in 2010 of an Expert Panel on the Constitutional Recognition of Aboriginal and Torres Strait Islander Peoples by the Gillard government. In its

[1] Australian Government (2017).

B. Harris, *Constitutional Reform as a Remedy for Political Disenchantment in Australia*, https://doi.org/10.1007/978-981-15-3599-4_9

report presented in 2012,[2] the Panel made a number of recommendations, including the removal of constitutional provisions which could be used to discriminate against Indigenous people, the replacement of the existing races power with a power to make laws relating to Indigenous people, the inclusion in the Constitution of a right not to be discriminated against on grounds of race and an acknowledgement that Indigenous languages form part of Australia's heritage This was followed by the establishment of a Joint Select Committee on Recognition of Aboriginal and Torres Strait Islander Peoples. Its report, presented in 2015,[3] recommended that the various options for constitutional change be further investigated, and that the government establish constitutional conventions both for the public as a whole and for Indigenous people specifically, to consult on the various options. This led to the appointment of a Referendum Council, which was tasked with engaging in public consultation and advising on the next steps towards Indigenous recognition. The final stage of the consultation process was the holding of the National Constitutional Convention of Indigenous people at Uluru, which in 2017 produced the Uluru Statement from the Heart.[4] The Statement called for the establishment in the constitution of a first nations' Voice to Parliament, a body that would advise parliament on the effect of proposed legislation on Indigenous people and the establishment of a Makarrata Commission which would guide the making of treaties between Australian governments and Indigenous peoples and which would also engage in a process of truth-telling about colonisation and its consequences. This recommendation was adopted by the Referendum Council in its 2017 report.[5] Following this, in 2018, a parliamentary Joint Select Committee on Constitutional Recognition relating to Aboriginal and Torres Strait Islander Peoples recommended that steps be taken to establish the Voice to Parliament, albeit without defining by what mechanism the Voice should operate.[6] Yet, after all these years of consultation and reports, and despite governments saying that the process should result in concrete rather than merely symbolic change, the proposal that there should be a Voice to Parliament was entirely too concrete for the government, which rejected it out of hand.[7]

9.2 A Question of Terminology

The general failure to appreciate what is involved in this debate is reflected at the most fundamental level in the habitual use of the term 'constitutional recognition of Indigenous people.' Even the name of the organisation whose mission it is to

[2] Commonwealth of Australia (2012).

[3] Parliament of Australia (2015).

[4] Referendum Council (2017a).

[5] Referendum Council (2017b).

[6] Parliament of Australia (2018).

[7] Australian Government (2017).

advance the constitutional position of Indigenous people – Recognise – reflects this phrase, no doubt because the concept of 'recognition' has become too familiar to the public for other words to be used. But use of the word 'recognition' is in reality indicative of a general misunderstanding both of the nature of the task at hand and of the nature of a constitution. A constitution, like any law, is not a document in which facts are 'recognised'. It is one in which rights and duties are created. So simply to include in the constitution a statement of recognition, to the effect that Australia has Indigenous people and that they were the original inhabitants of the continent – worthy as that might be of inclusion in a preamble – would have no effect in addressing the concerns of Indigenous people. There is irony in the fact that at the same time as he was arguing that Indigenous recognition should not merely be symbolic, John Howard advocated inclusion of recognition of Indigenous people in a preamble, which would have been of purely symbolic importance, but failed to propose constitutional change that would have affected the legal rights of Indigenous people. Use of the term 'recognition' thus masks the real issues involved, as it implies that the position of Indigenous people is something that can be satisfied by mere symbolism. Finding some term other than 'recognition' is therefore not just a matter of semantics, it is an important first step in ensuring that the debate focuses on the real issue, which is the acknowledgement of the *constitutional rights* of Indigenous people. This is the term that is used in this chapter.

Another preliminary issue that needs to be addressed is the claim that is often made that instead of focussing on the constitutional position, we should instead be thinking about 'practical' things, such as health, housing and education, as though the two were mutually exclusive. As was pointed out by Albie Sachs, former Justice of the South African Constitutional Court, respect for human dignity embraces both the right to freedom and the right to bread.[8] Thus, Indigenous people, like people everywhere, have a claim to both justice and material advancement – there is no reason why the former should be deferred in order to achieve the latter. Furthermore, as is argued towards the end of this chapter, constitutional rights can in fact play a powerful role in securing material advancement.

9.3 The Special Position of Indigenous People

Before discussing how the rights of Indigenous people might be protected by the Constitution, one needs to address the 'why'. Can the treatment of Indigenous people as a distinct group be justified in principle? Does not the idea that all people have equal rights derived from the value of dignity identified in Chap. 2, militate against differential treatment of Indigenous people? This is an important issue, because rejection of 'special treatment' of Indigenous people has provided opponents of

[8] Sachs (2009, p. 173).

inclusion of Indigenous rights in the Constitution with an emotive argument, manifested either in outright racism or in more subtle forms as in the government's statement that an Indigenous Voice to Parliament would be inconsistent with the equal civic rights of all citizens.[9] So on what ground might rights attach differentially to Indigenous people?

Key to answering this question is an appreciation that whereas some rights are individual, others are exercised either individually or in community, while yet others are by their nature purely communal. This is reflected in the fact that statements about the rights of 'Indigenous people' refer to the rights of Indigenous people as individuals, whereas statements referring to the rights of 'Indigenous peoples' refer to the collective rights of Indigenous communities. To take some examples: The right to be afforded due process upon detention is a right exercised by an individual. The right to religious freedom can be exercised either individually or communally. The right to maintain the very existence of a group – its identity and its sovereignty – is a communal right. No-one could deny that, if Australia was to be conquered by an invader, its identity as a state eliminated and its institutions of government suppressed, this would amount to a deprivation of the rights of the Australian community as a whole. One would surely feel great sympathy for all Australians in such circumstances and would argue that they were entitled to redress. Yet this is exactly what happened to Indigenous people at the time of acquisition of Australia by the Crown: Because of that acquisition, they became conquered people, and the question facing us today is how to redress the consequences of that fact. The fact that Indigenous Australians were exposed to the benefits of a modern and technologically advanced society does not in itself justify conquest, although it is frequently cited as such by conservatives:[10] One could imagine an alternate past, in which interactions between Britain and the Indigenous peoples were peaceful in nature and as a result of which modernity was adopted through processes of trade and cultural exchange.

The fact of conquest also makes apparent the difference between Indigenous Australians and the many other equally well-defined groups within Australia, such as of British, Irish, Chinese, Greek or Italian descent: Of all the ethnic groups who collectively comprise the population of Australia, only the Indigenous inhabitants were subject to conquest and were therefore involuntary participants in the union of cultures, and while it is true that many of the initial settlers were convicts transported to Australia against their will, they brought their law and culture with them. All subsequent migrants who came to Australia did so willingly, and accepting that although there was no impediment to their continuing to practice cultural traditions in their new country, they would nevertheless become members of a broader Australian body politic, of which their own culture would form a component. Indigenous Australians on the other hand had no choice as to whether to accept settlers and their imported culture, and within a century of colonisation, Indigenous

[9] Thorpe (2017).

[10] Karp (2018).

peoples found that their cultures had been displaced from their previous dominant position and that the success, and indeed survival, of Indigenous people was tied to adaptation to the culture of the colonisers. There is thus a clear difference between Indigenous and other Australians, in that the former were conquered peoples, whose sovereignty, law and culture were surrendered involuntarily. If one accepts that a community has a right to exist and not to have that existence terminated by conquest, it follows that the Crown's acquisition of sovereignty over Australia amounted to a breach of the communal rights of its various Indigenous peoples. The question which then arises is what these various communal rights are and how they can now practicably be afforded protection, notwithstanding the passage of time since settlement.

9.4 Sovereignty

Obviously the most fundamental right a community enjoys is that of sovereignty. Some people argue that Australian governments recognise that Indigenous peoples continue to exercise surviving pre-colonisation sovereignty, and should enter into treaties (either a single treaty on behalf of all Indigenous peoples, or individual treaties with them separately) as a means of regulating the relationship between them and Indigenous peoples. Opponents of this argument (not the least successive Australian governments) state that Indigenous sovereignty no longer survives and that therefore it is not possible to enter into treaties with Indigenous peoples. The truth lies between these two positions, and because the terms 'sovereignty' 'treaty' are frequently misunderstood, an important first step in understanding the issues is to appreciate what these terms mean.[11]

The term 'sovereignty' is used in both a political sense and in a legal theory sense.[12] In a political sense, sovereignty vests in whoever ultimately allocates political power in the state. In *McGinty v Western Australia*,[13] the High Court held that because political authority derives from the Constitution, and because the voters can change the Constitution, sovereignty vests in the people. However, given that the authority of the people to change the Constitution comes from the Constitution itself, the question which must then be answered is where does the authority of the Constitution come from? That is a question which can be answered by determining where sovereignty comes from as a matter of legal theory. This requires that one trace authority back though history until one reaches what the legal philosopher Hans Kelsen referred to as the *grundnorm* – the original source of authority, which always depends on some historical event. So, the answer to the question of where

[11] For an excellent analysis of sovereignty and its implication for treaty-making see Brennan et al. (2004).

[12] O'Sullivan (2007, p. 27).

[13] (1996) 186 CLR 140, 230.

the authority of the Constitution comes from is that it came from the Parliament of the United Kingdom which enacted it through the *Commonwealth of Australia Constitution Act 1900* (UK). But from where did the United Kingdom Parliament get its authority to enact a constitution for Australia? The answer to that question – further back than which one cannot go in Australia – is that authority was not obtained through any legal process but was simply taken by Crown when Australia was colonised. Therefore, although while it might be true to say that, from a political perspective, the Australian people are 'sovereign' in the sense that it is they who elect the government, the fact is that from a legal perspective, the ultimate source of the authority of the Constitution is the acquisition of sovereignty by the Crown. Therefore, to understand what happened to the sovereignty of the Indigenous peoples of Australia, one has to examine the legal basis for colonisation and compare what happened in Australia to what happened in other settler societies.

According to eighteenth century international law (and of course here we are referring to European notions of international law – not the law of the Indigenous peoples), acquisition of another territory could occur in one of three ways – by settlement of *terra nullius* (uninhabited territory), in which case, given the absence of any other law, the coloniser's law applied; by cession of territory by its previous sovereign, in which case the existing legal system carried on in effect unless modified by the colonising power; or by conquest, in which case the legal system of the conquered power remained in force until modified by the conqueror.

This taxonomy was however subject to an important qualification: A territory that was in fact inhabited was deemed to be *terra nullius* where its population lacked what contemporary Europeans considered to be the hallmarks of a 'civilised' legal system. For this reason, acquisition of sovereignty over Australia by the United Kingdom (proclaimed by Captain Cook in 1770, and re-iterated by Governor Phillip in 1788) proceeded on the basis that it had occurred by settlement, even though Australia was obviously inhabited by its Indigenous people who, moreover, lived in settled societies.[14] For this reason, English law was deemed to have become applicable upon settlement, and Indigenous law never to have existed.

The famous decision in *Mabo v Queensland (No 2)*[15] altered this view of the law. The case concerned the specific issue of whether Torres Straits Islanders had retained title to their land after colonisation. The High Court rejected the *terra nullius* doctrine and held that pre-existing Indigenous rights to land—referred to as native title—continued in existence after the assumption of sovereignty by the United Kingdom. People who could prove that they held native title, which would be done by reference to Indigenous customary law, would be entitled to continue to exercise the rights they had under such title unless it had been overridden by some positive legal act.

However it is important to understand that the High Court did *not* take the step of saying that sovereignty had been acquired over Australia by conquest or cession and

[14] For a comprehensive discussion of Indigenous society before colonisation see Pascoe (2018).
[15] (1992) 175 CLR 1.

that all Indigenous law not displaced by a positive act had survived – even though one might think this was the logical consequence of the court's rejection of *terra nullius*, and its statement that reference could be had to Indigenous law in proving the existence of native title. Instead, the court maintained the position that Australia had been acquired by settlement and that United Kingdom law had become the general law, but held that when sovereignty was acquired by the United Kingdom, native title continued in existence *as part of the common law of Australia*, not as the product of a surviving Indigenous sovereignty. Under this approach, Indigenous law is not recognised as being of effect – its contents are simply used as evidence in determining whether native title exists under common law and, if it does, then in which Indigenous community it vests. With respect, the decision in *Mabo*, while welcome, was contradictory, in that it mixed a consequence of acquisition by settlement (reception of the common law and obliteration of Indigenous law) with a consequence of acquisition by conquest (survival of Indigenous law, at least as a method of proving legal rights).

Unsurprisingly, under the received legal system (that is, the legal system brought to Australia from the United Kingdom and subsequently developed by Australian institutions), the Crown's acquisition of sovereignty is unchallengeable in Australian courts. This is because under both the common law and international law whether sovereignty has been acquired depends solely on whether or not the regime claiming it has been effective in asserting its control over the territory in question. In other words, whether the transfer of sovereignty was agreed to by the peoples from whom it was transferred is irrelevant from a legal point of view. Although this test leads to unjust results in that it validates conquest, there is no practical alternative way of determining whether a regime has acquired sovereignty: In circumstances where a new regime has succeeded in achieving control over territory and has supplanted the pre-existing regime, one would be left in the position of saying that no-one has sovereignty unless one recognised the effectiveness of the new regime. In other words, acquisition of sovereignty is as much a matter of historical reality as it is of law.

For this reason, the High Court has affirmed that nothing in the *Mabo* decision changed the prevailing legal position, which is that the acquisition of sovereignty by the Crown extinguished any Indigenous sovereignty that might have existed, along with Indigenous law.[16] This has significant implications for the claims that Indigenous peoples never surrendered their sovereignty and that therefore negotiations between Indigenous peoples and Australian governments must proceed on the basis that it is between sovereign entities. One has sympathy with this view, given that what the legal system refers to as 'settlement' was, in reality, conquest, slaughter and dispossession. Yet because given that the received legal system has asserted sovereignty over Australia, even if the government of the day wanted to recognise Indigenous sovereignty, it would have to do that by divesting itself of some of its

[16] See, for example, *Coe v Commonwealth (No 2)* (1993) 118 ALR 193, *Walker v New South Wales* (1994) 82 CLR 145, *Commonwealth v Yarmirr* (2001) 208 CLR 1 and *Members of the Yorta Yorta Aboriginal Community v Victoria* (2002) 214 CLR 422.

sovereignty – which is itself an exercise of its sovereignty. In other words, since under the rules of the received legal system Indigenous sovereignty was extinguished upon settlement, any successful appeal to that legal system to 'resurrect' Indigenous sovereignty would, as a matter of logic, amount to an acknowledgement that the legal system had acquired sovereignty from Indigenous people.

The legal position of Indigenous peoples in Australia differs markedly from that of Maori in New Zealand and native American tribes in the United States. This stems from the fact that in both countries, treaties regulate the relationship between the government and Indigenous peoples. In New Zealand colonisation was marked by the signing of the Treaty of Waitangi by representatives of the Crown and many, but not, all Maori chiefs. Interpretation of the Treaty is a vexed issue, made all the more so by the fact that there are two texts – in Maori and English – the meaning of which differ, not the least because some of the terms used in the English version had no exact equivalents in Maori. A key difference is that whereas the English text says that the Maori chiefs ceded 'sovereignty' to the Crown, the Maori text used the word *kawanatanga*, which means 'governorship,' rather than 'sovereignty'. Furthermore, the Maori text (but not the English) preserves the *rangatiratanga*, or 'chieftainship' of the Maori, which has been interpreted by some as the preservation of a right to self-determination. The Treaty also affirms that Maori retained their rights to land and 'taonga' – a term meaning 'treasures' which embraces both tangible and intangible property. The Treaty also conferred on Maori the full rights of British subjects. The subsequent history of New Zealand, and in particular the past 40 years, has seen attention focussed on determining what rights were reserved to Maori people under the Treaty.[17] In 1975 Parliament enacted the *Treaty of Waitangi Act 1975* which, although not making the Treaty part of statute law, established the Waitangi Tribunal, which hears claims for compensation or other restorative action for breaches of the Treaty, such as those relating to land, waterways and fishing rights, as well as in relation to language and culture. Legislation frequently imposes an obligation on the government to take the principles of the Treaty into account when exercising statutory powers.[18] An example of this is provided by s 9 of the *State Owned Enterprises Act* 1986 which, as held by the court in *New Zealand Maori Council v Attorney-General,*[19] imposed an obligation on the Crown not to exercise powers conferred by the Act without providing an opportunity for the Waitangi Tribunal to consider claims arising under the Treaty in relation to land that might be disposed of under the Act.

The position in the United States differs yet again as, in contrast to Australia where Indigenous sovereignty was lost, and New Zealand where the question is contested, there is no doubt that in the United States many Indigenous peoples succeeded in retaining a degree of sovereignty. Although many native American nations

[17] For a contemporary discussion of the issues see O'Sullivan (2018).

[18] An example of this is provided by s 9 of the *State Owned Enterprises Act 1986*, which provides that nothing in the Act permits the Crown from acting contrary to the principles of the Treaty.

[19] [1987] 1 NZLR 641 (CA).

were subjected to genocide by settlers as the United States extended its power westward, others survived and entered into treaties which preserved some aspects of their remaining sovereignty while ceding others to the federal government. The powers that these nations (which are referred to under United States law as 'domestic dependant nations') continue to exercise is founded on a residuum of the same sovereignty that existed in pre-colonial times – it was not conferred by the United States government.[20]

The different legal processes by which colonisation occurred in Australia on the one hand and New Zealand and the United States on the other explain why the acquisition of sovereignty over Australia cannot be undone and the original Indigenous sovereignty cannot be revived. From a legal perspective, the loss of Indigenous sovereignty is a *fait accompli*. Yet from a practical point of view, that fact is less important than one might think. It is obvious and uncontroversial to state that sovereignty is divisible – the existence of the states in Australia's federal system is evidence of that. Therefore, the fact that Indigenous peoples were deprived of their original sovereignty would not prevent an Australian government from conferring *new* sovereignty on them, albeit as a delegation of power by the received sovereignty rather than the continuation of Indigenous sovereignty.

The distinction between reviving pre-existing sovereignty and conferring new sovereignty may seem a fine one, but in discussing how Indigenous rights might be protected, it is far more useful to concentrate on how sovereignty might be acquired anew, rather than engaging in what, from a legal point of view, would ultimately be a fruitless argument directed towards reviving the sovereignty lost at the time of colonisation. In particular, the focus should be on acquiring the most important attribute of sovereignty, namely self-determination. Thus the acquisition of sovereignty by the Crown in the past is no impediment to the acquisition by Indigenous people of self-determination in future.

9.5 A Treaty

Before discussing how self-government could be achieved, it is necessary to examine the purpose that might be served by a treaty as a mechanism for recognising Indigenous rights. Many prominent Indigenous figures have argued that Australian governments, federal and state, should enter into a treaty or treaties with the Indigenous peoples of Australia. The establishment of a Makarrata Commission, to supervise agreement-making between the Crown and Indigenous peoples was one of the proposals contained in the Uluru Statement from the Heart. Unfortunately, the idea of a treaty has become linked with that of sovereignty, because in the minds of most people, treaty-making is one of the ways in which sovereign entities establish rules for their interaction. But if Indigenous peoples no longer have sovereignty,

[20] *United States v Wheeler* 435 U.S. 313 (1978), 328.

could there be a treaty or treaties between them and the Australian government? Can a country enter into a treaty with a sector of its own population or is it true, as John Howard stated, that a nation 'does not make a treaty with itself'?[21] The problem with this debate is that as with 'sovereignty', the term 'treaty' is clouded in misunderstanding.

When most people think of a treaty, they have in mind the meaning of the term in international law, which is that a treaty is an agreement between two sovereign states which is legally binding between them in their capacity as international actors. It is important to realise that although a treaty will be enforceable by each state against the other in international forums, it will not be enforceable in their domestic legal systems, unless the obligations arising under the treaty have been enacted into law. So, to take an example, if two countries signed a treaty in which each undertook to prohibit uranium mining and one of them breached the treaty, under international law the other could take action in accordance with whatever dispute-resolution mechanism was specified in the treaty.[22] However a person living in one of these countries could not take the government (or whoever was engaging in uranium mining) to court alleging that their actions amounted to an infringement of the treaty. Domestic enforcement would be possible only if that country had enacted legislation making the treaty part of domestic law. So although a treaty may be enforceable internationally, from a domestic perspective it will be of purely political importance.

Although treaties are usually entered into in the international sphere, the word 'treaty' can also be used in the different sense of a political agreement within a country. Examples of this are provided by Canada, which has negotiated treaties with Indigenous peoples even after the acquisition of sovereignty by the Crown, as well as by Norway, Sweden and Finland, where the governments have negotiated treaties with the Sami people inhabiting their countries. Again, such treaties will remain purely political documents, without any legal effect, unless and until they are enacted into law.

What the above shows is that there is nothing magic about the word 'treaty'. One could use the words 'Makarrata', 'agreement', 'compact', 'covenant' or 'accord' or 'treaty' to refer either to an agreement between sovereign states – or equally to an agreement between groups within a sovereign state. Furthermore, irrespective of what they are called, such agreements have no domestic legal effect unless enacted into law. In light of this, we can see how participants in the debate on Indigenous rights have for the most part been talking at cross-purposes, and why the idea of entering into a treaty has inspired both unreasonable fear in opponents of such a development and unreasonable hope in its supporters: Opponents of a treaty with Indigenous people think that, because treaties are usually entered into by sovereign states, Indigenous peoples cannot enter into treaties with Australian governments

[21] Australian Government (2000).

[22] This might lead to a body such as the International Court of Justice ordering the defaulting party to abide by the treaty – but even then the absence of any international enforcement agency means that treaties really depend on voluntary compliance by the parties to them.

because they no longer enjoy sovereignty. On the other hand, proponents of a treaty think that Indigenous people retain their sovereignty, that entry into a treaty would be proof of that fact and that a treaty would in itself confer rights on Indigenous peoples. Both sides are wrong: Although under Australian law Indigenous people no longer enjoy sovereignty, and entry into a treaty would not change that fact, the loss of sovereignty would not prevent Indigenous peoples entering into treaties with Australian governments. However, while a treaty could amount to an important and symbolic first step along the road towards recognising Indigenous rights, it would in itself not create legal rights. The potential usefulness of a treaty or treaties would lie in the fact that they amounted to the expression of political will to work towards agreed goals and outlined process to achieve those goals – but that potential would remain completely unrealised unless treaty commitments were converted into law. The real question is how the law would ultimately change as a result of the treaty process.

9.6 Self-determination as an Over-arching Right

The most fundamental right that a people has is self-determination. This right is protected by the Article 3 of the United Nations *Declaration on the Rights of Indigenous Peoples,* ratified by Australia in 2009. Article 3 states that

> Indigenous peoples have the right of self-determination. By virtue of that right they freely determine their political status and freely pursue their economic, social and cultural development.

Self-determination is thus an overarching right which embraces a number of other rights. I would argue that at a minimum, and in Australia's particular circumstances, constitutional recognition of the rights of Indigenous people requires that four key rights be recognised: the right to self-government, the right to culture, the right not to be discriminated against on grounds of race and the right of Indigenous people to be consulted through a Voice to Parliament.

9.7 The Right to Self-government

Article 4 of the *Declaration on the Rights of Indigenous Peoples* states that

> Indigenous peoples, in exercising their right to self-determination, have the right to autonomy or self-government in matters relating to their internal and local affairs, as well as ways and means for financing their autonomous functions.

The achievement of self-government would involve negotiation between the government and Indigenous peoples, in all likelihood resulting in different solutions in different circumstances. The creation of an institutional framework for Indigenous self-government would be complicated by the geographic distribution of Australia's

Indigenous population. While in some cases there are identifiable Indigenous peoples living in defined geographic areas, population movement – and in particular urbanisation – means that geographically-based models of self-government would not meet the needs of all Indigenous people. Nevertheless, in many instances it will be possible to establish Indigenous self-government institutions with geographically-defined jurisdictions.

An issue that would need to be addressed if the authority of Indigenous communities over defined areas was given constitutional recognition would be the status of customary law.[23] Surprisingly, Australian governments, and the public as a whole, have been less accepting of the concept of legal pluralism than far more conservative colonial societies: In South Africa, for example, statutory recognition was accorded to tribal courts (which hear civil matters arising under customary law and exercise limited criminal jurisdiction) in 1927, although the *de facto* operation of customary law had in fact continued uninterrupted by colonisation.[24] Indeed, customary law was recognised in most African colonies established by the United Kingdom, and customary law still remains in force in parallel with imported common law and subsequently-enacted statute law. There would be no reason why legislation conferring self-government on Indigenous communities should not include conferral of authority on them to apply Indigenous law. The most comprehensive study of the status of indigenous law in Australia was contained in the Australian Law Reform Commission's 1986 report on *The Recognition of Aboriginal Customary Laws*.[25] The Commission recommended that recognition be extended to Indigenous law,[26] but that no single method of recognition would suit all circumstances.[27] Although Indigenous law has been recognised for some evidentiary purposes in applying statutes (most significantly for the purpose of determining native title), it has not been recognised as being of force in itself.

A statute recognising Indigenous law would need to include provisions governing where, between whom and in relation to what areas of law Indigenous law would apply. Such conflict of law rules would be similar to those which are used in determining which law applies in the international sphere when questions arise as to which jurisdiction's law governs a case. They are also a feature of the domestic law of countries which recognise more than one legal system.[28]

---

[23] For a discussion of this see Harris (1999).

[24] See the *Black Administration Act* No 37 of 1927 ss 12 and 20 of which recognised the jurisdiction of Chiefs' and Headmen's courts) and the Law of Evidence Amendment Act No 45 of 1988, s 1 of which empowered other courts to take judicial notice of customary law. Section 211 of South Africa's post-apartheid Constitution (the Constitution of the Republic Of South Africa 1996) recognises traditional authorities and customary law.

[25] Australian Law Reform Commission (1986).

[26] Australian Law Reform Commission (1986, p. 194).

[27] Australian Law Reform Commission (1986, pp. 199–207).

[28] For an overview of how the South African legal system accommodates both customary and received law and determines the applicability of each see Bennett, T (1991) and Sanders A (ed) (1990).

An issue which attracts controversy whenever recognition of Indigenous law is mooted, is the compatibility of that law with human rights. In particular, adverse public comment has been aroused over issues such as the infliction of corporal punishment in accordance with Indigenous law. Interestingly, concern in respect of the incompatibility of Indigenous law with human rights has not been matched by equal public concern that provisions of common or statute law should be invalid if incompatible with human rights. And herein lies the solution: If the constitution contained a bill of rights, then all law – customary, common and statute – would be subject to its provisions, and any rule of law, irrespective of its origin, which failed the proportionality test contained in the bill of rights, would be invalid.

This discussion on Indigenous self-government thus far has assumed the existence of geographically-defined areas over which Indigenous peoples exercised authority. However, overseas experience shows that, even in the absence of geographically based self-government, a degree of control over its own affairs by a geographically-dispersed ethnic group is possible. The theory of consociationalism, developed by the Dutch political scientist Arendt Lijphart,[29] provides a model of how this can be done. The theory has been used as a constitutional device to defuse communal tensions in ethnically-divided societies, and one of its elements, 'segmental autonomy,' achieves that goal through the establishment of administrative arrangements which allow groups to manage their own education, health and other social services even if they live in the midst of other groups. In other words, segmental autonomy allows self-government – or at least elements of it – to be achieved on a communal and not just a territorial basis. Such arrangements would be of obvious benefit to Indigenous people who wish to exercise autonomy even though they do not live in cohesive, territorially-based, Indigenous communities.

9.8 The Right to Culture

Various Article of the UN *Declaration on the Rights of Indigenous Peoples* protects the right of Indigenous peoples to maintain and strengthen their cultures.[30] The right has several aspects, including rights of access to places of cultural significance, the right to education in accordance with culture and the right to maintain and use language, to name but a few. In Chap. 6 we saw that a distinction is often drawn between so-called first generation political rights and second generation socio-economic rights, in that whereas the first are said to require only state abstention from interfering in their exercise, the second require positive state action, which requires the expenditure of money. We also saw that this distinction, while useful, has its limitations, in that the vindication of some classic first generation rights – for example, the right not to be subject to inhuman treatment – will require state

[29] For an explanation of consociationalism see Lijphart (1969) and Lijphart (2008).

[30] See in particular Articles 3, 5, 8 and 11–16.

expenditure if they are to be protected. The right to culture has both first and second generation aspects to it: Sometimes the right is used to prevent interference in the exercise of culture. But, for a culture to flourish – particularly where that culture has been almost obliterated – something more is needed: In those circumstances, the state has a positive duty to take steps to ensure that Indigenous people have the resources necessary to maintain culture.

An excellent example of a formulation of Indigenous cultural rights can be found in s 19(2) of the *Victorian Charter of Human Rights and Responsibilities 2006* (Vic), which provides as follows:

> Aboriginal persons hold distinct cultural rights and must not be denied the right, with other members of their community:
>
> (a) to enjoy their identity and culture; and
> (b) to maintain and use their language; and
> (c) to maintain their kinship ties; and
> (d) to maintain their distinctive spiritual, material and economic relationship with the land and waters and other resources with which they have a connection under traditional laws and customs

I would suggest formulation be included in the constitution, with the addition of wording of the type used to protect second generation rights:

> The state must take reasonable legislative and other measures, within its available resources, to achieve the progressive realisation of each of these rights.

This would provide Indigenous people with a powerful tool for vindicating their rights, because if cultural rights were legally enforceable under the constitution, Indigenous people would not be dependant for the acknowledgement of those rights on the good will of government – an acknowledgement which will always be contingent on what is politic and which, since Indigenous people are in the minority, will always mean what is palatable to the non-Indigenous population. Having such a right embedded in the constitution would have an infinitely greater impact on the position of Indigenous people than would a merely symbolic declaration of recognition. It would have a more immediate impact than even a constitutional provision providing a mechanism for negotiations on self-determination, because while cultural rights could be vindicated through the courts as soon as they were incorporated into the constitution, negotiations on self-determination could take years, and possibly decades.

9.9 The Right Not to Be Discriminated Against on Grounds of Race or Ethnicity

The right not to be subject to discrimination on grounds of race or ethnicity was one of the rights discussed in Chap. 6, where the arguments against recognizing such a right (particularly as it applies to Indigenous people) were refuted. It would obviously be invidious, and insufficiently compliant with Australia's human rights obligations, for such a provision to prohibit only discrimination against Indigenous people – conformity to human rights principles requires that the constitution prohibit discrimination on grounds of race or ethnicity generally. Nevertheless, such a right would be of particular importance to Indigenous people in light of both historical and recent experience.

An issue of particular impact on Indigenous people arises from the fact that a constitutional right prohibiting racial discrimination could be interpreted as prohibiting laws that were for the benefit of particular groups in that, by conferring a benefit on one group, parliament would be discriminating against those groups which did not receive the benefit. As argued in Chap. 6, the bill of rights should include an exception to the equality right so as to permit affirmative-action legislation designed to remedy historical disadvantage. This would be crucial to giving redress to Indigenous people in particular for past wrongs.

It is also important to appreciate how the right to culture and the right to non-discrimination on grounds of race would be mutually-enforcing and would operate in tandem to work significant advantage for Indigenous people. The right to non-discrimination could, if accompanied by a rider permitting affirmative action (such as is contained in the text I have suggested above), be used as a mechanism for the redress of past injustices, because the inclusion of words permitting affirmative action would provide additional constitutional authority for positive treatment of the protection of the cultural rights of Indigenous people. A right to culture which included a provision requiring the state to provide resources to enable Indigenous people to maintain culture could, in combination with affirmative action, mean that the right could be used as a lever to obtain not just political advancement but material advancement as well – for example, by ensuring that the government provided adequate funding for Indigenous health and education. This is why it is a false to set up a dichotomy between 'political' and 'practical' advancement for Indigenous people. The two are not mutually exclusive – they are mutually supportive.

9.10 An Indigenous Voice to Parliament

The final key element in constitutional reform as it pertains to Indigenous people is the creation of an Indigenous representative body which would provide a national forum for the discussion of Indigenous affairs and for making representations to the government. This was a proposal contained in the Uluru Statement from the Heart which received so curt a dismissal from the government on the ground that it would not obtain majority support from the Australian people. Yet the proposal was modest in the extreme, and the government's response was not only dispiriting to Indigenous people but was also fundamentally dishonest: Contrary to the government's assertion, the proposed Indigenous Voice to Parliament would not have been vested with any legislative authority and would not have been a third chamber of parliament. The fact that the Indigenous assembly would have the role of commenting on legislation presented to parliament would not have detracted from the powers of parliament nor would it have meant that the consent of the Indigenous assembly would have been required before parliament could enact legislation – as was expressly noted in the Referendum Council's Final Report.[31] The assembly's role would have been purely consultative and advisory.

The government also argued that because the assembly would have been elected only by Indigenous people, it would have been inconsistent with the fundamental principles of 'one person, one vote' and of 'all Australian citizens having equal civic rights – all being able to vote for, stand for and serve in either of the two chambers of our national parliament.' This too is incorrect – no-one's right to vote or stand for parliament would have been compromised by the existence of an Indigenous assembly, and since the assembly would have been consultative, its establishment would not have meant that Indigenous people were being given any additional legislative power above that enjoyed by other Australians. The only differential treatment that would have been accorded to Indigenous people was that they would be afforded the opportunity, as a distinct community, to comment on legislation, a step which would be entirely justified – indeed barely sufficient – to redress the fact that, as was stated at the start of this chapter, they were people who were the original sovereigns of the country, who lost self-government, law, lands and sometimes lives, as a result of colonisation.

Perhaps the most cynical aspect of the government's rejection of the proposed representative Indigenous body was that the proposal was 'incapable of winning acceptance in a referendum'. Of course that would be the case if the government itself was putting its efforts into arguing why the proposal should not be accepted. But it is precisely here that the government faced a moral test – and one which it failed: Even if it was the case that a majority of voters would start from a position of being opposed to the idea of an Indigenous assembly, then instead of ruling the proposal out on the ground that it would not be acceptable to voters, surely a government that was committed to justice for Australia's Indigenous people should have shown leadership by putting its energy into persuading voters why the measure was justified? However instead of doing that, the Turnbull government's approach was to start by propitiating opponents of meaningful change by bargaining away the rights of Indigenous people – even before debate had properly begun – presumably in order to win conservative support for some as yet unspecified watered-down reform. Australia is – one would hope – a less conservative country than it was at the time of the 1967 referendum. Surely it would therefore not be too difficult a task – if our politicians could display moral leadership of the type that existed in 1967 – to overcome opposition to measures which Indigenous people have requested? Indeed, a 2017 survey by the Griffith University Centre for Governance and Public Policy found that 60.7% of respondents supported the idea of the establishment of a representative Indigenous body to advise the government on laws and policies affecting Indigenous people, and that 58.4% of respondents supported the idea of formal agreements between Australian governments and Indigenous peoples to recognise

[31] Referendum Council (2017b).

the rights of the latter.[32] What the history of the period 2007–2017 has shown is that the obstacle to the acknowledgement of constitutional rights for Indigenous people does not lie in uncertainty on how to achieve it. Rather it lies in an unwillingness on the part of governments to effect the necessary constitutional change and to foster the goodwill of the Australian public in support of such a project.

References

Australian Government (2000) PM transcripts – transcripts from the Prime Minister of Australia. 29 May 2000. https://pmtranscripts.pmc.gov.au/release/transcript-22788. Accessed 8 Oct 2019

Australian Government (2017) Response to referendum council's report on constitutional recognition. https://ministers.pmc.gov.au/scullion/2017/response-referendum-councils-report-constitutional-recognition. Accessed 8 Oct 2019

Australian Law Reform Commission (1986) The Recognition of Aboriginal Customary Laws (ALRC Report No. 31). Australian Law Reform Commission, Brisbane. https://www.alrc.gov.au/publication/recognition-of-aboriginal-customary-laws-alrc-report-31/. Accessed 8 Oct 2019

Bennett T (1991) A sourcebook of African customary law for southern Africa. Juta & Co, Cape Town

Brennan S, Gunn B, Williams G (2004) 'Sovereignty' and its relevance to treaty-making between indigenous peoples and Australian Governments. (2004) 26 Sydney Law Review: 307–52

Commonwealth of Australia (2012) Final report of the expert panel on recognising aboriginal and Torres Strait Islander peoples in the constitution. https://antar.org.au/sites/default/files/expert_panel_report_.pdf. Accessed 8 Oct 2019'

Harris B (1999) Indigenous law in South Africa – lessons for Australia? (1999) 5 James Cook University Law Review: 70–112

Karp P (2018) Australia day: Tony Abbott says British settlement 'a very good thing. The Guardian, 18 January 2018

Lijphart A (1969) Consociational democracy. (1969) 21 World Polit: 207–25

Lijphart A (2008) Thinking about democracy: power sharing and majority rule in theory and practice. Routledge, London

O'Sullivan D (2007) Beyond biculturalism – the politics of an indigenous minority. Huia Publishers, Wellington

O'Sullivan D (2018) 'Re-imagining the sovereign: an indigenous case study in citizenship, self-determination and democratic inclusivity. Discover Society. 6 November 2018, https://discoversociety.org/2018/11/06/re-imagining-the-sovereign-an-indigenous-case-study-in-citizenship-self-determination-and-democratic-inclusivity/. Accessed 8 Oct 2019

Parliament of Australia (2015) Joint select committee on constitutional recognition of aboriginal and Torres Strait Islander peoples (2015). Commonwealth of Australia, Canberra. https://www.aph.gov.au/Parliamentary_Business/Committees/Joint/2015_Constitutional_Recognition_of_Aboriginal_and_Torres_Strait_Islander_Peoples/Constitutional_Recognition/Final_Report. Accessed 8 Oct 2019

Parliament of Australia (2018) Joint select committee on constitutional recognition relating to aboriginal and Torres Strait Islander peoples (2018). Final Report. https://parlinfoaphgovau/parlInfo/download/committees/reportjnt/024213/toc_pdf/Finalreportpdf;fileType=application%2Fpdf. Accessed 8 Oct 2019

[32] Griffith University Centre for Governance and Public Policy, *Australian Constitutional Values Survey*, 2017 https://app.secure.griffith.edu.au/news/wp-content/uploads/2017/10/Griffith-University-UNSW-Australian-Constitutional-Values-Survey-Sept-2017-Results-2.pdf

Pascoe B (2018) Dark Emu – aboriginal Australia and the birth of agriculture. Magabala Books, Broome

Referendum Council (2017a) Uluru statement from the heart. Commonwealth of Australia, Canberra. https://www.referendumcouncil.org.au/sites/default/files/2017-05/Uluru_Statement_From_The_Heart.pdf. Accessed 19 Oct 2019

Referendum Council (2017b) Final report of the referendum council. Commonwealth of Australia, Canberra. https://www.referendumcouncil.org.au/sites/default/files/report_attachments/Referendum_Council_Final_Report.pdf. Accessed 21 Oct 2019

Sachs A (2009) The strange alchemy of life and law. Oxford University Press, Oxford

Sanders A (ed) (1990) The internal conflict of laws in South Africa. Butterworths, Durban

Thorpe N (2017) Turnbull government formally rejects proposal for indigenous voice to parliament. NITV News. 26 October 2017

Chapter 10
An Australian Republic

Abstract The chapter acknowledges that, while amendment of the constitution so as to make Australia a republic is the most often discussed constitutional reform, it is the least pressing. The chapter examines what is meant by the term 'head of state' and how the fact that that term is not included in the constitution has enabled monarchists to cloud debate over what the severance of the link with the Crown would – and would not – mean. The chapter explains how the conventions governing the exercise of the powers of the Governor-General operate and recommends that they be codified – as has happened in numerous Commonwealth countries, some of which have become republics, some of which have retained the Queen as head of state. Codification would reduce the uncertainty that led to the constitutional crisis of 1975, and would also assuage the fears of those who believe that having an elected president (the model clearly favoured by voters) would create the risk of a clash between president and prime minister. The chapter ends by recommending a similar model of elected president operating within the system of parliamentary government as that which operates in Ireland.

10.1 Framing the Debate

The question of whether Australia should become a republic is the most discussed potential constitutional reform, despite the fact that it is the least pressing of the issues confronting us. Yet a steady majority of voters – 53% in favour versus 43% against according to a 2016 survey[1] – would like Australia to become a republic. Despite the evident popularity of such a change, it has also given rise to an entirely unwarranted degree of concern about what its effects on the Constitution would be. The reality is that taking such a step would not be complex from a constitutional point of view. Debate on this issue is conducted almost entirely without reference to the experience of other countries, an examination of which would show that Australia's situation is not unique and that many countries have severed the link with the Crown without difficulty and without adverse consequences for the operation of their constitutions.

[1] Australian National University (2016, p. 80).

B. Harris, *Constitutional Reform as a Remedy for Political Disenchantment in Australia*, https://doi.org/10.1007/978-981-15-3599-4_10

The constitutional link with the monarch of the United Kingdom could be terminated without any alteration to the way in which executive power is exercised under the Constitution. Severing the link with the Crown would not have any effect – positive or negative – on the operation of the Constitution. However it would certainly be of great symbolic effect: Becoming a republic would remove the final remnant of our former colonial status and would signal to the world that we are wholly independent, both in appearance and in fact, because we would no longer have a foreigner as our monarch. It would also mean that the person who is the ultimate source of executive power in Australia would no longer be someone holding office by virtue of hereditary succession determined by the law of a foreign country, and that any Australian could aspire to be the person embodying the ultimate source of executive authority under the Constitution.

As in so many other areas, debate on a republic has been bedevilled by loose terminology and by misunderstanding of the Constitutional position, in particular about the powers of the Governor-General. The result is widespread confusion about what a change to a republic would – and, as importantly, would not – mean for the way the Constitution operates.

10.2 Who, or What, Is a 'Head of State'?

The first and most fundamental source of confusion arises from the use of the term 'head of state'. Possible correct answers to the question 'Who is our head of state?' are: no-one, the Queen or the Governor-General – depending entirely on what one means by the term. Since the term is not used in the Constitution, it would be most correct to say that no-one is head of state, as the office does not exist. But leaving that option aside, if one wants to determine whether the Queen or the Governor-General is head of state, one needs to examine what the Constitution says about their respective roles.

The constitutional position, as stated in s 61, is that executive power is vested in the Queen, and that that power is exercised 'on her behalf' by the Governor-General. It is therefore incontrovertible that the Queen is the source of executive power, even though the Governor-General exercises it for her. If there was no Queen, there would be no Governor-General. The Governor-General's powers are thus entirely derivative, however much monarchists seek to divert attention from this truth in furtherance of an argument that we have an 'Australian head of state' in the person of the Governor-General.[2]

From this it follows that, if by 'head of state' one means 'the person who is the ultimate *source* of executive power under the Constitution,' then the Queen is head of state. However, if by 'head of state' one means 'the person who actually *wields* executive power,' then it would be true that the Governor-General is head of state.

[2]As an example of this see Smith (2015).

The problem is that because the term 'head of state' is unknown to the Constitution, people are free to use it as they like, and while some use it to refer to the Queen, many use it to refer to the person who exercises powers on behalf of the Queen – which is harmless so long as there is clarity that the Governor-General's powers are not his or her own. It is because the legally accurate phrases 'the person who is the ultimate source of executive power' and 'the person who wields executive power' are clumsy that people have fallen into the habit of using the ambiguous term 'head of state', with all the attendant confusion that has caused. For this reason, the term is best avoided.

10.3 An Australian President

The simplest way of severing the constitutional link between Australia and the monarchy would be to amend the Constitution in such a way as to remove references to the Queen and state that her powers were vested in a person chosen by whatever method was prescribed by the Constitution (an issue which is discussed later). That person's title could be President, Governor-General or anything else that Australians wanted. The most natural title to use would be President because it is associated with republics, in contrast to the term Governor-General which was an office specifically created in British colonies as to serve as a delegate of the monarch. Having severed the link with the Crown, it would be decidedly odd to retain the title of Governor-General – yet some people have argued that doing so would increase the chances of Australians accepting a move to a republic because the title 'President' suggests that we would adopt a presidential system of government, such as operates in the United States, in place of the parliamentary system we currently have. That argument panders to constitutional ignorance. However allergic to the word 'President' some voters may be, the answer is not to retain the title of Governor-General, with its monarchical associations, but to demonstrate that having a President need not have anything to do with the presidential system. As evidence of this one can point to the many countries – as diverse as Ireland, Germany, Malta, Mauritius, Austria and India, to name but a few – which are parliamentary republics, in which a president acts in the same figurehead capacity as does the Queen in the United Kingdom, with actual executive power being wielded by a Prime Minister heading a government which is responsible to the legislature. For this reason, this chapter uses the term 'President' when referring to the person in whom executive power would be formally vested if Australia became a republic.

How an Australian President should be selected has been a matter of controversy. Surveys have repeatedly shown that most voters favour popular election of a President. This is why the republic referendum of 1999 was doomed to fail – not because a majority of Australians wanted to maintain the link with the

Crown – polls showed a clear majority in favour of a republic[3] – but because the Howard government put to voters a model under which the President would have been selected by Parliament that most republicans did not want.

Much has been made of the argument that having an elected president would be incompatible with the system of government embodied in the Constitution because, it is said, by having both an elected president and an (indirectly)[4] elected Prime Minister, one would be setting up a system in which the President might be tempted to use their popular mandate as justification for interfering in decisions made by the Prime Minister, in contravention of the conventions under which the Governor-General operates. Is this a real problem and, if so, how could it be remedied?

10.4 Law and Convention

Key to understanding this is an appreciation of the distinction between law and convention. This was outlined in Chap. 3, but it is useful to explain the difference here again: Law is made by a formal process and is enforceable by the courts which will give a remedy if it is breached. By contrast, conventions are political practices which, although they are regarded as being obligatory, develop informally and are not enforceable by the courts.[5] As an example of a convention operating in the United Kingdom is the rule that, although the Queen is legally entitled to refuse her assent to legislation enacted by Parliament, by convention she always signs bills into law. The last occasion on which a monarch refused to sign a Bill was in 1707, and it was the de facto shift in power from the monarch to Parliament which occurred in the late seventeenth and early eighteenth centuries which caused it to become accepted that the monarch would not exercise her power of veto, even though legally the power still existed (and indeed still exists). So it would be true to say that if the Queen was to refuse to sign a bill into law, that conduct would be unconstitutional (in the sense that it breached convention) but would not be unlawful. The idea that there can be rules which one is obliged to obey but which are not legal rules and are unenforceable is understandably confusing, particularly in the case of those conventions which provide for the direct *opposite* of what the law says, the obligation to assent to legislation being one such example. This gives rise to the obvious question of why the conventions should not be codified – that is, put into the form of legal rules – a step which is indeed recommended later in this chapter. For the moment however, let us assume the existence of conventions and examine their relevance to the office of Governor-General.

[3] Cassin (2009).

[4] As explained in Chap. 4, under the system of parliamentary government, voters do not elect the Prime Minister. Voters elect a Parliament, and a person becomes Prime Minister if they enjoy the support of a majority of members of the House of Representatives.

[5] For a general discussion of the nature of conventions, including their unenforceability by the courts, see *Re Amendment of the Constitution of Canada* (1981) 125 DLR (3d) 1, 84–6.

When the Commonwealth Constitution was drafted, it was on the assumption that the conventions which operated in the United Kingdom would operate in Australia. This had the consequence that crucial aspects of what the Constitution says are at odds with how it actually operates. In the case of the Governor-General this means that what he or she may do according to the law can be very different from what he or she can do according to convention. For example, while s 58 of the Constitution says the Governor-General can decide whether to assent to legislation 'according to his discretion', in reality convention dictates that the Governor-General must always assent to bills passed by parliament.

The importance of conventions to the office of Governor-General becomes clear when one considers that apart from a few powers which the Constitution regulates by expressly stating that they are to be exercised by the Governor-General on the advice of the executive Council (that is, the ministers),[6] the exercise of all the others is regulated by convention. Thus, even in the case of powers which are not *expressly* stated as having to be exercised on advice, it understood that where the Constitution gives a power to the Governor-General, that is subject to the convention that the Governor-General exercises it on the advice of the cabinet or relevant minister. So, for example, the s 58 power to assent or not assent to legislation is subject to the convention that the Governor-General cannot, in fact, withhold consent. The executive power in s 61 is subject to the convention that in reality, it is the Prime Minister and other ministers who run the government, and advise the Governor-General on the exercise of her powers. Similarly, the apparently unqualified discretion conferred on the Governor-General by s 64 to appoint ministers is subject to the convention that the he appoints a Prime Minister who is able to command a majority in the House of Representatives, and then takes that person's advice on whom to appoint as ministers in charge of the government departments.

Apart from the powers which the Governor-General exercises on the advice of the government (either expressly or by convention), there are four so-called 'reserve powers' which he or she exercises independently and not on anyone's advice. These are to appoint a prime minister, dismiss a prime minister, dissolve parliament, and refuse to dissolve parliament. But even the exercise of these powers is regulated by convention:

The power to appoint a Prime Minister is subject to the convention that the Governor-General must appoint whoever leads the party or coalition with a majority in the House of Representatives. The operation of this convention requires cooperation between politicians and the Governor-General: An incumbent Prime Minister who loses the majority in the House after an election must comply with convention and resign, leaving it open to the Governor-General to appoint whoever is able to command the support of the House. In the event that a general election produced a result where no one is able to command a majority in the House, convention would

[6] Examples of this are calling an election of the House of Representatives (s 32), creating government departments (s 64), appointing public servants (s 67) and appointing federal judges (s 72).

require the incumbent Prime Minister to advise the Governor-General to dissolve Parliament and call another election.

The power to dismiss a Prime Minister can be exercised where an incumbent Prime Minister loses his or her majority in the House of Representatives and refuses either to resign or to ask the Governor-General to call an election, where a Prime Minister who has lost an election refuses to resign and allow the Governor-General to appoint a new Prime Minister, or where a government persists in unlawful action. This power was exercised under controversial circumstances in 1975, as discussed below.

Usually, the Governor-General dissolves Parliament on the advice of the Prime Minister. However the Governor-General could exercise this power on his or her own initiative after dismissing a Prime Minister (in accordance with the rules described above) if there was no one else able to command a majority in the House of Representatives. In these circumstances the deadlock could be resolved only by Parliament being dissolved and an election being held.

Finally, some argue that if a government has recently been elected but shortly thereafter loses the confidence of the House of Representatives, the Governor-General has the power to refuse a request by a Prime Minister to dissolve Parliament if there is someone else who can command a majority of the House and thus form a government. However, given that the conventions all serve the doctrines of representative government, the better view is that a Governor-General can never refuse a Prime Minster's request to refer to the voters the question of who should form the government.

So, to return to the question which led to this discussion of conventions, is there a risk that a directly-elected president might breach the conventions and interfere in the conduct of government? The first and most obvious point to note is that a Governor-General is equally capable of breaching the conventions as is a President. Indeed opponents of Governor-General Kerr's actions in 1975 maintain that he did just that.

10.5 The Constitutional Crisis of 1975

The events of the constitutional crisis illustrate the inherent weakness of a constitution where fundamental rules are both disputed and unenforceable, so it is useful to examine what occurred. The origins of the crisis lay in the refusal of the Senate, in which the Coalition had a majority, to pass Appropriations Bills (legislation authorising the government to levy tax and spend money) which had been passed by the Whitlam Labor government in the House of Representatives. Without parliamentary authorisation, s 83 of the Constitution would make it unlawful for the government to spend money. This meant that once money granted under previous appropriations legislation ran out (which it would have done before the end of the year) the government would not be able to pay its running expenses, including the salaries of public servants. In early November, Kerr advised Whitlam that, as

Whitlam was unable to secure financial supply, he should resign. Whitlam refused, arguing that it was contrary to convention for the Senate to block supply. With less than 3 weeks' supply available, Kerr asked Chief Justice Sir Garfield Barwick to advise whether Kerr could dismiss Whitlam if Whitlam persisted in his refusal to resign. Barwick advised that he could, because his view was that under the conventions of responsible government, a Prime Minister who cannot secure the passage of appropriations legislation can no longer govern, and if such a Prime Minister refuses to resign, he can be dismissed by the Governor-General under the latter's reserve powers.

On 11 November, Kerr summoned Malcolm Fraser, leader of the Liberal opposition in the House of Representatives. Kerr advised Fraser that he would dismiss Whitlam and appoint Fraser as 'caretaker' Prime Minister, provided that Fraser agreed to instruct the Liberal majority in the Senate to pass the Appropriation Bills and to advise Kerr to dissolve Parliament once he was appointed as caretaker Prime Minister. Kerr then met with Whitlam and dismissed him. Fraser was appointed as caretaker Prime Minister and advised the Governor-General to dissolve Parliament. The Senate passed the Appropriation Bills. Meanwhile, in the House of Representatives, Whitlam succeeded in passing a motion of no confidence in Fraser's Government (which, of course, had no majority in the House of Representatives). Before the Speaker had the opportunity to convey the result of the vote of no confidence to the Governor-General, the latter's secretary read a proclamation on the steps of Parliament ordering the double dissolution that had been requested by Fraser. Fraser won the subsequent general election.

The following points can be made in relation to the constitutionality of the above: The Senate was fully within its rights under s 53 of the Constitution to block financial supply. Whitlam's argument, which was that because supply had never previously been blocked this meant that a convention had been established that supply could not be blocked was debatable. The argument was in any event irrelevant, given that in the event of a clash between a convention and a statutory provision, the latter must be followed,[7] that the text of s 53 clearly gives the Senate the power to block supply and that the Constitutional Convention debates of the 1890's reveal that s 53 had been designedly put into the Constitution upon the insistence of the smaller colonies.

Kerr should not have involved the Chief Justice in the controversy. The issues Barwick was asked to address could conceivably have come before the courts because, in dismissing the government, the Governor-General was acting under s 64 of the Constitution. In theory his exercise of this power could have been reviewed by the courts (although, given that s 64 says that ministers hold office 'at pleasure', review would have been unlikely to succeed). The Governor-General's proper legal adviser was the government's Attorney-General, although, understandably, Kerr would not have wanted to inform him of his plans to dismiss Whitlam.

---

[7] For a statements on the fact that conventions do not limit legislative capacity see *Madzimbamuto v Lardner-Burke* [1969] 1 AC 645, 722 G – 723 C.

So far as the dismissal itself is concerned, there is no doubt that s 64 gives the Governor-General the power to dismiss a Prime Minister, and so Kerr's action was certainly lawful. Whether it was constitutional – that is, whether it was in accordance with convention – is a point upon which people continue to argue.[8] It is clear that, under the conventions of responsible government, a government needs the support of only the House of Representatives to remain in office. Whitlam argued that this meant he was entitled to continue in government even though he could not get his Appropriation Bills through the Senate. However, this is to ignore the *rationale* for the rule that the party that has a majority in the House of Representatives is entitled to govern, which is that that entitlement to govern stems from its ability to govern. A party that is unable to obtain supply is unable to govern, and the inherent problem in the Australian Constitution (which was not remedied even in the wake of 1975) is that the Senate – the house to which the government is not responsible – has the power to block supply, and thereby deprive the government of the ability to govern. It is upon this reasoning, which certainly makes sense from a practical point of view, that Kerr relied in asserting that convention dictated Whitlam ought to have resigned and that Kerr himself was acting in accordance with convention in dismissing him when he (Whitlam) did not.

Given that Kerr's actions were legal, the question as to whether they were in accordance with convention ultimately boils down to one of timing: It could be argued that Kerr acted prematurely and should have waited a few more days to see if the political impasse might break before taking the step of dismissal. Whitlam might have resigned or the Senate might have passed the Bills, which would have averted the crisis. The problem was, however, that there was a high level of anxiety in the community over the continued payment of government salaries, as the government's authority to spend money would have expired in less than 3 weeks. Furthermore, of major concern to Kerr was the fact that, had he warned Whitlam that he was risking being dismissed if he did not resign, Whitlam could have asked the Queen to dismiss Kerr. According to convention, the Queen would have been bound to accede to such a request, whereupon Whitlam could have replaced Kerr with a compliant Governor-General – although the fact that there is correspondence in the National Archives between the Queen and Kerr which the Archives has successfully resisted making available to the public raises the question as to what stance of the Queen would in fact have adopted in such circumstances.[9] Had Whitlam been allowed to stay in office until after supply ran out, expenditure of government money would then have been unlawful under s 83 of the Constitution. Persistence in unconstitutional activity would have given Kerr a different ground upon which to dismiss Whitlam, but that would have been available only once the courts had found the government's conduct to be unlawful. Should Kerr have waited until the country

[8] For two recent books see Kelly and Bramston (2015) and Hocking (2015). Still unknown is what correspondence between Kerr and the Queen would reveal, particularly with regard to whether Kerr raised with the Queen what would happen if Whitlam asked the Queen to dismiss Kerr, which is what Kerr feared might happen if he had forewarned Whitlam that he would dismiss him.

[9] See Hocking (2018).

reached that position? Most people would probably answer 'No', in which case Kerr was right to stand on the power that s 64 of the Constitution undoubtedly gave him to dismiss Whitlam.

The 1975 crisis – which could arises again, as nothing has been changed in the Constitution to prevent it – reveals the danger not only in having law and convention running in parallel, but also with law and convention providing conflicting rules and with conventions not providing what should happen in the circumstance where a government *can* govern in the sense that it has a majority in the House of Representatives yet at the same time *cannot* govern because it cannot get appropriations legislation through the Senate. The problem is compounded by the bizarre circumstance that the Governor-General and the Prime Minister each have the power to dismiss the other (assuming that the monarch complies with convention and accedes to a Prime Minister's request to dismiss the Governor-General) and so the resolution of any confrontation between the two is determined by whoever reaches for the telephone first.

10.6 Codifying the Conventions

While it would certainly be possible to have what has been referred to as a 'minimalist' republic, with a President replacing the Queen and Governor-General, the text of the Constitution remaining otherwise unchanged and the conventions continuing to operate, the obvious solution to the uncertainty caused by the conventions would be to codify them – in other words to put them into the Constitution, thus converting them into enforceable rules of law. This would ensure that that the Constitution read in the same way it operated and would address the concern that some people have that an elected President would be tempted to depart from the rules by usurping the powers of the Prime Minister. However it is important to recognise that codification would be beneficial whether Australia became a republic or not – indeed, significant as severing the link with the Crown would be from a symbolic point of view, codification of the conventions is of far greater importance from a practical point of view because it would have a beneficial effect on the day to day operation of the Constitution. The Constitution would reflect how constitutional rules actually operate, and all participants would know that the rules would be enforceable by the courts.

Constitutional conservatives have an almost mystical attachment to the conventions. Yet what many people do not realise is that these conventions arose by accident rather than design, and are, at base, the product of laziness in eighteenth and nineteenth century Britain, where no-one bothered to put new constitutional rules into legislative form. It was these rules that were assumed to operate when parliamentary governments were established in the Australian colonies and, subsequently, when the Commonwealth Constitution was drafted.

Setting aside emotional attachment to the conventions, arguments against their codification usually focus on the supposed impossibility of putting the conventions into words or, alternatively, on the supposed 'flexibility' they allow in the operation of the Constitution.

The argument based on impossibility is easily refuted by the fact that many Commonwealth countries – some of which have retained the office of Governor-General and the link with the Crown,[10] others of which have become republics with presidents[11] – have codified the conventions. In simple terms, if language is capable of stating what the conventions are, then surely those statements can be put into the form of legal rules? The fact that the impossibility argument continues to be made despite the evidence from overseas reflects the insularity of debate in Australia – although it is difficult to determine whether that is the product of genuine ignorance of what goes on in other countries or of determination on the part of constitutional conservatives to keep quiet about facts that are inconvenient to them.

The argument based on flexibility – that codification would not be inadvisable because it would (somehow) prevent the Governor-General from responding to the exigencies that might arise[12] – is curious and is fundamentally at odds with the importance those advancing it place on the conventions as a key part of the Constitution. The argument seems to be founded on the view that constitutional practice is somehow different from all other areas of human endeavour and incapable of being captured by comprehensive rules. Perfection is, of course, unattainable in any area of law, but there is nothing *qualitatively* different about constitutional law that makes it any more difficult for drafters of its rules to anticipate the various circumstances that might arise in the exercise of a power. Furthermore, just as one would not want uncertainty in the rules defining what constitutes the crime of murder, or defining one's tax liability or what procedures must be adhered to when registering a corporation, surely one would equally not want uncertainty in the fundamental rules of the Constitution? Leaving rules 'flexible' (which in reality means ambiguous), as well as unenforceable by the courts, is fundamentally incompatible with the doctrine of constitutionalism and with the rule of law, which require that rules be certain in their content and application and able to be enforced by judicial remedy when they are breached. Again the experience of overseas jurisdictions exposes the invalidity of the 'flexibility' argument, as constitutional draughtspersons in those countries have had no difficulty in framing the rules directing the powers of a Governor-General or President with sufficient specificity as to cover the eventualities that might arise in the relationship between head of state, Prime Minister and parliament.

Before examining how an Australian President could be chosen, we should note that, if the conventions were codified, there would be no need to have an office of head of state at all. Although there might be good reasons why we would want a

[10] See, for example, the *Constitution of Barbados* 1966, Arts 61, 65, and 66; the *Constitution of Bahamas* 1973, Arts 73, 74 and 66; the *Constitution of Grenada* 1973, Arts 52 and 58; and the *Constitution of Jamaica* 1962, Arts 64, 70 and 71.

[11] See, for example, the *Constitution of Dominica* 1978, Arts 59, 60 and 63; the *Constitution of Malta* 1964, Arts 76. 79, 80 and 81 and the *Constitution of Mauritius* 1968, Arts 57, 59 and 60.

[12] McGarvie (1999, pp. 161–2).

human being to personify the country and operate the levers of the Constitution, it would be possible to draft the constitution in such a way as to have the rules currently applied by the Governor-General become self-executing. So, for example, instead of the Constitution stating that the Governor-General/President must appoint as Prime Minister whoever had a majority in Parliament, the Constitution could simply state that whoever is able to command a majority in Parliament would be Prime Minister.[13] All the other powers of the Governor-General could be dealt with in the same way. Remedies for non-compliance would be available from the courts, just as they would be if there was a Governor-General or President applying the rule and either they had exercised their powers inconsistently with the rule or had lawfully exercised their powers but had been disobeyed. In other words, if the powers of the head of state were codified, they could be enforced by the courts irrespective of whether the rules were applied by an office-holder or operated automatically.[14]

However, people may prefer to have a human being at the apex of our Constitution, simply because we are used to having someone in that role who personifies the nation. That is a perfectly good reason to have such an office-holder, so assuming that we did want to retain that system, how should a new head of state be chosen?

10.7 Choosing a President

As already stated, polls posing the question of what method people would prefer for choosing an Australian President have consistently shown that direct election is the most popular option. The 1999 referendum failed – indeed, was arguably set up to fail by the Howard government – because it presented voters with the choice between a republic with a President chosen in a manner that most republicans did not want, or no republic at all. The mechanism for choosing a President was one which would have involved a nominations committee putting forward names to the Prime Minister who, along with the leader of the opposition, would then have proposed that person for approval by a joint sitting of the House of Representatives, which would have to have approved the nomination by a two-thirds majority. The 1999 proposal did not include any codification of the powers of the Governor-General, and so, despite requiring approval of *appointment* by parliament, it left intact the Prime-Minister's power of *dismissal*. In other words, just as a Prime Minister can dismiss a Governor-General simply by means of a request to the Queen (who must, by convention, agree with the Prime minister's request), under the 1999

[13] Such a system already exists in part in the ACT, where s 40 of the *Australian Capital Territory Self-Government Act 1988* (Cth) states that the Chief Minister is elected by the Legislative Assembly. Section 48 states that if a motion of no confidence is passed in the Chief Minister and the Assembly does not elect a new Chief Minister within 30 days, the Assembly is dissolved and elections must be held.

[14] Here it would be essential to have broad rules of standing which enabled citizens to enforce the Constitution. The issue of standing is addressed in Chapter 11.

proposal the Prime Minister could similarly have dismissed the President without the approval of parliament.

Accepting then, as one must, that a model providing for direct election of a President is the only one which is likely to succeed at a referendum, what type of election could one expect? An election for the presidency would admittedly be a tame affair, as none of the candidates could promise to 'do' or 'not do' anything, because they would be running for an office where their decisions were prescribed either by convention or, more preferably, by the Constitution if the conventions were codified. Nevertheless, the example of Ireland shows that it is possible to have elections to an office even where the office confers no discretionary powers. In that country, which has a parliamentary system of government, the Constitution provides for an elected President[15] against the backdrop of codified rules which determine how the head of government (the *Taoseach* or Prime-Minister) is selected.[16] On several occasions since Ireland became a republic in 1949 there has been only one candidate for President. On other occasions there have been contested elections, but such campaigning as there has been has not revolved around party politics or policy platforms – they could not have done – but around the personalities of the candidates and who voters thought would best personify the country and represent it on the world stage.[17]

The Constitution would also need to make provision for the dismissal of a President. The Prime Minister's control over dismissal of the Governor-General is an obvious flaw in our current Constitution. This became evident during the constitutional crisis of 1975, because the two major protagonists each had the power to dismiss the other – Kerr could have dismissed Whitlam, and Whitlam could have contacted the Queen and requested her to dismiss Kerr. The possibility of being dismissed was a factor in Kerr's mind in deciding how long to allow the impasse between the government and the Senate to persist. Had Kerr not had the threat of dismissal hanging over him, he might well have allowed a few more days to pass before deciding to dismiss Whitlam. Certainly had Whitlam got wind of Kerr's plan to dismiss him, the risk of Whitlam launching a pre-emptive strike would obviously have been very great. It clearly makes no sense for each of these figures to have the power to dismiss the other, yet that is how the Constitution currently operates.

The most obvious politically-neutral way of providing for the dismissal of a President would be for the Constitution to contain a mechanism for impeachment of the President upon application to the High Court on grounds of misbehaviour or incapacity. If impeachment was successful, some other figure – perhaps the Speaker of the House of Representatives – could become Acting President, pending the election of a new President.

[15] *Constitution of Ireland* 1937, Art 12.2.1.

[16] *Constitution of Ireland* 1937, Art 13.1.1 and Art. 28.10. For a discussion of the constitutional provisions relating to the powers of the President see Duffy (1993, pp. 120–8).

[17] Ibid 146–7.

Both the will (judging by public opinion polls) and the means exist to make Australia a republic. But as this chapter has shown, however important that symbolic step would be, and irrespective of whether Australia became a republic, it would be infinitely more important for us to codify the conventions, so that the rules we operate by actually conform to the rules as written.

References

Australian National University (2016) Trends in Australian political opinion – results from the Australian election study, 1987–2016. https://australianelectionstudyorg/publications/. Accessed 8 Oct 2019

Cassin R (2009) Unpalatable choice sank the republic. The Sydney Morning Herald, 6 November 2009

Duffy D (1993) Ireland. In: Republic Advisory Committee (1993) An Australian Republic – the options. Australian Government Publishing Service, Canberra

Hocking J (2015) The dismissal dossier: everything you weren't meant to know about November 1975. Melbourne University Press, Melbourne

Hocking J (2018) Relics of colonialism: the Whitlam dismissal and the fight over the palace letters. The Conversation, 5 February 2018

Kelly, P Bramston, T (2015) The dismissal: in the Queen's name. (Penguin Australia, Melbourne

McGarvie R (1999) Democracy – choosing Australia's republic. Melbourne University Press, Melbourne

Smith D (2015) The Governor-General is Australia's head of state. Aust Law J 89: 857–866

Chapter 11
Access to Constitutional Justice

Abstract This chapter discusses the process by which judges are selected and recommends that judicial selection be placed in the hands of a judicial services commission on which would serve representatives of the legal profession, the bench and the public, and that the government would be restricted to choosing judges from candidates put forward by the commission. The chapter also discusses the rules on standing, which have the effect of restricting who may initiate legal action to enforce the constitution. The chapter argues that because everyone has an interest in seeing that the constitution is complied with, different rules of standing should apply in constitutional matters than do in other types of litigation. It draws on the *actio popularis* of Roman law, and its parallels in other constitutions, as a model for how this could be achieved.

11.1 The Role of the Courts

Although their effect on government is less obvious than is that of parliament and the executive, the courts are the lynchpin of constitutional government. This is because unless people are able to challenge unlawful governmental action in the courts, and unless the government respects judgments of the courts, the rules of constitutional law become pointless and government becomes arbitrary and unrestrained. This is of course true of any legal rule: A law is effective only to the extent that those who allege that it has been infringed can approach the courts to have the rule enforced. This principle is encapsulated in a Roman law maxim: *ubi ius ibi remedium* – where there is a right there must be a remedy. How the courts are structured, who chooses (and dismisses) judges and who has the right to enforce a rule of law before the courts (referred to as having 'standing') are therefore important questions relevant to determining how effective our constitutional system is.

B. Harris, *Constitutional Reform as a Remedy for Political Disenchantment in Australia*, https://doi.org/10.1007/978-981-15-3599-4_11

11.2 The Structure of the Courts

Because the federal system means there are nine separate legal systems in Australia, we have nine separate court systems, one for the Commonwealth and one for each of the eight states and territories. This has led to significant complexity in the administration of justice.

There are three levels of Commonwealth courts: the Federal Circuit Court, the Federal Court and the High Court. The Federal Circuit Court has jurisdiction which is limited by statute. The Federal Court has unlimited jurisdiction, which means that it can hear any matters arising under Commonwealth law. The Federal Court is divided into two divisions. The trial division consists of courts presided over by a single judge. The Full Court consists of three or more judges and hears appeals from the Federal Circuit Court and from the trial division of the Federal Court. The High Court has the dual function of hearing certain matters as a trial court and in hearing appeals from that jurisdiction and from the Full Court of the Federal Court.

Each state and territory has its own court structure. The usual hierarchy is of a Magistrates Court and a District Court which have jurisdiction limited to the amount involved (in civil cases) and types of offences (in criminal cases). Above the District Court is the Supreme Court, which has unlimited jurisdiction and which is divided into a trial division (where cases are heard by a single judge) and a Court of Appeal (where cases are heard by three or more judges). Appeals from the Magistrates Court can be heard by the District Court, while appeals from the District Court and the Supreme Court trial division are heard by the Court of Appeal. Because it can occur that a dispute between litigants may involve issues arising under both state and Commonwealth law, the Commonwealth enacted the *Jurisdiction of Courts (Cross-Vesting) Act 1987* (Cth) which confers jurisdiction on state and territory courts to hear Commonwealth matters.

The state and Commonwealth court systems are linked by virtue of the fact that the High Court hears appeals not only from the Federal Court of Appeal but also from the various state and territory Courts of Appeal.

The structure of the court system is illustrated by the diagram below. The names of the state and territory courts may differ among the eight jurisdictions, but for sake of convenience only one state hierarchy is shown here (Fig. 11.1).

The abolition of the federal system would greatly simplify the administration of justice in Australia, because as there would be a single legal system for the entire country, there would also be a single court hierarchy. If we had a single national court system, the opportunity should be taken to re-name the courts: An oddity of Australian court nomenclature is that while the state courts are called 'Supreme' Courts (which suggests that that court that is at the top of the hierarchy), the highest court in Australia is called the 'High' Court. Since the state Supreme Courts would no longer exist, it would more accurately reflect the character of the highest court in the country if it was re-named the 'Supreme Court', and a court lower in the hierarchy called the 'High Court' – as is the case in the United Kingdom. In addition, it would be anomalous, if Australia was a no longer a federation, to continue to use

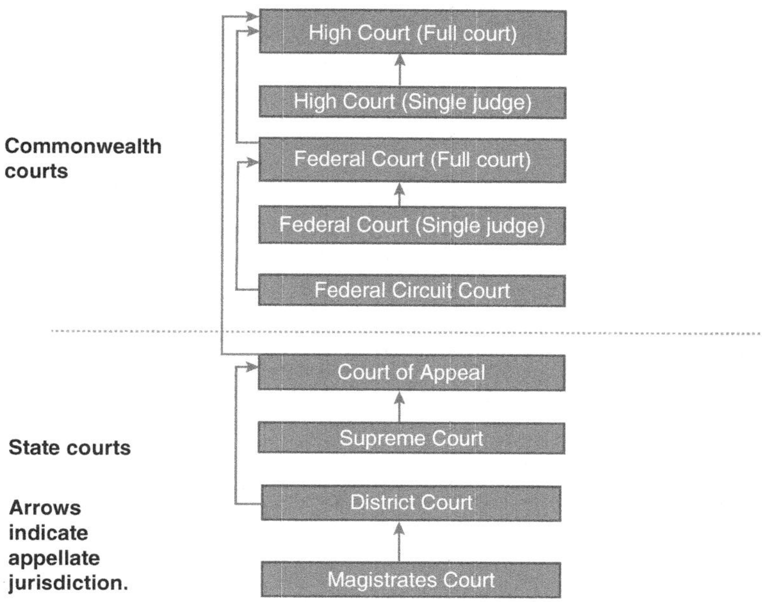

Fig. 11.1 Court structure

names such as 'Federal' Magistrates Court and the 'Federal' Court. Therefore I would suggest that the new hierarchy of courts be as follows: Magistrates Court, District Court, High Court, Court of Appeal and Supreme Court. This proposed hierarchy is represented in the following diagram (Fig. 11.2).

11.3 The Appointment of Judges

The process by which judges are selected and dismissed is critical to the impartial functioning of the justice system. Although Australia is fortunate in having a highly-regarded judiciary renowned for its professionalism and impartiality, the appointment of judges in all jurisdictions remains under the sole control of the government. It has also frequently been noted that the composition of the bench, in particular in so far as gender, ethnicity and social background are concerned, does not reflect society as a whole. The desire to reduce political factors in appointments and to broaden the composition of the bench have led to calls for reform of the method by which judges are chosen.

As matters stand, at Commonwealth level s 71 of the Constitution states that judges are appointed by the Governor-General in Council, which means by the Governor-General on the advice of the government. Section 7 of the *High Court of Australia Act 1979* (Cth) states that an appointee must be a judge of a federal or State court or must have been a legal practitioner for at least 5 years. Section 6 of

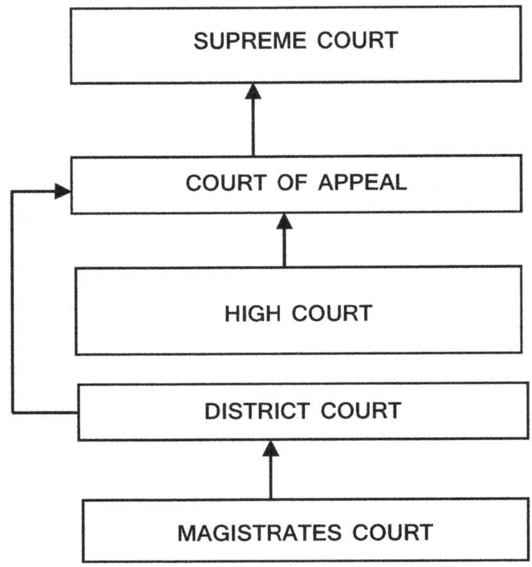

Fig. 11.2 Proposed court structure

the Act states that before making an appointment, the Commonwealth Attorney-General must consult with the Attorneys-General of the states. Other than that, the appointment process is both non-prescriptive and closed in the sense that no-one knows how the government determines who among the range of suitably qualified potential candidates should be considered for appointment, who apart from the Attorneys-General of the States the Commonwealth Attorney-General consults (although it is thought that consultations extend to existing members of the judiciary as well as bodies representing the legal profession) and how often the cabinet rejects the person recommended by the Attorney-General, requiring the process to begin again.

There is undoubtedly a natural tendency on the part of a government to select judges who it thinks might have the same approach to the law as it does. Although in Australia governmental deliberations over judicial appointments occur out of the public eye, it is understood that governments take into account what they think appointees' approaches to the law are likely to be – particularly in so far as constitutional interpretation is concerned.[1] Of course, sometimes governments miscalculate, and judges turn out to hold views that governments did not predict. The point however is that a government's political views should, as far as possible, be removed as a consideration affecting judicial appointments.

There has been debate over a number of years on the question of whether the method of appointing judges should be reformed so as to make it less subject to

[1]An example of this being exposed occurred in 1913, when Albert Piddington was appointed to the High Court. It emerged that the government had, through an intermediary, sounded out his views on Commonwealth-State relations prior to making the appointment. The resulting controversy caused Piddington to resign a few weeks after accepting his appointment, never having hear a case.

political considerations. There have also been calls to make the bench more reflective of the population in so far as race, gender and other characteristics are concerned.[2]

In some countries – in particular in some states in the United States – judges are popularly elected. However that practice is fundamentally incompatible with the maintenance of judicial independence and impartiality. The judicial role is not, and can never be, 'representative' in the sense of being exercised in accordance with what is popular. It requires the impartial application of the law to all litigants irrespective of public opinion. The election of judges is incompatible with judicial independence because elected judges are reliant for their tenure on retaining popular support. It is also incompatible with impartiality, because a judge who has his or her eye on whether decisions were likely to be popular would tend to decide cases in accordance with that criterion, rather than on their merits.

An alternative both to appointment at the sole discretion of the government and to popular election, is the de-politicisation of the judicial appointments process through the establishment of a judicial appointment body to advise the government on who should be appointed. There has been some movement in this direction in Australia so far as appointments to state and territory Supreme Courts are concerned. In Western Australia, the Northern Territory, Queensland and Tasmania, a panel advises the Attorney-General on whom to appoint. The panels vary widely in terms of their composition, ranging from current and past members of the judiciary, representatives of the legal profession, nominees of government departments and nominees of the Attorney-General. In most of these jurisdictions vacancies are publically advertised and prospective candidates may lodge an expression of interest in being appointed. After considering prospective appointees (interviews are not held, although in Western Australia may be at the discretion of the panel) the panels in these jurisdictions present their Attorney-General with names of those deemed suitable for appointment from which the Attorney-General selects one for consideration by the cabinet.

Although these panels have the advantage of removing the selection of judges from the sole discretion of the government, they suffer from the weakness that their composition is relatively narrow. In other Commonwealth countries the process has gone further, with judges selected by more broadly-composed bodies. In South Africa, for example, the Judicial Service Commission includes government and opposition MPs, representatives of the legal profession as well as representatives of the judiciary and of academia.[3] In the United Kingdom the 15-person Judicial Appointments Commission consists of judges, legal practitioners and six lay (that is, non-lawyer) members, one of whom is appointed Chairman.[4] In Canada the Independent Advisory Board for Supreme Court of Canada Judicial Appointments consists of a retired judge, legal practitioners, a legal academic and three other

[2] For a detailed discussion see Williams (2008, pp. 165–6).

[3] See s 178 of the *Constitution of the Republic of South Africa Act* 1996.

[4] See s 2 of Schedule 12 of the *Constitutional Reform Act 2006* (UK).

members, two of whom musty be non-lawyers.[5] In the case of each of these countries, after evaluating candidates, the selection body recommends a list of those it considers suitable for appointment, from which the government selects one.

Apart from de-politicisation of the appointment process, a judicial selection commission can help address the other criticism of the current method of judicial appointment, which is that it leads to a bench lacking in diversity in terms of gender, ethnicity and social background. The issue of judicial diversity is controversial. Given that the judiciary discharges an expert role which requires specific qualifications and experience, its membership cannot be expected to reflect the population as a whole. Yet public confidence in the judicial system would be enhanced if the bench reflected the broadest possible range of social backgrounds and experience possible from within the pool of qualified candidates.[6] In the long term, the best hope for achieving a diverse judiciary is to ensure that diversity is fostered in access to law schools and in advancement in the legal profession. But even in the short term, the establishment of a judicial selection commission could effect positive change, in that the composition such a commission would affect who it recommended for appointment to the bench – in other words, the more diverse the background and experience of the members of the commission, the more diverse one would expect its choices would be.

Taking all of the above into account, and drawing on the experience of other countries, I would suggest that a judicial selection commission should consist of three members of the judiciary, two nominees of the legal profession and four non-lawyers appointed through a public selection process. This structure would ensure that as well as the judiciary and the profession, who have always traditionally been consulted, lay people would have a role. Judicial vacancies should be advertised along with the criteria that the commission would take into account in assessing candidates, and candidates should be interviewed by the commission. The commission should provide the Attorney-General with three names from which he or she should make an appointment.

11.4 Dismissal of Judges

No less important than the process of appointing judges is the process by which they are dismissed. Security of tenure (until retirement age), along with protection against reduction in judicial salaries, are important elements of judicial independence, which were first put into legal form in the United Kingdom in the *Act of Settlement 1700* (UK) and in Australia are contained in s 72 of the Constitution. These rules serve to protect the judiciary from pressure by the executive and, like so many of the doctrines of our Constitution, were born out of the bitter struggle between parliament and the monarchy in seventeenth century England, when the

[5] The composition and functions of the board are outlined in Trudeau (2017).

[6] See the discussion in Harris (1993).

monarch would dismiss judges whose decisions he disagreed with. Under s 72, a judge can be dismissed only by a joint address to the Governor-General by both houses of Parliament on grounds of proved misbehaviour or incapacity. No Commonwealth judge has ever been removed from office under s 72.

The reference to 'proved' misbehaviour or incapacity, suggests that removal requires that parliament engage in a judicial process. Yet the Constitution does not specify what process is to be used. A suitable process was proposed by the 1988 Constitutional Commission, which recommended that the Constitution be amended so as to provide for a Judicial Tribunal, staffed by superior court judges to hear cases, and to make recommendations to the legislature.[7] Thus only if a judge had been found by the Tribunal to have engaged in misbehaviour or to be incapable of discharging their office would the matter come before parliament for a vote. The Constitution should also specify that evidentiary rules guaranteeing a fair hearing would also be applicable. It should also be made clear that 'misbehaviour' refers to the judge's conduct while in office, rather than to conduct prior to appointment, as it would be inconsistent with the doctrine of security of tenure if a judge was able to be dismissed for conduct engaged in before being appointed to office. On the other hand, 'misbehaviour' should be interpreted as involving not just misconduct in the performance of judicial duties, but also serious breaches of the law and other behaviour engaged in after appointment which demonstrates unfitness to hold office,[8] which would be achieved through the inclusion of the word 'unfitness' in the relevant constitutional provision. The Constitution should also make provision for the suspension of judges while an inquiry is in progress, as continued discharge of judicial duties while a hearing is in progress would impact upon public confidence in the integrity of the courts.

11.5 Judicial Salaries

An important rule protecting judicial independence is that judges' salaries should not be able to be reduced. This is provided for in s 72 of the Constitution. Some attention should also be paid to the issue of the amount of judicial salaries, and the potential for them to be eroded by inflation. If judges were appointed on the recommendation of a commission, it would seem appropriate that the same body should be vested by the constitution with the task of determining judicial salaries, subject to the requirement that judicial salaries should increase each year by at least as much as the consumer price index.[9] This would not involve any drastic change from current practice, as the salaries of judges are currently set by remuneration tribunals in the case of the Commonwealth and all states bar Tasmania (where they are set by a formula calculated by reference to judicial salaries in other states).

[7] Constitutional Commission (1988, pp. 180–203).

[8] Campbell and Lee (2001, pp. 110–11).

[9] See the discussion of the quantum of judicial salaries in Winterton (1995, pp. 26–7).

11.6 The Problem of Standing

As stated at the start of this chapter, a legal rule is only effective in so far as someone can enforce it in the courts. Unfortunately, in Australia there are many instances where there is no right to go to court to challenge governmental action or where rules of standing limit who may approach the courts in order to enforce legal rules.

Whether a person may enforce a legal rule in the courts is governed by the law on 'standing'. Only a person with standing in a dispute can go to court to have it resolved. The need for rules of standing is obvious when one considers a simple scenario involving a contract of sale between A and B, where A promises to pay B the amount of $ 100 and B promises to deliver his TV set to A. If A pays B the $ 100, but B refuses to deliver the TV set, C cannot take B to court to force B to perform under the contract. Only A can do that, because only A's rights have been affected by B's refusal to perform. In this instance, one would say that A has standing but C does not.

Although the rules of standing are easy to apply and are fair in their consequences when disputes involve easily defined plaintiffs whose rights have been affected, they tend to have adverse effects in cases where large groups of people are affected. The underlying common law rule in Australia is that for a person to have standing, they must be vindicating their own private right or, where rights that the public as a whole are entitled to are in issue, a person must be able to demonstrate that their interests are particularly affected above and beyond those of the general public.[10] This was illustrated by *Australian Conservation Foundation v Commonwealth*,[11] a leading case on environmental law, in which the court held that in order to vindicate a public right or enforce a public duty, a plaintiff must be able to demonstrate a special interest in the matter – in other words, must stand gain some advantage or avoid some disadvantage in bringing the action. Importantly, the court held that a mere emotional or intellectual concern did not amount to a sufficient interest. For this reason the court denied standing to an environmental group seeking to challenge the government's decision to approve a resort on the grounds that the government had failed adequately to consider an environmental impact report, holding that, apart from sharing an interest in the environment, the members of the group had failed to show how they personally would be affected by the approval of the resort.

A more liberal approach to determining what constitutes a special interest was evident in *Onus v ALCOA of Australia Ltd*,[12] in which the court held that members of an Aboriginal group had standing to challenge the construction of a smelter at a sacred site because they were the traditional custodians of the site, there was a special cultural and spiritual significance to the site and the group visited the site regularly. Although this approach was more generous than that in *Australian*

---

[10] *Anderson v Commonwealth* (1932) 47 CLR 50.

[11] (1980) 146 CLR 493.

[12] (1989) 149 CLR 27.

Conservation Foundation, the court still retained the special interest test. Gibbs CJ held that a mere intellectual or emotional concern was insufficient to found standing,[13] while Brennan J held[14] that for standing to exist, a plaintiff must show that

> …he has been specially affected, that is, in comparison with the public at large he has been affected to a substantially greater degree or in a significantly different manner.

This common law requirement for a special interest has affected the way the courts interpret the Constitution. Under sections 75 and 76 of the Constitution, jurisdiction is conferred on the courts to decide 'matters' arising under Commonwealth law. The High Court has interpreted the word 'matters' strictly, holding that for there to be a matter, there has to be a dispute between parties who have standing in the sense explained above.[15]

The operation of the rules of standing are particularly problematic when it comes to the enforcement of constitutional law. The insistence that a litigant be able to demonstrate a personal interest in a matter order to have standing - and the corresponding denial of standing to a litigant who has 'only' a general interest in the maintenance of the constitutional order – places an obstacle in the way of the rule of law, which relies for its effectiveness of the ability of people to force governments to comply with the Constitution.

As explained earlier, the rules of standing require proof of differential operation of unlawful conduct in relation to a specific plaintiff as distinct from its effect on the broader public. Yet, in many instances, differential effect on the individual may be slight and the interest or concern of the public as a whole may be of far greater importance – particularly in cases involving compliance with the Constitution. In *Onus v Alcoa,* the court took spiritual matters into consideration in assessing the interests of the applicants. Is it not anomalous that the courts do not similarly consider philosophical concerns as being sufficient to found standing? The decision in *Onus v Alcoa* was undoubtedly liberal so far as Indigenous rights and spirituality were concerned, but it was still conservative in its requirement that there be 'something more' than emotional or intellectual concern to establish standing. Why should a secular concern for compliance with the Constitution be any less entitled to be taken into consideration as a ground for standing than spiritual concerns relating to land use? Unfortunately, the High Court has set its face against the conferral of standing on plaintiffs simply because they are citizens with a general interest in the enforcement of the Constitution.[16] The only exception to this trend was a

[13] (1989) 149 CLR 27, 35.

[14] (1989) 149 CLR 27, 74.

[15] This rule was first enunciated in *In re Judiciary and Navigation Acts (Advisory Opinions Case)* (1921) 21 CLR 257.

[16] See *Victoria v Commonwealth and Hayden* (1975) 134 CLR 388, 402; *Attorney-General (Commonwealth), ex rel McKinlay v Commonwealth* (1975) 135 CLR 1, 26: *Ingram v Commonwealth and Peacock* (1980) 54 ALJR 395, 397 and *Attorney-General (Victoria); ex rel Black v Commonwealth (DOGS Case)* (1981) 146 CLR 559, 589.

decision at state level in *McDonald v Cain*,[17] where the court held that voters had standing to seek a declaration that it would be unlawful to present a Bill changing electoral boundaries for assent where the Bill had allegedly not been passed in accordance with the Victorian Constitution.

The prevailing approach in Australia thus focuses on the impact of law on the individual, rather than the impact of law on society as a whole. Yet where the law in question is one relating to the constitution, surely it should not be necessary to seek out a single, particular person who will be 'sufficiently' harmed or benefited by the law? The fixation on finding an individual with standing seems particularly inappropriate to field of constitutional law, as infringements of the constitution necessarily affect all individuals in society, and ought therefore to be remediable on the suit of any member of society.

Under the current approach, breaches of the constitution will be left unremedied in circumstances where no-one with a personal interest initiates legal action. In other words, whether an alleged breach of the constitution is able to challenged depends on whether an individual finds it to their own advantage to initiate a challenge rather than on the legal merits of the issue. This means that meritorious challenges may not be heard, and constitutional breaches thereby allowed to stand, simply because no self-interested litigant comes forward. This is surely a paradox – the rules of standing are supposedly justified on the ground that they prevent litigation based on individual caprice, yet their effect is precisely the opposite: Only those legal questions in which some individual is found to have an interest will be litigated, while those that may be of great importance to the commonweal, but which do not serve an individual interest, will not be. The result of this is that the law effectively favours the selfish over the selfless.

Another paradox in the law is the fact that the rules of standing appear to operate differently when it comes to politicians. Standing is frequently accorded to political actors without any exploration of whether they have a personal interest, in contrast to the 'ordinary' litigant, who has to demonstrate that they are able to surmount the interest hurdle. In other words, the current law of is not only founded on a bad rule, it appears that that the rule applies unevenly. This is evidenced by a number of constitutional cases in which the standing of plaintiffs was assumed (at least apparently - as the issue was not argued) because of their political status. For example, in *Cormack v Cope*,[18] the High Court heard a challenge brought by two opposition senators alleging non-compliance with the process contained in s 57 of the Constitution for resolving disputes between the House of Representatives and the Senate. Similarly, in *Victoria v Commonwealth (PMA Case)*[19] and *Western Australia v Commonwealth (First Territorial Senators Case)*,[20] the plaintiff states brought actions challenging compliance with s 57, along with the additional issue in the lat-

[17] [1953] VR 411.

[18] (1974) 131 CLR 432.

[19] (1975) 134 CLR 81.

[20] (1975) 134 CLR 201.

ter case of whether parliament had the power to give representation to the territories in the Senate. The territorial senators issue was again litigated at the instance of a State in *Queensland v Commonwealth (Second Territorial Senators Case)*.[21] In *Combet v Commonwealth*,[22] two members of the court[23] held that the shadow Attorney-General, in her capacity as an opposition Member of Parliament, had standing to challenge the validity of the expenditure of public money.

In none of these cases did the courts address the issue of *why* politicians or states should have standing. Plainly one can understand why opposition senators would have a *political* interest in challenging the procedures whereby the government had passed legislation, and why, in a legislative chamber where representation is state-based, states would similarly have a political interest in not having their power diluted by conferring representation on territories. But if members of legislative chambers and the entities to which seats are allocated in them are assumed to have standing to bring actions to ensure compliance with the Constitution, why should not individual citizens, who after all form the foundation of the state, not also have standing to do so?

Furthermore, what if it was *not* in the political interests of actors such as senators and states to challenge a particular breach of the constitution? The result then would be that the constitution would remain unenforced because its enforcement would be hostage to the interests of political actors. A counter-argument that might be raised is that in most, perhaps all, instances where a law has been invalidly enacted, there will eventually come a time when a plaintiff will be able to show that they have been personally affected through its operation, and that they will then have standing. That may be true in some instances but will not necessarily be true in all, and in any event misses the point that, as shown in the cases discussed above, political actors have not been required to wait until the law has operated on them – they have been deemed to have standing to initiate an immediate challenge. So the question remains as to why similar immediate standing should not be conferred on ordinary subjects of the law? In some cases their interest may be no less partisan than that of political actors. However in other cases, their interest may be altruistic rather than partisan, being motivated solely by a desire to uphold the doctrine of constitutionalism, particularly in circumstances where politicians have failed to take action to enforce the constitution because it was not in their interests to do so.

Perhaps the most glaring anomaly of all is provided by s 44 of the Constitution, the operation of which felled several MPs and senators in 2017 and 2018. Under s 353 of the *Commonwealth Electoral Act 1918* (Cth) the High Court may hear petitions that an electoral return (that is, the declaration that a person has been elected) is invalid. Under the rules of standing, such a petition could be brought by anyone with a particular interest, which could be either a defeated candidate or a voter in the electorate (in the case of House of Representatives seats) or in the state (in the case

[21] (1977) 1329 CLR 585.

[22] (2005) 224 CLR 494.

[23] McHugh J, 556–7 and Kirby J, 620–1.

of Senate seats). However, once a person has been sworn in as a member of either house, s 47 of the Constitution provides that each house of parliament that has jurisdiction to determine whether a person is qualified to sit. Under s 376 of the *Commonwealth Electoral Act 1918* (Cth) a house of parliament may (but does not have to) refer such a case to the High Court for determination. In *Alley v Gillespie*,[24] the High Court held that these are the only processes whereby the validity of an MP or Senator can be tested – in other words, a voter does not have standing to do so. The effect of this is that compliance with Constitution is held hostage to political interests, because in any decision under s 47 of the Constitution and any decision as to whether a case should be referred to the High Court, the relevant chamber will divide along political lines. This clearly demonstrates the inappropriateness of vesting in a political body the power to determine a question which should be decided on its legal merits. This was illustrated in 2018 when an opposition motion to refer Peter Dutton to the High Court for breaching s 44(v) was defeated by a government majority.[25] In other words, whether an MP or senator is compliant with the Constitution is ultimately determined by politics rather than by law, which is scandalous.

11.7 Reform of the Rules of Standing

In light of these problems, Australian academics have called for reform to the rules on standing. The arguments presented by Patrick Keyzer are particularly cogent. He started from the proposition that since the Constitution governs all, all should have the opportunity to ensure its compliance through the courts, and that therefore anyone who has a serious and arguable case relating to compliance with the Constitution should have a right to approach the courts for relief.[26] He advances three arguments in support of this.[27] The first is that litigation can provide a vehicle for freedom of political expression, as it is a method of arguing against the validity of government action. The second is that the rule of law confers a legitimate interest on everyone to know what the law – particularly the law of the Constitution - is, and to have available to them the remedy of declaration of invalidity where a law is unconstitutional. The third is that since sovereignty ultimately rests in the people, the people should have a right to approach the courts to ensure that the government is acting lawfully. Standing in constitutional matters therefore warrants special treatment.

[24] [2018] HCA 11.

[25] Johnston (2018).

[26] Keyzer (2010, p. 42).

[27] Keyzer (2010, pp. 123–4).

In addressing the counter-argument that such a broad rule of standing might open the floodgates of litigation, Keyzer states[28] that standing would still have to be demonstrated, but that

> …the courts ought not exclude a person from access to constitutional justice on the basis of *who they are*. Instead, the courts can exclude people from access to constitutional justice on the basis of *what they have argued*.

In other words, under Keyzer's approach, the law would assume that all people have standing to ensure compliance with the Constitution and so whether the courts would intervene would depend only on whether a plaintiff could demonstrate that there is a justiciable question to be heard. Keyzer's argument is therefore not that no interest is required, but rather that the law should recognise a *different type* of interest – in other words, his argument reconceptualizes what an interest entitled to its day in court is, and recognises that a litigant acting in the public interest is as much entitled to standing as one acting in their own personal interest.

The idea of having broad rules of standing is not new – in fact its roots can be traced back to Roman law, under which the *actio popularis* (or popular action) conferred standing on individual citizens to enforce public duties, even in the absence of a personal interest.[29] The *actio* reflected Roman ideas of citizenship, to which the fact that Rome was a republic is critical to an understanding. As the *res publica* – the 'public thing' – the republic was thought of as something in which all citizens had an interest.[30] This interest was not only a generalised one as a member of the body of citizens, but a personal one as well: Every citizen had a duty to intervene when the *res publica* was threatened.[31] Therefore, just as a person could hold enforceable legal rights such possession and ownership in relation to a *res,* or thing, under the law of property, so too did he enjoy rights in relation to the *res publica* which could be vindicated by means of a specific legal action, the *actio popularis*.[32] The *actio popularis* therefore gave practical form to the values underlying the Roman concept of citizenship and so legal action to ensure that public duties were complied with was viewed as a natural activity for the citizen. The adoption of an interventionist stance by the citizen was thus seen as a public benefit – an attitude which contrasts sharply with the characterisation in modern case law of the public interest litigant without a personal stake in a controversy as an 'officious busybody' to whom standing should be denied.[33]

In modern times, rules of standing in constitutional matters have been broadened in many countries. The process of democratisation after the fall of communism in

[28] Keyzer (2011, p. 73).

[29] *Digest of Justinian*, D 47.23.1, Mommsen et al. (1985, p. 794).

[30] Lacey (1978, p. 93).

[31] Rawson (1975, p. 247).

[32] Bolgar (1959, p. 53).

[33] See *United States Tobacco Co v Minister for Consumer Affairs* (1988) 20 FCR 520, 527 and *Onus v Alcoa of Australia* (1981) 149 CLR 27, 35.

Eastern Europe saw a number of countries[34] enact constitutional or statutory provisions giving citizens the right to challenge non-compliance with the constitution, in accordance with the idea that protection of the democratic order would be maximised if citizens had the capacity to take legal action to defend it.[35] This trend was followed in a number of other European jurisdictions.[36] In Croatia for example, Art 38(1) of the *Constitutional Act on the Constitutional Court of the Republic of Croatia 2002* states that

> Every individual or legal person has the right to propose the institution of proceedings to review the constitutionality of the law and the legality and constitutionality of other regulations.

Similar developments have occurred elsewhere in the world: In Nepal, Article 133(1) of the *Constitution of Nepal 2015* states, in relation to the jurisdiction of the Supreme Court, that

> Any Nepali citizen may file a petition in the Supreme Court to have any law or any part thereof declared void on the ground of inconsistency with this Constitution because it imposes an unreasonable restriction on the enjoyment of the fundamental rights conferred by this Constitution or on any other ground, and extra-ordinary power shall rest with the Supreme Court to declare that law void either ab initio or from the date of its decision if it appears that the law in question is inconsistent with the Constitution.

In Uganda, s 137(3) of the *Constitution of Uganda 1995* states that
A person who alleges that—

(a) an Act of Parliament or any other law or anything in or done under the authority of any law; or
(b) any act or omission by any person or authority, is inconsistent with or in contravention of a provision of this Constitution, may petition the constitutional court for a declaration to that effect, and for redress where appropriate.

Finally, s 38 of the *Constitution of the Republic of South Africa Act*,[37] states:

38. Anyone listed in this section has the right to approach a competent court, alleging that a right in the Bill of Rights has been infringed or threatened, and the court may grant appropriate relief, including a declaration of rights. The persons who may approach a court are—

    (a). anyone acting in their own interest;
    (b). anyone acting on behalf of another person who cannot act in their own name;

---

[34] Sadurski (2005, pp. 5–6).

[35] See the discussion in Popescu (2014, pp. 162–4 who points to Estonia, Lithuania, Romania and Venezuela as jurisdictions in which an *actio popularis* is available.

[36] Kilinç (2016) cites Lichtenstein, Malta, Croatia, Georgia and Macedonia as jurisdictions which have created statutory *actiones populares*.

[37] No. 108 of 1996.

(c). anyone acting as a member of, or in the interest of, a group or class of persons;
(d). anyone acting in the public interest; and
(e). an association acting in the interest of its members.

Section 38(d) is obviously the most important of these provisions in so far as enforcement of the Constitution by individuals is concerned. Furthermore it is important to note that although the text of s 38 applies to remedying infringements of the Bill of Rights, in *Ferreira v Levin*[38] the Constitutional Court held that a broad approach to standing should be taken in relation to the enforcement of all parts of the Constitution. Thus in *Freedom Under Law v Acting Chairperson: Judicial Service Commission*,[39] the court held that the applicant organisation had standing to seek review the respondent's dismissal of a complaint made by members of the judiciary against a judge who they alleged had attempted improperly to influence members of the Constitutional Court. The court held that Freedom Under Law had a right, acting in the public interest, to ensure that the independence of the judiciary was upheld[40] and indeed that[41]

> …every South African citizen has an interest to be served by judges who are fit for judicial office, and by courts which are independent and impartial.

In similar vein, in *Democratic Alliance v The Acting National Director of Public Prosecutions*,[42] the court held that a political party had standing both in its own interests and in the public interest to ensure that the rule of law was upheld.[43] On this basis the court held that the appellant could initiate litigation seeking judicial review of the respondent's decision to discontinue a prosecution of President Jacob Zuma for corruption.

The importance of these cases lies in the fact that under the South African Constitution, citizens are viewed as legitimate intervenors in public affairs through their enforcement of constitutional obligations against the branches of government, even in the absence of a personal interest being at stake,[44] an approach that is radically different from that which has thus far prevailed in Australia.

These examples come from a variety of jurisdictions with different legal systems, however the philosophy underlying them is the same - that because every person has an interest in ensuring that the organs of government discharge their duty to comply with the constitution, and because that duty is owed not to any specific individual but rather to the people as a whole, everyone should have the

[38] 1996 (1) BCLR 1 (CC), 99.
[39] 2001 (3) SA 549 (SCA).
[40] 2001 (3) SA 549 (SCA), 556 B-C.
[41] 2001 (3) SA 549 (SCA), 557 D-F.
[42] 2012 (3) SA 486 (SCA).
[43] 2012 (3) SA 486 (SCA), 504.
[44] For a discussion of the application of rules of standing following the enactment of South Africa's post-apartheid Constitution, see Swanepoel (2014) and Swanepoel (2016).

right to act in the public interest and to ask the courts for a remedy when the constitution is breached.

References

Bolgar V (1959) The concept of public welfare: an historical comparative essay. American Journal of Comparative Law 8:44–71

Campbell E, Lee H (2001) The Australian judiciary. Cambridge University Press, Cambridge

Constitutional Commission (1988) Final report of the constitutional commission. Australian Government Publishing Service, Canberra

Harris B (1993) Appointments to the bench - the role of a judicial services commission. Adelaide Law Review 15:191–207

Johnston D (2018) Vote to send Liberal Peter Dutton to High Court defeated 69–68. The Border Mail. 23 August 2018

Keyzer P (2010) Open constitutional courts. Federation Press, Leichhardt

Keyzer (2011) Standing to raise constitutional issues reconsidered, considered. Bond Law Review 22:60–77

Kilinç B (2016) Individual application in Turkish constitutional adjudication. Key, Palermo

Lacey W (1978) Cicero and the end of the Roman republic. Hodder and Stoughton, London

Mommsen T, Kreuger P, Watson A (trans. and eds) (1985). The digest of Justinian. University of Pennsylvania Press, Philadelphia

Popescu R (2014) The forms of direct democracy and their role in ensuring good governance. Romanian Journal of Comparative Law 5:126–184

Rawson E (1975) Cicero – A Portrait. Allen Lane, London

Sadurski W (2005) Rights before courts: a study of Postcommunist courts in central and Eastern Europe. Springer, Dordrecht

Swanepoel C (2014) The judicial application of the "interest" requirement for standing in constitutional cases: "a radical and deliberate departure from common law". De Jure 47(1):63–84

Swanepoel C (2016) The public interest action in South Africa: the transformative injunction of the south African constitution. Journal for Juridical Science 41(2):29–46

Trudeau J (2017). Independent Advisory Board for Supreme Court of Canada judicial appointments. https://pm.gc.ca/en/news/backgrounders/2017/07/17/independent-advisory-board-supreme-court-canada-judicial-appointments Accessed 9 Oct 2019

Williams G (2008) High court appointments: the need for reform. Sydney Law Review 30:163–169

Winterton G (1995) Judicial remuneration in Australia. Australian Institute of Judicial Administration, Melbourne

Chapter 12
Civics Education and Reform Strategies

Abstract Although the Australian electorate is notoriously conservative when it comes to constitutional reform, a 2014 survey in questions which were prefaced with an explanation of what the implications of various reforms would be produced results which indicated a greater receptiveness to reform than one might initially have thought. A key impediment to reform is lack of knowledge about the constitution. The chapter discusses the poor state of civics education and analyses the Civics and Citizenship component of the Australian Curriculum, concluding that whereas it explains the constitution well, it does not equip students with the intellectual skills – particularly a background knowledge of political philosophy – to enable them to critique the constitution. The chapter criticises politicians who, out if self-interest, promote fear of constitutional reform, and the legal academic community which displays little interest in it. The chapter discusses reform strategies, advocating the establishment of a constitutional commission at which the entire range of possible constitutional reforms could be canvassed. Failing that, the chapter recommends that because of the obvious unfairness of the electoral system, a campaign focussing on electoral reform would stand the best chance of success as an initial measure. This would in turn lead to a re-alignment of power in parliament which was more conducive to broader constitutional reform. The chapter concludes by urging Australians to adopt a positive, principled and optimistic attitude towards reform.

12.1 Impediments to Reform

The reluctance of voters to approve constitutional change is notorious. Of 44 referenda held since 1901, only eight have been successful. An important contributing cause of this is widespread lack of understanding of how the constitution works. People are, understandably, unwilling to interfere with a mechanism when its operation is a mystery to most of them.

The degree of ignorance about the constitution is profound. A 1992 survey found that only 67% of Australians knew that we have a constitution.[1] In 1994, a report by

[1] Muller (1992).

B. Harris, *Constitutional Reform as a Remedy for Political Disenchantment in Australia*, https://doi.org/10.1007/978-981-15-3599-4_12

the Civics Expert Group, a panel appointed by the government to inquire into the standard of civics education in Australia, found that only 18% of respondents said that they had some understanding of the constitution, only 40% could correctly name both houses of parliament, and 62% thought we have a bill of rights.[2] A 2015 survey found that only 65% of Australians knew that we have a constitution – a lesser proportion than in 1992.[3] Of course, people cannot be blamed for lack of knowledge if it has not been provided to them in the first place. What is almost worse than lack of knowledge, is half-knowledge – enough to give people a misplaced degree of confidence to engage in debate, but insufficient to avoid serious error when they do.

Ignorance is not something for which people can be blamed – the fault lies in the shortcomings in civics education, which are discussed later in this chapter. But voter ignorance provides only one obstacle to constitutional reform. Of equal importance – and certainly blameworthy – is the conduct of politicians and other public figures who misrepresent how the constitution works and what the effects of reform would be. To take some examples, John Howard famously refused to issue an apology to the Stolen Generation in parliament, saying that this would attract financial liability to the Commonwealth (which is untrue, since nothing said in parliament can be used as evidence in litigation). Kevin Rudd in framing the terms of reference for the National Human Rights Constitution implied that the constitution does not have justiciable rights (also untrue). Frank Brennan said that having a right to equality coupled with affirmative action would be too complex for the courts to interpret (true only if one believes that Australian judges are less able than their counterparts in the many other countries which have such provisions), while Malcolm Turnbull said that the proposed Indigenous Voice would amount to adding a third chamber to parliament (untrue as the Voice would have only an advisory and not a legislative function).

All the statements in the previous paragraph could be easily rebutted if analysed by anyone with a basic knowledge if constitutional law, yet they appear plausible to those who do not – which unfortunately means most people. The reason why such statements are so effective at derailing constitutional reform is that because people are unaware of the truth, they err on the side of safety and reject reform. This is precisely the effect hoped for by constitutional conservatives, whose members are found within the ranks of both main political parties and who have a vested interest in maintaining the status quo.

We therefore face a dual challenge, the first element of which is to improve the standard of civics education so as to equip people with the necessary knowledge – and skills of critical thinking – to enable them to participate in debate and to differentiate what is true from what is false. The second element is to counteract those conservative forces which oppose reform, whether simply from unreasoning and

[2] Civics Expert Group (1994).

[3] Miller (2015).

instinctive opposition to change, or from self-interested determination to preserve existing power-relationships.

12.2 Public Attitudes to Constitutional Reform

Turning first to the question of public knowledge of constitutional matters, despite the depressing view given by the surveys cited above, it is important not to be too pessimistic. Voters are educable and capable of recognising injustice. The evidence for this is provided by a survey on attitudes to constitutional reform conducted in 2014.[4] The survey consisted of 26 questions, designed to ascertain the views of respondents in six key topics: knowledge of the constitution and experience of civics education, views on the electoral system, a bill of rights, parliamentary scrutiny of the executive, the future of federalism and whether Australia should become a republic.

Although a disturbingly high 51% of respondents said that they had never been taught how the constitution works, an overwhelming majority (95%) supported the proposition that school students should be taught more about the constitution.

When asked whether they thought that, under the current system of elections for the House of Representatives, parties obtained seats in proportion to their share of the national vote, 33% of respondents said yes, 25% did not know and only 43% correctly responded in the negative. What was significant was when asked in the next question whether parties *should* obtain a share of seats proportional to their vote, 75% of respondents said yes. Most significantly of all, when asked which of three objectives of an electoral system were most important, 46% said providing voters with local representatives to whom they could take their concerns, 42% chose fairness in accurately representing which political party voters supported, and only 12% chose the formation of government by a single party – a result which is contrary to the argument put forward by the major parties when electoral reform is suggested.

As a preface to the next question, respondents were given the following background statement:

> Under the current electoral system for the House of Representatives, MPs are elected in single-member electorates. A single party usually gets enough seats to form government, but parties do not get representation in proportion to their support nationwide. This can even lead to a government coming to power with fewer votes nationwide than were received by the opposition. By contrast, under a proportional representation system, parties always get seats in proportion to their share of the national vote. Governments are usually formed by a coalition of parties which, in combination, will always represent a majority of voters.

---

[4] The survey data was drawn from a randomly selected sample representative of Australian voters.

In light of that, 58% of respondents supported a proportional system whereas 42% supported the current system. In other words, when first given an *explanation* of the realities of the effect of different electoral systems, there was a clear preference among voters to a fairer system.

When it came to protection of human rights, 81% of respondents said that there should be certain fundamental rights which a parliament elected by the voters should not unreasonably be able to limit or remove. The significance of this question lies in the fact that it included the phrase 'a parliament elected by the voters,' because it required respondents to confront the key issue underlying the constitutional protection of human rights, which is that it puts a limit on the democratic will. In full knowledge of that, an overwhelming majority of respondents agreed with the proposition put to them. Furthermore, when asked what they were asked which of three methods they felt would be most effective in protecting rights, 66% chose obtaining an order form the courts, 20% petitioning the government and only 14% seeking change at the next election – a clear understanding that it is justiciability that gives effective protection to rights. Disturbingly however, a majority of respondents either did not think that the constitution currently protected rights (13%) or said that they did not know whether it did or not (51%). In other words, most people would wrongly assume that the constitutionalisation of rights would be a novelty in Australia.

As a prelude to the next question, respondents were informed that the constitution does in fact protect four express rights and empowers the courts to invalidate legislation which unreasonably limits those rights. Respondents were then asked whether they thought that the constitution should protect the full range of rights contained in the international human rights documents which Australia has agreed to uphold, and 59% answered in the affirmative. As a follow-up, respondents were then asked which of a list of 20 rights should be protected by the constitution. In each case a clear majority agreed that the rights should be protected – indeed, protection of 16 of the rights was supported by more than 90% of respondents. When asked in a separate question about socio-economic rights, 76% of respondents agreed that they should be given constitutional protection, subject to what resources were available to the government.

The next set of questions related to parliamentary control of the executive. After given information that, under the current system, the Speaker of the House of Representatives is elected by a simple majority of MPs and that this means that both the election and the dismissal of the Speaker are controlled by the government, 60% of respondents were of the view that the speaker should instead by elected by a 2/3 majority of MPs. When asked whether ministers should be obliged to answer questions put to them by Parliament, an overwhelming majority of 96% responded in the affirmative,[5] while 78% said that a refusal by ministers to respond to questions should attract a penalty. Similar majorities of 96% and 89% were obtained when the

[5] Indeed this was the highest positive response to any of the questions in the survey except for the right to trial by an independent judiciary, supported by 98%.

same question was put in relation to answering questions put by parliamentary committees. Finally, when asked whether the validity of ministerial refusal to answer questions on grounds of public interest should be accepted without question or should be determined by the courts, 85% of respondents chose the latter option.

On the question of federalism, and after being given the definitions of a federal and a unitary state and information on the costs of the federal system, 55% of respondents said that they preferred a federal system whereas 45% supported a unitary system. This response is surprising given that it is at odds with the findings of a Galaxy poll in 2013, which found that 78% of respondents favoured having a single set of laws for the country[6] and a 2014 survey by the Griffiths University Centre for Governance & Public Policy which found that 71% of respondents favoured changing the current system (among whom there were differing preferences for the allocation of functions to national, regional and local governments).[7]

The final set of questions related to the powers of the office of Governor-General and to whether Australia should become a republic. After reading an explanation of the nature and importance of conventions and the fact that they are unenforceable, 64% of respondents agreed with the proposition that the conventions should be incorporated into the constitution as legally-enforceable rules. As to whether Australia should become a republic, 52% supported such a change. When asked by what method a president should be chosen if Australia did become a republic, an overwhelming majority of 73% supported election by the people. Finally, while 56% of respondents said that they would be concerned that an elected president might be tempted to use their powers contrary to the conventions, 71% said that that concern would be met if the conventions were to be changed into legally-enforceable constitutional provisions.

What does all this tell us? First and foremost it tells us that, given widespread lack of knowledge of the constitution, the giving of background information is crucial to obtaining an accurate impression of voter attitudes to constitutional reform. Furthermore the results demonstrate that if provided with such information, Australians are by no means as averse to constitutional reform as is commonly supposed – indeed, quite the opposite, because the results indicate that significant majorities support the adoption of a fair electoral system, constitutional protection of human rights, the independence of the office of Speaker, the imposition of a requirement that ministers answer questions put by parliament and its committees (with sanctions if they do not), codification of the powers of the Governor-General (or President, if Australia became a republic) and, if only by a narrow margin, the move to a republic.

These are all major reforms, and the positive response to them highlights that it is lack of knowledge about the constitution that is the key barrier to reform. The challenge then is how to address that problem.

---

[6] Galaxy Research (2013).

[7] Brown (2014, p. 15).

12.3 Reform of Civics Education

The current programme of civics education in Australia, like all other elements of the Australian school curriculum, had its origins in the *Melbourne Declaration on Educational Goals for Young Australians*,[8] which laid out the goals for education in the twenty-first century. Goal 2 stated that students should be able to become 'successful learners, confident and creative individuals, and active and informed citizens.' The Declaration further stated that active and informed citizens 'are committed to national values of democracy, equity and justice, and participate in Australia's civic life.'

In the years following the Melbourne Declaration, the new Australian Curriculum was developed by the Australian Curriculum, Assessment and Reporting Authority (ACARA). The Australian Curriculum Civics and Citizenship (ACCC) is one of the 16 areas into which the national curriculum is divided, and outlines civics and citizenship education for Years 3–10. In primary school (Years 3–6), the curriculum is integrated into a broad subject area called Humanities and Social Sciences (HASS), which embraces history, geography, business and civics and citizenship. The curriculum for secondary school (Years 7–10) is it presented as a discrete subject. Its lack of status as an independent subject in the primary years has been identified as a weakness both in its identity and effectiveness.[9] Nothing is provided for students in Years 11 and 12, so exposure to more advanced civics education depends on students choosing to undertake a subject such as politics or legal studies.[10] Use of the national curriculum is not mandatory – education is controlled by the states, so it is up to each state to determine whether and how the curriculum is taught, and this has led to variation across the country.[11]

The content of the Civics and Citizenship curriculum,[12] provides students with comprehensive explanation of the origins and operation of the system of government, treating progressively more complex material from year to year. The key issue from a constitutional reform perspective is to what extent the curriculum focuses on critique of the constitution and consideration of how it might be improved. Although students are called upon to apply critical skills at different points of the curriculum, they generally do so by analysing how the constitution works rather than by discussing what its shortcomings might be. Despite the fact that the curriculum and encourages students to develop 'justice-oriented citizenship' and 'critical citizenship' by exposing them to social diversity and problems such as racism,[13] it does so within the framework of accepted institutions – it does not invite students to critique those institutions or discuss how they might be reformed. As one commentator stated, the

[8] Ministerial Council on Education, Employment, Training and Youth Affairs (2008, pp. 8–9).

[9] Print (2017, p. 20).

[10] Tudball (2017, p. 27).

[11] Print (2017, pp. 19–20).

[12] Australian Curriculum, Assessment and Reporting Authority (2019a).

[13] Tudball (2017, p. 33).

problem with the curriculum is that it can lead to a 'non-critical understanding and assessment of what democracy is, and what it should be.'[14] This clearly does not satisfy the requirement of 'critical citizenship.'

To take some examples: In the Year 7 curriculum, students discuss 'how ministers are subject to the scrutiny of other members of the parliament led by an officially recognised opposition,' – but that statement presumes that ministers *are* indeed subject to scrutiny, it does not question whether scrutiny is effective. A positive inclusion in the Year 8 curriculum is debate on the question of whether parliament or the courts are best placed to resolve conflicts between various rights and freedoms, although the opportunity is not taken to determine whether the range of rights protected by the constitution is adequate. The Year 9 curriculum includes the only explicit reference in the 7–10 curriculum to critique of the constitution, in that students are asked to develop their citizenship skills by posing questions which evaluate Australia's democracy such as 'how equal?', 'how representative?' and 'how accountable? Finally, although in Year 10 students are introduced to comparative material, this aspect of the curriculum is limited to consideration of the constitutional system of a single Asian country, and students are asked only to compare the differences between the operational characteristics of that system and Australia's. While the focus on Asia is to some extent understandable given Australia's location, I would argue that the point of comparison should not be on a different region or regions, but rather on different *institutions* (wherever they may be drawn from), and that the question students should discuss is not just how systems differ in relation to how they operate but how they differ in relation to consistency with constitutional *values*.

There is no doubt that the Civics and Citizenship curriculum goes long way towards remedying the lack of knowledge of the Australian constitution, but whether it will enable future generations to be more critical of the constitution is doubtful. Apart from the comparative sparseness of opportunities for critical evaluation discussed in the preceding paragraph, the curriculum has the shortcoming of failing adequately to help students develop an ethical framework against which to evaluate institutions. The centrality of values to civics education is recognised by educators in the field.[15] However, although in Year 7 students study a module on 'How values, including freedom, respect, inclusion, civility, responsibility, compassion, equality and a 'fair go', can promote cohesion within Australian society,' nowhere in the entire curriculum is there coverage of philosophy, without a knowledge of which one surely cannot evaluate the values underlying a constitution. This is a critical omission. As one researcher in the field of civics education writes[16]

> Of all the learning areas in the curriculum, civics and citizenship is uniquely placed to provide opportunities for young people to develop their ideals, values, morals and ethics as

---

[14] Zyngier (2012).

[15] Petersen and Bentley (2017, p. 147).

[16] Henderson (2017, p. 42).

individuals and as members of society, and to learn how to act in accordance with them in various contexts.

One of the general capabilities that the Australian Curriculum requires to be developed across the different curriculum areas is Ethical Understanding,[17] yet how can this be achieved unless students are exposed to the foundation of ethics, which is philosophy? Of course this would have to be done with regard to the level of complexity that secondary students could cope with, but it is naïve to think that students can properly understand the meaning of concepts such as 'democracy' and 'freedom' without some prior knowledge of political philosophy. In common with other English-speaking countries, Australia has lagged behind in introducing philosophy to the high school curriculum. We compare unfavourably with European countries, where philosophy is an accepted part of the curriculum. In some, such as France, Spain and Italy, philosophy is mandatory in the final years of high school.[18] The thinking underlying this policy is that a knowledge of philosophy is necessary not only to produce citizens who are capable of analysing the ethical questions arising from the study of civics, but also to produce well-rounded people whose concerns arise above the mundane.

In the *Shape of the Australian Curriculum: Civics and Citizenship Paper* (drafted to guide the Civics and Citizenship curriculum)[19] ACARA stated that

> The values on which Australia's democracy is based include freedom of the individual, government by the people through a representative parliament, free and fair elections, the rule of law, equality of all before the law, social justice and equality, respect for diversity and difference, freedom of speech and religion, lawful dissent, respect for human rights, support for the common good, and acceptance of the rights and responsibilities of citizenship.

Yet nowhere in the curriculum is there a recognition that what each of these concepts means ultimately depends upon values, that the content of these concepts is contested and that in certain circumstances they may indeed clash with each other – a clash which can be resolved only through the application of value-based judgements. Elsewhere ACARA states that the rationale for the civics and citizenship subject is to 'help students develop inclusive attitudes and beliefs and liberal democratic values.'[20] But this presumes that liberal democratic values are to be preferred. Why? To be devil's advocate, why should society not be based on some other value-system, such as benevolent dictatorship? As was discussed in Chap. 2, the answer ultimately depends on Kantian notions of dignity, but without knowing that, students lack the intellectual tools required to understand – and defend – liberal democracy.

The curriculum therefore needs to go behind labels such as liberal democracy, the rule of law, equality and human rights and explore the philosophy which

---

[17] Australian Curriculum, Assessment and Reporting Authority (2019b).

[18] See Humphreys (2013) and Le Roux (2011).

[19] Australian Curriculum, Assessment and Reporting Authority (2012, p. 5).

[20] Australian Curriculum, Assessment and Reporting Authority (2012, p. 2).

underpins them. Unless it does so, students will not only fail to understand the constitution, but will be unable to evaluate the extent to which the constitution does in fact embody these institutions and, therefore, how it might need to be reformed. In short, what the curriculum needs to do is teach students about justice as a necessary corollary of teaching them about law – and this can be done only by introducing philosophy as a key part of the civics and citizenship curriculum.

12.4 Conservatism as an Obstacle to Reform

At the start of this chapter I identified the public's lack of knowledge of constitutional matters as the first impediment to constitutional reform. The second is the influence of conservatism in Australian society.

What is conservatism? This is a broad question with a range of possible – and sometimes conflicting - answers. The most common definition of conservatism is that it is a political philosophy which looks to the values of the past and upholds traditional institutions such as family, church and nation. Conservatives also generally reject the idea that it is the role of politicians to reform society, preferring instead that society evolve without state direction. However this definition is subject to significant exceptions. Conservatives may initiate radical reform if in order to return society to what they see as its previous ideal condition – Margaret Thatcher's privatisation of industries previously nationalised by post-World War II Labour governments being a good example. Conservative antipathy to state intervention might logically be thought to lead to them supporting constitutional protection of rights. However this is not necessarily the case, because although conservatives generally favour protection for economic freedoms, many are wary of constitutionalising other rights lest this provides individuals with a tool which could be used to restrain the power of government and to effect social change through litigation. Conservatives are tolerant of inequality, satisfied to let the free interplay of political, social and economic forces elevate some and subordinate others. For this reason, they oppose social engineering designed to produce levelling, even in the face of socio-economic conditions which are objectively unjust. Conservatives also generally oppose measures designed to achieve racial, gender and other forms of equality. The overall effect of conservatism is that it preserves the status quo and thus benefits the powerful to the detriment of the weak.

Conservative opposition to constitutional change in Australia stems from two different groups, although their membership can overlap. The first is made up of what one might call ideological conservatives of the type described above, who resist reform because they see it as threatening those power structures and institutions which conservatives traditionally privilege. A good example of this mindset is represented by those who opposed marriage equality because they believed that by permitting same-sex couples to marry, marriage as traditionally conceived would be undermined – although how this would actually occur was never articulated. Another example is provided by those who refused to participate in the apology to the Stolen

Generation because they saw the apology as an admission of guilt in relation to how Indigenous people had been treated. Indeed conservative attitudes with regard to many Indigenous issues, such as whether and when Australia Day should be celebrated and whether Indigenous constitutional rights should be recognised, are coloured by a concern that the founding of the nation through a process of colonisation should not be seen as morally blameworthy.

The other strain of constitutional conservatism derives from political self-interest. Such opposition is not 'conservative' in an ideological sense. Indeed its hallmark is that it crosses party lines because its wellspring is not a political value but rather a purely pragmatic concern that the power of government (by whomever it may be formed) should not be weakened. Thus neither Labor nor Coalition politicians support electoral reform, as it would sound their political death-knell in that neither bloc would ever be able to govern on its own. Similarly neither of the major parties support enhanced scrutiny powers for parliamentary committees – in fact, they have long colluded in ensuring that no a minister has ever been sanctioned for refusal to answer questions put by a parliamentary committee, as illustrated by Labor's failure to use contempt powers against former Liberal government Defence Minister Peter Reith during the Children Overboard affair, discussed in Chap. 7. So far as human rights are concerned, neither Labor nor the Coalition have supported the constitutionalisation of additional rights – even a right as fundamental as that to racial equality.[21] In so doing, both parties betray their self-professed fundamental values – individual freedom in the case of liberals and social justice in the case of Labor. Radical reforms of the type advocated in this book would attract vehement opposition from both the major parties, as most of the changes would alter the distribution of power in Australia in a manner favourable to the individual and disadvantageous to government in general and the major parties in particular. The likely opposition that such reforms would attract would be proof both of their necessity and of their likely effectiveness in addressing the power imbalances enabled by the current constitution.

A perhaps surprising source of conservatism is the academic community, who one would expect to be most eager to critique institutions and to find solutions to contemporary problems. Unfortunately, apart from spasmodic debate on a republic, which fails to address the key issue of codification of the conventions, and the occasional suggestion that Australia should have a statutory (that is, non-enforceable) bill of rights, the legal academic community is notable for stultifying thought – or lack of thought – about constitutional reform, and for a lack of curiosity about how overseas constitutional arrangements might be adopted in Australia. For the most part, academic lawyers are happy to confine their efforts to interpretation of what is, rather than on thinking of what might be.

To take some examples, the Centre for Comparative Constitutional Law at the University of Melbourne, which is staffed by many experts in the field of Australian

[21] Indeed then Prime Minister Tony Abbott rejected the idea of a constitutional right to equality. See Williams (2014).

constitutional law, regularly holds seminars at which overseas experts explain developments in their countries – but that is as far as it goes. Largely absent from the scholarship produced by the Centre is any exploration of how these developments could be applied in Australia. It is as if despite our unfair electoral system, our lack of executive accountability and our failure adequately to protect human rights, everything is fine in the Antipodean house and nothing or neighbours has to offer is of any use. Another concrete illustration of self-satisfied uncritical isolationism is provided by a special issue of the *Federal Law Review* published in 2004 which was devoted to electoral law, but in which not one article questioned the lack of representivity of the current system. There was only one article on proportional representation – and that consisting of a description of the New Zealand electoral system, which contained no reference to what lessons that system might have for Australia. The same conservatism is evident in the attitude of the Constitution Education Fund. While this organisation (whose CEO was leader of the No campaign during the 1999 republic referendum) has the laudable aim of promoting public knowledge of the constitution, entirely absent from its programme is an attempt to educate Australians about underlying constitutional *theory* or on how to evaluate the Constitution in the light of theory. Nowhere is there discussion as to whether our electoral system is fair, whether rights are adequately protected, whether there is effective parliamentary scrutiny of the executive, or whether unwritten conventions provide sufficient certainty and protection against abuse of power. Instead of being presented as something living and amenable to improvement, the Constitution is presented as though inscribed on Mosaic tablets: complete, unchanging and – even more significantly – as not requiring change. The document is presented as representing the apotheosis of constitutional development, which this book has shown it clearly is not.

The constitution is plainly defective. It fails to provide for fair representation, adequate supervision of the executive by parliament or protection for human dignity in the face of majoritarianism. It is built on a denial of Indigenous self-determination and on the formal vesting of executive power in a foreign monarch. It embodies a federal system that has no rational basis and serves no useful purpose. The rules of standing restrict the rights of citizens to enforce their constitution. Why, in the face of all this, is the academic community not leading the charge in arguing for reform? Possibly the answer is that they consider that the difficulties involved are so insuperable as to make the debate not worthwhile. But to adopt that attitude is to surrender to pragmatism rather than to fight for the principles upon which the constitution should be based.

12.5 Identifying the Path Forward

The Constitution is deeply flawed and in need of thoroughgoing reform. However, given the notorious difficulty of amending the Constitution, the changes recommended in this book would take decades to achieve if done piecemeal. Furthermore, given that the different parts of the constitution interact with each other, changing one part usually has implications for others.[22] There is therefore a strong case to be made for undertaking a general review of the Constitution with a view to drafting a completely new one.

The question is how such a monumental task as a complete redrafting of the constitution is to be achieved. A major part of the problem is getting constitutional reform onto the national agenda. The first step should be one of conscientisation – a campaign to make people aware of the defects in the constitution and how they impact negatively on their lives. The key objective would be to overcome the prevailing sense of disengagement from politics which is inimical to reform and to convert disillusionment and inertia into outrage and action. Such a campaign could co-ordinated by a pressure-group such as GetUp! or, alternatively, by an organisation established for the specific purpose of mustering support for constitutional change (as for example Recognise did in relation to Indigenous constitutional recognition). In conducting a campaign for change it would be important to bear in mind that success will depend as much upon emotional factors as it does on technical arguments. An important element of the campaign should be an appeal to people's sense of fairness: The electoral system, which denies so many votes any effect on the composition of parliament, is an obvious example of an aspect of the constitution which could be targeted because of its inherent unfairness to the individual voter. In relation to other issues however, the best appeal may be to self-interest. Here the federal system, which imposes practical burdens on people moving from state to state, which absorbs billions of dollars that could otherwise be used to improve services and which is in part responsible for the high cost of housing, is an obvious target. The problem is that at the moment, people think of the constitution as something remote from them, irrelevant to their everyday lives. Arguments such as the ones presented in this paragraph will bring home that in reality the constitution pervades every aspect of their existence and impacts directly on their personal interests.

Another avenue that might lead to constitutional reform is the holding of a general review into the Constitution. The Constitution was last reviewed in 1988, and reviews prior to that occurred in 1959 and 1929. By contrast, Australia's corporations legislation went through no less than nine stages of reform during the period 1997–2004.

But if the opportunity for wholescale reform did not present itself, then which of the many possible reforms should be given priority? In my view, reform of the electoral system offers the greatest chance of success, simply because the unfairness manifested by the current system is so glaring that it would not be difficult to engen-

[22] For example, if Australia was no longer to be a federation, the Senate would become redundant. This would remove whatever scrutiny (however limited) there is of the government, and so would necessitate reform of the committee system of the House of Representatives so as to enhance their power to sanction recalcitrant ministers. The abolition of federalism would also require a reorganisation of the court system.

der support for change if a concentrated campaign was mounted. To return to the theme this book started with, in an era of increasing disillusionment with the political system, a reform which held out the promise of people being able to choose a parliament which actually reflected their views would surely stand a good chance of succeeding. The adoption of a more representative electoral system would of course be bitterly resisted by the major parties, but that is perhaps the best demonstration to the community of how worthy a step it would be.

12.6 Attitudinal Change

Key to the achievement of any constitutional reform is changing the way Australians think about the constitutional matters in general and constitutional change in particular. There are a number of dimensions to this:

First, and most important, is the need to overcome the reflexive pessimism with which constitutional reform proposals are met. The most common reaction to such proposals is that since reform is so difficult, there is no point in thinking about it. But this misses the point that it is in large part *because* people think in this manner that reform is difficult. Thinking reform is difficult is itself the greatest hurdle to reform. We should instead realise that while there may be difficulties associated with reform, with sufficient effort they can be overcome, as is the case in any other area of human endeavour. We need to normalise discussion of constitutional reform rather than seeing it as something outlandish or bizarre, and we need to approach constitutional questions with an attitude of optimism, thinking about things not just as they are but as they could be. The results of the 2014 survey discussed at the start of this chapter show that if people are made aware of constitutional problems they are willing to entertain reforms which conventional wisdom usually suggests are far too radical to be approved of by Australian voters. We also need to abandon the idea that we should adopt watered-down half-measures in order to secure the support of those resistant to change. Propitiation of those who are hostile to change is a recipe for mere tokenism, as the debate on Indigenous constitutional rights has demonstrated. Constitutional change is worthwhile only if it has a real impact on existing power allocations, and achieving it requires that its opponents be confronted head-on, and their arguments firmly refuted.

Second, we need to overcome the tendency to abandon reform proposals as soon as the first negative argument is raised against them. For example, anyone who argues that we should have a full bill of rights receives the response that that would confer excessive power on the courts. A proposal to abandon federalism elicits the objection that Australia is too big to govern without the states. Each of these arguments is easily countered, yet they have achieved the status of conventional wisdom instead of being seen for what they are – self-serving attempts by those with vested interests to preserve a system from which they benefit. As this book has shown, an expansion of the range of rights protected by the constitution would not only not confer a new function on the courts but is the only mechanism that is capable of protecting individual dignity from the overweening power of the state. Similarly there is no practical reason why Australia could not be governed by a national government which delegated powers to regional or local governments. The reason why naysayers are so easily able to capture the field in such debates is that, for the most part, people do not have the necessary knowledge of constitutional law which is needed to counter these poorly founded objections – which again highlights the need for civics education of a type which equips citizens with the skills necessary to critique the constitution. There is no doubt that engaging in constitutional debate is hard work. It requires people to think deeply and confront difficult questions. It also requires them not to accept facile and superficial objections to reform at face value, but to challenge them instead. The benefit to society of engaging in this work would undoubtedly be worth the effort.

The third dimension of attitudinal change follows from the previous one. There is a tendency in Australia to consider obstacles to constitutional reform before analysing the rationale for reform. This is to put the 'how' cart before the 'why' horse, which has the inevitable effect of starting consideration of constitutional reform from a negative position – and often of preventing such consideration taking place at all. This way of thinking is also irrational – the logical order of addressing a problem is first to accept that there is a problem, and then to work out how to solve it, weighing the benefits and costs involved. Starting by looking for reasons *not* to solve a problem means that the benefits of doing so never receive proper consideration. Furthermore, as so often happens when problems arise in any field of human endeavour, solutions which no-one would previously have conceived of when the project began are discovered during its course – but the prerequisite for that is of course the decision to embark upon the project in the first place.

Fourth, we need to abandon pragmatism in favour of principle. As discussed in Chap. 2, the Constitutional Conventions of the 1890s were notable for the absence of a discussion of values upon which the constitution should be based. The objective of the drafters of the constitution was entirely practical – how to structure a deal that would satisfy the political and commercial interests of the colonies. The result was that the Australian constitution was built on a foundation of pragmatism rather than principle. This created a predisposition to analyse constitutional issues from a utilitarian rather than from a values-based perspective, an attitude that persists to this day. To take an obvious example, the idea that the electoral system should be reformed so as to be more proportionate in its effect almost always meets with argument that since proportional systems inevitably lead to coalitions, and since coalitions are unstable, such a change should be rejected in order to maintain political stability. Leaving aside the flawed link in this chain of reasoning that coalition governments are inherently unstable, the more disturbing aspect of this chain of reasoning is the subordination of a pragmatic concern such as stability over the principle that each voter should be entitled to equal influence over the political process as every other. In other words, even if it *was* the case that electoral reform led to less political stability, that would provide insufficient reason to justify breaching the fundamental principle of voter equality. Therefore, a critical aspect of attitudinal change to constitutional debate must be an appreciation of the need first to determine what values should underlie the constitution, of analysing the constitution in light of those values – and then determining what changes to the constitution adherence to those values requires. The idea that the constitution should be values-based was fundamental to the drafting of South Africa's post-apartheid constitution, and led to human dignity – the value discussed in Chap. 2 – being the first of the fundamental values listed in the founding provisions of the Constitution.[23] Importantly these values are not found in the preamble (which, as a matter of statutory interpretation, would mean that they were not part of the text of the constitution itself) but are contained in s 1 of the Constitution, which means that the courts are required to take them into account in cases where textual ambiguity arises. I would argue that in drafting a new Australian constitution we should do so not only in light of what human dignity dictates, but that that value should similarly be included as a principle guiding the interpretation of the constitution.

Fifth, we need to confront the insularity – sometimes bordering on xenophobia – that features prominently in the attitudes of constitutional conservatives. This attitude is retrograde and unscientific because development and progress in all fields of knowledge rely on comparing different experiences. Australians would be astonished if medicine or engineering were practised as they were in 1901, with no account taken of developments which have taken place in those fields in the intervening 119 years, both here and overseas. Why then should we be resistant to amending the constitution so as to take account of developments in constitutional theory throughout the world over the same period? To take one example, our constitution still does not take into account the international consensus regarding the moral bankruptcy of positivism which emerged in the aftermath of the post-World War II war crimes trials, and which led to the adoption of the Universal Declaration on Human Rights. Despite the prominent role played in the development of human rights jurisprudence by H.V. Evatt, the constitutional protection of human rights in Australia is no further advanced than it was 60 years ago.

As this book has shown, other jurisdictions provide a wealth of ideas which we could draw upon to remedy each of the flaws in the constitution. All the problems discussed in this book have been successfully addressed in other countries. Therefore an important element of overcoming resistance to constitutional reform lies in combatting insularity. We need to be open, in addressing the shortcomings in our constitution, to adopting institutions and practices which the experience of overseas countries has shown to be useful. In that way we could devise a constitution which incorporated the best that the rest of the world has to offer. Why should we not aim for a powerful system of legislative scrutiny over the executive as operates in the United States? Why not see the formation of coalition governments as a positive side-effect of a fair electoral system as it is in New Zealand, Switzerland or Germany, where politics is far more consensual than in Australia? Why not model a bill of rights on that contained in the South African constitution, which is based on human dignity as the supreme value? Why not codify the conventions governing the office

---

[23] Section 1(a) of the *Constitution of the Republic of South Africa Act No. 108 of 1996.*

of head of state as has been done in so many Commonwealth countries, and why not have an elected presidency operating in tandem with parliamentary government as in Ireland? Why not recognise self-determination of Indigenous peoples as in the United States, Canada or New Zealand? So long as our attitude to constitutional change remains closed, insular and incurious, our constitution will lag behind the rest of the world.

Finally, we need to abandon the conventional wisdom that bipartisan consensus is the only basis for constitutional change. Since much worthwhile change – for example reform of the electoral system, the enhancement of the scrutiny powers of parliament and the inclusion of a full bill of rights in the constitution – would have consequences inimical to the interests of the major parties, it is naïve to expect that they would willingly co-operate in bringing such changes about. Believing that change will occur only with the concurrence of the major parties is to give them a veto over reform and allows them to perpetuate the status quo. If we continue to let the parameters of reform be determined by those who are opposed to it, it should come as no surprise that meaningful reform does not take place. Real constitutional change is therefore likely to occur in spite of, rather than because of, the major parties, and as the result of organised popular pressure of the type discussed earlier in this chapter.

12.7 Conclusion

This book began by analysing how dissatisfaction with the way politics is conducted has undermined public confidence in the way we are governed. Unfortunately, our disillusionment with our politicians – justified as it is – has had the negative effect of making people fearful of change on the pessimistic assumption that any political change is bound to have adverse consequences for them. The irony is that voter resistance to constitutional change has the bizarre consequence of benefitting the very politicians with whom people feel such disillusionment. We need to discard our history of inertia and paralysing fear which unintentionally perpetuates the way politics are conducted.

Finally, I would suggest that the best way to think about the constitution is as follows: If we were given the task of drafting a constitution today, would we really opt for an unfair voting system which can allow a government come to power with fewer votes than the opposition; minimal protection for individual rights in the face of state power; paltry parliamentary powers to scrutinise the executive; a purposeless and expensive federal system; disregard for the status of the Indigenous people from whom the country was taken; a link to a foreign monarchy, coupled with a failure to specify in the constitution key rules governing the operation of the executive, and a justice system which obstructs the right of people to enforce the constitution? If we would not do those things now, why retain the constitution which does do them? It is only by adopting this blank slate approach that one realises just how obvious is the need for constitutional reform, and that what we need is a completely new constitution, rather than just amendment of the existing one. In light of that, the Appendix to this book contains a model constitution which incorporates the changes for which I have argued.

There is no doubt that constitutional reform is extraordinarily difficult, given the hurdles presented by s 128 and the political forces that have an interest in preserving the status quo. But every great project is difficult – indeed, it is the need to overcome difficulties which in part makes it great.

References

Australian Curriculum, Assessment and Reporting Authority (2012) Shape of the Australian curriculum: civics and citizenship paper. http://docs.acara.edu.au/resources/Shape_of_the_Australian_Curriculum__Civics_and_Citizenship_251012.pdf. Accessed 22 Oct 2019

Australian Curriculum, Assessment and Reporting Authority (2019a) Civics and citizenship. https://www.australiancurriculum.edu.au/f-10-curriculum/humanities-and-social-sciences/civics-and-citizenship/. Accessed 11 Oct 2019

Australian Curriculum, Assessment and Reporting Authority (2019b) Ethical understanding. https://www.australiancurriculum.edu.au/f-10-curriculum/general-capabilities/ethical-understanding/. Accessed 11 Oct 2019

Brown A (2014) Australian constitutional values survey 2014. Griffith University, Nathan

Civics Expert Group (1994) Whereas the people…civics and citizenship education – report of the Civics Expert Group. Australian Government Publications Service, Canberra

Galaxy Research (2013) Australian laws study. http://members.webone.com.au/~markld/PubPol/GSR/Polls/Galaxy%20Australian%20Laws%20Study%20February%202013.pdf. Accessed 8 Oct 2019

Henderson D (2017) Current practice and future challenges in teaching civics and citizenship. In: Petersen A, Tudball L (eds) Civics and citizenship education in Australia. Bloomsbury, London

Humphreys J (2013) Philosophy in schools: how other countries do it. The Irish Times. 19 November 2013

Le Roux G (2011) Are French students taught to be more philosophical? France 24. 16 June 2011

Miller N (2015) More than one third of Australians have not heard of the Constitution, survey finds. Sydney Morning Herald. 21 February 2015

Ministerial Council on Education, Employment, Training and Youth Affairs (2008) Melbourne declaration on educational goals for young Australians. http://www.curriculum.edu.au/verve/_resources/National_Declaration_on_the_Educational_Goals_for_Young_Australians.pdf. Accessed 22 Oct 2019

Muller, D (1992) Most want constitution changed once they work out what it is. Sydney Morning Herald. 3 July 1992

Petersen A, Bentley B (2017) Connecting values and religion with civics and citizenship. In: Petersen A, Tudball L (eds) Civics and citizenship education in Australia. Bloomsbury, London

Print M (2017) The recent history of teaching civics and citizenship education in Australia. In: Petersen A, Tudball L (eds) Civics and citizenship education in Australia. Bloomsbury, London, pp 1989–2015

Tudball L (2017) Theoretical perspectives and pedagogical possibilities in the new civics and citizenship curriculum. In: Petersen A, Tudball L (eds) Civics and citizenship education in Australia. Bloomsbury, London

Williams G (2014) How would a referendum change Australia's racist laws? Sydney Morning Herald. 22 Sept 2014

Zyngier D (2012) Monash University press release. Monash University. 20 August 2012 https://www.monash.edu/news/opinions/teaching-for-democracy-not-just-about-it-how-should-we-teach-civics. Accessed 11 Oct 2019

Appendix – Commonwealth of Australia Constitution Act 2020

Preamble

We, the people of Australia, recognising the inherent dignity of every human being enact this Constitution.

Chapter 1 – The Constitution

1 The Constitution

This Constitution is the supreme source of law in Australia and is based on the principles of human dignity, fundamental rights, democracy, equality, accountability and the rule of law.

2 Supremacy of the Constitution

Any law, whether statute law, common law, or Indigenous customary law, is invalid to the extent that it is inconsistent with this Constitution.

3 Remedies

Anyone listed in this section has the right to approach a competent court, alleging that this Constitution has been infringed or is about to be infringed, and the court may grant such relief as it sees fit including, but not limited to, declaring a law or conduct to be void, issuing a declaration or injunction and awarding damages. The persons who may approach a court are –

(a) anyone acting in their own interest;
(b) anyone acting on behalf of another person who cannot act in their own name;
(c) anyone acting as a member of, or in the interest of, a group or class of persons;
(d) anyone acting in the public interest; and

B. Harris, *Constitutional Reform as a Remedy for Political Disenchantment in Australia*, https://doi.org/10.1007/978-981-15-3599-4

(e) an association acting in the interest of its members.

Chapter 2 – The Bill of Rights

4 Recognition of rights

The rights listed in this Constitution are recognised as belonging to all persons, natural and legal. Nothing in the Constitution shall be construed as denying any rights not mentioned therein.

5 Application of rights

The rights stated in this Chapter and in Chapter 6 apply to all law, and binds the legislature, the executive, and the judiciary and all persons, both natural and legal both within Australia and extra-territorially.

6 Limitation of rights

The rights in the Bill of Rights may be limited only in terms of law of general application to the extent that the limitation is reasonable and justifiable in an open and democratic society based on human dignity, equality and freedom, taking into account all relevant factors, including

(i) the nature of the right;
(ii) the importance of the purpose of the limitation;
(iii) the nature and extent of the limitation;
(iv) the relation between the limitation and its purpose; and
(v) the availability of less restrictive means to achieve the purpose.

7 Life

Every person has a right to life. The death penalty shall not be imposed in Australia.

8 Liberty

(1) All persons have a right to personal liberty.

(2) Any person who has been deprived of liberty must immediately be informed in a language they understand or through an interpreter

(i) of the reason for the deprivation of their liberty
(ii) of their right to contact a chosen family member, chosen legal advisor and chosen medical practitioner without delay and
(iii) of their right to silence and of the consequences of waiving that right.

(3) Any person who has been deprived of their liberty must be charged with an offence or released within 24 hours.
(4) Any person who has been charged with an offence must be brought before a court of competent jurisdiction within 24 hours in order to have the validity of the continued deprivation of their liberty determined.

(5) A person deprived of liberty has a right to apply for bail.
(6) A person charged with an offence has a right to a fair trial in an open and impartial court, at which they are present and where they and their legal representative have the opportunity to hear and challenge all evidence against them and to present a defence case, within a reasonable time.
(7) A person charged with an offence has the right to be presumed innocent until proven guilty and the right not to be compelled to give evidence in their trial.
(8) A person who has been tried and acquitted in relation to an offence may not be charged or tried in relation to that same offence again.
(9) A person who has been convicted of an offence may not be charged, tried or punished in relation to that offence again.
(10) In any criminal proceedings a person has a right to have the proceedings interpreted into a language they understand.
(11) Evidence obtained in contravention of this Constitution must be excluded from proceedings if admission of that evidence would render the proceedings unfair.

9 **Search and seizure**

Every person has the right not to be subject to arbitrary

(i) search of their person or home;
(ii) search of their property;
(iii) seizure of their possessions; or
(iv) infringement of the privacy of their communications.

10 **Retrospective criminal laws**

(1) A person must not be found guilty of a criminal offence as a result of conduct that was not a criminal offence when the conduct was engaged in.
(2) A penalty imposed on a person for a criminal offence must not be greater than the penalty that applied to the offence when it was committed.
(3) If a penalty for an offence is reduced after a person committed the offence but before the person is sentenced for that offence, the reduced penalty should be imposed

11 **Slavery, forced labour, torture and cruel or inhuman treatment or punishment**

No one may be subject to slavery, forced labour, including military or civil conscription, torture or cruel or inhuman treatment or punishment.

12 **Expression**

(1) Every person has the right to freedom of expression, which includes the right to

(i) impart and receive information
(ii) engage in scientific research and artistic activity
(iii) impart and receive ideas and opinions
(iv) to engage in peaceful public assembly or protest.

(2) This freedom does not extend to incitement of harmful acts.

13 **Voting, candidacy and elections**

(1) Subject to the provisions of sections, every adult citizen has the right to an equal, secret vote and, if registered as a voter, and subject to the provisions of section 43 of this Constitution, to stand for election to public office.

(2) Every citizen has the right to register to vote and to participate in free, fair and regular elections for Parliament.

14 **Association**

Every person has the freedom to associate and to decline to associate with others.

15 **Religion**

No law shall be made for the establishment of any religion, or for the imposition of any religious observance, or for prohibiting the free exercise of any religion.

16 **Privacy**

Every person has a right to privacy in relation to the collection, dissemination, verification and correction of personal information relating to them.

17 **Personal autonomy**

Every person has a right to autonomy in relation to intimate choices relating to reproduction, bodily integrity and personal relationships and not to be subject to medical or scientific experiments without their informed consent.

18 **Equality**

(1) Every person has the right to equality. No one may discriminate against another person on any of the following grounds:

(i) gender
(ii) sexual orientation
(iii) trans-gender status
(iv) residence in a particular part of Australia
(v) marital status
(vi) pregnancy
(vii) family responsibility status
(viii) breastfeeding
(ix) age
(x) ethnicity or race
(xi) impairment
(xii) physical features
(xiii) religion or ethical belief
(xiv) political belief or activity
(xv) trade union activity
(xvi) lawful sexual activity

(xvii) association with a person with any of the attributes mentioned in subsections (i)–(xv) of this section

(2) Nothing in the foregoing shall prevent the enactment of laws or the taking of measures to overcome disadvantage or to ameliorate past discrimination.

19 **Movement**

Every person has the right to freedom of movement.

20 **Commercial activity**

Every person has the right to engage in commercial activity.

21 **Children**

(1) Every child has the right

(i) to parental care or to appropriate alternative care when removed from the family environment;
(ii) to be protected from maltreatment, neglect or abuse;
(iii) if detained, to be kept separately from detained persons over the age of 18 years.

(2) A child's best interests are of paramount importance in every matter concerning the child.
(3) In this section "child" means a person under the age of 18 years.

22 **Water, food, shelter, medical care and education**

(1) Every person has, subject to the resources available to the state, a right to basic water, food, shelter, medical care and education.

(2) The state must take reasonable legislative and other measures, within its available resources, to achieve the progressive realisation of these rights.

23 **Environment**

(1) Every person has a right to the protection of the environment, subject to the resources available to the state.

(2) The state must take reasonable legislative and other measures, within its available resources, to achieve the progressive realisation of this right.

24 **Culture**

Everyone has the right to use the language and to participate in the cultural life of their community, and to educate their children about their language and culture.

25 **Access to information**

Every person has a right to access to information held by the state, subject to the defence of public interest, or that the provision of the information would place an unreasonable financial or administrative burden on the state, the onus of which is on the state to prove.

26 Administrative action

(1) Every person has a right to receive written reasons for any administrative decision or action that is adverse to their interests.

(2) Every person has a right to judicial review, including review on grounds of reasonableness, of administrative decisions or actions.

27 Property

(1) Every person has the right to possess, own and exercise other rights in relation to property, which includes the rights Indigenous people have to property rights under Indigenous customary law.
(2) Every person is entitled to just terms compensation for deprivation or destruction of property by the state.

Chapter 3 – The Executive

28 Executive power

Subject to this Constitution, the executive power of Australia vests in the President of Australia, and consists of such powers vested in the executive by this Constitution, by Parliament and by the common law, including the powers formerly exercised by the Crown in right of the Commonwealth of Australia.

29 The President

The President shall be directly elected by the people of Australia for a term of five years.

30 Impeachment of the President

The President may be impeached on application to the High Court on grounds of misbehaviour in office or incapacity.

31 Acting President

If the President retires, is impeached or dies in office, the Speaker of the House of Representatives shall become Acting President pending the election of a new President, which must occur within 60 days.

32 The Cabinet

The President shall be advised by a Cabinet consisting of the Prime Minister and other Ministers who direct the departments of state who must be members of the House of Representatives.

33 Exercise of power by the President

(1) All references to the President in this Constitution are to be taken as references to the President acting on the advice of the Cabinet, unless the reference is to

the President acting on the advice of some other person or body, or as directed by this Constitution.

(2) The powers of the President include the power to summon, prorogue and dissolve Parliament and to be Commander-in-Chief of the defence forces.

34 Appointment of the Prime Minister

Subject to section 35(3), when the Prime Minister resigns, dies or is dismissed, the President must appoint as Prime Minister the person who has the support of a majority of members of the House of Representatives.

35 Dismissal of the Prime Minister

(1) The President must dismiss the Prime Minister when

(i) the Prime Minister no longer has the support of a majority of members of the House of Representatives or

(ii) the House of Representatives has rejected a proposed law for the appropriation of money or the imposition of taxation and, in either of the circumstances mentioned in (i) or (ii), the Prime Minister refuses either to resign or to advise the President to dissolve the House of Representatives.

(2) The President must dismiss the Prime Minister when the Prime Minister has refused to comply with an order made by the Supreme Court.

(3) If the President dismisses the Prime Minister in accordance with sub-section (1)(i) of this section, and there is no other person who has the support of a majority of the House of Representatives, or if the President dismisses the Prime Minister under sub-section (1)(ii) or (2) of this section, he must immediately dissolve Parliament.

(4) If the President has dissolved Parliament under sub-section (3) of this section, the President must appoint as Acting Prime Minister the parliamentary leader of the political party which has the most numerous members in the House but which did not have any members who were Ministers immediately before the dismissal of the Prime Minister. The Acting Prime Minister shall hold office until the day upon which the House of Representatives meets after a dissolution contemplated by sub-section (3) of this section.

36 Appointment and dismissal of members of the Cabinet

The President, acting on the advice of the Prime Minister, shall appoint and dismiss members of the Cabinet.

37 Dissolution of the House of Representatives

The President must dissolve Parliament when and only when the following circumstances exist:

(i) the President is advised to dissolve Parliament by the Prime Minister or

(ii) the Prime Minister has been dismissed in accordance with section 35(1)(i) and there is no other person who has the support of a majority of the members of the House of Representatives or
(iii) the Prime Minister has been dismissed in accordance with section 35(3).

38 **Liability of the executive**

(1) The executive is liable for its acts and omissions under both procedural and substantive law.
(2) The liability of the executive under subsection (1) of this section attaches to the executive even in cases where a servant or officer of the executive is exercising an independent discretion in the course and scope of their duties.
(3) Where an award of damages has been made against the executive, the judgment shall be satisfied from the Consolidated Revenue Fund.

Chapter 4 – The Legislature

39 **Legislative power**

(1) The legislative power of Australia is vested in a Parliament, which consists of the President and the House of Representatives.
(2) Subject to this Constitution, Parliament shall have the power to make laws for the peace, good order and government of Australia.
(3) Without limiting the generality of sub-section (2) of this section, Parliament may make laws delegating legislative and executive powers to local and regional governments and Indigenous authorities.

40 **Sessions of Parliament**

(1) After an election for the House of Representatives, the President must summon the House of Representatives to meet not later than 30 days after the day the election was held.
(2) The President must convene a session of Parliament at least once in each calendar year.

41 **Composition and election of the House of Representatives**

(1) The House of Representatives shall consist of members elected in accordance with this section.
(2) Australia shall be divided into electorates with as equal a number of voters in each as is reasonably possible to achieve and with each electorate returning seven members of the House of Representatives, provided that one electorate shall be formed by the island of Tasmania.
(3) Every registered voter attending a voting station on a day set for a House of Representatives election shall receive a ballot paper on which they may indicate ordered preferences among as many of the candidates as they choose.

(4) Candidates may indicate a party affiliation or independent status on the ballot paper.
(5) The quota of votes required for election to the House of Representatives from an electorate shall be the one vote plus one eighth of the total number of valid votes cast in that electorate. A candidate who has obtained sufficient votes to reach the quota shall be declared a member of the House of Representatives.
(6) When votes are counted, the first preference vote of each voter shall be allocated to candidates. If no candidate reaches the quota, votes shall be transferred from one candidate to the next in accordance with the preferences indicated by voters, until a candidate reaches the quota. Where a candidate reaches the quota, the number of his or her votes in excess of the quota shall be distributed among the remaining candidates in proportion to preferences they received from voters. If no candidate reaches the quota after a redistribution, the candidate with the lowest number of votes shall be eliminated, and his or her votes distributed among the remaining candidates. This process shall continue until seven candidates have reached the quota or, if a seat in an electorate remains to be filled and no remaining candidate has received the quota, then the candidate with the highest number of votes shall be declared elected.

42 **Vacancies**

(1) If any vacancy shall occur in a seat in the House of Representatives through death or retirement of a member, a recount shall take place in which the votes of the member of the House of Representatives whose seat has become vacant shall be distributed among unsuccessful candidates, after which the count shall proceed in the manner described in section 41(5).
(2) If a candidate who is successful after a recount is no longer alive or no longer willing to become a member of the House of Representatives, the recount shall continue after redistribution of the votes of that candidate.
(3) If no candidate is alive or willing to become a member of the House of Representatives, the candidate's seat shall remain vacant until the next election.

43 **Term of the House of Representatives**

(1) Every House of Representatives shall continue for three years after the date upon which it assembled after the last election and no longer, but may sooner be dissolved by the President in accordance with this Constitution.
(2) The President must proclaim an election for the House of Representatives following a dissolution of the House of Representatives in any of the circumstances mentioned in section 37(1) of this Constitution.
(3) An election must be held within 30 days of a proclamation being issued by the President under sub-section (2) of this section.

44 **The Speaker of the House of Representatives**

(1) The House of Representatives shall choose a member to be the Speaker of the House by a two-thirds majority, and whenever the office of Speaker becomes vacant, the House shall choose another Speaker.
(2) When a person is elected as Speaker, his or her seat in the House of Representatives becomes vacant, and the party which the Speaker represented shall appoint another person to that seat or, if the Speaker had no party affiliation, then the Speaker may appoint a person as a member of the House, to serve until Parliament is next dissolved.
(3) The Speaker shall continue in office until retirement or death.
(4) The Speaker may be removed from office by a vote of no less than two-thirds of the members of the House of Representatives.
(5) Before or during the absence of the Speaker, the Speaker may choose a member to be Acting Speaker, who shall exercise the powers of the Speaker, until the return of the Speaker.

45 **Procedures in the House of Representatives**

(1) The quorum for the conduct of any business of the House of Representatives shall be one third of the whole number of its members.
(2) Questions arising in the House of Representatives shall be determined by a majority of votes of members present and voting. The Speaker shall not vote unless the numbers on either side of a question are equal, whereupon the Speaker shall have a casting vote.

46 **Misbehaviour by members of the House of Representatives**

(1) The Speaker may suspend a member of the House of Representatives for up to seven days for misbehaviour on his or her own initiative.
(2) Without limiting the power of the Speaker under sub-section (1) of this section, an allegation of misbehaviour by a Member of the House of Representatives may be considered by a committee of the House of Representatives, which shall then report to the Speaker.
(3) After considering the report of the committee, but without being bound by it, the Speaker shall determine whether misbehaviour has been proved, whether such misbehaviour shall be punished and, if so, whether to impose a punishment of suspension from the House of Representatives for no more than 6 months, a fine of no more than $ 10 0000 or such other amount as Parliament may by an Act of general application set, or imprisonment for not more than 6 months

47 **Disqualifications**

(1) Any person who

(i) has been convicted of treason, or has been convicted and is serving a sentence of imprisonment for more than a year for any offence punishable under the law of Australia; or
(ii) holds a judicial office; or

(iii) is a member of the public service; or
(iv) is a member of the defence forces; or
(v)or is an officer or employee of a public authority;

shall be incapable of sitting or being chosen as a member of the House of Representatives.

(2) A person who falls within a disqualifying category listed in sub-sections (1) (iv)-(vi) of this section may be chosen as a member for the House of Representatives, but shall be deemed to have ceased to hold the disqualifying position on the day immediately before the day they are elected to the House of Representatives.

(3) If a member of the House of Representatives becomes subject to any of the disqualifications mentioned in sub-section (1) of this section, the seat of that member of the House of Representatives shall thereupon become vacant.

(4) Any question respecting the qualification of a member of the House of Representatives, or respecting a vacancy in the House of Representatives, and any question of a disputed election shall be determined by the Supreme Court of Australia.

48 **Privileges**

(1) Subject to this Constitution, Parliament shall have the power to make laws relating to the powers, privileges and immunities of the House of Representatives of its members and of its committees.

(2) The House of Representatives or any of its committees or any member of a committee may summon any person to appear before the House of Representatives or a committee and give such evidence as may be requested.

(3) Subject to the defence of public interest immunity, failure of a person to appear and give evidence under sub-section (2) of this section shall be an offence prosecutable before the High Court and punishable by a fine or imprisonment of no more than one year.

49 **Enactment of laws**

(1) A proposed law shall be taken to have been passed by the House of Representatives when it has been assented to by a majority of members present and voting.

(2) When a proposed law has been passed by the House of Representatives in accordance with this Constitution, the President must assent to it forthwith, whereupon it becomes law.

50 **Proposed laws appropriating money or imposing taxation**

(1) A proposed law appropriating money shall deal only with such appropriation, and a proposed law imposing taxation shall deal only with the imposition of taxation.

(2) A proposed law shall not be taken as appropriating money or as imposing taxation by reason only of its containing provisions for the imposition or appropria-

tion of fines or other pecuniary penalties, or for the demand or payment or appropriation of fees for licences or fees for services under the proposed law.

51 Taxation and appropriation of money

(1) No taxation shall be raised or money appropriated other than by a law enacted by Parliament.
(2) All moneys received by the executive shall form one Consolidated Revenue Fund, to be appropriated in accordance with the Constitution.
(3) Subject to sections 38(3) and 53(1)(iii) of this Constitution, no money shall be drawn from the Consolidated Revenue Fund except by appropriation made by law.

Chapter 5 – The Judiciary

52 The judicial power of Australia

(1) In accordance with the doctrine of separation of powers, only courts may exercise judicial powers, no court may exercise non-judicial powers, and no judicial officer may hold office in the executive or legislative branches of government.
(2) The judicial power of Australia is vested in the Supreme Court of Australia, the Court of Appeal, the High Court, the District Court and the Magistrates Court.
(3) The Supreme Court of Australia has jurisdiction to hear appeals from the Court of Appeal, subject to the Supreme Court of Australia granting leave to appeal.
(4) The Court of Appeal has jurisdiction to hear appeals from the High Court and from the District Court, subject to the Court of Appeal granting leave to appeal.
(5) The High Court is a court of unlimited original jurisdiction above such jurisdiction as is conferred on the District Court.
(6) The District Court has such original jurisdiction, and jurisdiction to hear appeals from the Magistrates Court, as is conferred on it by Parliament.
(7) The Magistrates Court has such original jurisdiction as is conferred on it by Parliament, and may have a separate small claims jurisdiction conferred on it.
(8) The Supreme Court of Australia shall consist of a Chief Justice and six other judges.
(9) The Court of Appeal shall consist of ten judges, and each case before the court shall be heard by a bench of five judges.
(10) The High Court, District Court and Magistrates Court shall consist of benches of judges and magistrates allocated to different geographical regions.
(11) A bench of the High Court, the District Court and the Magistrates Court shall consist of one judge or magistrate.

53 Appointment of judges and magistrates

(1) The Chief Justice and judges and magistrates of the courts created by section 52(1) of this Constitution

(i) shall be appointed by the President;
(ii) shall not be removed except by the President acting in accordance with an address made by the House of Representatives requesting removal on the ground of proven misbehaviour while holding judicial office, unfitness or incapacity;
(iii) shall receive such remuneration as is fixed by the Judicial Services Commission, provided that such remuneration shall form a permanent charge on the Consolidated Revenue Fund, shall not be diminished during the judges' continuation in office, shall increase annually at least the level of increase of the consumer price index and shall be equal in the case of all judges of the same court.

(2) In making appointments under this section, the President shall be advised by the Attorney-General.

54 The Judicial Services Commission

(1) The Judicial Services Commission shall consist of

(i) the Chief Justice of the Supreme Court of Australia
(ii) the most long-serving judge of the Court of Appeal
(iii) the most long-serving judge of the High Court
(iv) two nominees of the legal profession;
(v) four persons not falling into categories (i) – (iv) appointed by a process determined by Parliament.

(2) The Judicial Services Commission shall, in respect of any vacancy to a court created by section 52(1) of this Constitution submit to the Attorney-General the names of at least three persons from whom the Attorney-General shall select an appointee to be appointed by the President in accordance with section 53.
(3) In determining whom to nominate under subsection (2) of this section, the Judicial Services Commission shall select from applicants who are, or have been, judges of an Australian court or who are admitted as a legal practitioner whose abilities and breadth of background and experience indicate that they merit appointment.
(4) Notwithstanding the anything contained in section 51(1), judicial salaries shall be paid from the Consolidated Revenue Fund upon the direction of the Judicial Services Commission.

55 Removal of judges

(1) An allegation that there are grounds to remove a judge from office on the grounds mentioned in s 53(1)(ii) shall be made to a Judicial Tribunal, which

shall consist of three persons who are judges of the Supreme Court of Australia, the Court of Appeal or the High Court appointed by the President for terms of five years.

(2) Where the Judicial Tribunal finds that it has been presented with evidence which supports a prima facie case of misbehaviour in office, unfitness or incapacity, it shall request the President to suspend the judge against whom allegations have been made pending the outcome of proceedings mentioned in subsection (3) of this section, and the President shall suspend the judge.

(3) If a prima facie finding has been made under subsection (2) of this section, the Judicial Tribunal shall conduct a conclusive hearing into the question of whether a case of misbehaviour in office, unfitness or incapacity has been proved, and shall advise Parliament accordingly.

(4) In conducting proceedings under subsection (3) of this section the Judicial Tribunal shall be bound by the rules of evidence.

(5) No address mentioned in section 53(1)(ii) may be made by the House of Representatives to the President unless the Judicial Tribunal has made a finding of proved misbehaviour, unfitness or incapacity.

56 **Liability of judicial officers**

A judicial officer exercising judicial power shall not be liable in tort for any judicial act done within jurisdiction, nor for any judicial act done outside jurisdiction unless it is proved that such act outside jurisdiction has been performed with actual knowledge of want of jurisdiction.

57 **Exercise of judicial functions by military tribunals**

Nothing in this Chapter shall prevent the exercise of jurisdiction by military tribunals in relation to the conduct of persons while members of the defence forces of Australia.

Chapter 6 – Indigenous People

58 **The status of Indigenous people**

The Constitution acknowledges the original habitation of this country by Aboriginal and Torres Strait Islander peoples, their original ownership its lands and seas, and their continued enjoyment of indigenous rights

59 **Treaties and self-determination**

Indigenous peoples have a right to self-determination, and the government of Australia may enter into treaties with Indigenous peoples to provide for the realisation of that right, including by the establishment of self-government institutions and the application of Indigenous customary law.

60 Indigenous cultural rights

(1) Indigenous peoples hold distinct cultural rights and must not be denied the right, with other members of their community:

(a) to enjoy their identity and culture; and
(b) to maintain and use their language; and
(c) to maintain their kinship ties; and
(d) to maintain their distinctive spiritual, material and economic relationship with the land and waters and other resources with which they have a connection under traditional laws and customs

(2) The state must take reasonable legislative and other measures, within its available resources, to achieve the progressive realisation of each of these rights.

61 Voice to Parliament

(1) Indigenous people have a right to provide advice to Parliament on proposed and existing legislation

in so far as it affects Indigenous people.

(2) Advice to Parliament shall be provided through the Voice to Parliament, a body elected by

Indigenous people in accordance with legislation enacted by Parliament after consultation by the government with Indigenous peoples.

CHAPTER 7 – TRANSITIONAL PROVISIONS

62 State Constitutions and law

Until Parliament enacts legislation to the contrary, all law of the States and Territories that was in force immediately prior to the coming into force of this Constitution, except the Constitutions or Self-Government Acts of those States and Territories, shall remain in force.

63 Location of Parliament

Parliament shall meet in Canberra.

Chapter 8 – Amendment

64 Amendment of the Constitution

(1) This Constitution may be initiated either by the approval of a proposed amendment by Parliament or by a petition proposing an amendment signed by no less than ten percent of registered voters.

(2) A proposed amendment must be put to voters in a referendum within 90 days of the fulfilment of sub-section (1) of this section.
(3) Subject to sub-section (4) of this section, an amendment will become law if approved by a majority of votes cast at the referendum.
(2) A proposed amendment which would amend any provision contained in Chapter 1, Chapter 2, Chapter 5, section 60 or this Chapter will become law if approved by 75% of the votes cast at the referendum.

Chapter 9 – Interpretation

65 **Meaning of words**

Words in this Constitution bear the following meaning unless the contrary is indicated

'amendment' includes repeal.

'Indigenous' in relation to a person means an Aboriginal person or a Torres Strait Islander

'seat' means a seat in the House of Representatives representing a geographic electorate and filled by a member.

Index

B. Harris, *Constitutional Reform as a Remedy for Political Disenchantment in Australia*, https://doi.org/10.1007/978-981-15-3599-4

1157191217 1828240320

The manufacturer's authorised representative in the EU is Springer Nature Customer Service Centre GmbH, Europaplatz 3, 69115 Heidelberg, Germany. If you have any concerns regarding our products, please contact ProductSafety@springernature.com

Printed and bound by CPI Group (UK) Ltd, Croydon, CR0 4YY

30/09/2026

02225510-0008